Curious Subjects

Curious Subjects
Women and the Trials of Realism

Hilary M. Schor

OXFORD
UNIVERSITY PRESS

Oxford University Press is a department of the University of Oxford.
It furthers the University's objective of excellence in research, scholarship,
and education by publishing worldwide.

Oxford   New York
Auckland   Cape Town   Dar es Salaam   Hong Kong   Karachi
Kuala Lumpur   Madrid   Melbourne   Mexico City   Nairobi
New Delhi   Shanghai   Taipei   Toronto

With offices in
Argentina   Austria   Brazil   Chile   Czech Republic   France   Greece
Guatemala   Hungary   Italy   Japan   Poland   Portugal   Singapore
South Korea   Switzerland   Thailand   Turkey   Ukraine   Vietnam

Oxford is a registered trademark of Oxford University Press
in the UK and certain other countries.

Published in the United States of America by
Oxford University Press
198 Madison Avenue, New York, NY 10016

© Oxford University Press 2013

All rights reserved. No part of this publication may be reproduced, stored in a
retrieval system, or transmitted, in any form or by any means, without the prior
permission in writing of Oxford University Press, or as expressly permitted by law,
by license, or under terms agreed with the appropriate reproduction rights organization.
Inquiries concerning reproduction outside the scope of the above should be sent to the
Rights Department, Oxford University Press, at the address above.

You must not circulate this work in any other form
and you must impose this same condition on any acquirer.

Library of Congress Cataloging-in-Publication Data
Schor, Hilary Margo.
Curious subjects : women and the trials of realism / Hilary M. Schor.
p. cm.
Includes bibliographical references and index.
ISBN 978-0-19-992809-5 (hardback)—ISBN 978-0-19-992810-1   1. English fiction—
19th century—History and criticism.   2. Women in literature.   3. Women and literature—
England—History—19th century.   4. Women—Identity.   I. Title.
PR868.W6S36 2013
823'.8093522—dc23
2012034350

ISBN 978-0-19-992809-5

CONTENTS

Acknowledgments   vii

Introduction: The Curious Princess, the Novel, and the Law   1

PART ONE: Forming the Novel
1. The Making of the Curious Heroine: Enlightenment, Contract, and the Novel   15
2. Reading for the Test, Trying the Heroine: The Curiosity Defense   42
3. Alice and the Curious Room   69

PART TWO: Crossing the Threshold
4. Was She Guilty or Not? The Curious Heroine Meets the Wicked Novelist   99
5. *Bleak House* and the Curious Secrets: "Who Copied That?"   133
6. The Bluebeard of the Classroom: Bad Marriages, General Laws, and the Daughter's Curiosity   163
7. George Eliot and the Curious Bride: Ghosts in the Daylight   189

Conclusion: The Clockwork Princess, or Justice for the Dolls   230

Notes   249
Index   267

ACKNOWLEDGMENTS

In the years in which I worked on this book, curiosity proved a flighty and quicksilvery topic, but the one constant was the loyal affection and unceasing interest of my friends. Without their curiosity, mine might have given out much sooner! As with everything I have done in the last twenty-five years, this book owes the most to my colleagues at the University of Southern California, particularly those in the English department and the Gould School of Law. To my co-conspirators and friends in the Center for Law, History and Culture, particularly Ariela Gross and Nomi Stolzenberg, I owe debts beyond any acknowledgment I could make. Beth Meyerowitz, then dean of faculty of the college, found me a leave when I most needed one, and Associate Dean Scott Altman found me an office at the law school in which to work; they are my heroes. Support from outside sources was also crucial, particularly the John Simon Guggenheim Foundation, which made possible a full sabbatical year and a wonderful immersion in London curiosity. The clear-eyed editors at Oxford University Press, including Shannon McLachlan and Brendan O'Neill, the fabulous reports from the anonymous press readers, and the generous intervention of Kevin Dettmar, made these final revisions imaginable.

My friends and family rallied not only through the turmoil of writing but also through surgeries, physical therapies, emergency visits, and months of driving me around (and listening to me qvetch!). Helena Michie surpassed all known limits of friendship by staying with me after my hip replacement surgery—and, of course, by writing her own brilliant work, which has inspired so much of my own—she is the compleat friend. The friends who hosted me during periods of intense writing, especially Jim English, Eileen Reeves, Phiroze Vasunia, Miriam Leonard, and Meg Wiggins; the cafés that sheltered me; the colleagues who threw out ideas over lunches and dinners and phone calls and coffees and workshops, including Paul Saint-Amour and the wonderful participants in our NEH seminar, Elinor Accampo, Emily Anderson, Alex Capron, Carolyn Dever, Mary Favret, Alice Gambrell ("luna and curious!"), Nora Gilbert, Barry Glassner, Sarah Barringer Gordon, Devin Griffiths, John O. Jordan, Peggy Kamuf, Rebecca Lemon, Deidre Lynch,

Eric Mallin, Natania Meeker, Richard Menke, Andrew Miller, Robert Newsom, Stephen Park, Rob Polhemus, Robert Post, Arden Reed, Michael Shapiro, Norman Spaulding, Simon Stern, Garrett Stewart, Jennifer Urban, Robyn Warhol, Robin West, Erika Wright, and particularly Karen Pinkus, in the blissful, clear days at the Getty Research Institute, reminded me daily that writing, however solitary, need not be lonely—their gifts are too many to mention. Special thanks to those who gave me a forum for presenting work in progress: Josephine McDonagh at Oxford; Joe Childers at UCR; Jonathan Grossman and the nineteenth-century group at UCLA; Ann Coughlin and Peter Brooks in a wonderful law and literature conference at the University of Virginia; Joe Litvak at Tufts University; Elaine Auyong and John Plotz and the nineteenth-century group at Harvard; the departments of English at Indiana University, Vanderbilt University, and the University of California, Berkeley; Franco Moretti, Alex Woloch, and the Center for the Study of the Novel at Stanford; and the wonderful audiences at the Dickens Universe at the University of California, Santa Cruz. Jayne Lewis read and loaned me books and listened, always; Michael Quick forced me to think critically about sympathy and curiosity and gave me Kate Atkinson; the luminous Sally Ledger reminded me that this was a nineteenth-century book; Martin Jay gave me Hans Blumenberg; Cathy Gallagher and D. A. Miller remained what they always are—the two most brilliant Victorianists in the universe, who have given me the enormous gift of love and attention, and show an utterly unnatural willingness to continue to write letters of support. Thank you.

Three other kinds of obligation stand out. The first is to my family, who never, ever, ever for one minute stopped believing in me, even through the longest book revision in the history of the world—their care and love are the air I breathe. In particular, without my sister Renée, I might never have written about Alice or Nell—imagine! (Sorry about the pirates.) The second great debt is to the people who were my writing partners in completing this book, friends who read every word over and over and made every word better. Sarah Raff came to this project as it first became a book and in the first meeting of our writing group taught me more than I had learned in the previous ten years—she is the dearest, loveliest presence. Ned Schantz has been part of this book from the first of its glimmers through the shadows of its completion—I'm sure he thought it would follow us to our graves, but no, Ned, it is only my affection that will do that! The book really is done this time! And Laurie Novo, who has always been my first and best reader, is that, and so much more, always.

Finally, the greatest and most unexpected joy of this project has been rediscovering my debt to the magisterial and charming scholars who came before. Without the thankless (at the time) labors of critics like John Butt, Gordon Haight, Humphry House, Gordon Ray, and Kathleen Tillotson, I could not have done any of this work. To spend hours in their presence, reading diaries and letters and editions they created when the Victorians were abandoned to the dust heaps of literary history is to realize again what scholarly courage means—the courage to do the first work before you, and do it well. And I have been truly blessed to work with one of the great scholars of Victorian literature for the last twenty-five years, and to have had him as my reader (devoted and constant and true) at every stage of the project. To my dear friend and stalwart colleague, Jim Kincaid, this book is dedicated, as am I. And because there are always new books to write, to him, as to all my collaborators, I say, the mistakes are mine; the joy came from you; and what larks!

Hilary Schor
Los Angeles, 2012

Curious Subjects

INTRODUCTION

◈

The Curious Princess, the Novel, and the Law

As for what motivated me, it is quite simple; I would hope that in the eyes of some people it might be sufficient in itself. It was curiosity—the only kind of curiosity, in any case, that is worth acting upon with a degree of obstinacy: not the curiosity that seeks to assimilate what it is proper for one to know, but that which enables one to get free of oneself. After all, what would be the value of the passion for knowledge if it resulted only in a certain amount of knowledgeableness and not, in one way or another and to the extent possible, in the knower's straying afield of himself? There are times in life when the question of knowing if one can think differently than one thinks, and perceive differently than one sees, is absolutely necessary if one is to go on looking and reflecting at all.

Michel Foucault, "Preface," History of Sexuality, Vol. 2

Miranda: You have often
Begun to tell me what I am, but stopt
And left me to a booteless Inquisition,
Concluding, stay: not yet.

Shakespeare, The Tempest (1.2. 33–36)

She had an immense curiosity about life and was constantly staring and wondering.

Henry James, The Portrait of a Lady

Once upon a time there was a princess, who was beautiful, wise and good—or, as she was familiarly known by her subjects, "Handsome, clever and rich." The princess lived in a kingdom crowded with objects. The world was filled with furniture and pianos and clocks, with barometers and weather and clouds, with clothing and jewels and paintings and omnibuses

(1)

and trains. The princess walked on roads and rode in automobiles and went wherever she pleased and did whatever she liked, and in all the land there was only one law, and it was "Thou shalt not be curious."

The country I am describing is, of course, the landscape of the realist novel; the princess is its heroine; and its law is the subject of this book, for the English novel is full of interdictions, denials, and surreptitious glances at curiosity. "Never wonder," says Thomas Gradgrind to his daughter Louisa. "Without thinking myself a Fatima, or you a Blue Beard, I am a little curious about it," says Esther Summerson, who "wondered all day" and "now I thought it might be for this purpose, and now I thought it might be for that purpose, but I was never, never, never, never near the truth." "I see you would ask why I keep such a woman in my house: when we have been married a year and a day, I will tell you; but not now."[1] *Hard Times*, *Bleak House*, *Jane Eyre*: it is only by breaking the interdiction against wonder, repeatedly, obsessively, and each time as if it were for the first time, that the novel gets its plot. The story of the realist heroine and her transgressive curiosity is the story that I shall tell here, and my argument is not only that without curiosity there would never be any such thing as the realist novel, but that it was the novel that brought the modern feminist subject into being.

What is the relationship between the realist novel, the heroine's curiosity, and her emancipation? To tell that story we might look no further than an afternoon in Oxford in the 1860s, when Charles Dodgson took a boat ride with a young girl, as she grew larger and smaller and larger and smaller and (of course) curiouser and curiouser. We could note that at roughly the same moment Matthew Arnold was standing in a lecture hall, also in Oxford, reminding his listeners that it was curiosity, a trait that he described as "the most un-English trait I know," the mind turning on itself, which was the essence of a liberal imagination. Meanwhile, in London, John Stuart Mill was introducing into the debate over the second Reform Bill language that would, for the first time, make women legal "persons"—and Robert Browning was noting the same disappearance of wives into their husband's identity with his fierce and terrifying poem, "A Woman's Last Word":

> What so false as truth is, false to thee?
> Where the serpent's tooth is, shun the tree.
> Where the apple reddens, never pry,
> Lest we lose our Edens, Eve and I.

The Victorians understood, that is to say, that there was something powerful, alluring, dangerous, and lost about female curiosity.[2]

This is not where other histories of the novel begin. Realism in the novel has traditionally been allied not so much with knowledge as with stuff, with the world of material objects, the world that we could similarly have found in Oxford at the Ashmolean Museum, the repository of Tradescant's rarities, ethnographic, botanical, and artistic curiosities long since moved from their first home in a London tavern.[3] That version of realism has no happier home than that described by George Steiner decades ago in a review of James Middleton Murray and the Web of Words:

> Did Victorian pundits need less sleep than we do? Consider the facts. They tramped miles over brake and through briar before breakfast or after high tea. At either or both of which collations they would consume flitches of bacon, grilled kidneys, silver-sides of Scotch beef, a garland of mutton chops, kippers and bloaters in silvery shoals, and half a dozen cavernous cups of Indian tea. They sired more offspring than Jacob the Patriarch. They breathed Homer and Catullus, Plato and Vergil, Holy Scripture and Bradshaw's Railway Guide through their stentorian nostrils. When they voyaged, it was either through Turkestan with a walking stick and one change of flea powder or to the spas of Europe with a pride of steamer trunks, portable escritoires, tooled-leather vanity cases, and mountainous hampers. . . . [After the morning service on Sunday] a second service, with an average of eleven hymns, four homilies and assorted benedictions, followed in the afternoon. After which there would be Mendelssohn's "Songs without words" at the piano, a reading out loud of two or three of the shorter epics by Clough or Tennyson, a charade featuring General Gordon's celebrated descent of a staircase at Khartoum in the face of death. . . . Victorian memories ingested epics, Biblical family trees, the flora of Lapland, Macedonian irregular verbs, local topography, and the names of third cousins with tireless voracity. Victorian wrists and fingers wrote, without typewriters, without Dictaphones, to the tune of thousands of words per diem. Histories of religious opinion in six volumes, lives of Disraeli ditto, twelve tomes of "The Golden Bough," eighteen of Darwin, thirty-five of Ruskin.[4]

Steiner brilliantly sums up that world of objects against which the modernists and we so powerfully rebel—think of Miss Kilman, in *Mrs. Dalloway*, stumbling into the steamer trunks in the department stores as she leaves her tea with Elizabeth Dalloway, brokenhearted, or the perfectly prepared layette of a doll called "Princess Daisy," preserved intact in the Bethnal Green Museum of Childhood.

But if we strip the novel bare of material culture, layettes and epics and the flora of Lapland, we are left instead with the heroine's imagination, testing itself against the world, trying to know something outside itself. In a particularly sharp chapter from Elizabeth Gaskell's *Ruth*, the heroine, near the end of the novel, finds herself staring out a window:

> Everything seemed to change but herself. . . . She and the distant hills that she saw from her chamber window, seemed the only things which were the same as

when she first came to Eccleston. As she sat looking out, and taking her fill of solitude, which sometimes was her most thorough rest—as she sat at the attic window looking abroad—she saw their next-door neighbour carried out to sun himself in his garden. When she first came to Eccleston, this neighbour and his daughter were often seen taking long and regular walks; by-and-by his walks became shorter, and the attentive daughter would convoy him home, and set out afresh to finish her own. Of late years he had only gone out in the garden behind his house; but at first he had walked pretty briskly there by his daughter's help—now he was carried, and placed in a larger, cushioned, easy-chair, his head remaining where it was placed against the pillow, and hardly moving when his kind daughter, who was now middle-aged, brought him the first roses of summer. This told Ruth of the lapse of life and time.[5]

The "kind daughter," now middle-aged, brings the "first roses of summer." This is the other thing we look to the novel to do: to locate us in space and time; to give us a sense of our own subtle transformation through the three volumes of its progress, each page we turn bringing us, like the characters, closer to death.

My sense of realism is of something that vibrates between these two possibilities: the novel of steamer trunks and the novel in which a character looks out and says, as Clarissa Dalloway will some seventy years later, "here was one room; there another."[6] This is what Ian Watt referred to as the realism of referentiality, a "full and authentic report of human experience," but one that gets beyond the mere world of stuff, that is, as Elizabeth Ermarth writes, "relatively careless of the concrete." In this sense, as Watt, Ermarth, George Levine, and others have made clear, "formal realism is, like the rules of evidence, only a convention," one which connects its readers to a series of (individual) perspectives, gathering consensus as it gathers events.[7] But my definition of realism depends further on a sense of doubleness, one that I connect not only to Watt's classic distinction between the realism of "presentation" and the realism of "assessment" but also to the doubled nature of curiosity: that curiosity is both something you have ("I am so curious about Isabel Archer; what will she do?") and something you are ("Isabel Archer is so very curious; what a curious vase that is!"). By curiosity, then, I will throughout this book mean several aesthetically and historically complicated things: a form of inquiry; an innate sense of wonder; a subject unduly interested in looking; an object of true or imagined singularity; and that world of objects cunningly made. That world delights and bewilders us: "Spanish fans, Spezzin straw hats, Moorish slippers, Tuscan hairpins, Carrara sculpture, Trastaverinini scarves, Genoese velvets and filligree, Neapolitan coral, Roman cameos, Geneva jewellery, Arab lanterns, rosaries blest all round by the pope himself, and an infinite variety of lumber," to quote one such novelistic list.[8] But I do not want to lose that other sense of curiosity that realism conjured: the subject who, looking out at the world, sees only herself, looking. This book argues that the dialectical relationship between these kinds of curiosity was present at the creation of the novel, that this dynamic sense of curiosity is peculiarly fitting to the formal requirements of the realist novel, and that curiosity is a powerful engine of plot-making and readerly desire.[9]

Why, then, the curious heroine? We need think no further than Crusoe on his island, measuring the weather and counting the goats, to place ourselves in the plot of exploration; a hero like Pip, ambitiously looking around him (in however purblind a fashion), offers a curiosity of his own, of course. In fact, from that perspective, it is a rare heroine who displays any curiosity at all—like the virtuous heroine of Charlotte Lennox's *The Female Quixote*, who has not only no story but also no unseemly curiosity. When the Bennet sisters cluster around the window to see the soldiers passing by, Elizabeth and Jane hold back; when Mr. Rochester asks Jane, "Will you accept my answer?" she does. If, as narrative theory has taught us, "Men have plots of ambition and women have plots of love," it would seem that female curiosity, far from the key to the realist novel's form, is precisely what it must exclude. No man, as Darcy and Rochester remind us, will marry a woman who not only cannot keep a secret but also yearns to know (let alone to publish) yours.[10]

My point is not that there are no female Crusoes (contemporary narrative experiments such as Jane Gardam's *Crusoe's Daughter* and Marianne Wiggins's *John Dollar* put the lie to that idea), but rather that a very different form of female curiosity not only informs but also shapes the realist novel. That curiosity is one perhaps best summed up by the heroine of the film *The Lady Eve*, when she informs her deluded fiancé that "all women are adventuresses." They have to be, she points out, in the marketplace of female sexuality, to negotiate the high seas of romance, to (as Henry James put it in the preface to *The Portrait of a Lady*) "affront her destiny."[11] "Well, what will she *do*?" is the novelist's as well as the reader's question; the author's question is, "What will she *see*?" The heroine's question is, "What is this world in which I must make my way?" And in her way, the question that lies before her most often is, "whom shall I marry?"

It may be, in fact, that heroines are the keys to readers' curiosity precisely because the high seas are largely denied to them—as are bastions of male authority and male debauchery. Coming to Europe may be a "mild adventure" for Isabel Archer compared to Crusoe's island, but her entry into the clutches of Madame Merle and the sterile, dark rooms of Gilbert Osmond, to whom she all too quickly promises herself, are as terrifying as any cannibal Crusoe confronts. The question for Isabel Archer, for all the "frail vessels" of this tradition, is precisely that of escaping the curio cabinet, of moving freely in the world, of choosing for themselves, in a world that is structured (and here I mean both the novel and Anglo-American society) to allow them one and only one choice: that of a husband.

In short, my view of female curiosity places it securely within two sets of law: the first, the laws of genre that we recognize as the realist novel; the second, the legal constraints of Anglo-American marriage, in which a marriage contract literally "contracts" around the heroine. What the laws of genre and the laws of marriage share is an interest in singular answers, one at war with my sense of doubleness, but what I am arguing for curiosity is precisely a moment of hesitation in the imposition of law, a kind of gap that breaches those laws. The plot of the curious heroine builds into these contracts a suspension, a delay, a space for a curiosity however insufficient to its task, however much always slightly belated in its perspicacity. How is it that the heroine can find out what she needs to know in the time allowed to her to investigate, when what she needs to know awaits her only on the other side of the threshold, the other side of the marriage plot? Or, as Cinderella beautifully puts it in Stephen Sondheim's *Into the Woods*,

> How can you know what you want
> Till you get what you want,
> And you see if you like it?[12]

This is the essential realist question: how can you know? If we take seriously the realist novel's centrality as an interrogative place for characters and readers alike, a place that teaches us not only what but also how to know, then the curious heroine's attempts to gather information, and the risks of these trials, are the novel's central function. What does the curious heroine need to know? Islands, not so much; the marriage bed, all of us, perhaps.

This is the odd relationship of curiosity to desire, even as narratologists such as Peter Brooks have defined it. Is curiosity merely (sexual) desire, displaced always and only into a seduction plot? There is a bluntness overall to the usual solution of the heroine's plot that cuts off interrogation, which in turn blunts the heroine's curiosity. The assumption of many readers of *Emma*, *The Portrait of a Lady*, *Middlemarch*, or *Daniel Deronda* is that there is a single thing the heroine doesn't know, and that is the mystery of sex. No heroine who knew "that" would marry Gilbert Osmond or Edward Casaubon or Henleigh Grandcourt—or, to take the obverse, what the heroine needs is a good fuck, and then she will have all the answers; she will finally know what everyone else knows that she doesn't know; she will have "caught up" to the world. But if that were true, of course, the books could end after the marriage—or more accurately, the heroines would not need to go on learning after their marriages; they would not need an education beyond their husbands' creepy touch in bed; they would not need the law, or its ferocity in interrogating *them* about what kinds of subjects (legal and literary) they want to be.[13]

What holds my two views of curiosity together (the world of objects and roads and omnibuses and the world the heroine sees) is the idea of a subject who can contract; who can *bind* herself through time; who *tries* the world, and finds it lacking; who moves through the world *choosing*—a realm of legal subjectivity unique to the modern world, which goes by the literary shorthand of the marriage plot. The test; the choice; the contract; the world afterward: how are we to live "here—now—in England," as Dorothea Brooke puts it in *Middlemarch*. Realism is where she learns; the uneasy space *between* the asking of a question and the *learning* of an answer, even if that space is one of error, mistake, confusion, and even misery—or, the space more accurately known as marriage. Marriage, curiously, offers in the realist novel exactly what John Stuart Mill imagined for the liberal subject: persistent exposure to that which is most alien. In the novel, a bad marriage is central to the heroine's curiosity, to her movement through realism into full subjectivity—or, as George Eliot again put it, "Doubtless a vigorous error vigorously pursued has kept the embryos of truth a-breathing: the quest of gold being at the same time a questioning of substances, the body of chemistry is prepared for its soul, and Lavoisier is born."[14]

I think this matters because it has stopped seeming obvious to us that realism is a game with knowledge—and even when we did know that, we didn't know it was a game best played by marriageable women. Catherine Gallagher's exploration of women and fictionality reminds us that the heroine who is (in a sense) in pursuit of her own property as well as her own name made the exactly right kind of vessel for fiction: one that is general enough for us to follow her adventures and insert ourselves; one that is named enough to give us a place for our sympathies. But what she is doing is testing the reality of the world against precisely her expectations for the future, a story that will recur in our explorations as the problem of the cruelty of the test in *Clarissa* and *The Golden Bowl*, the problem of probable knowledge and statistical justice in *Hard Times*, of criminal knowledge in *Vanity Fair*, and the deadly doubling of knowledge in *Bleak House*. But it is the heroine's desire to know, and the hints of both cruelty and terrible loss behind it, that runs through all of these texts—the heroine must play the game well; she must learn what she is never to know; she must know without (while) seeking to know too much, and she must do it backward, as Governor Ann Richards said of Ginger Rogers, in heels. When Barbara Stanwyck invokes the pirate heroine, she does so not only as an adventuress of the high seas (for whom the ship's decks are her business office) but as "The Lady Eve," the heroine who, like the first Eve, like Pandora and Psyche, travels beyond the expected realms of knowledge. (The adulteress, as Angela Carter notes, "if she plays her cards right, may evolve into the adventuress, whose status in life . . . has always been that of a free woman.")[15] Only when a curious woman, call her Eve, or Pandora, or Psyche, reaches out her hand, holds up a lamp, and opens a door, can the plot begin; and paradoxically, only by choosing badly does the heroine then get the power to choose well, to enter the law, and to take the law in her own hands. The doubling of the heroine offers the text's meditation on its own status as representation—but it also serves a pedagogical purpose for both the hero and the heroine, one that (in a pattern we will see throughout this book) cannot be overcome through law, but only through the law's higher knowledge. As "Jean" says to Hopsy, now "Eve's" husband, when he warns her he is married—"Why, Hopsy, so am I," and the law has (inadvertently?) performed its work as magical arbiter of romantic destiny.

If that structure reverberates primarily as mythic, Eve dropping apples repeatedly on the hapless, tripping-over-his-own-feet hero's head, it also echoes as a fairy tale, precisely the one Jane Eyre invokes when Rochester asks her *not* to ask her question. Jane has come into Thornfield Hall after standing out on the leads: "Anybody may blame me who likes, that then I longed for a power of vision that might overpass that limit." Instead of finding that vision, Jane returns to the corridors of Thornfield, which stretch before her "narrow, low, and dim, with only one little window at the far end, and looking, with its two rows of small black doors all shut, like a corridor in some Bluebeard's castle." But the presence in Jane Eyre's gritty material world of the Gothic, the romance, the curious, is no accident, reader.[16] It is instead a heightening of the realist "and then . . ." that reminds us that beyond the promise of law lies its threat: the ghosting of the married woman, as she disappears into coverture, all ability to choose, to know, to *contract*, dissolved by her initial promise, the successful completion of the marriage plot. What better story for that than the Bluebeard story, in which the wife, wooed by the very world of materials objects, riches, jewels, all that might tempt the princess from her solitary tower, is trapped in the palace, bound by the very beauty of her clothes and the richness of all that surrounds her, handed a single key, and told, thou must not seek to know. Instead, she goes farther: she walks down the dark corridor, runs down the slippery stairs, opens the doors, and knows the worst—that her body is forfeit; her promise is forever; she herself is contracted away.

What is this knowledge—and what kinds of curiosity does the novel render legitimate and illegitimate? How is the curious heroine ever to be curious enough—and how can the novel create the space for her new knowledge, without blasting open its own most treasured form, the marriage plot? Or, again, as Stephen Sondheim said,

> Now I know:
> Don't be scared.
> Granny is right,
> just be prepared.
> Isn't it nice to know a lot?

And a little bit not. (p. 69)

The heroine's curiosity must walk a similarly fine line: the heroine must have enough curiosity to start a plot, not so much as to overwhelm it (or, put another way, not enough to become herself fallen, beyond the reach of middle-class representation)—but she must also be free to use her knowledge, and that commits the novel not only to the Gothic possibilities Jane Eyre invoked (a surprise that might make us afraid) but to exactly that wider vision that Jane herself longed for from the leads of Thornfield Hall. In the nineteenth century, such knowledge was political, and it linked the curious heroine to a world far beyond her dissatisfied marriage bed; it brought her into the world of choosing that few thought women could enter, the world of legal and political representation. However much the nineteenth-century novel may mock political aspirations, it indulges in them with equal force, particularly when it comes to the romance of women's rights. So when Jane Eyre leaves Rochester because "I respect myself," she sounds less like Eve or Bluebeard's wife than she does like John Stuart Mill, who said, "The question [of what they are to do] rests with women themselves—to be decided by their own experience, and by the use of their own faculties. There are no means of finding what either one person or many can do, but by trying—and no means by which any one else can discover for them what it is for their happiness to do or leave undone." At the moment when Mill is introducing into Parliament a bill for women's right to the franchise, the language of choice, of experience, of *trials*, is rendered political, even where we might least expect it to be, in the heart of the realist novel, when the novelist (and the reader) must ask, "What is she to *do*?"

This intervention of John Stuart Mill's political radicalism into what seemed to be the fairy-tale world of the novelist suggests the way the Anglo-American tradition of the novel has been misread precisely because of the absence of any recognition of feminism as a revolutionary movement. Readers of the novel, following Franco Moretti, have been able to dismiss the marriage plot and fairy tale (and along with them, the realist novel itself) as quietist in the face of the more radical continental novel, arguing, as Moretti does, that "the fairy tale reassures," and hence is the most appropriate narrative genre for "the task of creating a universal culture of law," one which assimilates its subjects into the happy endings of the marriage plot.[17] Of a novel such as *Jane Eyre*, he claims, it offers only the "most irrational escapism," as the heroine on one hand flees sexual pleasure in the name of law, and on the other returns to a quiet happy ending within marital bliss. Moretti here is participating in a much older line of critique of the novel, particularly the Victorian novel of marriage, as Queenie Leavis also scorns Jane Eyre's sexual puritanism, and Virginia Woolf the limitations of being "always a governess, always in love."[18] But this is to miss the central critique of these novels, and what their use of the curious heroine's fairy tale travails makes clear. For what Moretti claims is merely "fairy tale justice" is precisely what these endings trouble, and the disappearance of the wife into the legal structures of marriage (again, what frightens Jane Eyre away from Rochester's domination in the first place) is not the successful completion of but rather the first step in what he rightly declaims as the real plot of the novel: "In the life of the individual, maturity now means one thing only: knowledge" (139). What Moretti does not ask is knowledge of what? And what would it mean if we saw the novel's quest for knowledge, its delay of the marriage plot, its hesitation over the wife's disappearance into her husband's arms and a *new* dispensation of the law, as a quest for a knowledge that goes beyond what every "mature individual" should know; a quest for different knowledge; a new form of curiosity? Then the novel's ambivalent relationship to contract, particularly to the dangerous forms of the bourgeois sexual contract, might have that revolutionary edge that Moretti bemoans in the dispersal of the Chartist revolution and the failure of England to join in wider continental struggles; it has a curious struggle of its own to pursue.

For as Stanley Cavell remarks in discussing the comedy of remarriage, "the achievement of human happiness requires not the perennial and fuller satisfaction of our needs as they stand but the examination and transformation of those needs."[19] This is not a book about sexual prudishness (the heroine just needs to learn about sex) or about individual happiness ("If only he would choose me . . .") or even about certainty of vision. It is instead a book about error, wandering and seeking—about taking seriously *for women* the "examination and transformation" of what it means to be a person capable of choice, however constrained or confused (or even wrong) that choice might be. It is that transformative power that this book claims for female curiosity and the realist novel: a woman reaches out her hand; a woman climbs the tower; a woman walks out into the world and (perhaps) casts a ballot, as did the unexpected heroine Lily Maxwell, who, in defiance of the law, found herself registered as a householder in Manchester and took the opportunity to vote for representation in Parliament.[20] The unhappiness of Gwendolen Harleth, the rape of Clarissa, Jane Eyre out on the leads of Thornfield Hall longing for "a wider power of vision," the misery of Isabel Archer's sterile marriage, Dorothea Brooke's desire to do something heroic "here— now— in England"—these are part of a larger questioning that is at the heart of the realist novel; the novel's curiosity about what *it* is to do. Put the heroine on trial; use the heroine to put the world on trial; "what to do, what to do?" as Angela Carter will ask of the heroine's plot in the twentieth century. "I would like to know . . ." says Offred in *The Handmaid's Tale*. "Know what?" the Commander asks her. What's beyond the door; what's beyond the wall; what is it I want; "whatever there is to know," I say; but that's too flippant. "What's going on."[21]

By the time I reach the end of my tradition, these questions will be very dark indeed: in the world of *The Handmaid's Tale*, women can no longer read or write; their bodies are (at best) vessels; their names are not their own. (She is "Offred" because she is "of Fred," and her name is lost to history.) But the literary practices on which I focus throughout, the "serious pleasures of suspense," as Caroline Levine describes them, the force of law (as both fictional device and extra-diegetic reminder of the real-world limits on the heroine's imagination) and the power of curiosity to shatter expectations—these hold out a possibility for a peculiarly modern subject that the curious heroine represents.[22] The story ends not only with forms of rethinking traditional realism but also with a new vision of social fictions, with the fractured automaton, no longer a purely Miltonic subject, but a figure who raises the question put best by Donna Haraway, "The cyborg would not recognize the Garden of Eden; it is not made of mud and cannot dream of returning to dust."[23]

Of what does she dream? What will the heroine do with her new knowledge; what new forms of desire are available to her; what new legal subjects are born; what happens to the form of the realist novel, which holds at its chilly heart the structure that Roland Barthes claimed all narrative offers, a "proposal and [a] suspended answer"?[24] I want to suggest one final transformative element of the heroine's curiosity, something that frees us to see the marriage plot, with all its dark shadows, as a space of knowledge and possibility, as something that goes beyond mere courtship; beyond the question we must always ask, "Why always Dorothea?" There are other figures that lurk at its edges, not only single women and tricksters and pirates, but figures of friendship, artistry, doll-makers, other purveyors of curiosity. What makes the marriage plot so powerful is precisely that it recognizes that it is a means to an end, not an end in itself; it need end neither in remarriage nor marriage itself, but in self-knowledge alone. Toward the end of *Sense and Sensibility*, Marianne Dashwood finally realizes how miserable her sister Elinor has been through the whole novel, and asks her, how did she bear (and even conceal) her unhappiness, knowing that she loved Edward Ferrars so passionately.

> But I did not love only him;—and while the comfort of others was dear to me, I was glad to spare them from knowing how much I felt. Now, I can think and speak of it with little emotion. I would not have you suffer on my account; for I assure you I no longer suffer materially myself. I have many things to support me. I am not conscious of having provoked the disappointment by any imprudence of my own, I have borne it as much as possible without spreading it farther.
> . . . And after all, Marianne, after all that is bewitching in the idea of a single and constant attachment, and all that can be said of one's happiness

depending entirely on any particular person, it is not meant—it is not fit—it is not possible that it should be so.—[25]

Austen unexpectedly suggests here a different reading of the marriage plot—that while it may structure a heroine's progress into the world and organize a reader's experience, while it may pose *one* game of curiosity, it is not the only game, nor is it the only trial. In that view, marriage exists not as an answer to a question, but as an *opportunity* to *pose* a question—for not everyone, as Elinor Dashwood reminds us (though of course, she herself will), enters into the marriage plot single and exits married.

This is the final sense of curiosity to which this book is committed, and it is one beautifully summed up by George Toles in a sentence with an echo of Jane Austen at its heart: "The best cure for a bewitching assertion is the positing of a more spacious question."[26] That might be the best way of suggesting what I am trying to approximate here, at the threshold of Bluebeard's chamber. In the realist novel, women do not "choose" in order to get married; they enter the marriage plot because it was the one place where they had anything that looked like choice. They didn't choose to marry, they married in order to choose, and they do so in a world of myth, fairy tale, contract and law. Marriage was never the question; the question was the question. The marriage plot, at this moment in the history of the novel and of women's progress toward emancipation, is simply a brilliant way, however bitter the road to enlightenment and through however many dark chambers, for the curious heroine to ask the question.

PART ONE

Forming the Novel

CHAPTER 1

The Making of the Curious Heroine

Enlightenment, Contract, and the Novel

The values of this bourgeois public sphere [are clear]: its members held reason to be supreme; everything was open to criticism (the public sphere is critical); and its participants opposed secrecy of all sorts.[1]

Curiosa et captiosa interpretatio in lege reprobatur—a curious & captious interpretation is to be disapproved.[2]

What is a series of actions? The unfolding of a name. *To enter?* I can unfold it into "to appear" and "to penetrate." *To leave?* I can unfold it into "to want to," "to stop," "to leave again." *To give?*: "to incite," "to return," "to accept." Inversely, to establish the sequence is to find the name: the sequence is the currency, the *exchange value* of the name. By what divisions is this exchange established? What is there in "Farewell," "Door," "Gift"?

Roland Barthes, *S/Z*

"Do not consider me as an elegant female intending to plague you, but as a rational creature speaking the truth from her heart." With this claim, Elizabeth Bennet marks herself as precisely the kind of subject in which I am interested—one capable of choosing, one capable of thinking, one also capable (as Mr. Darcy's aunt, Lady Catherine de Bourgh, will put it many chapters later) of being "tried," for "I came here to try you." Interestingly, for my purposes, her avowal comes at a moment when she has just chosen, and chosen to say no, refusing the proposal of the all-too-absurd Mr. Collins. But her declaration of independence comes, as we have already seen, at the price of a certain renunciation of curiosity as well—Elizabeth Bennet, for all her enlightenment, can only afford a cautiously deployed, carefully concealed, form of curiosity.[3]

The heroine, like the realist novel as a genre, bears a vexed relationship to enlightenment, the historical transformation that begins with the injunction "Dare to know." The philosophical movement that took as its figure Prometheus stealing fire from the heavens always carried its own shadow with it. As Horkheimer and Adorno wrote, "The prime cause of the retreat from enlightenment into mythology" lies "in the Enlightenment itself," the awareness that "the fully enlightened world radiates disaster triumphant."[4] Roy Porter has stressed the way that "poets, critics and authors" played a crucial role "in debates over identity, individuality and subjectivity . . . the role of the imagination in the politics of the gendered self,"[5] and I follow him in taking the novel seriously as not only a form of enlightenment but also a weapon for estrangement. To the extent that the novel is a product of enlightenment thought, directing the quest for knowledge both inside the individual and into the wider world, the subject it creates, a liberal subject capable of choosing and one also capable of curiosity, also carries a fear of going too far—the shock of enlightenment, the fury of lightning. Even Mary Shelley, remember, is reluctant to display the technology of animation that creates her modern Prometheus, leaving it to generations of filmmakers to depict the bolt of electricity at which she only hints.[6]

Within the world of the realist novel, which flavors the coming of enlightenment with the shadow of disenchantment in its own ways, we might think that the heroine bears an especially onerous burden—the necessity of balancing enough curiosity to generate a plot with sufficient modesty to resist the blows of events, the perdition of knowing too much, the anxiety of knowing too little. Proscriptions against female knowledge, prescriptions of female propriety—as Angela Carter cries out in mock despair, "Prescribe. Proscribe. What to do, what to do?"[7] From *Paradise Lost*, with which I will mark a certain form of modernity, to Richardson to Austen to the Victorians, I will be arguing against too easy an assumption of the heroine's retreat from knowledge. Instead, we will see that it is in fact the heroine's curiosity that repeatedly shocks the novel into being, that jump-starts the plot, that engineers the progress, however jagged and dangerous, to a liberal self. Without it, as Carter also remarks of "the interesting Justine," "though she is virtuous, she does not know how to be good" (55).

If this is surprising, we might think back to the origins of curiosity itself—to Oedipus and the question of the Sphinx. For there, too, the curiosity comes not from the hero but from the heroine, the Sphinx with her questions. A riddle is not necessarily the most interesting form of curiosity, but to the extent that all riddles invite a paradox (as Oedipus's riddles undoubtedly do), they suggest a world of wanting-to-know, of subjects waiting to know the answer to the questions, who am I? where am I going? what will come next? In Muriel Rukeyser's retelling of the Oedipus story, as Teresa de Lauretis reminds us, Oedipus actually blew the quiz because he missed the ambiguity: when he answered that it was man who goes on four feet, two feet, three feet, he forgot to say "woman."[8] "Everyone knows man includes woman," he replies. "Hmmmph," says Rukeyser's Sphinx.

Enlightenment, that is to say, is a tricky business—and it yields unwieldy subjects. The novel tends to treat enlightenment, as we will see in what follows, as a function of what Roland Barthes called the "hermeneutic code," a form of suspense destined to be fulfilled. It is that—but it is also a process of curiosity, shock, and (perhaps) renewed curiosity that forms a curious subject capable of choosing, choosing badly, choosing again—one capable of forming connections, signing contracts, questioning her place in the world. This chapter begins with the history of curiosity and its dense entanglement with women and the novel. For this, we will need to tease out more of the ambivalence of enlightenment: the curious object in the museum, the curious readers in the novel, the curious wife in the fairy tale. From object to subjects, curiosity tracks a complicated path. But all this will culminate for us in the complexities of *The Portrait of a Lady*, for it is with the novel's creation of the curious heroine in all of her contradictions that feminism, too, will get a curious subject.

When Oedipus answered the question of the Sphinx, he was entering into an even earlier myth: that of the princess who trapped her would-be suitors. As an early fragment of Pindar puts it succinctly, her question was "the riddle from the jaws of the savage maiden."[9] De Lauretis notes further that though the princess and her quest have been repeatedly rewritten into female stasis and male mobility, *all* plots used to begin with women's questions and with the heroine's quest. The princess must be wedded, but the hero's power comes from exciting her desire; agency is hers, and only very late in the story does she become a monster, hideous and terrible. The same inversion occurs in what Freud observes in the story of the three caskets, when the suitors among whom Portia is choosing must follow her father's tyrannical will and choose among the caskets. As Freud notes, choosing the casket is an inversion of the original heroine's choice—in the folk tale, it is her consent that truly charges the narrative.[10] After Oedipus, the question will belong to the hero prince, but female curiosity still remains: it is her plot that gives us the "unfolding."

"To enter, to begin, to leave . . ." We begin here as well, for Barthes echoes, however inadvertently, a series of myths of female curiosity that undo the customary masculine prerogative of choosing. While Prometheus brings fire, Pandora opens the vase that unleashes the problems of mankind; Psyche, bending with her lamp over the beautiful, sleeping Cupid, spatters him with wax and sets herself on her wanderings; Eve, in the garden, stretches out her hand, seizing knowledge, reaching beyond her own grasp, tumbling us into history. These myths are not synonymous, but they all offer ways of generating new worlds of narrative. Pandora, having opened the box and unleashed disaster, is also the source of hope, just as, repeatedly, in the novel, the story of a curiosity that goes too far offers the metaphor for experimental science. (Imagine if Frankenstein were not the modern Prometheus, but a modern Pandora.) Psyche, too, offers a metaphoric cluster for the empirical imagination: after the midnight look at her beautiful lover (a gaze that enacts the ancients' view of curiosity as the snare of the eye), she wanders the world and undergoes a series of tests, of forms of sorting and knowing. Only after she has separated the seeds of a thousand grains into piles, counted and numbered and named the world, can she be freed into the romance plot again. But it is Eve, putting herself on trial when she imagines testing her strength against God's commandment (thou shalt not eat; stretching forth her hand, she ate . . .) who provides the central metaphors for my study: the woman who wants to know as God knows, who chooses without knowing what she is choosing (What is death?) and then, in choosing grace, must choose again. Or, take a moment from a nineteenth-century Eve: imagine Fatima, the wondering wife of the Bluebeard story, anxiously crossing the threshold into the locked room. As Angela Carter recounts the tale in "The Bloody Chamber," the heroine freely confesses her audacity in unlocking the door and entering the secret room but reminds her lover that she is being killed for a disobedience that her husband demanded, that "I only did what he knew I would do." The lover replies simply, "Like Eve."[11]

Curiosity, like love and pretzels, has a history, but as these earliest myths suggest, curiosity is always, like the fire of enlightenment, both a way of starting things and a potentially dangerous force, something that takes people beyond their sphere and imagines a way of knowing best left to the divine. For that reason, Aristotle and the ancients doubted curiosity; Augustine and Aquinas inveighed against it; even Pascal feared it. Augustine in particular understood the dangers of curiosity unleashed, in particular the curiosity of the eye, as Eve says in *Paradise Lost*, praising "this fruit divine, / Fair to the eye, inviting to the taste, / *of virtue to make wise*" (Book 9, 776–78; emphasis added)[12] As Hans Blumenberg summarizes, *curiositas* represents "'ocular desire' (*concupiscentia ocrulorum*), the pure functional drive of the organ of sensation, which finds satisfaction even in the most trivial object and is defined as the futile and inquisitive appetite for sensual experience" (312).[13] This "self-satisfaction of instinct through surrender to the world of appearances" dresses itself up in "the great words and the images of supposed values in whose terms the human spirit conceived of its destiny and dignity, as knowledge and science," but it is a vice in that it enjoys exactly "the degree of difficulty and remoteness of its objects" (312) As Blumenberg notes in his sophisticated history of curiosity and modernity, precisely that distance is at the heart of our modern fascination with our own curiosity: curiosity is a "temptation . . . in the double sense that to test oneself on and with what is resistant and uncommon ... is at the same time to be tempted." The intermingling of the test and the temptation is what marks the modern, for with the Renaissance, we see a rebirth of curiosity, no longer Augustine's "amusement at a mutilated corpse, theatrical shows ... and the investigation of nature and ... the magical arts," but an "interest in invisible things within the world," the mind that "does everything in order to know itself." (361, 360). By the time of Galileo, curiosity "has already separated itself from the structure of personality, from the psychic motive forces, and has become the mark of the hectic unrest of the scientific process itself" (396). With the virtuosi comes curiosity's enshrinement at the heart of scholarship and hence of wonder, the bringing down of the heavens to material reality.[14] In this way, curiosity is the sign as well as the agent of secularization, replacing "God [as] the primary 'object' of one's attention in the 'beyond.'" But curiosity also has a sacred history: the earliest "curios" are saints' relics, and they bring with them "cure," at the same time that other "curios" mark the "care" of those who made them, and still others the "curiosity" of those who observe them.[15] Curiosity retains this doubled nature of sacred and profane, in its own faith in "anticipation," the "beyond" of religion of metaphysical systems; as even Blumenberg stresses, "To understand the process of the legitimation of theoretical curiosity as a basic feature of the beginning of the modern age certainly does not mean to make curiosity into the 'destiny' of history, or one of its absolute values" (240). But he argues that what we experience as that peculiar openness of the mind to all kinds of experience is not merely the secularization of an earlier curiosity (once forbidden, now unleashed) but something different in itself—some striving after more which, along with voyages of discovery and Faustian quests of inner experience, created the modern world, the force that allows even Freud to invoke the "self-ascription of knowledge appetite," when he writes in *Beyond the Pleasure Principle*, "What follows is speculation, often far-fetched speculation, which the reader will consider or dismiss according to his individual predilection. It is further an attempt to follow out an idea consistently, *out of curiosity to see where it will lead*" (448, emphasis added).

The *OED* tracks for us the journey of curiosity in England, a history that suggests a world at once highly ordered (neat, precise, careful, almost obsessively so) and richly (even unnervingly) furnished with a cheerful and disorderly plenitude. It tells us that in a person, curiosity is a carefulness, an observation, as well as a desire to know. Curiosity is inquisitiveness (including about other people); scientific or artistic interest (that of a "virtuoso"); a pursuit or a hobby; "a desire to make trial or experience of anything novel." Curious people over the centuries have been "careful," "anxious," "cautious," "observant," "fussy" ("nice"), "accurate," "ingenious," "desirous of seeing or knowing; eager to learn; inquisitive. Often with condemnatory connotation: Desirous of knowing what one has no right to know, or what does not concern one, prying." (This, as the *OED* notes, is "the current subjective sense.") The curious are "minute in inquiry; discriminating"; they are even "devoting attention to occult art." And in things? Curiosity is "careful or elaborate workmanship; perfection of construction; elaborateness, elegance; artistic character." "The quality of being curious or interesting from novelty or strangeness; curiousness," "a matter upon which undue care is bestowed; a vanity, nicety, refinement," "an object of interest; any object valued as curious, rare, or strange." Curiosity can be applied to a person who is "'queer' in his appearance, habits, etc.; cf. oddity." Something curious can be something "deserving or exciting attention on account of its novelty or peculiarity; exciting curiosity; somewhat surprising, strange, singular, odd; queer." (This, says the *OED*, is "the ordinary current objective sense.") The danger of a curious thing? It is "used as a euphemistic description of erotic or pornographic works," the equivalent clearly of the occult in people—sex, darkness, excitement, singularity.

Curiosity enters the modern world not only as Augustine would have it, as a lust of the eye, what Eve calls "a longing of the eye." But to the extent that curiosity remains an optical obsession, it enters culture through a closet: a place of privacy, interiority, secrets, and treasures; a junkbox.[16] The cabinet of curiosity, the *Wunderkammer*, served a variety of purposes: it contained the artist's collection of rare objects, the budding scientist's proofs of observation, the tourist's memorabilia, and the affluent collector's evidence of his own interest and wealth. Gradually, the private collection gave way to public museums—or, as we might think of it, the artist's or curioso's hobby became a place of public veneration.[17] The metamorphosis is hardly complete. The continued connection between pornography and curiosity suggests the ways curiosity is still linked to things that are hidden: peepholes, pinholes, keyholes, even the rabbit hole of *Alice in Wonderland*.[18] Curiosity, in the eighteenth and even the nineteenth century, has yet to shed all those erotic trappings—nor has the curious heroine completely separated herself from her purely pornographic double, all hole, but curiosity has certainly grown more respectable.[19] Indeed, in the time I have been working on this book, curiosity has left the closet and gotten a room of its own. Several museums have paid elaborate tribute to their own origins in similar ways, re-creating the *Wunderkammern* at their heart, but one gallery in particular, the Gallery of Enlightenment (1680–1820) at the British Museum, offers a uniquely self-conscious view to its own creation.[20] A shrine to Hans Sloane and his original "cabinets of curiosity," the gallery occupies the room once held by King George's library, which is now, of course, the core of the collection of the British Library. It begins as a monument to the idea of "classifying" the world, but an hour's wandering in the gallery suggests the ambiguities that haunt the study of curiosity. The exhibit aims to represent "how different collections formed during the course of the 18th century were arranged to gain knowledge about the world, past and present," and the cases cover such subjects as "The Revolution in Science," "King George's Library," "Natural History Drawings," "Customs of Ancient Times," and "Seeing Progress in Variety." At the center of it all stands the case of "Curiosity and Curiosities." Divided into the areas of "craftsmanship," "marvellous works of man and nature," "the habits of man," "portraits and curiosities," and "artificial curiosities," the objects on display include "life size portraits in oil," ivories, "a rhinoceros horn cup [that] was an antidote to poison for those who drank from it, a translucent agate made into a casket and tiny 'naturally occurring' dice," and "a nautilus shell," which "inside was carved into the shape of a helmet with a visor," whose "interior was carved with a scene of the 1639 defeat of the Spanish by the Dutch admiral Maarten Tromp in the English Channel off Dover." The desire to get infinitely lost in the ephemera, the wonders of microscopy, the enormous pull that curiosity exercises on all of us, all illustrate the brilliant statement of Lorraine Daston and Katharine Park that "collectors [of curiosities] did not [merely] savor paradoxes and surprises; they piled them high in over-flowing cupboards."[21]

But the exhibit also plays up the irony of any such collection, one that, as we shall see, shadows the novel as its own kind of curiosity collection, and that is the uncertainty of its own epistemological ground. The exhibit begins with confidence, for "Sir Hans Sloane's collection was typical of many European 'cabinets of curiosities.' Here was the world in miniature, a collection that set out to show all the wonders of God's universe to mankind." The museum marks itself as a place at the heart of culture: typical, one of many, European. Then the specific: "Displayed in Montague house, the original home of the British Museum, Sloane's collection stimulated wonder and provoked curiosity. By emphasizing the rare, the exotic and the exceptional, visitors [sic] were encouraged to speculate on the mystery of nature and on human ingenuity at its centre." Barring the misplaced modifier, the museum imagines that gift of "paradox," the inability to understand curiosity always at curiosity's heart—that is, curiosity begins as collective and returns us to singularity, like the "curiosos" who populate the OED's definitions of curiosity. And yet, no sooner does the museum stake its place than it disavows it. In the final paragraph of the "Curiosity and Curiosities" description, the curators strike a different note. "In creating a cabinet of curiosities, Sloane was old-fashioned even by the standards of his own day. But his careful cataloguing, and insistence on representing living as well as past culture, are evidence that the Enlightenment had begun to shed its light on his collection." What began as a "typical" European collection, and then became "rare" and "mysterious," is now revealed as purely idiosyncratic—"old-fashioned even by the standards of [its] day," and only barely touched by the light of the Enlightenment.

The museum's *twinned* sense of curiosity, at once a sharp and brilliant moment of *éclaircissement*, and a shower of dingy objects undifferentiated in their plenitude, awaiting a sorter who will never appear, helps us understand why this room shares more than dates (1680–1820) with the rise of the novel. When we stand in that room, bewitched and a tad dizzy, are we standing in the space of the novel? The most cynical answer might be yes, that the novel is no more than an advertisement for the commodities of culture. The best illustration of this is Thackeray's when he suggests, in a sketch published in *Punch* in 1847, composing a novel entirely of objects, each of them brought forward with corporate sponsorship. The speaker in "A Plan for a Prize Novel," says to his protégé, "Walk into the shops, I say, ask for the principal, and introduce yourself, saying, 'I am the great Snooks; I am the author of the 'Mysteries of May Fair;' my weekly sale is 281,000; I am about to produce a new work called 'The Palaces of Pimlico, or the Curse of the Court,' describing and lashing fearlessly the vices of the aristocracy; this book will have a sale of at least 530,000; it will be on every table."[22] What could be easier, he asks?[23]

> For instance, suppose it is an upholsterer. What more easy, what more delightful, than the description of upholstery? As thus:—
>
> "Lady Emily was reclining on one of Down and Eider's voluptuous ottomans, the only couch on which Belgravian beauty now reposes, when Lord Bathershins entered, stepping noiselessly over one of Tomkins's elastic Axminster carpets. 'Good heavens, my lord!' she said—and the lovely creature fainted. The Earl rushed to the mantel-piece, where he saw a flacon of Otto's eau-de-Cologne, and," &c.

Long before Fay Weldon "received a substantial—but undisclosed—sum of money from the Bulgari jewelry company to feature the company in the written work" in *The Bulgari Connection*, Thackeray imagined the novel's true destiny to be a series of self-perpetuating, almost self-generating commodities, perfectly assembled into a simulacrum of the material world.[24]

But the space of the mad collector, dense with objects and alive with nouns, is precisely what early critics of the novel feared, and it is why curiosity gets such a bad name early on. Edmund Burke famously remarked in his essay on the Sublime, although "the first and simplest emotion which we discover in the human mind, is Curiosity," by which he means "whatever desire we have for, or whatever pleasure we take in novelty," "those things which engage us merely by their novelty cannot attach us for any length of time." Curiosity, he says, "is the most superficial of all affections . . . [and] incapable of affecting the mind with any other sensations than those of loathing and weariness."[25] E. M. Forster, in the twentieth century, continued to strike this note. He says: "Curiosity is one of the lowest of the human faculties. You will have noticed in daily life that when people are inquisitive they nearly always have bad memories and are usually stupid at bottom." And, he goes on to state, novel readers are no different. Nothing is less interesting than a man who asks you a thousand questions; nothing less engaging than a novel that offers you nothing but a thousand incidents, "and then . . . and then . . . and then."[26]

As Forster famously says, "We are all like Scheherazade's husband, in that we want to know what happens next," but such curiosity is never enough. Not only is such curiosity linked fatally to the feminine, as the reference to Scheherazade suggests, but it is merely a "story," and not an interesting one at that. For as we all know, for Forster

> a story [is defined] as a narrative of events arranged in their time-sequence. A plot is also a narrative of events, the emphasis falling on causality. "The king died and then the queen died," is a story. "The king died, and then the queen died of grief," is a plot. The time-sequence is preserved, but the sense of causality overshadows it. Consider the death of the queen. If it is in a story we say "and then?" If it is in a plot we ask "why?" (86)

Forster imagines the opposite of story to be not curiosity but mystery, which demands intelligence and memory on the part of the reader, asking us to remember incidents and create connecting threads between them, for since a plot "cannot be appreciated without intelligence, part of the mind must be left behind, brooding, while the other part goes marching on." Curiosity in this view becomes a kind of death march, endlessly gathering new details to it, never shaping any of them into a sequence of causality.

At this point in our abbreviated cultural history, unexpectedly, curiosity and women begin to find each other again. Anna Wulf, in *The Golden Notebook*, says, "I have only one, and the least important, of the qualities necessary to write at all, and that is curiosity," a quality she links to the increasing sociological, journalistic yearnings of the novel, its retreat from the great intellectual or passionate inquiries of Eliot, Tolstoy, and Thomas Mann.[27] But surely part of her aversion, the note of anxiety, if not downright aggression, is how often the curiosity of details, the realm of small things beautifully but uselessly depicted, has been imagined as the way women writers in particular enter the novel. For John Stuart Mill, it is this attention to details, to objects, to curiosity as a mere cabinet (not so much a *Wunderkammer* as a file cabinet, perhaps, or recipe box) that outfits women to be novelists—but novelists only of a lower order. "Our best novelists in point of composition, and of the management of detail, have mostly been women," Mill notes, but "their compositions are mostly grounded on the existing fund of thought, and their creations do not deviate widely from existing types. This is the sort of inferiority that their works manifest: for in point of execution, in the detailed application of thought, and the perfection of style, there is no inferiority."²⁸ Women, free to observe the world around them, can acquire the "detail" they need—and manage it as if it were another form of huswifery—but they lack as yet the wider experience of free-ranging thought that would allow those details to blend into the "intelligence" Forster also praised. Ian Watt, a hundred years later, in *The Rise of the Novel*, will again single out the detail work, the curious collections, of women writers, interestingly citing Mill as well: "[Jane Austen's] example suggests that the feminine sensibility was in some ways better equipped to reveal the intricacies of personal relationships." Watt goes on to link this attraction to minute detail, what Henry James calls women's quality as "delicate and patient observers; [their ability to] hold their noses close, as it were, to the texture of life,"²⁹ to the (limited) success of women novelists—and, we might say, the sadly limited quality of curiosity itself, once again like Sir Hans, trapped between wonder and enlightenment, doomed always to inquire and gather, always to ask "and then?" and "and then?" never to see or to *know*.

This is one answer to the initial paradox ("Prescribe. Proscribe. What to do, what to do?") I posed about women, curiosity, and the novel. To the extent that she is enflamed with curiosity, drawn beyond the door, excited by what she does not know, the heroine is doomed; to the extent she is chaste, refusing curiosity's lures, proceeding in willed ignorance, she is (equally) at risk. If they are not Pandoras, delving after forbidden, Promethean knowledge, women are mere housekeepers, trapped, fatally, in the trivial. The novel is similarly vexed, poised like a golden-haired doll, perched on the threshold, torn between too much curiosity, too little, and just enough.

If, as I am suggesting, this oscillation is crucial to the formation of the realist project, the "serious pleasures of suspense" or, more precisely to my purposes, the dangerous pleasures of the suspended question, this remains a dilemma for contemporary critics, seeking and at times disparaging the heroine's role in the evolution of the novel. The novel, as I began by suggesting, plays a complicated game of knowledge, one caught up in debates over statistics, criminal law, evidence, and testimony, questions that will recur throughout this book, explicitly in some chapters and more covertly in others. But these ways of knowing are ways of being known in the world as well. They are ways of becoming liberal subjects with all the ambivalence that carries with it. Critics today who take the novel more seriously (if also critically) as a tool of subject formation are similarly skeptical, in particular about the role of women in acquiring knowledge. To them, women's access to the forms of culture is yet another weapon of domestication, part of the dangerous Enlightenment (for which read Benthamite) project of subject formation. Novels work by mastering and subduing curiosity, by making it part of the forces of order, making curiosity (again) trivial. There is a crucial element in this analysis, one necessary to any feminist history of the novel, and that is seeing the novel's cultural work as a gendering of the subject. We might join Nancy Armstrong in locating the modern subject as a woman, the unexpected victor (like Pamela or Jane Eyre) in a Gothic marriage plot.[30] Armstrong's argument overlaps with mine in crucial aspects: she notes that novels work for women precisely because women are denied adventures: in fact, novels are less dangerous for women precisely because "girls must soon perceive the impossibility of their rambling about the world in quest of adventures" like Robinson Crusoe (16). But as she argues, Robinson Crusoe actually becomes the perfect model of female subjectivity, which developed, as it did for Crusoe, in "a totally self-enclosed and functional domain where money did not really matter." For Armstrong, that enclosed domain is marriage and domesticity, and she not only sees marriage as a realm for women that dissolves the social contract into the marital contract (blaming John Stuart Mill for this cultural sleight of hand) but also sees the novel as carrying out precisely the same substitution. In short, novels are dangerous after all, for they convince us to follow sexual plots in lieu of social plots, and hence ignore the way erotic victory (by Jane Eyre, by Elizabeth Bennet, by Pamela) has been manufactured in order to make social problems and class conflict disappear altogether. "The sexual contract cancels out the political one," as she claims of Mill (39); "the union miraculously transforms all social differences into gender differences and gender differences into qualities of mind," as she argues of *Pride and Prejudice*; and "social competition could be sexualized and therefore suppressed even while it was being experienced" (51). For Armstrong, this suppression reaches its apogee in *Hard Times*, where "in a novel rumbling with labor unrest and crises within the educational system, Dickens pursues the sexual theme with perfect aplomb, as if he knew that in fiction at least these volatile political issues could be resolved simply by subjugating the female," in this case the "otherwise unnoteworthy bourgeoise," Louisa Gradgrind (55). Poor hoodwinked readers, willing to follow the uninteresting heroine into the marriage bed, abandoning both the heroine's visions of more (which of course are also unrealized by this plot) and the social desire for more, all for the sake of Mr. Darcy's strong arms. But I think Armstrong in turn is a little hoodwinked by the seductive nature of the marriage plot, imagining that the woman who signs the marriage contract has an unambivalent or even unambiguous relationship not only to that contract but also to the social contract at which it always hints. That moment of contract seems to me far more complicated, as the heroine maintains her position as a choosing subject only by entering a far more dangerous plot—which is also to say that Jane Eyre and her sisters are far less complicit subjects than Armstrong's analysis suggests, and Louisa Gradgrind is far from an "unnoteworthy bourgeoise."

But Armstrong's social critique is not the only path available. Narrative theory also highlights that moment of choosing as a moment of dangerous inscription into a preordained status quo, but it draws closer to my interest in the curious heroine by suggesting something far more alluring in that figure—and something already anxious in her presence in the narrative contract. Roland Barthes in particular marks the moment of female curiosity as the start of what he tellingly calls "contract narratives": a moment of transformation within sexual and social relations.

For Barthes, narrative desire does not float free. Rather, it exists in a world of social relations. "Narrative: legal tender, subject to contract, economic stakes, in short, *merchandise*," he says in *S/Z*: "What should the narrative be exchanged for? What is the narrative worth?" (89) "Sarrasine" is not the story of a castrato, but of a contract; narrative is determined not by a desire to narrate but by a desire to exchange: "It is a medium of exchange, an agent, a currency, a gold standard." And who is the agent of the narrative? It is the heroine, sitting outside the locked door, looking at the picture of the Adonis. It is with her question to the narrator, "What did that mean?" that the story gets under way; with her insistence, "No, I want to know now" that the contract is formed. Without her curiosity, no story, no enigma, no contract.

For Barthes, woman is not herself a "locked door" but the attempt to penetrate one: here, the woman desires an answer, an entrance into narrative. For that reason, she asks the question and enters the contract. And Barthes means this contract literally: while Peter Brooks, air-lifting Barthes's sense of contract out of history, claims that contract is a static force, for Barthes it is real and motile.[31] The contract is "tit for tat," a night of love for a good story, but it is also the woman's attempt to gain not only knowledge but also power, a power she retains in the end only by breaking the contract, asserting her own secrets: "No man will have known me." But while the story is going forward, it is a story of pure exchange: pure "fable," in Barthes's terms. That story (a "contract of prostitution" in "Sarrasine," but also the "purchase [of] life itself," as it is in *The Thousand and One Nights*) is not merely a story of female sexuality, but a story of the heroine's attempt to gain knowledge otherwise closed to her—something that is outside, forbidden, unknowable except through a contract with a (predatory) man.

"What is there in farewell, door, gift?" They remind us that both narrative theory and the law in the nineteenth-century novel depend on a nuanced and even dangerous sense of contract and its relationship to curiosity, a relationship enshrined in the marriage plot. The intersection of the two creates the puzzle of modern identity: what does a contracting subject need to know to promise, and how do the limits of female curiosity mark the limits of a contracting, promising self? These are questions that matter as much for readers as they do for heroines. The novelist, the wife, and the suffragette come together—and together they enter the curious room.

And so from the *Wunderkammer* to the rise of the novel to contract theory and the modern subject, for path is where liberal theories of law begin as well. Contract *is* the sign of the modern world. In Sir Henry Maine's famous formulation, we mark the move from ancient to modern by the move from status to contract, and with the freedom to contract comes the emancipation from all the traditional trappings of status, being placed where you are born, being set in professions and religions, in caste and class. John Stuart Mill, who did more than any other thinker to connect feminism and liberalism, identifies the change as even more dramatic: it is, he writes, the move from fisticuffs to business; it is the moment when the modern world begins.[32]

What are the implications of this freedom of contract for women? In one view, women are the thing that is exchanged. They are the merchandise, the goods—and that is one sense of curiosity; a woman is a curio. As in Barthes, this seems initially a pornographic move. It imagines culture as the "traffic" in women, a world in which women are either goods exchanged "between men," moving from their fathers' to their husbands' houses, or are furniture upon which you parade your other commodities, as Dickens suggests in calling Mrs. Merdle "the Bosom," a mantel which her husband can decorate with jewels. The darkest instance of that alienation in English literature is Blake's "London," in which the exchange of women ("the youthful harlot's curse") blasts the newborn infant's tear and blights with plague the marriage hearse.

But Blake's nightmare world of "charters" reminds us unexpectedly of the more positive (or at least agentive) views of contract. The tradition of the English novel and of Anglo-American law is to move women away from commodities and toward agency: in the novel, as in (aspects of) the law, women are contracting subjects, capable of promising. Anglo-American law is unusual in requiring "consideration," in that there is no contract without exchange: in law, you can never contract to give "something" for "nothing"; you cannot bind yourself in slavery. Within that model of reciprocity if not total equality, marriage stands (however ironically at moments) as the model of all contract. The marriage contract requires consent on the part of the woman—a moment in which she is not just property. A woman must "bind" herself—and women, like readers, must be imagined as capable of promising and remaining true.

When John Stuart Mill first suggested that the law might consider women to be legal "persons," and in particular suggested they might represent themselves in the franchise, he framed the problem this way: "The law would cease to declare them incapable of serious things; would cease to proclaim that their opinions and wishes are unworthy of regard, on things which concern them equally with men, and on many things which concern them much more than men. They would no longer be classed with children, idiots, and lunatics, as incapable of taking care of either themselves or others, and needing that everything should be done for them, *without asking their consent*. If only one woman in twenty thousand used the suffrage, to be declared capable of it would be a boon to all women. Even that theoretical enfranchisement would remove a weight from the expansion of their faculties" (emphasis added).[33] This is the central question of legal and parliamentary reform in the middle of the nineteenth century, when Mill, inspired and badgered by a brilliant circle of feminists, first proposed in parliamentary debate over the Second Reform Bill that a woman might be a legal person, that the law might "make the woman a moral agent in these matters." For Mill, this begins precisely with the power of contract—and then, subtly but brilliantly, leads first to suffrage, then to marriage reform, and then to a fully fledged curiosity, in both senses of the word.

Mill's attention to marriage law and the law of coverture, under which wives are no longer legal persons, losing the freedom to sign contracts, to write wills, to inherit property, throws us back on the novel—and in particular on the marriage plot—with a new sense of why women need *curiosity*. "Marriage is the only actual bondage known to our law. There remain no legal slaves, except the mistress of every house" (196). Women (most women, and certainly most heroines) will make one and only one choice. They will have exactly one chance to "choose [their] pursuits," one moment when they have "liberty to govern their conduct by their own feelings of duty," and that is the moment of consenting to marry. At that moment, they disappear as legal persons, and they will lose even the right to own their own curiosity, to wander at will. Mill points out in essence what subsequent feminist critics will observe: first, that a slave does not ever have choice in the way that Enlightenment theory imagined, so a woman's "choice" needs to be understood differently; and second, that a "contracted heart" in that way, given the constraints on female choice, is a form of prostitution, a contract in which women trade their services for support; in which they have given away their right to bargain, to contract again, to choose "their own feelings of duty."

Strange then to say that curiosity is what restores to women that quintessential freedom, but so argues John Stuart Mill. For Mill, marriage is not only "bondage" and the serial violence of Bluebeard's castle; it is also a potent site of political and "theoretic" emancipation. Marriage is for him a Miltonic utopian ideal, for it is the place where true companionship obtains. It is also, or rather it should be, the place where we learn sympathy—as Mill poignantly puts it, to the possible disbelief of anyone actually raised in a family, it is a "school of sympathy in equality." Most important, it is the perfect laboratory for what Mill values—the exposure to opinions utterly unlike our own. Mill believes in the total freedom of expression because he thinks that "he who knows only his side of the case" (as he quotes Cicero) "knows little of that," and it is only through adversarial debate, the exploration of that which is most unlike oneself, that one can come to a free conclusion. Testing as much as sympathizing creates the perfect union. We need to dwell with what we do not like in order to think more clearly and independently— and is there a better definition of marriage than consistently, over time and of necessity, dwelling with what we do not like? So marriage is on one hand the obvious sign of inequality, a world of in which "the vilest malefactor has some wretched woman tied to him, against whom he can commit any atrocity except killing her, and, if tolerably cautious, can do that without much danger of the legal penalty" ("Subjection of Women," 151). And yet on the other hand, marriage in its more ideal form becomes a place for Mill where two curious minds can encounter one another and test the world. Marriage takes its place alongside the franchise as offering women the necessary education in choosing that will allow them to become ever more conspicuously individual.

Mill's prescription for female emancipation is certainly unorthodox, but it is entirely seductive and curiously novelistic. It has powerful implications for the Victorian marriage plot with which it is coincident, as George Eliot, more than any other writer, will discover. What women lack in the world as it is currently organized is the chance to fulfill that striving after something original only they can see. Eliot articulates something very similar in *Felix Holt*, when Esther Lyon says to Felix, "Women choose meanly because only mean things are offered them," and Felix wishes for Esther "a good strong terrible vision" that will save her.[34] The novel imagines that their marriage could be something as yet unseen, something visionary and radical. Mill's relationship with an extraordinary woman (and the eccentric marriage he eventually formed with her, attempting to renounce his property rights in flagrant defiance of what the law forced on him) provided Mill with the model of that more perfect union which, however extralegally, emancipates both parties, imagines a different compact. This is what he imagines for women, this freedom to choose something that as yet does not exist, something that takes a form that others cannot see, a "good strong terrible vision." Until conditions of freedom obtain, until people are free to choose the unexpected, to shock their neighbors and perhaps surprise themselves, neither party can be said to contract; neither party can be said truly to choose. And here is the question all the novels in this book will take up with even more intensity at the moment when curiosity gains a political standing: *what happens after that first choice?* Once a woman begins to understand the implications of her choice, how can that woman become free to experiment—to test, to wander, to be curious, to choose again?

This question returns us to the model of the Bluebeard plot and narrative theory—to curiosity. In this view, the first choice a woman makes is of a husband, and only by making that choice can she learn about choosing, but that first choice runs the grave risk of being a fatal error. Given the compulsion to marry, however, a woman may be truly free to choose only *after* she learns from that initial mistaken, uninformed choice. Only then is she the independent thinker, the person freed from convention, whom Mill imagines.[35]

Mill formulates an essentially novelistic equation: as you choose, so shall you live. What the realist novel adds to that narrative is the possibility that even a bad choice can become a good choice, can bring you knowledge, courage, eccentricity, curiosity. Whereas Mill both embraces the possibility of good marriages and suggests subtly the useful frictions of an imperfect marriage, the novel of the curious heroine goes further, claiming that a bad marriage, all but inevitable for a woman of intelligence in the world as it is, can still be a coming to wisdom. It is through narratives of bad marriages (ill-conceived, ill-matched, ill-fated) that the heroine increasingly comes to test the contractual model of marriage and conceive a new law and new plot possibilities for women. Even as it seems to erase a woman's legal identity and capacity for choice, marriage can be an instrument of education, not only "a school of sympathy in equality" but a school for individuality and for moral choice.

Think back, then, to *S/Z*, and the moment when the curious heroine stands outside a door, waiting to hear a story. For Barthes, as in the marriage plot, curiosity is eroticized, but Barthes, as we saw, noticed something else: that under this erotic contract, women do not want sex for its own sake, or even to gain other material pleasures. Instead, they are trading sex for knowledge. This is what readers do as well. We bind our desires; we "charter" them; we render them licit; we lock them up. But this story does something else. Barthes's "pensive" marquise, like the heroines of George Eliot, retains the power to enter the law, to inscribe a story of judgment. The question is always, what would it take for her to enter? What would it mean for this story to be a story of moral choice? If she did, and if the modern woman became the subject of some different power to choose *and then choose again*, contract would cease to be merely circulation; curiosity would be more than dilatory interest; the heroine's questions would become significant, ethical, matters of life and death—as they are, repeatedly, in the Victorian novel.

In *Middlemarch*, George Eliot called this vision "a sudden letting in of daylight, waking her [Dorothea] from previous stupidity and *incurious* self-absorbed ignorance." This is the progress of the curious heroine, removing herself from the classification of "children, criminals and idiots," and choosing to care, choosing (we might say) her "curiosity." It is that, as Eliot says later in the novel, which "asserted itself as acquired knowledge asserts itself and will not let us see as we saw in the day of our ignorance." But there is another story for this "letting in of daylight," and its name is Bluebeard. This Gothic tale might seem to have little to do with the realist novel, but it offers us a powerful fable for the story of curiosity, consent, and marriage we are telling; what we might call the nontrivial (or even ethical) version of curiosity. This tale is darker, what Eliot elsewhere will call "ghosts in the daylight," a story of willful self-alienation, of a fatal curiosity that risks everything but that yields the whole story, though Fatima almost breaks her neck (then almost loses her head) to get it. What price knowledge? In terms that Mill might recognize, the price is total self-alienation, an abandonment to everything but wanting to know, to finding the forbidden self behind the locked door. Bluebeard's wife, removing the forbidden key from the chain and opening the door, entering the bloody chamber, asks, what else might be behind a door? Nothing less than the same modern subjectivity posited by the curators of the British Museum and modern feminism: a post-Enlightenment subject; one poised and ready to contract.

Where better to find a contract than in a fairy tale? This one, in particular: once upon a time there was a man with a blue beard—in search of a wife. And in another part of the same story there was a woman, a woman with a sister, a woman who knows better but marries the man with the blue beard anyway . . . and is drawn into a mystery. Having agreed to one contract, the marriage contract, she finds herself bound by another: a promise not to open a closed door. Open it she does, tripping down the steps in her eagerness—and what she finds is a series of her predecessors, all drawn by the same curiosity. It is no accident that Charles Perrault's version of the Bluebeard story entered English culture in the late eighteenth century alongside the beginning of the new self-consciousness we have been tracing about the laws of coverture, and it comes to us as a cautionary tale, one suited for a world in which women are themselves objects of curiosity, discouraged from any interest in a wider world. Perrault's first moral confirms this: "Curiosity, in spite of its appeal, often leads to deep regret. To the displeasure of many a maiden, its enjoyment is short lived. Once satisfied, it ceases to exist, and always costs dearly."[36] But his unusual second moral hints at some anxiety about this conclusion, an anxiety much celebrated by subsequent revisions: "No husband of our age would be so terrible as to demand the impossible of his wife, nor would he be such a jealous malcontent," it says. "For, whatever the color of her husband's beard, the wife of today will let him know who the master is."

Angela Carter's twentieth-century revision draws our attention away from the tidy moral to an unexpected liberatory promise. The heroine of Carter's Bluebeard tale, "The Bloody Chamber," discovers in herself a Blakean capacity for pain and pleasure, a "potentiality for corruption," she did not know she had (11). This is the knowledge that her husband, dead at the end of the story, shot by "a single, irreproachable bullet through [the] head," always carried with him: "a man who lived in such strange, secret places that, if I loved him enough to follow him, I should have to die" (35). As in Perrault's version, the woman who marries against her best judgment a man with a "curiously blue beard" enjoys his wealth and power but must transgress, against his express command, the limits he sets upon her. Taking the smallest key on the chain he leaves with her and entering the forbidden chamber, she finds the bodies of his previous wives, left in a pool of their own blood. In her terror she drops the key, then retrieves it—but the telltale stain remains, and when the husband returns, he knows where she has been, and he knows what she knows. The husband knows in advance the extent of his wife's curiosity: as Carter's heroine says, it was "the secret of Pandora's box, but he had given me the box, himself, knowing I must learn the secret." But in Carter's story, unlike Perrault's, there is another secret, and that is the secret of Bluebeard's emptiness: when the heroine reenters his room, "carrying the bunch of keys that jangled at every step like a curious musical instrument," her husband is sitting on the bed, "his head sunk in his hands. And it seemed . . . he was in despair." When he looks at her, she observes: "[He] stare[s] at me with his blind, shuttered eyes as though he did not recognize me," and she feels "a terrified pity for him." "The atrocious loneliness of that monster!" the heroine remarks, and yet an atrocious loneliness is the mark of individualism in the story: "I knew . . . that henceforth, I would always be lonely," she says of her marriage, and to be married is to be "afraid of myself."

It is also to be curious: the product of their marriage is not a child but "a sleepless companion, my dark newborn curiosity" (22). That curiosity is both a curse and the thing that produces a plot. For however dark it seems, this is still a story of enlightenment, as the heroine crosses the threshold and moves toward knowledge: I stood there and was blind; I moved forward, and now I see. Space and time; here and there; then and now. And yet, the story also poses the paradox of a subject who must choose while being trapped, frozen in a moment of insufficient knowledge and of legally contravened subjecthood. However sanguinely the story may transpire for Perrault (the husband dead, the wife the inheritrix, the family settled, and the moral applied), the wife must break her word, cross the threshold, and desire to "know too much" for all these things to happen. In order to have a narrative, the wife must be curious, but to enter the marriage plot, she must have promised not to inquire too much—as the conclusion will tell us, an "impossible promise," one that makes and unbreaks her as a subject. It is by promising that she gains a story, and by breaking the promise, by being curious, that she gets an interesting story. The plot's great appeal is its double-edged sword, not only that the wife cannot ever know enough but that she will come to know too much—and only then can she choose. Curiosity is finally less what causes one to seek knowledge than the creation of new knowledge, the realm of the *Wunderkammer*, the magical chamber, the cluttered space of the novel, what Henry James calls in his preface to *The Portrait of a Lady* "the dusky, crowded, heterogeneous backshop of the mind."[37]

Is Bluebeard right? Is there always an earlier wife? How did the first wife get into the chamber? This is the question the story never asks—and yet, the novel does. Answering the question draws us all the way into enlightenment: I once was blind, but now I see; beginning to see the light; a terrible vision is born. In the novels that follow Bluebeard's entrance onto the English stage, one heroine after another will be struck by that lightning: in *Jane Eyre*, haunted by the as-yet-unseen Bertha Mason, the newly engaged Jane and Rochester stand by a lightning-blasted tree; in *Middlemarch*, after Dorothea leaves behind the blue room in Casaubon's house, she and Will Ladislaw are thrust into each other's arms by the shock of lightning; most directly and fatally, in Sade's *Justine*, the heroine is enlightened to death. And as for the paradigmatic heroine I invoked in my introduction ("What will Isabel Archer do?") she will, it would seem, be struck dumb.

For if we begin in the middle of the novel, Isabel Archer can do precisely nothing. As Madame Merle, the mistress of Isabel's husband and the mother of the girl whom Isabel believes to be Gilbert and his first wife's daughter, says of our heroine: "She seemed in a very simple, almost in a stupid, state of mind. She was completely bewildered" (426). She is bewildered precisely because she is beginning to see the light—she is, almost literally, dazed by enlightenment. We tend to forget this, for it is the beginning of *The Portrait of a Lady* most readers remember, the start of the journey, and the curious heroine's thirst for experience. Isabel Archer, the brave-hearted American girl, raised on promises, comes to England and captivates the imagination of all she meets: her uncle; her sickly, ugly cousin Ralph; the distinguished Lord Warburton; and the impetuous American, Caspar Goodwood. Everyone is curious—but no one as curious as she. She remains curious, singular, uncaptured, a perfect denizen of liberty ("If ever a girl was a free agent, she had been"[333]) until she meets Gilbert Osmond, another deracinated American, the friend and former lover of the serpentine Madame Merle, wife to a blameless Swiss man and secret mother of the lovely Pansy. Into this tangle of relations Isabel plunges, ignorant and wild and free and imaginative, only to choose to marry the one man in the world who does not love her for her imagination—or rather, would love her if she used her imagination only for his own purposes. Far from gaining her more freedom or more experience, her choice entraps her: "Her mind was to be his—attached to his own like a small garden-plot to a deer-park." Or, as she further thinks, "He didn't wish her to be stupid. On the contrary, it was because she was clever that she had pleased him. But he expected her intelligence to operate altogether in his favour" (355).

Osmond's expectations for Isabel operate as a kind of Bluebeard's castle: there is a dead wife; there is the haunted Madame Merle; there is Isabel's own incarceration. "Between those four walls she had lived ever since; they were to surround her for the rest of her life. It was the house of darkness, the house of dumbness, the house of suffocation...." (353). At first it seems that this is the bloody chamber, that this is Gilbert's form of wife-murder; but it is not. Instead the "darkness and suffocation" are the preparation for Isabel's real moment of choice, the moment when she chooses to cross another threshold, when she chooses not to renounce her own curiosity.

For if the first half of *The Portrait of a Lady* is the novel in which Isabel Archer, thinking she is choosing freely, is acquired by Gilbert Osmond, the second is the one in which she takes the full measure, as James would put it, of the curiosity shop in which she is enclosed. Here, Isabel realizes that although she still thinks, wrongly, that she chose freely, her choice has made her unfree, that it is, as Ralph once said it would be, "a cage." All marriage is, she said blithely, thinking she has chosen her cage ("If I like my cage, that needn't trouble you," she says; and the countess says, "I never congratulate any girl on marrying; I think they ought to make it somehow not quite so awful a steel trap" [294]), but the second half of the novel consists of the *rebirth* of her curiosity, her ability to precisely measure the dimensions of where she is "placed," and perhaps to free herself (or be forced into freedom by a knowledge she does not entirely choose) through her *second* education, the one that comes once she begins to defy her husband. Isabel's decision to marry Gilbert, her seemingly fatal choice, took place off stage, but this second choice takes place very much before our eyes—and is a provocation to our enlightenment as well.

How does Isabel Archer learn? Through a kind of terror. At first, to know things is horrible and is to be lost—a different version of the wideness of the world:

> Now that she was in the secret, now that she knew something that so much concerned her and the eclipse of which had made life resemble an attempt to play whist with an imperfect pack of cards, the truth of things, their mutual relations, their meaning, and for the most part their horror, rose before her with a kind of architectural vastness. (457)

How did that vision "rise before her"? The answer is an unexpected form of enlightenment. For the series of revelations that come to her almost unbidden, some of them from people who, in the words of the Countess Gemini, "have been so bored with your not knowing" (443), some of her own making, as Isabel's curiosity begins slowly to recover from the blow of her marriage, all come in startling bursts of light. When Isabel first comes on Madame Merle and Gilbert Osmond alone, her friend standing and her husband sitting, she receives "a sudden flicker of light" (458). After that scene, Isabel views Madame Merle "with a different eye" as she "seemed to wake from a long pernicious dream." As Madame Merle turns on Isabel ("Let us have him!" she pleads, about Lord Warburton's lapsed pursuit of Pansy) and Isabel responds, shocked, "What have you to do with me?" Isabel looks up at her, "her face ... almost a prayer to be enlightened," "but the light of this woman's eyes seemed only a darkness" (564). The Countess Gemini, with her "glittering eyes," asking "did you never guess" that Gilbert's wife had no children, reports, "My poor Isabel, you're not simple enough." The answer ("whether to this intimate friend of several years the great historical epithet of wicked were to be applied") comes in a "glare of intention," as the countess rises "while her gathered perversity grew vivid and dreadful." And when Isabel sees Madame Merle at the convent where they have both gone to visit Pansy, "Madame Merle was already so present to her vision that her appearance in the flesh was like suddenly, and rather awfully, seeing a painted picture move. Isabel had been thinking all day of her falsity, her audacity, her ability, her probable suffering; and these dark things seemed to flash with a sudden light as she entered the room. Her being there at all had the character of ugly evidence, of handwritings, of profaned relics, of grim things produced in court. It made Isabel feel faint" (449).

But Isabel does not faint. Instead, she chooses again, unexpectedly, her own curiosity. In the brilliant scene midway through the story, the scene that James himself considered the prize of the novel, "the vigil of searching criticism," Isabel shockingly thinks, "She would have been willing, however, to renounce all her curiosities and sympathies for the sake of a personal life, if the person concerned had only been able to make her believe it was a gain!" (361). All of this is horrible to the reader, who thinks she is capable precisely of this act of renunciation. But she is not. When her aunt, Mrs. Touchett, writes to tell her of Ralph's final illness, the message reads: "You used to talk a good deal about your duty and to wonder what it was; shall be curious to see whether you've found it out. Ralph is really dying, and there's no other company" (443). And Isabel, miraculously, becomes curious again.

Yet crucially, it is not exactly the same curiosity that Isabel experiences. Much as her aunt's telegram, which "seem[ed] to admit of so many interpretations," had sparked the entire plot in the first chapter ("Taken sister's girl, died last year, go to Europe, two sisters, quite independent"), this telegram opens again narrative possibilities, but here they form a moral question: "shall be curious to see whether you've found [your duty] out." With that provocation, Isabel starts on her second journey across the threshold, not the one that led her into the closed room of her marriage ("She was as perfectly aware that the sight of her interest in her cousin stirred her husband's rage as if Osmond had locked her into her room—which she was sure was what he wanted to do," she said in that long, quiet night before the dying fire) but the one that leads her into a railway car, across Europe and into Charing Cross station.

What does Isabel Archer want to know? Not, I think, what most critics have thought that women want to know, which is the secret of sexual pleasure. In that reading, what Isabel doesn't know is what everyone else knows—that sex with Gilbert Osmond will not be fun. As I suggested earlier, that is one way of reading the entire tradition of the curious heroine and the marriage plot: in that version, women could be properly schooled, and Dorothea Brooke would never choose Edward Casaubon nor Gwendolen

Harleth Henleigh Grandcourt. After all, say the critics, the hero's sadism is only thinly veiled, and only a woman not in on the secret would miss so enormous a clue. It is easy enough simply to subsume the Bluebeard plot to this larger cultural narrative of female ignorance and male insensitivity—in that way, even the end of the Bluebeard plot is easily read, the substitution of marital violence for conjugal sex; a dark awakening at a moment when the scimitar flashes; when in the brief illumination one sees the bodies of one predecessors and thinks, before the sword falls, ah, this was the law all along. Or, as we might rephrase it, whatever was I thinking when I married a man with a blue beard?

But that is not what Isabel Archer learns. For Isabel Archer *believes* in enlightenment. She believes herself free; she believes in her own ability to choose; she believes in her ability to judge for herself and to *contract*—she believes, in short, that she is an individual, in her majority, knowing for herself. This is the heart of her fury at Gilbert Osmond—not that he has used her, but that he didn't tell her. "A man might marry a woman for her money perfectly well; the thing was often done. But at least he should let her know" (425). Without that knowledge, how can Isabel even pretend to have assented; how can she presume to choose again?

The violence threatened against Isabel, her near terror of Madame Merle and Gilbert Osmond, the courage of her decision to visit the dying Ralph, is precisely her assertion of her ability to choose, to want to know something forbidden, something not only about the world but about herself. The violence directed at the heroine in *The Portrait of a Lady* is not so much erotic as it is designed precisely to destroy her individuality, her ability to choose, her ability even to know where she stands—to complete her inventory, that heart of the realist novel. It is in that way that the knowledge Isabel gains is what we familiarly call pornographic, for while pornography hangs in our imagination as the dark underside of enlightenment, it is but the fabular and stark version of other accounts of the modern world, including both the collection of curiosity and the realist novel This, rather than the secret of jouissance, is what Isabel Archer learns, though she would not phrase it as Angela Carter does:

> In a world where women are commodities, a woman who refuses to sell herself will have the thing she refuses to sell taken away from her by force. The piety, the gentleness, the sensitivity, all the qualities she has learned to admire in herself, are invitations to violence: all her life, she has been groomed for the slaughterhouse. And though she is virtuous, she does not know how to be good. (55)

This is Carter's brilliant cynicism, of course—but it is central to the novel tradition as well. What does it mean to be good? Goodness is not the same as virtue, which is nothing but the lamb's ability to walk to the slaughterhouse. Instead, goodness is choosing, as Isabel does, to defy convention, to risk her husband's rage, to walk out the door and visit a dying man whom she loves; a man who has not, unlike her husband, used her.

For this is the secret: again, that when she thought she was contracting freely, Isabel was most bound; when she thought she was most herself, she was most someone else's. This knowledge is what lies inside the bloody chamber, and this secret what sets Isabel free, makes her able finally to choose. Before, she lived in a world of false choices—false enlightenment. It takes the immersion in the world of the users, the cruel ones, to understand that what she had before was not true freedom. What Isabel had before was theories—or, as the novel says at different points, "She was wrong, but she believed; she was deluded, but she was dismally consistent. It was wonderfully characteristic of her that, having invented a fine theory, about Gilbert Osmond, she loved him not for what he really possessed, but for his very poverties dressed out as honours" (288). That is Ralph, of course, but later, "Isabel's cheek burned when she asked herself if she had really married on a factitious theory, in order to do something finely appreciable with her money. But she was able to answer quickly enough that this was only half the story" (351). We might add, that finding out her mistake (her "generous mistake") is the other half—and that without the mistake, that discovery would never have occurred.

What James has done in *The Portrait of a Lady* is illuminate the gap between theory and practice, expectation and reality, between the world Isabel expected to find and what she found behind the door. Isabel again, thinking that "if any woman was free she was," is wrong. To return to Freud and the choice of the caskets with which we began this chapter, there is "the illusion of choice where there is only necessity, or destiny." Or to give it a modern, feminist spin, as Carter suggests when she quotes a woman who spoke to Margaret Sanger about birth control, "it's so different a life from what all girls expect"(38). The curious heroine's progress, as we used to say, falls into that gap—and in that fall, she finds an unexpected and largely unwanted freedom, not the freedom they had imagined (says Carter, "Justine's life was doomed to disappointment before it began, like that of a woman who wishes for nothing better than a happy marriage"[50]) but something more terrible, more "grim," as Isabel would say. The plot forces on them a more radical form of freedom, a more radical choice, one almost outside the law. That is the realm Angela Carter seeks out in *The Sadeian Woman*, as she imagines the plot of that seemingly incurious heroine, Justine. Justine, as Carter notes, is another Clarissa, but one even more radically innocent—and nowhere is the tension between innocence and ignorance more clearly marked. But Carter says of the blankly virtuous Justine, "She is a free woman, in spite of herself"; though she hides from choice whenever she can (virgin and empty, not good) she has her "freedom thrust upon her, she has not seized it for herself" (51). Juliette may choose her freedom (strike out for herself), but even Justine can be struck by lightning.

And so, despite her dislike of "crude revelation," can Isabel Archer be (dumb)struck. Here Angela Carter helps us return to the great tradition of the English novel: the heroine's curiosity and her tricky progress toward knowledge. The realist novel, as I have suggested, has a series of stories of enlightenment marked by fire. The most striking (no pun intended) is Sade's *Justine*, where

> Justine dashes to the windows which are already being broken; she would do battle with the wind, she gives a minute's fight, is driven back and at that instant a blazing thunderbolt reaches her where she stands in the middle of the room . . . and transfixes her. Mme de Lorsange emits a terrible cry and falls in a faint; Monsieur de Corville calls for help, attentions are given each woman, Madame de Lorsange is revived, but the unhappy Justine has been struck in such wise [that] hope itself can no longer subsist for her; the lightning entered her right breast, found the heart, and after having consumed her chest and face, burst out through her belly. The miserable thing was hideous to look upon; Monsieur de Corville orders that she be borne away.[38]

That strategic, deadly lightning snakes a path through the nineteenth-century novel. When Jane Eyre and Rochester have their fierce confrontation in the garden, it is after a lightning storm, and Jane finds out the next day that an honored old tree at Thornfield Hall has been destroyed in the blast ("the great horse-chestnut at the bottom of the orchard had been struck by lightning in the night, and half of it split away"); later, Rochester himself is blasted and describes himself as "no better than the old lightning-struck chestnut-tree in Thornfield orchard." It reappears in *Middlemarch*, where it remains behind glass, but is forceful enough to throw Dorothea and Will into each other's arms:

> While he was speaking there came a vivid flash of lightning which lit each of them up for the other—and the light seemed to be the terror of a hopeless love. Dorothea darted instantaneously from the window; Will followed her, seizing her hand with a spasmodic movement; and so they stood, with their hands clasped, like two children, looking out on the storm, while the thunder gave a tremendous crack and roll above them, and the rain began to pour down. Then they turned their faces towards each other, with the memory of his last words in them, and they did not loose each other's hands.[39]

The central image is straight out of *Paradise Lost*, where Adam and Eve leave the garden and head toward mortality hand in hand (Will has just said to Dorothea, "Think of me as one on the brink of the grave"), but the lightning flash (like "the terror of a hopeless love") is rather like the regenerative spark in a Frankenstein movie, promising both monstrosity and unity, as if the heavens fiercely smiled upon them and a new life were beginning.

No such theatrics for Henry James, of course—and yet, the touch of melodrama enters *The Portrait of a Lady* as well, in its final moments of "revelation" and the glare of spectacle. The countess "had expected to kindle some responsive blaze," and though it is delayed, the lightning does come. It arrives after the great revelation, the single day in which Isabel "seemed to-day to live in a world illumined in lurid flashes," first Gilbert's refusal of her request that she visit Ralph, then her conversation with the countess, then the visit to Pansy, in which she confronts Madame Merle. At that moment, "on the other side of the window lay the garden of the convent; but this is not what she saw; she saw nothing of the budding plants and the glowing afternoon. She saw, in the crude light of that revelation which had already become a part of experience and to which the very frailty of the vessel in which it had been offered her only gave an intrinsic price, the dry staring fact that she had been an applied handled hung-up tool, as senseless and convenient as mere shaped wood and iron" (451). That same evening she boards the train in Rome and appears in England, meeting Henrietta and Bantling, leaving the lurid flashes of Rome behind. After that, twilight: the world of Gardencourt to which she has returned is a world of grayness, in which there is only "dim light" and "a shaded candle," and even Ralph's ghost is merely "the darkness beg[u]n vaguely to grow grey" (ch 55). The scene we expect to be the final scene of revelation, Isabel's final conversation with Ralph on his deathbed, is almost entirely in darkness, and Isabel does not claim any special form of enlightenment: "I only know today because there are people less stupid than I." The blast of knowledge comes later, from Caspar Goodwood's kiss:

> His kiss was like white lightning, a flash that spread, and spread again, and stayed; and it was extraordinarily as if, while she took it, she felt each thing in his hard manhood that had least pleased her, each aggressive fact of his face, his figure, his presence, justified of its intense identity and made one with this act of possession. So had she heard of those wrecked and under water following a train of images before they sink. (482)

This is "enlightenment," and James, with this metaphor, is playing artfully with the series of scenes from the literary past, but he is also rejecting the vision of sudden and irrevocable transformation, of the inevitable cosmic electric signal:

> But when darkness returned she was free. She never looked about her; she only darted from the spot. There were lights in the windows of the house; they shone far across the lawn. In an extraordinarily short time—for the distance

> was considerable—she had moved through the darkness (for she saw nothing) and reached the door. Here only she paused. She looked all about her; she listened a little; then she put her hand on the latch. (482)

Isabel does get an answer, a final revelation, for "she had not known where to turn; but she knew now." "There was a very straight path," says James—but neither he, nor she, says what it is; all we know is that when Caspar goes to seek her in London, she is not there, and Henrietta, with "cheap" patience, tells him she has gone back to Rome.

Here is where James confronts us with our own curiosity, at last. Caspar has asked Isabel what she will do and proposes himself as a solution—in much the same spirit that she herself has wondered if, had her aunt never taken her to Europe, she would have married Caspar in the first place. Is the entire adventure, in short, a mistake—can it be undone? Can the knowledge, we might ask, be unlearned? Her aunt, interestingly, posed much the same dilemma at the beginning of the book, questioning her own behaviour: "You may say I shouldn't have enlightened her," she says to Ralph in chapter 5, but the book will never say that, but nor does it ever say what this gift of enlightenment means or why, as at least seems true, it has led her backward into Bluebeard's castle, instead of forward into the future—or at least, as we might hope, into a divorce court.

James left himself open to several critiques in writing the book, and the ending, as he acknowledges, is one of them: he will be blamed for leaving his heroine "en l'air," and he hints that he might have written a sequel, perhaps as he did with *Roderick Hudson* and *The Princess Casamassima*. But there is much that is deliberate in his abandonment of his heroine to the middle of her story. For one thing, he has told us that the story was the thing of least interest to him: instead, he says, sounding the littlest bit like Forster, the point of most interest is the scene *before* the revelations tumble in upon Isabel, the scene where she sits up, thinking, in "the vigil of searching criticism." But for another thing, we might imagine, he has rejected the chance to make "use" of Isabel, to find the proper place for her in his collection. "Do with her?" Aunt Lydia says, under Ralph's repeated questioning: "Do with her? You talk as if she were a yard of calico. I shall do absolutely nothing with her, and she herself will do everything she chooses" (48). Isabel is not, after all, a yard of calico. "Why shouldn't Pansy be married as you would put a letter in the post-office?" (358), Isabel thinks, and then stops the marriage, just as she tries to stop Gilbert from "playing theoretic tricks on the delicate organism of his daughter" (435). Gilbert, the mad curioso, with his collection; Ralph, with his promise of forgiveness for a generous mistake; Isabel, with her faith in contract and enlightenment.

Isabel Archer is very much the princess before the Sphinx, the heroine with her choice of suitors—"the illusion of choice where there is only necessity, or destiny," as we saw Freud claim; "the passion which seemed to point to freedom even though it was actually fulfilled neither in marriage nor anywhere outside," as Horkheimer and Adorno put it (107). But the novel does not end there: Isabel escapes the collection; the letter does not get mailed; the objects get up and walk away; the heroine, no longer stupid, is given a new curiosity. She is, after all, free—the question, which is the question feminism will ask as well, is, what will she do with that freedom? From *Paradise Lost* onward (which is to say, everywhere in the modern world) that is the question for the novel as well. That curiosity, that test of the heroine, which is the heart of the novel, is where we must now turn.

CHAPTER 2

⚜

Reading for the Test, Trying the Heroine

The Curiosity Defense

All the characters are on trial in any civilized narrative.
  William Empson, *Milton's God*[1]

For God shal bring euery worke into iudgement, with euery secret thing, whether it bee good, or whether it bee euill.
  Ecclesiastes 12:14

And I perhaps am secret. . . . Heav'n is high . . .
  John Milton, *Paradise Lost*

Till this moment I never knew myself.
  Jane Austen, *Pride and Prejudice*

How many are the trials of the curious heroine! Not that the heroine doesn't wriggle. The beginning of the previous chapter invoked one of the most beloved scenes of *Pride and Prejudice*, that in which Lady Catherine de Bourgh arrives to interrogate Elizabeth Bennet. "I came here to try you," asserts Lady Catherine, and the trial seems to consist largely of Elizabeth parrying Lady Catherine's thrusts: "I am almost the nearest relation he has in the world, and am entitled to know all his dearest concerns," says Lady Catherine. "But you are not entitled to know mine; nor will such behaviour as this, ever induce me to be explicit," responds Elizabeth. Over and over, Elizabeth is allowed to finesse the question. She need say neither "Yes, I want to marry your nephew" nor "Yes, he has proposed to me," but rather she can, delightfully, frustrate Lady Catherine's curiosity: "I do not pretend to possess equal frankness with your ladyship. You may ask questions which I shall not choose to answer." But even Elizabeth Bennet must, in the end, give way, and her very refusal to promise *not* to marry Mr. Darcy is answer enough—both for Mr. Darcy and his aunt. The contract of narrative curiosity requires some answer, or at least the absence of a clear negative, to keep readers reading. But what, then, is the relationship between the heroine's comic and triumphant victory over Lady Catherine and Elizabeth's refusal (however temporary) to agree to another contract, her refusal to marry Mr. Darcy? What are the complicated games that the heroine plays in testing and being tested?

My argument in this chapter has to do with that fascinating delay, the space of curiosity, between the proposition and the contract—the trial that is the heart of the realist novel, and that makes possible (or not) the eventual marriage. Austen keeps both her promises: she reveals to all the characters the mystery behind Lady Catherine's questions, and she also fulfills her other promise to us, to lead the characters, as well as the readers, into the contract of marriage. But realism itself, as we have seen, is also a contract: a contract into which the reader enters, a contract that provides belief. Robert Newsom has pointed out the ways that this corresponds to formal philosophical ways of knowing, particularly through probability and problems of "credit," what he has called the antinomy of fictional knowledge, but it also, as Ian Watt observed, corresponds to courts of law and other forms of scientific knowledge, to what Catherine Gallagher has called fictional "nobodies" who carry out *our* research for us, testing and weighing the world, at the same time they make it a little smaller, a little more knowable, a little more mapped.[2] Works of formal realism, then, will correspond to a known world; they will contain characters who in at least some ways resemble people we might know or be; they will (in the most cynical reading) turn us into (proper) subjects, prepared for a world of (constrained, contracted) choice.[3] To say that is also to say that realism is always a made thing—an optical device for gathering perspectives, a machine for generating feelings, a collection of human oddities—and hence, as we have also seen, something disturbing, a touch uncanny, something that denaturalizes at the same time that it naturalizes the world. The realist novel always proposes a limit case—something that exists outside its boundaries, outside the contract. That is why, as Raymond Williams has remarked, the realist novel always functions a little like its most monitory characters, saying to rebels and readers alike, "Let's be realistic, [which] probably more often means 'let us accept the limits of this situation'"—count your money; hoard your opportunities; do not squander your desires.[4] Without it, as Mrs. Cadwallader reminds Dorothea Casaubon, you will sit alone in the library at Lowick, and fancy yourself ruling the weather.[5] To be in a realist novel is at once to be in a world of plenitude and certainty, and another world of potential loss and chaos—or as Adam Phillips says of the child's rejection of realism, "Our curiosity depends on a shrinking horizon. Good stories of profit and loss are bewitching."[6]

But to the child, as to the curious heroine, wishing may be the sign of loss. In the realist novel we "want . . . things to be otherwise because they are not as they are supposed to be," and "to live [our] curiosity is itself an acknowledgment of loss, of wanting as the sign of life" (15). The realist novel shows signs of life most stridently when it rejects the very limits it invokes, when it delays or hesitates or wonders. Mimesis is always a world of not-quite, and, as Christopher Prendergast reminds us, a contract is similarly a sign of distrust, not trust—a sign that we expect to be defrauded.[7] When we say a novel is realistic, that it is *vraisemblable*, that it is credible, we are saying that it accords with our beliefs, that it resembles the world in which we are supposed to live. To be incredible, to be incredulous, to want more, is to challenge not only the fiction but the world itself—the limits within which the novel exists, within which the contract is binding. Realism, that is to say, always invites, nay requires, a test. And it is the curious heroine, remember, who is particularly adroit at crossing thresholds—indeed, she exists for little else.

I want in this chapter to use realism's adversarial, duplicitous nature, its peculiar reliance on the trial, not so much to explore the persistence of legal forms in fiction (something brilliantly done in recent studies by critics such as Jonathan Grossman and Alexander Welsh) as to imagine how the curious heroine uses the trial to acquire information and plot a path, even if the forms of trials may ultimately defeat her ingenuity as well as her curiosity. Grossman's study of alibi in the light of emerging practices of character testimony and Welsh's careful study of the highly fungible forms of circumstantial evidence in fiction and law (objects that once "spoke for themselves" increasingly become seen as needing a story to give them meaning) parallel many of the changes I am charting.[8] As the novel evolves, so does the heroine's desire to testify on her own behalf—and her sense that her testimony itself will be disbelieved in a world framed by other narratives. But as both these critics remind us, realism's roots in skeptical philosophy and its primal role in shaping the culture's idea of what makes for a "proper story" also give the curious heroine a cultural power as strong as her own curiosity. In texts ranging from Milton's *Paradise Lost* to Samuel Richardson's *Clarissa* and Henry James's *The Golden Bowl*, we see the heroine try (sometimes successfully, sometimes in vain) to use her curiosity to gain a power beyond the one grudgingly granted her by the novel's ostensible framework. Realism, that is, allows the curious heroine, like Adam Phillips's reluctant child, like Elizabeth Bennet, a space for invention, a period of delay before the signing of the final contract, an interval in which she can instantiate a trial of her own making.

From the trial to the novel to modern feminism: the notion of realism as a form of trial goes back at least as far as Ian Watt who famously, in *The Rise of the Novel*, linked the novel, as I have, to epistemological forms nascent in the seventeenth and eighteenth centuries. For Watt, formal realism (like science, like philosophy) takes the form of a trial, a set of evidence presented to those keen masters of empiricism, the jury of your peers. The novel must feature ordinary people with commonplace names, people doing things in time and space in a manner recognizable to the jurors, their readers, who are also imagined as ordinary people with commonplace names. Watt's influential study has withstood many attacks, not least from feminists, but it provides a fascinating starting place, for imagining the novel as a form of trial offers more than mere events and consequences. If the novel is a place where, as Isabel Archer put it, "grim things are produced in court," it is also a place of (internal) discovery for the curious heroine, a trial of subjectivity. The trial becomes again what it was before it was "twelve good men and true," a place of moral testing, a space much more ambiguous, darker, violent.

But Watt's introduction of this metaphor offers us even more. Unexpectedly, in his discussion of *Clarissa*, Watt sets the terms for the analysis I will follow through in this chapter, a peculiarly feminist twist to the heroine's trials. This turn occurs when he approaches the moment when Clarissa does not marry Lovelace: "If Richardson had stopped here," Watt says, "Clarissa would have been a work analogous to such later portrayals of the Puritan tradition of the tragedy of feminine individualism as George Eliot's *Middlemarch* and Henry James's *Portrait of a Lady*" (234). These three works, Watt says,

> reveal the all but unendurable disparity between expectation and reality that faces sensitive women in modern society, and the difficulties that lie before anyone who is unwilling either to be used, or to use others, as a means. (234)

What Watt imagines as the "tragedy of feminine individualism" is what we have been talking about as the possibilities of female curiosity, but here he draws our attention brilliantly to the gap between expectation and the world—or put another way, between the "fiction" of the heroine's expectations of the world and the "reality" within the fiction.

This is the structure that Watt identifies, then: the heroine tests the world by testing the maxim. This is not just the bride test, in which the heroine's worth is measured, but the test in which she holds the world to a higher standard. To carry out that test, she must cross the threshold, enter modern society, turn herself into what Terry Castle would refer to as a "thermometer." This is in part the test that we have been carrying out through the Bluebeard plot, in which the wife risks her own life to open the locked door, but it is also the test the heroine carries out before her marriage—and in the case of Clarissa, at least, it will make marriage itself unimaginable.

But it is crucial that Watt imagines this not as fairy tale but as myth—and not any myth, but John Milton's "Puritan tradition," the tradition of Eve in the garden, and afterward. For Puritan individualism incorporates not only Eve's curiosity but also Milton's, the invention of the liberal choosing *marital* subject in "The Doctrine and Discipline of Divorce." For Watt, who imagines the novel as a post-Lockean form, the world of Milton is just a half step away, the world in which the moment of crossing the threshold, turning east of Eden, is inevitable.

Milton's Eve can be imagined as the first and most dangerous individual, as the model for the novel's heroines, insisting on taking the active role in her own trial and then proving the dilemma of "innocent ignorance." For *Paradise Lost*'s plot only begins at the moment when its heroine asks for a blue book. It is Eve's test that takes the place of the original subject of Milton's great project, "to *justify* the ways of God to man" by arguing against Satan, "the Adversary." The trial gets under way at the moment when Eve asks Adam to allow her to work in the garden alone—arguing that she should be allowed to face her own trial. By her logic, he has already been tested—she has not. Eve says to Adam, "And what is Faith, Love, Vertue unassaid / Alone, without exterior help sustained?" and he answers her in a firestorm of key words:

> Trial will come unsought.
> Wouldst thou approve thy constancy, approve
> First thy obedience; the other who can know,
> Not seeing thee attempted, who attest?
> But, if thou think, trial unsought may find
> Us both securer than thus warned thou seemest,
> Go; for thy stay, not free, absents thee more.[9]

Whereas Eve imagines "vertue" sustained under "assault" or "assessment" (the opposite of vertue unassaid), Adam plays brilliantly with testimony and test: "trial," he says, will come "unsought": she needs to "approve" her constancy by "approving" her obedience; more, he reminds her, if she is not "attempted" in the sight of another, who will "attest" to her? No testimony, he seems to be saying, no test.

This language of "proving" and "testifying" merges with the language of curiosity at the very moment when, we might point out, Eve fails the test— or perhaps, proves something she hardly set out to prove, precisely by wanting to know what the law is:

> What fear I then? rather, what know to fear
> Under this ignorance of Good and Evil,
> Of God or Death, of Law or Penalty?
> Here grows the Cure of all, this Fruit Divine,

> Fair to the Eye, inviting to the Taste,
> Of virtue to make wise: What hinders then,
> To reach, and feed at once both Body and Mind?
> So saying, her rash hand in evil hour
> Forth reaching to the Fruit, she plucked, she eat. (9: 773–81)

Apart from its remarkable use of rhetorical questions—since the response to "What hinders then / To reach?" is obviously and only God's command, that is hardly a difficult riddle to answer—the most striking thing in this passage is Eve's desire to achieve at one moment knowledge, wisdom, and the end to "this ignorance." "Curiosity" here carries its own "Cure," "this Fruit Divine." The serpent's best arguments (such as they are) have to do with the imparting of this cure, the knowledge that will equal Adam's. But this moment would not be possible without Eve's earlier desire. More than the fairness of the fruit, Eve craves the fairness of her own trial.

But locating the trial is harder than it looks, for there is no moment of choosing: instead, there is only eating. Not a single moment of reflection comes between the question and the answering hand: "What hinders then / To reach, and feed at once both body and mind?" Without a pause, *"So saying* / her rash hand in evil hour Forth reaching to the fruit, she plucked, she eat!" Eve "says," and then, without an answer, even as she is speaking, she "reaches"—or rather, "her rash hand in an evil hour / Forth reaching." We need to wait until the middle of the next line for her agency ("she plucked"), but the feeling, if not entirely the sense, of the sentence is that it is her hand, not she, that is rash; her hand that plucks; almost her hand that eats. The moment of choice is obscured; the moment Eve decides to eat, unnarrated. Is it the evil hour (surely outside human agency?) that is to blame? Or the evil hand? Or the fruit? It must, of course, be Eve herself, and yet the syntax almost allows her to slide out from under judgment.

If this cannot be done by the poet in order to unindict his heroine (and it cannot, for indictment is the point—their fault, not God's), it must in some sense be done precisely to highlight for us the precarious nature of choice, and done to throw our gaze on the later moment of choice, the moment after the fall, when Eve again chooses. This is the trial that she and Adam do not notice initially, the one that asks, "What do you do *after* you have sinned?" This is the question that matters for the novel for (independent as we are of talking serpents) this is the question that will come to all its readers. "What to do next?" Our virtue cannot (like Eve's) be proved before the fall but can only be tested after. And this is the trial at which Eve does succeed, the test in which she reasons out the correct answer, which is "we must repent and beg God's forgiveness." It is Eve, not Adam, who guesses correctly this time—and again, Adam comes in second, following Eve's lead, as it is Eve who names the game. This suggests not only that the first test wasn't the real test, designed as it was (like Bluebeard's) to make everyone fail ("Sufficient to stand, but free to fall"), but also that there is a better test to follow—and that test is, as the final lines put forward, "theirs to choose / Which way to go." It is this moment, the exile from paradise, that forms the moment of choice—their "wand'ring steps and slow" are their own, and they are solitary both because they are, in a small way, lost to each other, and more sublimely, because they are lost to, or lost from, God. But the world lies all before them, and the choice is theirs.

Paradise Lost evolves into the first great novel of companionate marriage,[10] but it takes its place as a narrative of choice alongside Milton's theories of divorce and of individual liberty. At the poem's climax, book 9, Adam and Eve dissolve into the most perfect pair of bickering spouses—or would, if so much were not at stake. But they agree on the grounds of the challenge: that "my default, or will of wand'ring, as thou callst it," as Eve puts it, is the result of her feeling "secure / Either to meet no danger, or to find / Matter of glorious trial." Wandering, fault, the "need to approve" are all the source of their current unhappiness. But Milton in his prose endlessly reflects on the need for a trial: "The Doctrine and Discipline of Divorce" begins by "openly protest[ing] against and provok[ing] [my opponents] to the trial of this truth before all the world" (702). Similarly, in "Areopagitica," "I cannot praise a fugitive and cloistered virtue. . . . That which purifies us is trial" (728). Marriage in turn is to be praised only to the extent that it is the "apt and cheerful conversation of man with woman," an exchange, a "remedy to loneliness" and dread singularity; a lonely marriage, a miserable marriage, "change[s] the blessing of matrimony into a familiar and coinhabiting mischief, at least into a drooping and disconsolate household captivity" (703). Marriage must be a genuine and an ongoing choice, an active trial of virtue, for "the trial of virtue [is] the exercise of truth" (733). A marriage without choice is meaningless, is merely "striving to glue together an error where God and nature will not join," for "such a marriage can be no marriage," just as (as Milton puts it in "Areopagitica"), "Reason is but in choosing, for [man] had else been a mere artificial Adam, such an Adam as he is in the motions," an Adam in a puppet show (711, 707, 733). Without choice, without proving, without a trial, there is no human identity, no true liberty, at all.

With this linking of female curiosity (the "will of wand'ring"), marital freedom and individual liberty, the realist novel can begin, for "the trial of virtue and the exercise of truth" sounds like nothing so much as Richardson's Clarissa.[11] If the heroine did not say, "What is virtue unassaied?" then she might say the following: "I have no patience, Sir, to be thus constrained. Must I never be at liberty to follow my own judgment? Be the consequence what it may, I will not be thus constrained."[12] Clarissa's "set of narrative procedures," which offers "a full and authentic report of human experience," in turn sets the formal rules for the novel as a "court of Justice," in Watt's phrase, but it reminds us also, as he does, that the novel "is not afraid of singularity." If anything, it will create it where it does not find it—and yet, painfully and resentfully, it will punish it just as severely. George Rousseau has pointed out the ways the new form of curiosity centered on the self "was not focused on narcissistic or demented persons but directed at selves zealous to learn anything possible about the human psyche and mind."[13] The trials of Clarissa, like the trials of the sister-novels to follow, prove that there can be no modern subject without a test, but they also prove that there is no curiosity that will go unchallenged—nor, for that matter, unchastened.

"Those who can bear much will have much to bear." If the novel begins as a machine for testing reality in general and individuals in particular, then *Clarissa* should be seen as proposing itself as a laboratory for testing the hypotheses of proverbs against the "examples" of plot,[14] and for testing its heroine against maxims of her own excellence. From the beginning of the novel, she is "the subject of the public talk" (1: 39); it is impossible but that "whatever relates to a young lady, whose distinguished merits have made her the public care, should engage everybody's attention"; she is a pattern young lady and "everybody pities you" (1: 39). More than a mere example, Clarissa is also a test of others, for "who, indeed, can be worthy of Miss Clarissa Harlowe?" (37: 173). This perfection is not only obnoxious to her family ("No more of your merits, Clary!" [17: 94]) but also a challenge to herself: when "persons of prudence, and distinguished talents like yours willfully err, how great must be the fault! . . . What a loss likewise to the world! What a wound to virtue!" (39: 180). In fact, Clarissa's exemplarity (what will be said of her?) becomes a magnet for such challenges for the world: "You see what you draw upon yourself by excelling all your sex"; "every eye, in short, is upon you with the expectation of an example" (1: 40). Her parents both praise her virtue and use it as a weapon against her, to try to force her behavior. Clarissa cannily quotes her mother as saying, "You are a dutiful, a prudent and a wise child, she was pleased to say (in hope, no doubt, to make me so); you would not add, I am sure, to my trouble" and then quotes the maxim meant to buttress her own behavior: "Obedience is better than sacrifice" (16: 89). "A young creature of your virtuous and pious turn," her mother counsels her, "cannot surely love a profligate" (16: 90). That "cannot" carries all the prescriptive power of any "realistic" description, the attempt to contain what it wishes were not true, but beyond its ambivalent status (prescribe, proscribe, to recall Angela Carter's description of the heroine's fate) lies the novel's curiosity: what kind of creature is this?[15]

How shall we try Clarissa? She gives us our first warning, quite literally: "How am I punished, as I frequently think, for my vanity in hoping to be an example to young persons of my sex! Let me be but a warning" (120: 453). Not just her virtue, but her assurance that she can preserve it, seems to mark Clarissa as a target.[16] Clarissa begins by thinking she knows herself, but what she knows turns out to be far more limited—and the test is perversely designed to reveal those limitations. Here it is linked to the second aspect of the trial, the ways in which Clarissa must learn the relationship between her maxims and the world in which she acts; she must test her theories against a world of practices, corrupt and otherwise. Precisely what she is testing is her own confidence in her ability to be an entire world unto herself—or, as we might put it, her ability to know herself in isolation. As she herself says, "To excel in theory, and to excel in practice, generally required different talents" (47: 221). When the book begins, she is, as Lovelace calls her, "a mere novice . . . as to practices, as to experimentals" (158: 538), but the novel gives her considerable practice. To read the novel as a test partly of Clarissa's making, one that allows her the epistemological education of maxim-testing, is curiously in line with the novel's interest in Clarissa's beatification, her qualification to "shine the brighter for the trials she may be exercised with" (301: 981). But that shining can occur only through a self-inflicted (and then self-consciously understood) pain.[17] In this novel, that is, practice makes perfect, but it is also a perfectly designed (almost controlled) experiment. "Your present trial is but proportioned to your prudence" (1: 40), Anna says, and repeats it later: "I told you some time ago that I thought your trials but proportioned to your prudence" (15: 86). Anna is in fact only echoing Clarissa herself when she says to her, "Your observation is verified, that those who will bear much shall have much to bear" (19: 105). But it is Lovelace who takes on the challenge of "trying" the near-angelic Clarissa. After all, as he asks, "Has her virtue ever been proved? Who has dared to try her virtue?" (110: 427); as Lovelace himself puts it, "To the test, then" (429).

As Ned Schantz has noted, the most ominous part of Clarissa's "test" is the way she must prove her humanity—and in part, can prove it only by dying.[18] Like a witch in a pond, only her drowning will get her out of this particular examination. A similar paradox underlies Lovelace's test: if she gives in to Lovelace's erotic seduction, he has won, but if he can "win" her, she is ordinary and must be ruined; on the other hand, if she doesn't give in but continues to resist, she remains a subject of the test forever. But what is the test of the heroine? Lovelace himself can never state clearly what the grounds of the test are: when Belford reproaches him, "If the trial only was thy end, . . . thou hast enough tried" (222:714), or, a little later, "You only proposed to try her virtue," Lovelace responds, "Is she not now in the height of her trial?" (244:836). As it becomes clearer that he is losing the trial, that he is unable to prove her like all other women (unable to make her no longer a "curiosity," nor to diminish her own interest in the world), Lovelace, too, joins the parade of her admirers: "What a triumph has her sex obtained in my thoughts by this trial" (225: 727). But he also becomes obsessed with the things his test cannot probe or prove: "What have been her trials? Have I had the courage to make a single one upon her person, though fifty upon her temper?" (216: 694). When he realizes that he can break her will only by drugging and raping her—both, in a sense, inimical to the original "trial" of her virtue, her ability to enact her own purity—he must turn against his own explanations of the test. Contradicting what he said earlier (202: 657), he now says, "There's no triumph over the will in force . . . but have I not tried every other method?" (256: 879). Suddenly, the trial isn't to test her, but to win her for himself, even if that victory will destroy Clarissa.

This is one aspect of Ian Watt's version of the realist dilemma: the plight of the heroine who wants to stand intact, who says, as Clarissa does, "I am nobody's." But that is only part of the novel's test, and the other deserves our particular attention here: what of the heroine who wants to test, to examine, the world; the heroine who is *curious* about the things around her; what if we were to read for *her* test? The Clarissa of the novel's opening is a remarkably fearless inquisitor, and an excellent companion for the reader.[19] She is funny, witty, savage. Her comments about her family, particularly her brother and sister, are worthy of Jane Austen, as when she says of Arabella "my poor sister is not naturally good-humoured . . . [and] appeared to great disadvantage when she aimed to be worse-tempered than ordinary" or that "the poor Bella has, you know, a plump, high-fed face" (2: 43; 7: 60). Her brother, she says, is a "plotter without a head, and a brother without a heart." Clarissa Harlowe is no mealymouthed utterer of platitudes and dutiful nothings. She is not only a better curioso but also a better libertine than Lovelace, more willing to follow the evidence where it leads, and smarter about the physical world. It is Lovelace, after all, who insists on living by a single code, the "rake's creed," defending his behavior "upon the foot of maxims we have long held and pursued" (223: 719). Clarissa pursues a different road. Indeed, her education into the world of "practices" rather than "theories" is extremely thorough, and although she chooses to leave the world of mere appearances at the end of the novel, by that time she has become extremely adept at reading and manipulating the visible world and its representations. She says, sounding remarkably like a free thinker, "I never thought it right to give more than a second place to the world's opinion" (368: 1139). She learns to control appearances, learns to detect and disarm traps, consistently does the best with what information she has. Lovelace says of her early, "We are all very ready, thou knowest, to believe what we like" (217:696), but she learns quickly to distrust benevolent as well as threatening events—and learns, even more to her dismay, to distrust her own "readiness" to believe.

Notice how very curious she is. Despite Lovelace's staging of the fire in the house and his assertion that "you will be convinced by ocular demonstration" (225: 726), she isn't, and provides a very clear explanation of why the behavior of the house's inmates made the fire's unimportance evident. She distrusts the carriage plot, with which Lovelace hopes to take her in; she comes to distrust Colonel Tomlinson, and even the "fine ladies" Lovelace presents as his female relations. When she is still living with her family, she studies their treatment of her and learns to prepare for it: she observes Betty counting her clothes (69: 281); she watches the family maneuver, saying, "I began to think it was a contrivance" (78: 311); she hides her pens and writes false letters to trick them. The result of her observation is to make her sneaky: as she says, "People suspiciously treated never, I believe, want invention" (69: 283); "I am grieved to be driven to have recourse to the following artifices" (90: 365).

The great lesson of the novel is not that Clarissa is a passive victim, nor even that she is defeated by the trickier Lovelace, for she is his equal in observation and detection, but that the very structures of curiosity allowed to the heroine are designed precisely to shield her from untoward knowledge—which is the only knowledge she needs. She is no less observationally acute than he: as she says, "We are both great watchers of each other's eyes" (125: 460). If anything, she is putting him to his own test: "He offered to vindicate himself: but I told him I would judge him by his own rule—by his actions, not by his professions" (36: 171). As Lovelace well knows, he could fail not only her test but also his own: "It is I, not she, at this rate, that must fail in the arduous trial" (138: 493). Lovelace knows how watchful and careful she is ("never was there in a woman such a sagacious, such an all-alive apprehension" (117: 448), but he also knows very clearly her limits: "I was all her fear, I found; and this house her terror. . . . But her mistrust is a little of the latest to do her service" (256: 882). As he says later, she has been watchful and sagacious, "but not watchful, not sagacious enough" (316: 1016). As with her virtues, so with her caution: "My supposed advantages became a snare to me" (261: 891), and her very curiosity leads her into more snares, those left waiting for a (too) curious woman.

This disadvantaged investigation is shared by the reader, and critics have been to equal degrees savvy and peeved about it, quick to take their feelings of exclusion out on the heroine herself. Curious as we are, we, too, suffer frequent epistemological blackouts, unsure at times if Lovelace is telling us the truth, if signs are to be trusted, if the outside world is really still there. It is hard for us to judge how Clarissa is judging evidence, and hence hard for us to learn. The plots of her brother, the visiting sea captain, fires and ipecacuanha and carriages with old ladies, all rush by us. Sometimes we are in on the deception and screaming in silence at our heroine; at other times, we are as befuddled as she is. There is a jaggedness in our curiosity and hers— they never quite mesh. Oddly, this makes it harder to take the tests seriously. Since Clarissa gets out of so many traps, it's hard to believe (despite our pre-reading consciousness that this novel is a tragedy) that any of these tests will actually work; we are lulled by their very repetition. Our heroine seems too canny (and rather too satiric) for any of them.

But if it is impossible ever for Clarissa to learn enough, how are we in turn to assess the test? This is the point Watt raises when he says, "We realize that the code which might seem to make Clarissa too prudent is not prudent enough when measured against the outrageous means which men allow themselves to gain their ends." Clarissa's prudence (at once too much and too little) results in the failure of Lovelace's own test, but the force of that recognition drives Lovelace to commence mere physical trials against her. The rape is the sign, perverse as this seems, that she has won the initial trial. But it is also the end of Clarissa's libertinage, of epistemological freedom, of her ability to construct any new plot for herself but writing and death.

Here is where the reader's desire for a trial, for an instrument of curiosity, becomes most intense. Readers want to know, and a trial seems to be the most efficient, to use a modern term, way of finding out.[20] What happened? Who did what to whom? How are we to judge the outcome—and whom are we to blame? But here we face the central question of this chapter: what is the relationship between a trial as a form of legal advocacy, one in which the testimony of the heroine and the failure of witnesses against her might matter, and the "trials" of realism, the study of conventions, maxims, plots, and belief that have mirrored the heroine's progress? Isn't this where we expect law to step in, to sort the testimony, to offer a verdict, to, in a sense, trump realism itself? It would seem, if we believed Watt, that Clarissa would press Lovelace for damages of some sort: indeed, most of her advocates make a similar appeal to her. Anna Howe initially urged Clarissa to go to the law for her rights under her grandfather's will, arguing fiercely at the beginning of the book against Clarissa's "resolution not to litigate for your right" (47: 210), for although Clarissa has said, "I am determined not to litigate with my papa" (28: 134), her father has no such scruples. As she quotes him, he says, "But if she marry that vile Lovelace, I will litigate every shilling with her: tell her so: and that the will may be set aside, and shall" (39: 177); why does she threaten no countersuits? Anna's appeal to the law and to external notions of justice represents both the failure of "ordinary" plotting to save Clarissa and our own readerly curiosity—surely a trial will save the day? As with cousin Morden, whose late arrival seems to promise liberation for the captive heroine and then fails, "the law" is imagined as an engine of plot, one that will redress the physical and moral wrongs done to Clarissa, and restore readerly, as well as moral, order.

Initially, Clarissa seems to share Anna and Mrs. Howe's sense of law's usefulness, the alliance between law and curiosity: "The LAW shall be all my resource," she says to Lovelace, concluding, "I have my SENSES" (281: 950). But this sense of legal redress is actually the thing that does not survive the rape. Anna and Mrs. Howe's sense of justice (along with our desire for Lovelace's punishment) runs into the stone wall of Clarissa's sense of self. In part, Clarissa thinks herself responsible for her own violation (part of the process of self-love and vanity that led her astray, the "one dubious step of stepping out . . . [that] led me so far out of my path that I am in a wilderness of doubt and error") but in part, she also thinks the law of limited usefulness to her in attaining the exemplarity she wishes to claim. A liberal notion of rights merely gets in the way of Clarissa's idea of the virtuous soul, or of controlling her own trial: she begs, "don't let me be made a show of" (261.1: 895), not because she resists publicity but because she hopes at the end to control self-representation. As she says repeatedly, "I shall never be myself again" (261.1: 895); the trial, she thinks, would make of her something else altogether.

This has certainly been its effect on the critics, who seem intent on trying Clarissa over and over—unwilling, to borrow from Stephanie Jed's commentary on the status of the rape of Lucretia in humanist texts, to "look . . . at the legend of the rape of Lucretia from the perspective of its formation and transmission . . . [and make] the focus shift from 'what actually occcurred' when Tarquin entered Lucretia's room to our own agency in making this rape occur over and over again."[21] Only "by including ourselves at the end of the narrative," says Jed, can we "assume responsibility for the continued reproduction of the rape of Lucretia," and a similar blindness entangles readers of this novel. The criticism of *Clarissa* that puts the heroine on trial offers a way for critics to count themselves out of the criminal class, a move that should make readers of *Clarissa* nervous, ignoring their role in perpetuating her torture. But in this way, it would seem to make the heroine's point for her by making her into something not herself, making her the wrong kind of spectacle.

Not that Clarissa does not invoke the law as spectacle herself. As Linda Kaufmann notes, Clarissa carries on her own trial—as she says poignantly, "The will is far more than a distribution of material possessions; it is a final testimony for the defense" (145). But at the same time that Clarissa is mounting her own defense, she is also her own best cross-examiner. Sandra Macpherson points this out clearly, saying (very much along the lines of my argument), that as far back as the abduction, "Clarissa has taken to describing her fault as an overinvestment in her own agency and as a failure to take seriously Lovelace's 'encroachments'" (77).[22] But Terry Eagleton makes the point even more passionately, arguing that "Clarissa's self-castigation is quite unjustified" (70), that "the passage commonly quoted to demonstrate a rare moment of self-insight on her part in fact reveals a self-lacerating mystification." He phrases it in this way, of course, because he imagines himself Clarissa's defender ("To suggest a symmetry between Clarissa's partial, understandable self-deceptions and Lovelace's unremitting schizoid fantasies is to cast a slur upon Clarissa," he says [69]) and takes up arms against William Warner, Lovelace's great advocate. Eagleton lets Warner convict himself, quoting, with patent scorn, Warner's opinion that

"Lovelace's 'shortcomings, . . . are not held against him by the lover of comedy.'" "Clarissa," adds Eagleton, sounding like the world's best prosecuting attorney, "presumably, couldn't take a joke" (67). With that killer line, one would imagine, the defense could rest.

Or, perversely, Lovelace could take the stand, quoting Milton in his own favor—and Clarissa could ask him, as she does in the novel, when he signed his contract with the devil and what its terms are. Contract, and in particular the marriage contract, is at the heart of the novel, and one forgets in light of the violence of the rape how much time is spent seemingly negotiating a contract between Lovelace and Clarissa. Those critics who discuss the novel in terms of its failed romance (and Ian Watt, as we have seen, is one of them) can seem in particular to feminist readers as if they have missed the point: the question isn't whether Clarissa is Lovelace's secret sweetie, but if she is his chattel, and the debates over marriage highlight rather than disguise that question.

But Lovelace himself imagines this contractual relationship in two ways that turn us back toward the connection between realism, contract, and curiosity. The first is when he protests that "all women keep some final secret" and seems at this moment (only shortly before the rape) to hone his anger on this point: he is a man who will find the final secret out; he is the man who will "penetrate" even the woman of surpassing penetration, Clarissa. He does not imagine himself as holding secrets, but as the possessor of the secrets of others—as the reader, we might speculate, instead of merely the author of plots. (He plots, that is, in order to read—and for that reason, among others, so resents Clarissa's attempts at plotting.) But his second great scheme is explicitly legal, and that is for annual (and annually dissoluble) marriages. Lovelace imagines this as a world of endless choice. I hate compulsion, he says, even as he admits that he hates therefore being compelled to be the rascal that he is. For this reason, as he admits to Belford, he has become "a machine," but if it weren't for his fear of "being compelled" to be "married for life," he would marry Clarissa. How ideal it would be, then, he imagines, if all marriages were only for one year, if couples could dissolve them affectionately, if freedom and marriage were not incompatible. No more adultery, no more fornication, no more polygamy—oh, and annual parliaments as well.

In this way, Lovelace claims, there would be no more spinsters—for every woman could "have her *twelvemonths' trial*" (874; emphasis in the original). At that moment, the word *trial* has gathered around it all the meanings we have been suggesting: it is at once the torture that marriage seems to be for most women in the novel; it is the man's ability to "test" the woman and her patience as well as her character; but it is also the woman's freedom to run a test of her own. If only, he seems to be suggesting, his pursuit of Clarissa could be reimagined as romantic courtship, if their sexual relationship could be renamed an experiment, and if they could sample each other with no obligation other than politeness and the willingness to part amicably at the end. They would, in this way, stay Miltonian individualists, Adam without "the motions," capable of reason, choice, consent.

Reading the novel in that way, however perversely, makes *Clarissa* not a failed love story but a failed marriage plot, one in which the heroine attempts in vain to get exactly what Lovelace imagines, enough knowledge before marriage to choose freely, and in which the rape is a violation not only of her body but also of the implicit contract between two individuals: to test to the end, to allow the text to speak for them, to *read* for themselves. Reading the novel in that way in fact suggests that even from the origins of the novel the marriage contract, like the reader's contract, is always a problem of knowledge as well as consent, one that opens up the space Barthes would imagine later as "the pensive text," the one in which the heroine stares into the distance, refuses the contract (sex-for-story) and instead promises to keep herself intact. Clarissa, like the Marquise and like Eve, demands a trial, but, like Adam Phillips's child, refuses the conclusions we would draw from it: the test is unfair; knowledge comes too late; freedom was illusory; the freedom comes from instigating yet another trial—this one, in her father's house, on her own terms. Having stepped out of the garden, into the wide world, having walked out of the closet and into the secret chamber, Clarissa says no—not just to the law, but to realism's claims of total visibility, a world of total penetration.

Thus, when Watt argues that the "rape is the least convincing moment in the novel," his pun not only anticipates the difficulties his ordinary jury might encounter in such a trial (particularly with a heroine who can no longer utter a coherent sentence about whatever it was that happened to her) but also accentuates what at other times is prominent even in his account: the limits of the very realism he seems to be espousing. At this moment in *Clarissa*, as at others, what is credible depends on points of view, on kinds of evidence, on our knowledge of character and the limits of the possible.[23] How to "prove" the rape? Who will testify? What is the critic's engagement in the heroine's violation? And who will acquit Clarissa's wandering foot, as it led her out of the garden and into the wild world? There are "no crimes without criminals," as Macpherson argues, but even Judith Wilt, who brilliantly undoes the novel's "evidence" to show the possibility of unindicting Lovelace, claims that "I don't say this to go to a court of law—"[24] though Sandra Macpherson again makes my point by asking, why not?

The Clarissa who surfaces after the rape, the witch who survives drowning, the adulteress who survives being pressed to death, is a very different kind of (eye)witness, and the novel hints at a turn away from the perfect realism epistolarity seemed to offer. Finally, as Richardson's tale has turned toward the Gothic, it is Lovelace who is in the dark, Lovelace who is tricked by the final test, the letter in which Clarissa promises to return to her father's house, only to use that contract as an alibi that allows her to slip (lengthily) into death. At that moment, it is we who want the trial, we who (like Lady Catherine, like a premodern divorce court) want evidence of betrayal; we want something the novel will not offer us, leaving us instead with the spectre of our own desire for certainty. What a far more interesting thing it is that this reading of the novel suggests—that the rape is not "convincing" not because we do not believe Clarissa, but entirely, and unfortunately, because we do.

The novel after *Clarissa* will by and large offer us these (faux realist) trials and the verdicts we crave, precisely to allow us to relax a little as readers. The sensation novel in particular, like the delightful Miss Hoighty of *The Law and the Lady*, will ask heroine and reader alike, "Are you like me? Do you like reading Trials?"[25] These novels will continue to exploit law for its possibilities of delay, of suspended judgment, but they will not grant the heroine the same power of choice in choosing her own trials. For as Judith Wilt put it, in linking *Clarissa* to Eve's trials, Clarissa "has already eaten the fruit; it remains only for her to be forced awake to the knowledge of her nakedness" (20). In the world of *Clarissa*, the plot and the form conspire to render the trial inadequate, the verdict uncertain, the prizes withheld, the heroine put back to sleep, this time forever; in the world after *Clarissa*, such sharp verdicts are all but unpalatable; no one really wants to know what happens on Dorothea Brooke's wedding night, or on Isabel Archer's, or Gwendolen Harleth's. Or put the other way, we have decided that we already know enough.

What does it mean for the trial to persist without the heroine's necessary curiosity? The interrupted marriage, the bigamous marriage, the wrongful conviction, and the show trial, all complicate plot in the name of knowledge—Jane Eyre waiting two hundred pages for Bertha Mason to die after Jane's uncle's lawyer disrupts the ceremony; Harriet Byron waiting for Charles Grandison to disentangle himself from a Catholic lady; Jem Wilson on trial for the murder of Mary Barton's lover; Valeria Woodville in *The Law and the Lady*, travelling like a dervish to overcome her husband's "Scotch verdict" of "not-proven guilty" of his first wife's murder. All of these novels in some way attempt to use law to palliate the deepest question (what I will loosely call the Clarissa question): is my husband also the man who is going to murder me? But they do not pose the same resistance to closure, the same libertinage, the same curiosity, that *Clarissa* did. As Anthony Trollope was to write of Wilkie Collins (and the sensation novel more generally) "it is all plot." Sounding like the cranky uncle of E. M. Forster, he continues, "One is constrained by mysteries and hemmed in by difficulties, knowing, however, that the mysteries will be made clear and the difficulties overcome at the end of the third volume. Such work gives me no pleasure."[26] That is to say that unlike *Clarissa*, which offers the heroine a different form of knowledge, one that, like Milton's lost husbands and wives, extends beyond the constraints of the initial marriage contract, these novels do little besides prepare wives for the slaughter. Or as Henry James was to put it in similarly describing the novel of all plot, the sensation novel, "*The Woman in White*, with its diaries and letters and its general ponderosities, was a kind of nineteenth century *Clarissa Harlowe*." "To Mr Collins," Henry James goes on to say, "belongs the credit of having introduced into fiction those most mysterious of mysteries, the mysteries which are at our own doors. This innovation gave a new impetus to the literature of horrors."[27] But James knows better, of course: his very invocation of Clarissa Harlowe reminds us that these indoor-mysteries long precede the domestic, and so does the heroine's trial. James takes Clarissa's trials, the test of "credibility" of the realist novel that Watt among so many other theorists of realism averred, very, very seriously. Give me a locked door and woman trying to cross the threshold, James might say, and I will give you another form of trial.

Emily Dickinson put it most fiercely, imaging herself in a Gothic nightmare, trying to enter the bloody chamber: "One need not be a chamber to be haunted, / One need not be a house; / The brain has corridors surpassing / Material place." The place of the trial moves increasingly inward, as James himself imagined: "a new impetus to the literature of horrors"—or, to return to George Rousseau's genealogy of curiosity, once we have turned from "objects to selves," we can "plac[e] the emergent practices of psychology and psychoanalysis in a longer tradition of fascination." This fascination is the realm of the James novel—and it reminds us how oddly Ruth Prawer Jhabvala, Ismail Merchant, and James Ivory, in creating their film adaptation of *The Golden Bowl*, misread the novel when they imagine a violent murder and adultery before the beginning, for they miss entirely what James, in that same review of Wilkie Collins, would call "the numberless possible forms of human malignity." Surely they must know, the monsters are all on the inside now?

But they are also ignoring what James would call the "numberless possible forms" of curiosity, and in particular the formation (and highly deliberate reformation) of the "felt element" of the heroine's curiosity.[28] *The Golden Bowl* is unique among James's novels and, I am arguing, in the longer tradition of the English realist novel, in that its heroine is someone who actually wants to know, and know the worst, and is allowed not only to know but also to judge. That knowledge, of course, carries with it an enormous price. Like the bowl itself, which moves through the story, as Peter Brooks wrote of the "unspeakable horrors of a French novel" in *The Awkward Age*, like a tracer dye, "revealing relations, making clear positions and motives that have thus far been uncertain,"[29] Maggie Verver's quest not only transforms those she comes to interrogate; it also leaves her a very different, and not altogether attractive, heroine. But it also suggests the way the novel becomes a dangerous and not altogether pleasant place to be. Unlike those finally congenial courtrooms, the dark house of the novel feels subaqueous and ominous and more than a little terrible. For in reversing the usual trials of the heroine, making her his prosecutor rather than his defendant, James turns the inquisition against us, as well, violating our contract, disturbing our rest, asking us what we think we know, and what we think the price of our own knowledge is. It is that ("what did you say to yourself?" as Ralph asks Isabel) which makes the golden bowl, as object as well as novel, "a rarity, an object of beauty, an object of price."

The golden bowl allows us to articulate what is most striking in this novel's view of curiosity. For it is the clearest "curio" we have had in this chapter, as if the novelist were intent on re-creating the history of curiosity itself, from pilgrimage to museum to Freud. Not only is the heroine perverse in her interest in digging up the truth, but in this novel, the objects themselves testify. This novel is truest to curiosity's objective core, as if the difference between people and the things they carried were increasingly hard to tell. The heroine is running the courtroom; the objects are speaking for themselves; there are no documents left to be read (gone, gone is epistolarity) and readers are confronted with the starkest of choices: which characters do we believe (the Clarissa question) has become which characters would you save—for in the terrible firestorm of curiosity in this book, not everyone wins our love. But that might be the final perversity of this novel—what if, at the end of the book, we cared for none of them? That might be the bowl's most dreadful secret—not only that it is one of those awful "tests" of reality (the murder weapon, the blood, the bone) but that it is truly, finally, empty.

How does this novel become a trial? It begins with the character trial with which we began, the world of the social novel, in which we are drawn to characters' testimony about themselves and each other. Volume 1 describes the eponymous "Prince" and the Prince's friend, Fanny Assingham, describes his former lover, Charlotte Stant, and this testimony gets us going. These are the two characters who are genuinely curious, in every sense of the word as we've been using it so far: Charlotte Stant, an American who has been travelling the continent trying to live (or at least to marry) well, and her former lover, Prince Amerigo, now engaged to an inexperienced, wealthy American girl, Maggie Verver, who travels with her father, the rich but also quite remarkably naïve Adam Verver. What will they do? we wonder—and so do they. By contrast, Maggie is initially not very curious at all. It is Charlotte, ironically introduced as "handsome, clever, and odd," who enters as an almost-Emma, the heroine whose cleverness, whose curiosity, will be our touchstone as the novel proceeds. Curiosity is in fact associated with Charlotte through most of the first half of the novel. That section may be called "The Prince," but

Charlotte is very much its object of interest—just as *Middlemarch* began as "Miss Brooke," so *The Golden Bowl*, Leon Edel tells us, began as "Charlotte." And Charlotte Stant is, as people continue to exclaim throughout the novel, "splendid. " For she has what the Prince calls "a curious world-quality, of which, in Rome, he had had his due sense, but which clearly would show larger on the big London stage"; she is ready to become spectacular.

And the Prince should know for he, too, is a curious object that "shows large." It is to him that Maggie says, before their marriage, "You're a rarity, an object of beauty, an object of price. You're not perhaps absolutely unique, but you're so curious and eminent that there are very few others like you. You're what they call a morceau du *musée*" (35). The Prince's curiosity, like Charlotte's, has a cosmopolitan, slightly scandalous air to it, but it seems something that can be tamed, possessed, made part of the Verver collection; like the golden bowl, which the Prince and Charlotte find in their illicit day of walking the London streets before his marriage, and like the shopkeeper who shows it to them, himself "the great curiosity they had looked at," the objects and people associated with curiosity are foreign, grand, inassimilable, and yet (strangely) always for sale. Again and again in book 1, curiosity swirls around people—moving from one character to another; from objects to the people who study them; from owners to possessions; to the very streets themselves. And yet, at least at the beginning of the book, curiosity repeatedly seems to fail the virtuous characters—while Adam Verver is initially "an angel with a human curiosity," by the time of his marriage to Charlotte (which very much reads like his purchasing of Charlotte), he chooses not to look at the telegram in which the Prince gives his opinion of the marriage. He "hesitated afresh, but as for amiability, not for curiosity." While Charlotte paces the streets of London, looking for the freedom she has lost, the days "when I could do as I liked," the good characters refuse to wander; they stay in their tracks; no ambitions, no desires, tempt them beyond their limits. And readers, we who live to wander, are of course drawn to the ambitious, vibrant, lonely Charlotte, with what James himself calls "her greater gaiety, her livelier curiosity and intensity, her readier, happier irony." If you took the edge out of Charlotte's irony (which would be quite a difficult thing to do), she might seem another Isabel Archer, challenging the world, asking it to meet her high expectations. Who wouldn't be on her side? And we are. Through her attempt to protect one secret day with her former lover, her day of postmarital wandering, as she calls it, "on the town," and her rekindling of her affair with Amerigo, we, too, are on the side of gaiety, irony, and curiosity, and our curiosity (as eroticized and fetishistic as theirs, trapped as we are in that world of people and objects) stays focused on the lovers.

Until, in the middle of the novel, James pulls the rug out from under us, or rather, tilts the board so the pieces fall to the other side. In the carefully plotted game of *The Golden Bowl*, with its few characters and highly limited moves, James turns the tables. For unexpectedly, after a half novel in which she has been placid, quiet, and good, and if anything (as she herself goes on to say) "stupid," Maggie Verver comes to curious life and decides to hold a trial. And with this move, our curiosity becomes more complicated as well: we suddenly know more than the characters who used to be our friends, Amerigo and Charlotte, and we cannot tell them what we know; on the other hand, we can no longer hear their thoughts, to which we are accustomed. Our curiosity, amazingly, is tied to that of a heroine with a single, familiar question: what has that woman to do with my husband?

The trial is staged with our participation, through a fascinating about-face, a formalist sleight of hand. Book 1 ends with Fanny Assingham and the Colonel discussing their visit to Matching, the country house, for a weekend—a visit that ended with Charlotte and the Prince going off together, ostensibly to see the cathedral at Gloucester, but clearly for a tryst. This scene, which we have already read in the previous chapter from Charlotte's perspective, is one of the most powerful erotic scenes in literature, and it takes much of its power from its secrecy. The Prince evokes the flaw in the golden bowl, remarking to Charlotte that he goes by his superstition; she answers, immediately, "I go by you," an avowal not just of passion but of total absorption, one that draws the reader in as well. What follows cements our bond with the lovers. When we read the subsequent scene with Fanny and the Colonel at the end of book 1, and participate in their laborious attempt to know if an affair has been going on, is going on, will go on, we are in a position to commend our own knowledge, and (a little bit) to scoff at their confusion—they will remain curious; they are unsure to what extent, having arranged the marriage of Maggie and the Prince and kept Charlotte's secret, they are complicit in the affair; they are entirely invested in a knowledge they cannot have, and that we hold fairly lightly. Accomplished readers of adulterous fiction, we know, after all, where we stand.

When the novel resumes, in part 2, however, we are asked to look back at our knowledge with (almost literally) someone else's eyes; and from that perspective, Charlotte Stant is not Isabel Archer but Madame Merle, staring at a cracked curio (as both women do), admitting her crimes and resigning herself to the dreaded return to America. How, exactly, does James turn our attentions around? It's a trick of time and space—he moves us forward in time, only to move us side to side in space: that is, book 2 begins with Maggie Verver, weeks later, thinking back to the night we have just read about in book 1, the night when her husband and stepmother returned from Matching. James takes us, as it were, across London, from the scene where Fanny and Bob Assingham assessed what they had just seen, to Maggie Verver, waiting in her drawing room, wondering what she has missed. In those final chapters of book 1, Fanny had referred to Maggie as both "blind" and as, for the first time, "a very curious little person," and announced that Maggie is now "awake." The second book begins by finding her, exactly, awake and waiting, as if fulfilling Fanny's prophecy that "her sense will have to open." We still have things we want to know, since we, too, left the lovers as they were going off on their own—voyeurs in our own right, we are waiting for some confirmation of what the Prince and Charlotte did, what Adam Verver knows, what Maggie knows and what she is willing to let the Prince know. But we are also, increasingly, waiting to see Maggie learn. The chapter is presented entirely in retrospect, a technique that usually calms readers down, with its confidence that someone has actually lived through whatever ordeal we are reading about, but here, the retrospection is incredibly agitated, as we share Maggie's anxieties on top of our own. Gradually, we pick up the details that seem to bring us back to specifics of time and place: the Prince's "advent," as Maggie puts it, being so late, dinner will be at nine; she has "merely driven, on a certain Wednesday, to Portland Place, instead of remaining at Eaton Square"; the Prince will expect her to be at Eaton Square—these details calm us, but only to prepare us for a new kind of doubt, for, even more gradually, we realize that Maggie has created a test for her husband, a way of learning what he expects, what he knows, what he has done. She has challenged him, as she says, with her "poor little behaviour," in a way that strikes him as "significant"—"and that this has a violence beyond what she had intended." This break, the moment of waiting ("for just how long? should she ever really know for just how long?") simply to see what her husband will say when he finds her exactly where she ought to be, becomes the great moment not just of violence but, the novel says, of terror: the moment of reckoning, the trial.

For the rest of the book, it is Maggie who stages these frightening tests—tests that so often depend on her merely being where she is supposed to be and saying what she is supposed to say, but knowing something that she was not supposed to know. In this way, she can accomplish the impossible—cross the threshold while sitting perfectly still, in her own drawing room. As she says to Amerigo when she confronts him with the golden bowl in the second test:

> "You knowing was—from the moment you did come in—all I had in view." And she sounded it again—he should have it once more. "You knowing that I've ceased—"
>
> "That you've ceased—?" With her pause in fact, she had fairly made him press her for it.
>
> "Why, to be as I was. *Not* to know." (437)

As she goes on to explain to her friend, "I put him in possession of the difference; the difference made, about me, by the fact that I hadn't been, after all . . . too stupid to have arrived at knowledge" (445). But what fascinates James is precisely that "arrival" at knowledge—the journey in which, for the first time in the novel, the language of curiosity clusters not around the tragic outsiders, but around the "poor dear little girl": "This charming grace of [Maggie's] curiosity"; "it immensely helped her . . . to be able at once to speak of the prince as having done more to quicken than to soothe her curiosity." "He had only made her more curious." In two pages, half a dozen times, Maggie is curiouser and curiouser.

This is what makes the trial so powerful as a way of knowing—even while the heroine continues to fear precisely the confirmation of her fears. When Fanny asks, "What then, dear Maggie, have you been thinking?" all she can say is, "Well, horrible things. . . . That there may be something—something wrong and dreadful, something they cover up." "What awfulness, in heaven's name, is there between them? What do you believe, what do you *know*?" she again asks Fanny—at the same time, as Fanny astutely notes, what she wants is as much "*dis*proof, as against herself, and has appealed to me, so extraordinarily, to side against her" (389). Look at the language: belief, proof, appeals, sides, disproof. The whole novel at last has become a trial: Maggie is "testifying"; Charlotte scares her by hinting at "the least approach to cross-examination"; Fanny cannot arrive at a "conviction"; "whatever [evidence] there may have been, it will also all have been buried on the spot" (391); "murder will out," says Colonel Assingham, thinking that there must be traces of the adulterous lovers all across London—"murder will," says Fanny, reopening our doubts, "but this isn't murder."

Maggie has become what James already was: a forensic epistemologist, looking for "proof" of a murder without a body. What she is doing at first resembles the trial structure of the sensation novel: replaying the facts of a crime through the eyes of an investigator, doing the work Peter Brooks identified as the business of plot, and reordering. But unlike Wilkie Collins, James resists the security of event, throwing us instead into the ambiguity of motive—how can Maggie be sure of what she knows, or be sure of the crime itself? This evidentiary obscurity is the state of the novel: everyone knows there is a crime, but no one is quite sure what it is; everyone fears and desires knowledge, but no one seems to know what knowledge would look like. That is, until the great climax of the book, when the golden bowl finally speaks. "Something very strange has happened, and I think you ought to know it," says Maggie, again retrospectively, to Fanny Assingham. And with that pronouncement, the certainty that she has knowledge to convey, we know that Maggie finally, herself, knows. But what—and how—and at what price?

In some ways, we know quite literally (well, this being James, almost literally) the price: Maggie has been wandering the streets of London, looking for a shop Charlotte once mentioned, "there being in Bloomsbury such 'funny little fascinating' places and even sometimes such unexpected finds." Maggie, as she says, ever attuned to "romantic impressions" in everything her rival mentions, has retained the impression and gone searching; what she found was, as any reader of novels would have foretold, the same antiquarian's shop that the secret lovers had found years before and the same golden bowl that the Prince had refused to allow Charlotte to purchase, because of its invisible flaw. Maggie has bought the bowl; the dealer, feeling guilty, has visited her to remonstrate with her, wishing to return her money, feeling he has taken advantage of her—but instead, waiting in the drawing room, he has seen the pictures of Charlotte and the Prince, and identified them as his glamorous visitors of years before. This will not surprise a careful reader—as Charlotte herself noticed, on that first visit, the dealer cares for his things, and cares that the right people see them: "'Didn't you see'—she was to ask it with an insistence—'the way he looked at us and took us in? . . . Yes, he'll remember us,' she says, with some apprehension." As for his return to their house, as if by magic—as the Prince says to Maggie, "I agree with you that the coincidence is extraordinary—the sort of thing that happens mainly in novels and plays. But I don't see, you must let me say, the importance or the connexion—" (432). But Maggie dismisses the mere "fictional" elements of it, the "sort of thing that happens mainly in novels and plays":

> It's not my having gone into the place, at the end of four years, that makes the strangeness of the coincidence; for don't such chances as that, in London, easily occur? (432)

What the strangeness consists of, as the man stands in the "red room," identifying adulterers from their photographs, is what Maggie calls "the whole case—the case of your having so long deceived me . . . that there had been so much between you before."

What James has done is to stage the arrival not so much of knowledge as of *conviction*, to use Ian Watt's word, in a single complicated and highly economical moment. As the bowl testifies against its admirers, as time and space collapse, the moment of the first visit to the shop must be superimposed upon the second, like a transparency; the shop itself, in the form of its fairy-tale owner, must come to the house and the street to the "red room." Why? So Maggie can come into possession "at least, I mean, of real knowledge"; so she can know precisely that she *didn't* know; that there *was* something to know;—or even more precisely, that there was something that she could have known, and that others knew, and, painfully, that others knew that she did not know. It is, of course, the Bluebeard moment, when she knows that her husband knew Charlotte before she did, that Charlotte is not locked in a red room but wandering around London—but she also knows something more awful still, that they knew how little she knew. As time, that anchor of realism, shifts before her, and the bowl re-creates the shop in her own home, she can stage her knowledge, formally, as a test of her husband. All of this, as she says, for the price of a bowl. "Shall you at least get your money back?" the Prince asks, after the bowl is broken. "Oh, I'm far from wanting it back," Maggie says. "I feel so that I'm getting its worth."

This is, even in a realist novel, a lot of value to get from a single object—and we might be forgiven for wondering if Henry James didn't find his bowl in Charles Dickens's Old Curiosity Shop. We know where he did get the bowl, of course—from the book of Ecclesiastes: "Or ever the silver cord be loosed, or the golden bowl be broken, or the pitcher be broken at the fountain, or the wheel broken at the cistern, Then shall the dust return to the earth as it was and the spirit shall return unto God who gave it. Vanity of vanities, all is vanity." Well, yes—the golden bowl, broken, is the sign of mortality, just as the lovers' betrayal is the reminder of the fall, and the red room, when it speaks truth, is a sign of the lovers' damnation. But as the chapter from Ecclesiastes ends, "For God shall bring every work into judgement, with every secret thing, whether it be good, or whether it be evil."

God and the novelist, of course, and the Prince's casual phrase (the sort of thing that happens mainly in novels and plays) reminds us of James's intense self-consciousness about not only the eponymous bowl but also the shop in which it was found. In the preface to the New York edition, James describes going around London with a photographer, looking to photograph the (of course fictional) shop for the frontispiece to the novel. That quest for the image of his shop, James says, was "the mere pleasure of exploration, abounding as the business at once began to do in those prizes of curiosity for which the London-lover is at any time ready to 'back' the prodigious city." And James captures the prize, his perfect shop, "which awaited in fact—but I check myself; nothing, I find now, would induce me to say where." James, unlike his bowl, stays mum. The shop, despite being, like the shop his heroine finds, "a concrete, independent, vivid instance, the instance that should oblige us by the marvel of an accidental rightness" must remain, as he says, "a shop of the mind."[30]

By the time Maggie Verver has staged her trial, has in essence re-created the antique shop in her own home, she has turned the "shop of her mind" into a courtroom as well. Throughout book 2 she is rummaging through it, her curiosity in danger of running amuck, her fear of what she will find endlessly outpacing the "horrors" she does, until she finds the true horror—the fact of the many relationships her husband has had with her stepmother, the fact of her own ignorance, the fact of "so much between you before." But making it a "shop" at the same time gives James another brilliant set of metaphors for female curiosity, one that will be as central to the novel's history as the courtroom. Again, the heroine steps into the garden and gathers "fruits," but here, the fruits of truly seeing, and seeing truth:

> It was as if she had come out—that was her most general consciousness: out of a dark tunnel, a dense wood, or even simply a smoky room, and had thereby, at least, for going on, the advantage of air in her lungs. It was as if she were somehow at last gathering in the fruits of patience; she had either been really more patient than she had known at the time, or had been so for longer: the change brought about by itself as great a difference of view as the shift of an inch in the position of a telescope. It was her telescope in fact that had gained in range—just as her danger lay in her exposing herself to the observation by the more charmed, and therefore the more reckless, use of this optical resource. (439)

Like the two other optical exhibits, the photographs of the lovers in the red room and the author's photograph at the beginning of the novel, Maggie's "shift of an inch" has brought an entire new world into relief, one that confirms that "I am not such a fool as you supposed me." Just as Maggie went from being the subject of curiosity in book 1 to the curious subject in book 2, so here she delineates both her own observations and the way that she herself becomes an object of curiosity, at once seeing and being seen—for remember, as she put it, "her telescope had gained in range," but her "danger lay in exposing herself to observation" precisely by her reckless "use of this optical resource." To see, in this novel, is always to risk dangerous observation.

James has transformed the spectacle of the trial into a different kind of spectacle altogether, a technology of optical devices, a technology for staging the truth without ever quite saying it. Hauntingly, Maggie's observation involves the oldest and the newest forms of interrogation: as in medieval trials, she has left the object alone to confront the criminal, as when a murderer would be asked to hold the murder weapon, or to visit the corpse, in the hopes that blood would speak, that murder would "out" itself. But as with that other optical trick, the Lumières' train racing toward its terrified audience a mere ten years before, something ordinary in everyday life here becomes frightening merely by being in the wrong place—a body in a locked chamber, a red room, a photograph, a blood-stained key, a mail train in a movie theatre. And as with the wife alone in the dark, even when the lights come back on, when, as Jane Campion's *The Piano* says of its Bluebeard show, "CHIEF and his party are shown the theatrical devices; the blood-bucket, the paper axe, the splits in the sheets," terror continues to hover around sight, whether we are seeing or being seen. Maggie's spectacle conjures again the story of the wife's doubled curiosity: when she realizes that the Prince has had "two relations with Charlotte, [he] may have had fifty . . . kept out of our sight," is Maggie different from any other Bluebeard's wife, finding the bodies in the chamber, wondering if she is next? Certainly, there is more than a hint that the Prince poses the threat of some unknown violence, some cruelty, which all the women in the novel fear: "Fanny Assingham was full of the special sense of his manner: it caused her to turn for a moment's refuge to a corner of her general consciousness in which she could say to herself that she was glad *she* wasn't in love with such a man" (206). The threat of the novel isn't precisely that of wife-murder; but by the time Adam Verver, following Maggie's terrible victory over Charlotte, takes his wife back to America, bound by a tiny invisible chain and uttering inaudible screams, we are further back in the realm of the Gothic than we might have imagined, and the more we know, the more exposed we feel.

But curiously, despite the fact that she averts her eyes "in pity and terror" at the end of the novel, Maggie seems to be the only person who isn't afraid. James may himself have been the novelist least frightened of female curiosity. In one of the great enunciations of the heroine's plot, George Eliot remarked, in *Daniel Deronda*, "Could there be a slenderer, more insignificant thread in human history than this consciousness of a girl, busy with her small inferences of the way in which she could make her life pleasant?" she asks. "What in the midst of that mighty drama are girls and their blind visions?" These are the lines that James himself quoted in the preface to *The Portrait of a Lady*, but as I have suggested, this novel is not quite as resigned to the heroine's fate as was the earlier book. *The Golden Bowl* suggests that, with a small shift of the optical apparatus, these visions might not be so blind after all.

This chapter began with Elizabeth Bennet's refusal of Lady Catherine de Bourgh's curiosity, leaving that powerful woman fuming with anger, outraged at her inability to penetrate every mystery, "every secret thing." When Charlotte carries off her departure at the end of *The Golden Bowl* with such aplomb, refusing to ask for Maggie's sympathy, is she presenting a similarly opaque surface to us, retreating into the silence of America? I suggested that *The Portrait of a Lady* offered a surprising window for sympathy with Madame Merle at the book's end, when she resigns her place in Gilbert and Pansy's life, and says, "I will go back to America"; something similar happens at the end of this book, when the verdict has been rendered, when not only Charlotte but also Adam Verver must return to that horrible place, not just America but "American City" America, and leave Amerigo, the better America, behind. If we aren't sure what Charlotte knows, we know even less about Adam Verver's knowledge—and is it he or Maggie who determines the resolution? Who is the criminal, who the judge? One of the most remarkable touches of this novel is to make the courtroom's answer far less satisfying than we might have thought: more even than Clarissa, James rejects the possibility that "knowing what happened" solves anything at all. Readers are left alone with Maggie and Amerigo at the end, and it is a poor showing we will make, for all our knowledge. Early in the novel, when Fanny Assingham is reminding her husband (and telling us) of the way Maggie and the Prince met, she says, "There are things, my dear—haven't you felt it yourself, coarse as you are?—that no one could tell Maggie. There are things that, upon my word, I shouldn't care to attempt to tell her now." "She'd be so scandalised?" asks the Colonel; no, says Fanny. "She'd be so frightened. She'd be, in her strange little way, so hurt. She wasn't born to know evil. She must never know it" (80). Readers, curious as we are, are now in the position of knowing evil—we, too, have crossed that threshold, and we are, aren't we? a little hurt.

At the end of *The Portrait of a Lady*, Ralph says to Isabel, "It hurts me as if I had fallen myself" (285), and Henry James takes seriously the hurt we feel when watching someone else fall. And this of all things takes us all the way back to Eve. It is as if our relationship with the heroine were not only voyeuristic, not only that of a juror waiting and watching to render judgment, but also almost maternal, caring, that other version of curious. Being a juror may not be quite as easy as it looks. Watchful, testful, wistful—knowledge is a peculiar trial to us, after all, and we share not only in the heroine's curiosity but also in her disillusionment, what Freud described so beautifully and seemingly inevitably in *Civilization and Its Discontents* as the result of a *failure* of law, when each of us must "give up as illusions the expectations [of our] . . . youth," and learn, as Maggie Verver does, "how much difficulty and pain has been added to her life by [others'] ill-will."[31] What is the position from which we judge that, when it is the job of the novel to render both our curiosity and our trials ever more strange to us, as well? That is the terror at the end of *Paradise Lost*, when the handed lovers walk into the wide world, with the flaming sword behind them, and it is the terror of the *Golden Bowl*— that however much Maggie Verver may hide her eyes at the end of the book, however much we are witnesses only to the final failure of any model of care, no novel could make us, more fiercely, want to know.

CHAPTER 3

Alice and the Curious Room

"What—is—this?" the Unicorn said at last.
"This is a child! We only found it today! It's as large as life, and twice as natural!"
Lewis Carroll, *Through the Looking-Glass*

Even though the exigencies of a "three wall" representation have in general forced certain departures from literal correctness, every effort has been made to preserve and emphasize the spirit of the room and to render it in accurate scale.
Mrs. James Ward Thorne, *American Rooms in Miniature*
(The Art Institute of Chicago, 1941)

This curious child was in the habit of pretending to be two people.
Lewis Carroll, *Alice in Wonderland*

"In the beginning was . . . what?" asks Angela Carter. "There's a theory," she says, "one I find persuasive, that the quest for knowledge is, at bottom, the search for the answer to the question: 'where was I before I was born?'" Unexpectedly, she answers the question:

> Perhaps, in the beginning, there was a curious room, a room like this one, crammed with wonders; and now the room and all it contains are forbidden you, although it was made just for you, had been prepared for you since time began, and you will spend all your life trying to remember it.[1]

Carter's answer to the question of origins is an uncanny echo of Kafka's parable, "Before the Law," in which the man spends his life in front of a door, only to find out it was his door; it was made for him; it was never locked; and now at his death it will disappear. But Carter's is a more specific fantasy, and it is the one we have been dreaming of since the opening chapter, when we gathered Tradescant's rarities in a pub in Oxford. The room is "curious"; it is "crammed with wonders" and full of things that are now "forbidden you," and you will spend your whole life "trying to remember it."

Carter's curious room appears in a sketch that is subtitled "The Curious Room" but whose proper title is "Alice in Prague," a tribute to Jan Svankmajer's film of *Alice in Wonderland*. Reenchantments of Alice dapple our culture, from Cecil Hepworth's brilliant 1903 film adaptation to Jefferson Airplane's terrifying paen to drug culture and Tim Burton's feminist explorer, recapturing "much of her muchness" and becoming again "the right Alice." Find a straight-haired girl with a level gaze, put her in an oversized hat, and hand her a teacup, and there's your Alice. But Carter's account consciously brings together the heroine and her cabinet, drawing us into that particularly "curious room" that is the space of the realist novel, the space in which, to borrow from that other theorist of uncanny houses, "that which is hidden is brought to light," something in particular in "that class of the terrifying which leads back to something long known to us, once very familiar."[2] From the "Wonder House" of Rudyard Kipling's *Kim* to Henry James's "house of fiction" with its "many rooms," characters wander realism in search of their double, the object that brings them (an otherwise ordinary object themselves) to life. The wonder room glitters, all crowded surfaces and busy corners, but it glistens with the promise of something (secret) inside; like a dollhouse, like the pinhole curiosa of Victorian erotic and pornographic books, like the realist novel, the curious chamber promises to double its readers as well—to allow us, like Alice, to "pretend to be two people."

This doubleness is part of the trickery of realism, which offers us both the curios of the real world and the curiosity of knowing we are in a fiction: what Robert Newsom has called the "antinomy" of realist belief is to know that we are choosing to believe in a fiction. Choosing to believe in a fictional character is a similarly complicated act, but even critics who are willing to challenge their belief in "characters" tend to believe in couches, railways, gardens, and stairways. As Freud says, "The situation is altered as soon as the writer pretends to move in the world of common reality". "by the time we have seen through his trick it is already too late and the author has achieved his object." But this is patently not the object for Angela Carter, for whom the imaginary room ("perhaps" a room) is an attempted act of memory, a re-creative act that is cunning and ingenious and clearly doomed to failure; try as you will, you cannot conjure the room that never existed. But it is the business of the realist novel to enter that fantastic space—as it does in fiction as various as *Alice in Wonderland*, *The Old Curiosity Shop*, and *Bleak House*. If the imagined space of the previous chapters was the courtroom, the room of forensic curiosity in which we master evidence and "try" the heroine, what matters in these books is another scene: the heroine crammed into a little house, stuffed in, until she must move her own head to keep from breaking her own neck. That moment presents a very different trial from those we have seen so far, the trials of a curio at war with her cabinet. Alice may wield her telescope with some of the bravado we saw in Maggie Verver at the end of our last chapter, her "reckless use of this optical resource" similarly "[bringing] about by itself as a great a difference of view as the shift of an inch in the position of a telescope," but for Alice, the primary object of investigation is her body itself and its own ability to "telescope." These novels pose a fascinating version of the question Henry James poses at the end of the century, when he asked what it was the heroine saw: "Place the centre of the subject in the young woman's own consciousness," he began, and ended, "put the heaviest weight into that scale, which will be so largely the scale of her relation to herself." This is what, unexpectedly, Lewis Carroll does, making "the scale of the heroine's relation to herself" a purely materialist question and the subject of the heroine's self-examination as well. For Alice asks not only what is the heroine, and what can she be thinking, but also exactly how *big* is she, and how can she survive an unreliable body in an ever-shifting world? In that way, after the careful realism of the epistolary novel or of *The Golden Bowl*, in these novels we reenter the fairy-tale chamber, cross the threshold into a darker form of curiosity, the world of dolls, of waxwork figures, of automatons, of "the wrong Alice." To take *Alice in Wonderland* seriously as realism and move from Carroll's world back to Dickens's is to see the fairy tale at the heart of the novel—and to see that for the curious heroine, as she walks into the haunted chamber, the line between what is matter-of-fact real and what is fantastically dreadful is a very thin line indeed.

Nothing crosses the line between the fantastic and the literal more than Alice Liddell's shape-shifting body. If, as Freud claimed in his essay on "The Uncanny," "the whole matter is one of testing reality," there is no more dangerous instrument for testing than Alice herself.

> "I almost wish I hadn't gone down that rabbit-hole—and yet—and yet—it's rather curious, you know, this sort of life! I do wonder what *can* have happened to me! When I used to read fairy tales, I fancied that kind of thing never happened, and now here I am in the middle of one! There ought to be a book written about me, that there ought! And when I grow up, I'll write one—but I'm grown up now," she added in a sorrowful tone: "at least there's no room to grow up any more *here*."[3]

For Freud, the uncanny lies not in any particular object, but in the traces of repressed knowledge that it brings with it, the gap that arises around something that (as Carter put it) we used to know but no longer (fully) know. The girl who "used to read fairy tales" and "fancied that kind of thing never happened" is *"now"* (no more forgetting) in the middle of one. Alice's knowledge is unable to keep up with her body: "I know who I *was* when I got up this morning, but I think I must have been changed several times since then.... I can't explain *myself*, I'm afraid, ... because I'm not myself, ... and being so many different sizes in a day is very confusing" (35). The shift in the telescope here is to see the world through the eyes of the estranged heroine, forced to experiment on herself.

This process of estranging oneself from one's own curiosity begins with the first scene of transformation, when Alice cannot get into the garden because she is too large. She drinks from the bottle and shrinks, only to be unable to reach the key on the glass table; she eats the cake and grows, only to become too large to fit through the door. To enter the beautiful garden, she is forced to experiment on herself, remaking herself to fit the "real world" she is suddenly in. But what is uncanny here is her perspective—to see herself as the subject of the experiment, to speak as the lab rat. There's a reason film re-creations of Alice dwell on this scene—it's a chance for them to show off their technical art but also to enact our estrangement, as we watch the heroine struggle ("Take the key with you," we want to scream to her, for we have played this game before). But critics who rejoice in their position outside the game, who chortle that Alice should rejoice in it as well ("she's no fun at all," they seem to say, in their "she's not the real Alice" voices) are essentially saying that she should lie back and enjoy it: they are missing the point.[4] Think back to Terry Eagleton's acerbic comment about William Warner's rebuke of Clarissa: that she simply doesn't get the joke. But something other than comic exuberance is going on in both texts, and reading Alice within this realist tradition of uncanny displacement violently forecloses the possibility of failed laughter, instead keeping us as curious as the heroine.

For the uncanny is all about misrecognition, or, as Freud might have put it, it's a question of whose dream you're in. In Tim Burton's *Alice*, the heroine repeatedly pinches herself, admonishing herself that this is her dream, that she can wake up at any time—something, of course, which is not true. For the reader, as Freud makes clear, the uncanny depends on our sharing the position of the person tricked, the person displaced, the person outside herself. Freud recounts the story of the princess in Herodotus, who holds the hand of the thief so that he cannot steal her father's treasure but must tell her a story. Instead, Herodotus says, the thief leaves the hand of his dead brother in hers, escapes to steal the treasure, and so delights the king with his effrontery that the king gives him the princess's hand in marriage. As Freud explains, we do not find this story uncanny, while elsewhere in his essay a dead hand left in ours would be the essence of the uncanny. But that is the point, Freud says: we do not find it uncanny because we share the perspective of the thief, not of the princess. If we had her point of view in mind, nothing would be more disturbing.

What does the doll see? Is she, to herself, merely a plaything, and how does the curio fight back? This is the question Alice asks, and it is at the heart of the novel's engagement with the curious heroine and with the problem of interiority, a problem crucial to the creation of female consciousness. Susan Stewart memorably describes the world of the dollhouse, our metaphor for the novel, as pure interior: "within within within."[5] So, too, does Freud describe the uncanny as not just a room "crammed with wonders" but a world of secrets, of things that are hidden, things that must be revealed. It is a land of homesickness, of nostalgia, of loss—but also of terrible things discovered, brought to light, brushing up against us in the dark. And at the heart, as Freud recounts in his anecdote of his own reflection in the train compartment, it is our confrontation with ourselves, ourselves but "not ourselves."

Unlike Richardson or James (or, for that matter, Angela Carter), Lewis Carroll did not have a terribly sophisticated language for this encounter with oneself in the wonder-house. He was an inveterate novel reader, with a full panoply of Victorian fiction in his library, but he did not turn to the novel when he went to explain what he was doing. Instead, his explanation of Wonderland was: "The heroine spends an hour underground, and meets various birds, beasts, etc. (no fairies) endowed with speech. The whole thing is a dream, but that I don't want revealed till the end." Carroll loved the idea of the dream vision, and the deadweight of the prose at the end (at the "reveal") suggests that he thought it was a very good trick, but it is not. Not only is it deeply disappointing to any reader who has "believed" in the world of Alice, but it is also a trick (and far from the only one) played on the novel's heroine, whom it wants to depict as naïve, untutored, and simply "taken in" by her adventures. The somnolent explanation, in short, is at war with the character Alice's own sophistication about her adventures and her growing narrative interest. But his other instinct, as that sentence reveals, was a better one: "various birds, beasts, etc. (no fairies)." The first thing that Carroll did when he began *Alice* was to borrow a volume of natural history, reaching less for the invention of the fabulist and more for the accuracy of a naturalist, and it is in that environment that we first begin to stare at Alice and ask, "What—is—this?" Alice's estrangement, like that of Little Nell and Esther Summerson, or the other occupants of the dollhouses to which I will subsequently turn, is that of the subject who finds herself the object of the experiment, who realizes that she is trapped in a world where she cannot make the rules, who cannot know herself, who asks of *herself,* "What is it?"—but who, nonetheless, believes that she will grow up, someday, and write about it.

How did the novel come to be the requisite domicile for the curious heroine? The Anglo-American tradition is full of heroines like Alice, turning from their books ("it had no picture or conversations in it, 'and what was the use of a book,' thought Alice, 'without pictures or conversations?'" [7]) into the real world, only to encounter the new strangeness of the world. Jane Eyre moves between Bewick's *History of British Birds* and her aunt's parlor and the quarrelling Reeds; Isabel Archer lifts her eyes from her novel, only to see her aunt, Mrs. Touchett, come to take her to a new world. So, in this chapter, Alice and her realist kin will repeatedly fall into another world—and they fall, as they inevitably do, both through and into curiosity. Alice may come later than most of these novels, but she gives us an excellent place to begin our wanderings, for both she and her novel are curious about so many things. Begin, as she does, with the rabbit and his pocket watch, the frog in footman's livery ("she felt curious to know what it was all about"), the Mad Hatter's watch, and what whiting are made of. Without saying whether or not she's curious about them, Alice notes that many things are "curious" in themselves: the duck and dodo and lorry and eaglet are all "curious creatures"; the door in the tree is "very curious"; the croquet game and the gardener painting the roses and the song about the whiting are all "curious"; and the Cheshire cat is "the most curious thing I ever saw in my life," which at this point in the book is saying a good deal. But Alice is curious in the other sense as well, for the "creatures" of Wonderland are just as curious about her as she is about them. "Your hair wants cutting," says the Hatter, "who had been staring at Alice for some time in great curiosity." More interesting, the longer Alice is in Wonderland, the more curious she becomes not just to the local inhabitants but to herself, and the more curious she is about her own experience: "What a curious feeling. . . . I must be shutting up like a telescope"; "it's rather curious, you know; this sort of life. . . . I wonder what's happened to me."; "everything is curious today." Or, as she retorts, in the one moment of such confusion that she fails to speak proper English, "curiouser and curiouser."

It is no accident that we owe that neologism to Alice, for she seems to have more than her share of curiosity—though it would be a strange person who didn't follow a rabbit with a pocket watch (and a pocket!) down a rabbit hole. But as we have noted, the thing that makes her most curious is her size[6]— and we have to ask, exactly how much of Alice is "left"? It is impossible to tell, and not only because she is always changing. Alice begins at "the usual size," which we must call size "X," for it is a size we cannot know. Once she falls wherever she falls ("many miles" from wherever she began, "near to the center of the earth," as Alice guesses, "four thousand miles down, I think," through to the "antipathies"), Alice is still, presumably, her "usual" size, but the objects are all wrong—or rather, they're not wrong in themselves, but they don't go properly with one another. Either, as she says, the locks are too big or the keys are too small, but nothing "fits." Faced with a three-legged table, a gold key, and a door that is fifteen inches high (a remarkably precise measurement for a girl who cannot say the word *antipodes*), Alice becomes the instrument of her own observation. Trapped in the realm of misfits, she wants to be the telescope—or rather, she "wishes she could shut up like a telescope, for she had begun to think very few things were really impossible." She "shuts up like a telescope" when she drinks from the first bottle, but she begins to worry instead that she is so small she might go out altogether, "like a candle." When she finds the "very small cake" (with the words *eat me* beautifully marked in currants) and eats it, in no time at all "she is opening up like the largest telescope that ever was" and is now "more than nine feet high." It is at this moment that she is forced to expand existing language like a telescope as well, to meet her needs—at this moment that she remarks that things grow "curiouser and curiouser," and so, of course, does she.

The story of Alice's many changes ("goodbye feet," tiny gloves, great pool, giant mice, "curious creatures," oh no!) nicely bridges what Carroll himself would call "laughing and grief," and it blurs literary genres as well as literary sizes. In some ways, all these transformations are a parable—Alice (named, of course, after the "real" Alice Liddell) has confused two states: growing up, as in taller, and growing up, as in older, and she does so throughout; this is both the running joke of a comic novel and the haunting tale of all living as a progress toward dying, the realization (as in "making real") that storytelling is always tinged with mortality, that mortality ("growing up" and then "going out like a candle") is always at the heart of fiction. But Carroll's interest in making puns literal, in making us *see* language, here connects back to the realist project with which we began. Taking Alice's measure is a way of measuring our relationship to the physical world, as in photographs that depict men standing next to monuments so we know just how big the buildings are. As Susan Stewart puts it, "The body serves as a 'still center,' or constant measure, of our articulation of the miniature and the gigantic" (102). But what if the heroine will not (cannot) stay still herself? As we track the transformations, Alice becomes more telescopy, rather than less. She goes into the rabbit's house and drinks from another bottle, growing so large she "finds her head pressing against the ceiling, and has to stop to save her neck from being broken"; the other animals throw stones, which turn into cakes, and (eating them) Alice shrinks again, only to be terrorized by a puppy and forced to fight it off with a stick; only when she finds the mushroom "about the same height as herself" can she begin to manipulate her own size, treating herself in fact as an experiment in size, and "succeeding in bringing herself down to her usual height."

But all of this must make us wonder: what, in this world, is the usual size? This is the pseudorealist question that interests me here—or rather, it's one that realism ought to be able to answer but cannot. How does Alice know that it is she, and not the tables, chairs, keys, locks, and even puppies that are moving? I offer this not just as a comic meditation, but as the necessary first step toward self-consciousness about both the heroine and her "cabinet," the fiction in which she is placed. Like the writerly Alice, who thinks there should be a tale about her, and that she will write it when she grows up, only to realize that "there's no room to grow any more here," being in the story seems here to preclude having room enough to reflect upon it in any meaningful way. Once we are in a fiction, we tend to think we know where we are. A novel begins with a fixed size and makes things larger and smaller; it's tempting to think we know how big they are. But this novel draws our attention to the instability of any such evaluations and to the question of how Alice can ever measure herself. At one point, she actually "holds her hand on the top of her head to feel which way it was growing, and she was quite surprised to find that she remained the same size." How could measuring yourself *with* yourself ever tell you anything?

From the moment she entered Wonderland, Alice has been trying desperately to find a stable element outside of herself to measure herself by; but what she is constantly doing instead is measuring herself by objects in a purely imaginary world. For this reason, in a strictly comic vein, she is frequently insulting the creatures around her (she tells the three-inch caterpillar that three inches is a wretched size to be; he says, "rearing himself upright as he spoke," "It is a very good height indeed"), but she is also attempting complicated reality games, which are never anything other than more elaborate forms of talking to herself. She is in fact imagining herself as two very different persons, one whose body is shifting, the other whose sense of self wants to stay still. Lewis Carroll in his letters and essays adapted the Thackerayan habit of referring to his characters as "puppets," presenting them as diminutive playthings to be picked up and put away in turn, but he has Alice do much the same thing when she knocks the jurors out of the jury-box and returns them promptly and carefully, thinking of them as like the goldfish she knocked out of their bowl the week before, in danger of dying outside their element. I think Carroll is right that we imagine fictional characters as at once life-sized, imposing, or even magisterial figures but also as miniatures, occupying a dollhouse of the mind, playing with fiction-sized furniture and cunning little objects, in a dream-house we half-occupy with them. This feeling is what we might think of as a "curiosity effect," for the original meaning of things made "curiously" is things made small, with enormous care. But this effect of the curious, something that all fiction, I would argue, creates, is writ large, as it were, by Alice's bodily woes, and it is both the primary effect of Alice as a novel and the sign of the "curiosity effect" in realist fiction.

Critics have not noticed this in part because of their own condescension toward Alice's narration and toward the threat of death that falls over the whole novel. Even Donald Rackin, one of the best Alice critics, has, I think, misread these passages, not noticing the doubled nature of curiosity: first, bringing what is hidden into the light; second, the literal doubleness of the heroine.[7] Rackin points out insightfully the gap between the child Alice and the adult narrator, arguing that the reader reads primarily with the narrator, as when Alice says she wouldn't cry out if she fell off the top of the house, and the narrator snarkily says, "which was very likely true" (meaning, of course, that she'd be dead—and I read the book several times before I got that joke), or when she tells herself, at a giant size, "You ought to be ashamed of yourself, a great girl like you to go on crying in this way!" and he adds, "she might well say this." But Rackin is much less convincing on the subject of the end of the novel, when Alice reflects on the trial. She says, "'I suppose they are the jurors.' She said this last word two or three times over to herself, being rather proud of it: for she thought, and rightly too, that very few little girls of her age knew the meaning of it at all." Rackin argues:

> This self-assured joke by the narrator, the "and rightly too," that gently, even lovingly perhaps, ridicules Alice who thinks that because she knows the names she knows the "meaning" of it all, but instead knows nothing of the meaning—this joke invites the adult reader to laugh at and, at the same time, love Alice. (5)

That's a sweet reading, almost dear, but I think it's ridiculous—and it doesn't seem true to the book. Rackin's analysis not only assumes our constant superiority to Alice, ignoring our dependence on her for any depiction of this strange world, but also assumes a fairly stable narrator and, oddly, a very stable Alice. In Rackin's account, the narrator always knows better, and Alice is always guessing a little, just what we'd expect from a heroine who consistently confuses "growing" and "growing up." But I don't agree that we are necessarily on the narrator's side in this, or that Alice is quite so ridiculous, and I want to draw our attention back to the curious child, who can not only pretend to be two people but also *know* that she's doing it—and who, it seems to me, has a better idea of what a jury does than anyone else in that particular courtroom. It is Alice who is most thoughtful about her own size—not only, as I have suggested, because of the threat her size poses to herself (a puzzle if there ever were one) but also out of a sheer fascination with her own experiments. Like John Snow, the Victorian epidemiologist, testing the effects of chloroform on himself with a stopwatch and a dropper, Alice can only know the effect of anything "real" by testing it on herself—and like Snow, she may not in fact survive the experiment.[8]

Taking the heroine's curiosity as not that different from either that of the "real world" or that of the trained professional gets us closer to defining this "fictional" world—and to what its uncanniness has to do with the heroine's curious body. What makes Alice so terrifying is not, as Carroll tried to tell us, that it is like a dream. Dreams contain fiction, make it banal, make it not matter. What is terrifying about this book is that it is so eerily like our world, so different and yet so immediately recognizable. Katherine Anne Porter expressed this beautifully in a radio broadcast about the novel in the 1940s. She says that as a child she feared *Alice*, unlike other books she read, precisely because "I believed in it entirely. The difference between it and the other fairy stories . . . is, that it all takes place in the setting of everyday life. The little glass table with the key on it, and the furniture and the gardens and the flowers . . . they were all things we knew, you see, familiar things dreadfully out of place, and they frightened me."[9] What a perfectly lovely description of the uncanny—what Dickens described in *Bleak House* as "the romantic side of familiar things," or, put differently, the principle that the uncanny begins at home. This is the world of Alice: a world of familiar things "dreadfully out of place" and equally of dreadful things making themselves quite at home in your parlor or at your tea party. Alice doesn't learn a new game, for she knows the rules of croquet; however, she must accomplish her goals while holding a flamingo still in her arms and chasing down her croquet ball, which alas is now a hedgehog and capable of wandering away. Nothing real is fixed; nothing fixed is real. No reader of *Bleak House* or *Middlemarch* will have trouble recognizing that universe—it's the universe of the realist novel.

If the uncanny does begin at home, how much more uncanny is a dollhouse? When Alice's house is growing in her own arms, we know we are in the presence of the uncanny (houses don't grow; children do) but more, we are back in the realm of curiosity. As Susan Stewart notes, dollhouses, like dolls, not only cross that uneasy border between childhood and adulthood, beginning with the crèche and moving on through mourning dolls, but also reside at the origins of the curiosity cabinet: "The art cabinets of sixteenth and seventeenth century Europe focused on the secular domestic interior as they displayed small objects made of silver, china, glass, and pewter as well as miniature furniture. Dutch miniatures of the time were often exact reproductions of the owner's household furnishings" (61). Like the realist novel, again, dollhouses both are and are not our world: "it's as big as life and twice as natural," but exactly how natural is something half the size of life? Contemporary fiction continues to puzzle over this: in A. S. Byatt's *The Children's Book*, the novelist Olive Greenwood writes a story called "The People in the House in the House" about a girl who, unhappy with the feeble dolls who inhabit her dollhouse, discovers "real" little people hiding in the park and brings them home to play in her dollhouse—where they baffle her attempts to feed and coddle them and pretend "to be dead."[10] She is slow to give up her experiments, for "she was stubborn, and lonely, and she meant well" (438), until to her horror she in turn is kidnapped by a (larger) child to whom she herself is a mere dollhouse creature. As she says to the little people, still within her house within the larger house, there is a monster out there—but they retort, to them, she is a monster. Nonetheless, they help her escape, for "we don't approve of locking people up and making them into toys" (442). Who does? we might ask at this moment in our investigations! But Kate Atkinson, in *Behind the Scenes at the Museum*, draws on an even more "realistic" fear of the dollhouse, a "big four-storey Victorian one," which has "pictures the size of postage stamps and postage stamps the size of dots; it has gilded chairs fit for a fairy-queen and chandeliers like crystal earrings and a kitchen table groaning under the weight of plaster hams and plaster moulded blanc-manges." But as her child-heroine Ruby says, "There's something eerie about it, with its microscopic plumbing (tiny copper taps!) and little, little leather-bound books (Great Expectations!)." Perhaps the twins, to whom it belongs, "with their galactic powers, will miniaturize me in the night and Auntie Babs will come in this room one morning and find the guest bed empty and the guest bed in the doll's house (much nicer than the camp bed) full of a doll-like Ruby Lennox clutching a teddy bear the size of an amoeba." But what is truly in the dollhouse is the secret, which here is the secret of the dead twin sister, the other self—where did *she* go?[11] To answer that, again, is to answer the question, where did I come from?

Dollhouses not only make us question (as do all curiosities, cunningly made) the size of our own relationship to the world but also promise a world of miraculous and open interiority. As Stewart again observes, the dollhouse is "the most consummate of miniatures." Using almost exactly Byatt's phrasing, she describes it as

> a house within a house. . . . Occupying the space within an enclosed space, the dollhouse's aptest analogy is the locket or the secret recesses of the heart: center within center, within within within. (61)

The dollhouse, she goes on to say, "is a materialized secret; what we look for is the dollhouse within the dollhouse, and its promise of an infinitely profound interiority." Like Alice, endlessly teased by unreachable keys to impossibly small doors, we imagine that behind each (false) front is a more real world—a garden, as Alice has it, in which the wonders of the world can be grasped in our hand, but which (however real they seem) baffle our attempts to reach out and touch them. The promise of something beyond—the promise of the garden, the promise of lost knowledge—leads us in, and under.

But how far under do we want to go? One reason Alice fears going out like a candle is that the voyage underground is usually into the land of darkness. Persephone, too, needed to be even more careful than she was about what she ate, and the Mad Hatter's tea party gives us the haunted feeling of Eve, who "knew not eating death." But the other fear is clearly of becoming inanimate in another way, of becoming the doll within the house, of being closed up, and of being "telescopic," becoming the mechanical doll of Freud's uncanny essay. This image of femininity haunts modern feminism, from

Ibsen's *A Doll's House* to Joss Whedon's *Dollhouse*. The fear for a woman is always of being trapped in the house, where law and culture put her—or, as Peter Goodrich brilliantly summarizes the history of English law, "woman is the gynaecum, she is a place, she is the inner household."[12] But law is also a threshold, residing, as Alice does, "on the boundary of knowing and being," straddling "inside and outside, exterior and interior," and the paradox for all these women, from Ibsen's Nora to Whedon's Echo, attempting to acquire a personality seemingly denied them, consists in turning themselves (back) into someone else's plaything. In the same manner, Alice both has interiority (she is conscious; she is her own narrator, in the habit of "pretending to be two people") and has none—she is the text's mechanical doll, instrumental, always at the command of others, in danger of being crushed by her own head. If the nineteenth century needed to develop a woman who had her own personality, who could cross that threshold into a full legal subjectivity, it needed to free her from the dollhouse—and yet, there is no more perfect way of understanding the subject than through its miniaturization, its transformation into a "curious object."

For that reason, the dollhouse proves a fascinating entry into the world of the realist novel—not only because it, too, presents us with a fiction of the real, all trompe l'oeil and missing fourth walls, but also because it helps us understand how completely odd it is that we sympathize with literary characters, those "little dolls."[13] We saw in chapter 1 the enormous anxiety the miniature generated among women writers in particular, the way Mill praised detail as women's work, the way Anna Wulf, the novelist-within-the-novel of *The Golden Notebook*, scorned her own curiosity as limiting her to the small, the particular, the sociological. The dollhouse is what the heroine as well as the author must leave behind, and the world of miniatures becomes increasingly what one recent, odd, scary book, *The Nutshell Studies of Unexplained Death*, imagines. In this extraordinary volume, a woman criminologist (and grandmother), Frances Glessner Lee, founded the Department of Legal Medicine at Harvard and (in the 1940s and 1950s) created a series of miniature crime scenes, in which we become detectives, looking for traces of arson, poison, and mayhem. As Corinne May Botz describes it, the "nutshell dioramas . . . display an astounding level of realism and precision: pencils write, window shades move, and every detail—a newspaper headline, a bloodstain on the rug, an outdated wall calendar, a cartridge casing—becomes a potential clue to the crime." We see less as a doll than as the doll's private investigator, but the novel as a rule takes that distance away from us: we are not diagnosticians; we are the *corps morcelé*.[14] The greatest trick of realism is the one Freud announced: to make us share the characters' perspective, to make us see the world through the doll's eyes. We usually think that the scariest thing about doll or replicant literature is the thought that one might, as in E. T. A. Hoffmann's story (or *Dollhouse*, or *Blade Runner*), accidentally have sex with a doll, but it is even stranger to think that one *feels with* one. To read as the doll reads is to experience the same estrangement I have been tracing between the curio and her cabinet, the heroine and her novel. Like Alice, writing a letter to her own feet, the fiction of curiosity gets at that sense of distance we feel is the root of consciousness: to be curious about oneself is to exist, but to see oneself as truly strange, to see oneself as not fully oneself, is to live in a terribly solitary world. Or as Alice puts it, "'Who am I then? Tell me that first, and then, if I like being that person, I'll come up: if not, I'll stay down here till I'm somebody else—but, oh dear!' cried Alice, with a sudden burst of tears, 'I do wish they WOULD put their heads down! I am so VERY tired of being all alone here!'"

So, before we turn to those other lonely, curious heroines, Little Nell and Esther Summerson, imagine the terrible loneliness of the dollhouse novel, a world peopled entirely with the consciousness of the inanimate. Like eighteenth-century fiction that tells the story of a coin or a carriage,[15] "dollhouse memoirs" trace the imaginary activities of very real objects—but in these cases, a reader's fantasies must begin with the idea that there is such a real object, the particular dollhouse narrated, in her world. In my first example, the artist Tasha Tudor built a dollhouse, had it photographed, and wrote a book about it and its inhabitants.[16] The fantasy (if it is such; the status of this object is not entirely clear to me) is that I could see the dollhouse if I wanted, just as I can visit the miniature Thorne Rooms at the Chicago Art Institute or the palace of Versailles itself: the fake house exists in the real world. More accurately, I could visit the same house twice (a fantasy to which we shall return in discussing *Bleak House*), for the artist built for her dolls a re-creation of her own house, and just as she furnished her own home, she had objects made for the dollhouse in turn. Some of the objects are historical collectors' items, but most are created specifically for the (little) house—and as Tudor recounts, she often bullied and charmed craftsmen into building miniature versions of the things they created for her own (big) house. She is certainly ingenious (she has a house for goats and uses peppercorns for goat droppings), but she is also pretty nutty. At one point, she creates a new doll to show a friend how it is done and falls in love with this doll—or rather, since she cannot, she has her male doll do so and promptly arranges a divorce for him, even though the dolls seem otherwise to live in the 1830s. (The newly married couple, at least at the book's publication, seems to be happily wed— no word on where the divorcée has gone. If Tudor built her a bachelor apartment, she does not say so.) The blended family of dolls continue to live in their perfectly realized world. They have a post office, one which Tudor developed at one and the same time for her children and her dolls, and the doll who is an artist just happens to paint like Tasha Tudor. It is not clear if Tasha Tudor knows her dolls are dolls—it is fairly clear they do not know they are not living. And just to be clear, they do celebrate Christmas, the kind of point that is important in dollhouse land. To the extent that dollhouses are always a compensatory fantasy, a world of better plots and clearer spaces, dolls need to get the best of our worlds and are spared the worst. In the most painful moment in the her account, Tasha Tudor expands the kitchen for her dolls, noting that she herself, when a child, did not have any such kitchen, for her mother (unlike the ur-artist, ur-mother Tudor) did not cook.

These dolls may have kitchens and goat droppings, but it is not clear how deeply Tudor is invested in their consciousness—nor in the fantasy that they can observe the world beyond their own. We need to turn to another amazing novel, *De Bever Hall: The Story of a Stately Dolls House*,[17] to take the fantasy one step further. In this book, the writer, the dollhouse owner, recounts her escapades, from the gift of the original dollhouse to all its transformations, through her subsequent purchases and her decisions about the house, but she does so not only from the perspective of the dolls ("look! we got new furniture!") but also as if they were the agents. It is the dolls who go shopping; they who decide where the piano must go; they who decide when the study becomes the kitchen, and so on. Here is where the uncanny quality of the dollhouse gets most interesting and reminds us again of the faux-naturalness of the natural heroine. Some characters—excuse me, residents—in the dollhouse are upset not by the intrusion of "the real world," but precisely by the dollhouse's *limited vraisemblance*. Lord de Bever is constantly worried about the lack of pipes on the bathroom and kitchen furniture. Just as Alice protests the absence of real-world rules in Wonderland, so he laments, "And worse still . . . not one of these baths or basins has any taps!" Finally, another character (resident? doll?) silences him by trumping his realist demands: why have faucets when there is no water? A deadly silence ensues. Like the comic (or is it?) version of a science fiction text in which characters only know they cannot walk beyond a certain street or open a certain door, or the moment in post–World War II novels when characters open a door to find out a room has been bombed out entirely and there is only air beyond, characters both resist and accept the limits of their world. Like Alice, they believe in a world elsewhere; unlike Alice, they seem largely unperturbed by the gray blobbiness of the world beyond their walls; and even more unlike Alice, they believe entirely in their own existence, never fearing that they will "go out like a candle." It is not possible that they will write poems to their feet or send letters to their feet; they are entire in themselves, the perfect version of mimesis, the dark side curiously integrated into their own displays.

Is this a novel? Is it a disguised autobiography of a young, cheerful dollhouse creator, a sort of portrait of the artist as a young miniaturist? The story of creating the dollhouse is literally a fiction—it is a making—but it is one that, like Lewis Carroll, seeks to reimagine itself in other, dreamlike terms—as Mrs. James Ward Thorne, the creator of the Thorne Miniature Rooms for the Art Institute of Chicago, discovered. In these perfect worlds, the tiny room is imagined as superior to the life-sized (because once lived-in) rooms that museums customarily re-created. One history of the rooms claims,

> Models such as these, in spite of their necessary limitations, some of which are by no means obvious, are in many ways superior to the so-called "period room" for presenting a complete picture of a type or style in its entirety. They offer a flexibility of lighting, setting and furnishing which the actual period room with its demand of piece by piece authenticity, its spatial requirements and the exigencies of lighting and accessibility, can never approach. Supplemented by displays of original objects and furniture, they would seem to offer an ideal solution of the hitherto unsolved problem of an adequate three-dimensional demonstration of the arts of decoration in the public museum.[18]

How did Mrs. Thorne "solve" the problem of "adequate three-dimensional" representation? She did so by precisely the standard we saw in Alice: things may shrink or grow, but they must remain consistent to themselves. Just as Alice's clothes expand or contract along with her (at no point is Alice swimming in clothes of a giant or bursting her seams), so the world of the miniature room remains constant.[19] Within it, one foot is always reduced to one inch—a creative solution Thorne initiated, which is now the standard in the field. In this way, of course, things always look "real"—which is to say, they look in harmony with the other (unreal) things around them. But while evoking the real, the Art Institute must also invoke the realm of the imaginary, to disguise a purely technical art with an imaginative one:

> Mrs. Thorne's solution to the problem of scale is almost magical. While recognizing that an absolute solution is practically beyond human capacity, she has succeeded to an unprecedented degree in relating each part so that a feeling of complete consistency has been attained. While in earlier series the majority of the tiny objects used were the result of years of collecting, in these rooms most of them were actually made to scale for their particular places. Special processes were developed for obtaining a hairline fineness in moldings and ornament and even the textiles were specially prepared in many instances to give the faery delicacy demanded. (p. 3)

While guides to miniature rooms obsess endlessly (sounding like Madame Merle and Gilbert Osmond, diagnosing a hairline fracture in an otherwise perfect teacup, or Ned Rossier, Pansy's would-be lover, and his bibelots) on the authenticity of their materials and the care with which they undertake their collections, they also need to disguise the clinical language they embrace, as much as they must disguise the sheer commodity fetishism behind the artistic (or in this case, the "fairy") labor behind it. While Mrs. Thorne relied on the skill of some very real craftsmen to do this work (wearisome work, as anyone knows who has built a parquet floor for a dollhouse by hand), by the time her admirers are done, one would think that fairies had assembled the houses in the night—or that they had been discovered in a random fall down a rabbit hole.

But let us return briefly to our central effect—telescoping heroines; larger, smaller, larger, smaller. The curious novel, I have been arguing, makes its point by acting out its curiosity on the uncertain size of the heroine, which is no joke to her. Her inability to measure herself, and her almost obsessive need not only to catalogue her world (no small collector, she!) and to talk about herself, mark her as the perfect embodiment of the novel's curiosity, and ours. Her hair wants cutting? What is she? How small is she? Is the world a real world or not, and however are we going to talk about it when we cannot see our own feet? That curiosity opens a gap in the forms of representation where the heroine can find a space to breathe—and where the novelist sees an opening as well. The curiosity of the heroine is where the novel owns up to itself, creates a space for the self-consciousness of feminism, by revealing precisely the mechanism by which the fantasy of the real is created. The size of the heroine is realism's "tell"—but by now, obviously, we have walked our way into a Dickens novel and a different version of the curious fantasies of realism.

From the loneliness of the dollhouse to the singularity of the heroine—and the odd shops of the Dickensian imaginary. *The Old Curiosity Shop* and *Bleak House* are not novels for children—nor are they really novels about children. But Alice's attempts to imagine a sunny dream of "laughing and grief" come directly out of Dickens's imagery of Little Nell asleep in the ghastly curiosity shop, and the dream world of *Bleak House*'s night vision, from Bucket's night walks to Lady Dedlock's last progress, takes on the same uncanny logic. If these books take on the qualities of dreams, Dickens also makes clear to us from the beginning that we are wandering in a child's nightmare, and the curious girl is trying to grow up. The always deluded Master Humphrey might end the first chapter by recounting what pleasure it gave him to imagine the little girl, sleeping in her little bed among the ghoulish antiquities of the old curiosity shop itself, "smiling through her light and sunny dreams,"[20] but this is as incongruous a thought as the picture Nell herself makes, the only lovely object among the curiosities—indeed, whenever Nell mentions her dreams, they are brutal; and when she takes her wicked grandfather away from shelter into the cold night, to keep him from carrying out a terrible murder and robbery, she does so in the name of a bad dream, in which evil men separate them ... something for which a reader can only hope! Dreams, in the world of the Dickens novel, are no sunny refuge—but then, there is very little sunshine in this world at all.

Dickens's touchstone in the mimetic imaginary here is initially less the dollhouse than the other symbol of curious things: the shop. To begin with *The Old Curiosity Shop*, we might begin with the old curiosity shop—and with the curious girl inside of it. The curiosity shop is at the heart of both Dickens's artistry in this early period and our understanding of Little Nell, who is imagined as its chief object and (once the novel is being purveyed) its chief commodity. The shop is so identified with Dickens himself that, despite the book's conclusion, which notes that "the old house had been long ago pulled down, and a fine broad road was in its place" (671), it existed for many years in Lincoln's Inn, and many a postcard of it remains around London, reminding us of the early and relentless commodification of Dickens's works overall (Pickwick figurine, anyone?). Dickens's craft and his persona were identified with the streets and their shops as well—not only the opening sketches by Boz, but Boz's own recollection of every street in London. As Walter Bagehot notes, with an affection close to contempt, Dickens "excels in inventories of poor furniture, and is learned in pawnbrokers' tickets." Dickens's London was the London of shops: "We have heard,—we do not know whether correctly or incorrectly,—that he can go down a crowded street and tell you all that is in it, what shop each was, what the grocer's name was, how many scraps of orange-peel there were on the pavement."[21]

In part, this suggests the young Dickens we are most familiar with: he is the master of a thousand streets, the collector of obscure characters and objects, the curator of his own museum. This is the Dickens of *Sketches by Boz*, who follows his "London Scenes" with "Shops and Their Tenants" and goes on to write brilliant accounts of a used-clothes shop in Monmouth Street, a sketch of pawnbrokers and their clients, and an amazing "inventory" of a broker's shop. From gin-shop to locksmith to stationer to bonnet-shape maker's, all the curiosities of London make their way into his early sketches, and this habit (of strolling down a street and speculating about it) remains throughout his novelistic career.

The first way that curiosity enters the Dickens novel is through the front door of the grandfather's shop—and an odd shop it is. It is described in detail only once: "The place . . . was one of those receptacles for old and curious things which seem to crouch in odd corners of this town and to hide their musty treasures from the public eye in jealousy and distrust. . . . The little old man . . . might have groped among old churches and tombs and deserted houses and gathered all the spoils with his own hands. . . . There were suits of mail standing like ghosts in armour . . ., fantastic carvings brought from monkish cloisters, rusty weapons of various kinds, distorted figures in china and wood and iron and ivory: tapestry and strange furniture that might have been designed in dreams" (47).These are a particular kind of curiosity, of course: they are antiques, gathered by an antiquarian who is himself a relic. These are hardly the riches of Dickens's usual shops: there are no Hindoo babies or articulated cats; there is no Pembroke table or "strings of coral" and "cards of rings and brooches, fastened and labelled separately, like the insects in the British Museum." In fact, we can't even purchase Dick Swiveller's wonderfully "deceptive" piece of furniture, which is "in reality a bedstead, but in semblance a bookcase," which he believes "firmly" to be a bookcase and nothing more. Though the curiosity shop is rumored to contain great secrets, it has (we might add regretfully) no such "secret conveniences." Instead, the shop is a compendium of inconveniences, odd objects, and uncomfortable surfaces—and even more uncomfortable deceptions. It doesn't have any of the things we might expect to find in a shop—prices, bargains, customers, or really, a single object we might desire. For all that critics see in the shop a representation of the vicious world of commodity-desire in Victorian England, the only desire expressed by the Curiosity Dealer is for his granddaughter, and that is the desire that she escape entirely the realm of desire: grandfather "would spare her the miseries that brought her mother, my own dear child, to an early grave. I would leave her—not with resources that could be easily spent or squandered away, but with what would place her beyond the reach of want forever" (71). To be beyond the place of want is to be beyond the world of objects as well—with that attitude, small wonder there are no customers! It is no accident that the one reference to what the grandfather might actually be buying and selling, diamonds, was excised from the manuscript by Dickens before publication; Nell herself, apart from a few sad flowers, is excused entirely from the world of buying and selling.

Although Nell and her grandfather walk away from the site of the shop in chapter 12, they find the idea of it much harder to escape. The curiosity shop itself does not exist after Nell and her grandfather leave—in fact, it returns in the blink of an eye to a state of deadness: "The place was entirely deserted, and looked as dusty and dingy as if it had been so for months" (162). But it may be so quick to empty itself of objects because it is merely reforming itself in every other space we visit. Every location, every "separate scene," to borrow another term from Bagehot, is dusty, crammed, antique, fantastic, distorted, and strange—and every scene finds Nell, again, the mistress of the curiosities, showing off whatever objects remain, telling their stories, lending them the coherence her beauty and youthfulness seem to add to every display—if only because, as the narrator tells us (and it is the secret of all curiosity shops), nothing reveals an object so much as contrast.[22] The puppet show in the graveyard, the churchyard, the fairs, all exist to put one odd object in contradistinction to another, with the resulting effect, strangely, of a singular uniformity.

People rather than shop-goods are the most powerful "objects" of desire in the novel—exerting a strange force over the other characters and seemingly pulling the very novel along with them—but Nell's role is not so doll-like as it might seem. Initially, of course, she is one of the curiosities, a version of the clockwork Sleeping Beauty of Madame Tussaud. While the children who visit the waxwork are "fully impressed with the belief that her grandfather was a cunning device in wax," they are far more impressed with her, for they "evidently supposed her to be an important item of the curiosities" (280). Throughout the book, she is an object of obsessive interest—not least, of course, because of her size. "Fine girl of her age, but small," as Dick Swiveller, with characteristic accuracy, notes—but it masks the darker plot that surrounds her: one in which she stands out from the crowd and is constantly observed, without noticing; one in which she is an unwitting sexual object; one in which, like Alice, she threatens to grow up unexpectedly. Much of the book depends on people making judgments based on her size—is she a child? is she a woman? is she a freak?—and then looking away from her. And we share in this as well: Nell is constantly offered up for delectation— Kit's, Quilp's, the waxwork customers', the drunken boatmen's, ours. Her very compactness makes her portable—and makes the novel the perfect *Wunderkammer*. But Dickens's view of this display is duplicitous, for Nell's singularity and delicacy similarly dissolve the longer and more carefully we stare. What Little Nell truly is, as the novel progresses, is a starving, battered young woman, footweary and heartsore; and much of what has torn her apart is the world of suffering through which she is wandering, about which she wonders, and of which she is increasingly a part—and hence, increasingly, not so singular after all.

But Dickens has made of Little Nell not only a metafictional heroine, a "cunning device" to interrogate his own curious realism, but a way of asking Lewis Carroll's question: what does it mean to have sympathy for the doll? Nell's entrance into the world of "exhibitions," when she joins up with Mrs. Jarley and her travelling waxworks, is certainly one of the most Alice-like sequences, for it plays mightily with our sense of large and small, real and unreal, novel and perspective box, but it is also one of the most pleasant sequences in the novel, not only because Mrs. Jarley herself is quite simply hysterically funny but also because these are the only scenes in the novel in which Nell is safely housed, fully fed, and not busy walking her feet into a bloody pulp. The mutual curiosity of Mrs. Jarley and Little Nell offers one of the rare moments of reciprocal and affectionate (rather than exploitative or scarily erotic) interest in the book. Mrs. Jarley produces an account of the waxwork that might almost be an ironic account of the initial chapters of the novel, with the boisterous Quilp, the clown-like Kit Nubbles, and the jostlings of Codlin and Short: when Nell asks if a waxwork is "funnier than Punch," Mrs. Jarley insists, no, it is nothing like that; instead

> it's calm and—what's that word again—critical?—no—classical—that's it—calm and classical. No low beatings and knockings about, no jokings and

squeakings like your precious Punches, but always the same, with a constantly unchanging air of coldness and gentility; and so like life, that if wax-work only spoke and walked about, you'd hardly know the difference. I won't go so far as to say, that, as it is, I've seen wax-work quite like life, but I've certainly seen some life that was exactly like wax-work. (271–72)

As critics have long noted, this is Dickens's comment on his own "waxworks," more animated than life itself, not just uncanny, but better than the real thing. But what strikes me is Nell's engagement with Mrs. Jarley—and Mrs. Jarley's with her—for as they continue to talk, the fascination shifts between the two of them:

"Is it here, ma'am?" asked Nell, whose curiosity was awakened by this description.
"Why bless you child, what are you thinking of—how could such a collection be here, when you see everything except the inside of one little cupboard and a few boxes? . . . It's gone on in the other wans to the assembly-rooms, and there it'll be exhibited the day after to-morrow. You are going to the same town, and you'll see it I dare say. . . ."
"I shall not be in town, I think, ma'am," said the child.
"Not there!" cried Mrs Jarley. "Then where will you be?" (272)

While first Nell's curiosity is "awakened," suddenly, Mrs. Jarley becomes the questioner—as if she were asking, where in the "wan" should she place Little Nell? And here, Nell's certainty falters in turn—for, as she says,

"I—I—don't quite know. I am not certain."
"You don't mean to say that you're travelling about the country without knowing where you're going to?" said the lady of the caravan. "What curious people you are! What line are you in? You looked to me at the races, child, as if you were quite out of your element, and had got there by accident."
"We were there quite by accident," returned Nell, confused by this abrupt questioning. "We are poor people, ma'am, and are only wandering about. We have nothing to do;—I wish we had."
"You amaze me more and more," said Mrs Jarley, after remaining for some time as mute as one of her own figures. "Why what do you call yourselves? Not beggars?"
"Indeed, ma'am, I don't know what else we are," returned the child.
"Lord bless me," said the lady of the caravan. "I never heard of such a thing. Who'd have thought it!" (272)

Notice how the conversation moves: initially, Nell is curious about the waxworks; gradually, Mrs. Jarley is curious about her. As she grows more amazed, she grows more like the waxworks themselves, "as mute as one of her own figures," but what turns her to wax is nothing remarkable at all—it is simply that Nell is, as she says, not "a curiosity" ("What curious people you are!") but the one thing about which no one is curious: "poor." "We are poor people, ma'am, and are only wandering about," and suddenly, Nell sees herself from the outside.

This is the moment in which Nell's wandering offers a very different version of Alice's, for just as Nell ceases to be a static object in a collection when she takes to the road, she also becomes a different kind of observer. That is, Nell's curiosity about the world changes, as does ours along with her. When Nell and her grandfather go to Birmingham to beg, they wander deeper and deeper into the horrors of industrialism, which make no impression on the grandfather but mark Nell deeply. At one cottage, where Nell and her grandfather go begging, a father stands in the doorway, and here is what he says:

> Do you see that? That's a dead child. I and five hundred other men were thrown out of work three months ago. That is my third dead child, and last. Do you think I have charity to bestow, or a morsel of bread to spare? (427)

What the novel registers at this moment is the contrast between Nell as a tiny, perfect icon of novelistic interest (reflecting that original use of "curiosity," to denote a small object perfectly crafted, showing the "care" of the artist) and the progress of Nell the poor child, walking in a world of other poor children, in which there is no useful ethic of care at all—as her grandfather remarks, finally, realizing that she is dying, "gazing as if for the first time upon her anxious face, her travel-stained dress and bruised and swollen feet, 'has all my agony of care brought her to this at last?'" (415). Much more than in *Alice*, and in a way that shifts us from allegory into social realism, curiosity itself seems to be indicted for its lack of interest—its detachment—its unwillingness to engage with the suffering of those in whom, repeatedly, it has claimed an interest.

Dickens does not rest there: whereas Carroll backs away from Alice's torment, retreating into the picture of a dream world, allowing the curious child to inhabit, despite his care, a fairy story after all, Dickens instead indicts his own novel, his own view of curiosity. Just as he drew our attention to the sufferings of the doll, to her ability to see herself from the outside, to be "two people," so, too, does he draw our attention to a larger social indifference: the limits of curiosity about the curious girl. In the original manuscript, at the moment just before the grandfather finally sees Nell's misery, Dickens imagined a larger response to the urban poverty he is everywhere depicting in this novel: he imagines a "portly gentleman," who stands "in the best street in the town that very night, as he went home from dinner," and who, "looking round him," says,

> Misery . . . Where is it? A splendid Town Hall—a copy from the antique—the finest organ in Europe, a Museum of Natural Curiosities, a Theatre, some capital inns, excellent shops where every luxury may be purchased at very little more than London prices; an elegant market-place, admirably supplied—what would they have? Misery! Pooh, pooh! I don't believe a word of it. (705)

Only Dickens could have written this character (is he not Mr. Bounderby, waiting to be born, twelve odd years later, in full bluster, in the middle of *Hard Times*), but only Dickens would also have included his own novel in the list of dreadful distractions from the dead, dying thus around us every day. Leave to one side the questions of what this tirade is doing there, how the narrator got to the "best street" in town, or what Little Nell is doing while the narrator flies around like the demon Asmodeus. At last, we know where all the real curiosities—the collections of fossils, shells, ornate sculptures, and mysterious bones—are hidden; they are not with the waxwork van, nor in the churches, nor in the curiosity shops: they are in a museum in an unnamed industrial city, waiting for the praise of a man of culture, a man who knows the cost of goods not only in his city but also in London, and not only the quality of every organ in Europe and the size of every town hall but also the ability of money to offset misery. Only Dickens would have placed a "Museum of Natural Curiosities" in his own old curiosity shop, as if to ask, does the novel itself do anything more to make us see, rather than merely walk by, true misery?

This scene, like the father of the dead children, argues for a different view of curiosity and the novel, for it is part of Nell's remarkable tour of industrial England, one which she takes in Dickens's own footsteps, undertaking the same trip he had carried out the year before he wrote the novel and looking about her. Dickens took this trip with his wife Catherine, his usual correspondent in those years, so he left no record of his travels, but he recorded it (and anticipated his own industrial fiction) through Nell's eyes. What does the curious heroine see? In the darkest portion of the novel, she makes her way into the heart of industrial England, its factories and fields and canals. She sees dying children, starving parents, anger and riots and rebellion. She not only travels through a land where "coal dust and factory smoke darken the shrinking leaves" and "strange engines spin and writhe like tortured creatures" and makes her way among "bewildering sights and deafening sounds" but also sleeps on a factory floor (412, 417). She grows hungrier, more tired, weaker; until finally she ceases to reflect at all (disappointingly) on what she has seen—in fact, she seems to abandon all curiosity not just about the world around her, but about her own story. After she makes her way through the nightmare industrial landscape, her story will be over, and there will be no plot left for her but the grave.

More than what she does or does not do or say, more even than what she sees, something important happens to Nell on this final journey: the waxwork child becomes ordinary. Earlier, she was "no more fit to fall in among people than people to count angels as their ordinary chums"; earlier, she was an object of extraordinary interest for us: a curious speculation, an object of pity, in the words of the earlier title, "THE CHILD." Here, she is absolutely unremarkable; nobody looks at her or asks her who she is or asks anything of her, except for the man who demands that she sing forty-seven songs. There is absolutely nothing curious about her; and until the long arm of coincidence reaches out to save her, leading her to faint at the feet of the schoolmaster, she is outside the world of interest altogether. "Misery, pooh, pooh!! I don't believe it!" Nell is finally in a position to be overlooked, as she is throughout her travels, as she is when she lies dead at the book's end, and her grandfather presents these same beloved objects, as if they had become saints' relics, and once again tries to tell Little Nell's story:

> "Her little homely dress—her favourite," cried the old man, pressing it to his breast, and patting it with his shrivelled hand. . . . "See here—these shoes—how worn they are—she kept them to remind her of our last long journey—You see where her little feet were bare upon the ground. . . .
> I often tried to track the way she had gone, but her small fairy footsteps left no track upon the dewy ground, to guide me." (468–69)

Nell's dress, her bird, her shoes: what kind of collection is this? The whole novel comes back as the story of one poor child's shoes—but the grandfather is still trapped in allegory, unable to echo the realism Dickens has precariously carved out of a fairy tale by making his curious heroine see. If we read only for the fairy tale, we willfully misunderstand the curiosity he imagines: "Look at me. I never will complain if you will not, but I have some suffering indeed" (415), Nell says; this is what a poor child says, as if afraid that she, too, a mere "atom" of suffering, would disappear without a sympathetic gaze, as if to be Alice without a looking glass is to cease to exist entirely.

Nell, like Alice, is multiply curious: she is small; she is delicate; she is a fairy; she is a freak surrounded by other freaks; she is also a character who walks out of the domestic world into the dreadful world of industrial England and looks straightforwardly at what lies in front of her. As with Alice, Nell's body is the place where the novel's progress is physically marked; unlike Alice, she lacks a certain resilience, even a willingness to eat and drink, which might save her. The readers who called out on the American shore,

"Is Little Nell dead?" are only fulfilling the book's terrible prophecy: the journey doesn't stop until the heroine lies buried at its end. In some way I have not entirely worked out, the point of *The Old Curiosity Shop* is to make curiosity redundant: can there ever have been a reader, all those Americans notwithstanding, who didn't know, from the absolute beginning of the book, when she lay sleeping in her fairy bed in the middle of all the dead, dead things, that Nell was as good as dead herself? The book may finally play only a death knell, but it forces us to take the curious heroine very, very seriously—we might say, as serious as death.

Esther Summerson, of course, is not dead—though, being a fictional character, she isn't alive either. Nor is she a doll, though she buries one at the beginning of her novel, *Bleak House*. But not only does she live in a house that is a compendium of mismatched tiny objects, a house that threatens to swallow her alive, she also has the habit "of pretending to be two people," and most certainly the habit of talking to herself—or, as she would say, "I have a great deal of difficulty in beginning my portion of these pages."[23] But how curious is she? Start with a moment when she looks, looks away, and looks again: she is in a small country church in Lincolnshire and looks up for "only a moment before I eased [my eyes] down again," catching only a glimpse of a woman "whose handsome proud eyes seemed to spring out of their languor, and to hold mine":

> Very strangely, there was something quickened within me, associated with the lonely days at my godmother's; yes; away even to the days when I had stood on tiptoe to dress myself *at my little glass, after dressing my doll*. And this, although I had never seen this lady's face before in all my life—I was quite sure of it—absolutely certain. . . . . But why her face should be, in a confused way, like a *broken glass to me*, in which I saw scraps of old remembrances; and why I should be so fluttered and troubled (for I was still), by having casually met her eyes; I could not think. . . . And yet I—I, little Esther Summerson, the child who lived a life apart, and on whose birthday there was no rejoicing—seemed to arise before my own eyes, evoked out of the past by some power in this fashionable lady, whom I not only entertained no fancy that I had ever seen, but whom I perfectly well knew I had never seen until that hour. . . . Neither did it revive for more than a few moments, when she once or twice afterwards *glanced at Ada or at me through her glass*. (225; emphasis added)

Esther Summerson, unlike the other heroines I have discussed, is not freakishly small—although she is called "little woman" by most of the characters around her, she isn't; she's a perfectly normal-sized woman in her early twenties trying to make her way, without fortune and eventually without her own face, through a fairly Darwinian Victorian London. But she raises for us a similar set of questions: How big is someone in a novel? How big is someone "inside," as opposed to the person "outside"? What happens when the woman steps out of the house—and what happens when the doll gets consciousness? What is remarkable in this stunningly rich passage is not just that Esther sees herself, instantly, as in a "broken glass," or that the mysterious Lady Dedlock in turn stares at Esther and Ada through "her glass," but that Esther imagines herself first standing "on tiptoe to dress [herself] in [her] little glass," and stands there not as herself but as "little Esther Summerson." Esther, we might say seriously, dolls herself up at this moment—her only hope of animation, that brief moment of "quickening," the moment when she curiously comes to life.

Of the many uncanny moments in *Bleak House*, the moments that seem so psychologically charged that they disrupt the ordinary progression of plots and characters, this is among the most striking: as Esther sees her own mother "in a broken glass," she also anticipates the moment when, after her illness, she will look at her own face behind a veil of her own hair, and it will be entirely new to her. She is also looking back, seeing her godmother's face, wondering if that could be where the uncanny resemblance lies, if only her godmother's expression of "stern decision" had not worn into her face "like weather into rocks." All these faces, and even more, all these Esthers, are present at once, despite the curious opacity of the scene. And as at so many moments in the novel, we can only echo Jo the crossing-sweep's woebegone plea when he sees Hortense, dressed up as Lady Dedlock, when she was dressed up as the poor woman: "Are there three of them then?"

I think there are three Esthers only in the sense that there are so many Alices: they are alternately tricks of size (three Esthers, all at different stages of the plot), or tricks of narration, or, depending on your perspective, tricks of the eye. What creates that "quickening" in Esther's perceptions at the moment of both intense trauma and intense pleasure—the moment of seeing (half-seeing, without knowing you are seeing, but also remembering, in the retrospective narration of *Bleak House*) the mother's (lost) face and (mis)remembering your own—is that moment of self-estrangement I have been connecting with realism, or more precisely, with realism's habit, which Esther quite literally personifies in the split narration, of talking to itself. This is what Alice desired: to be "in" the story and free to "reflect on it" at the same time—and it is what I mean by curiosity.

The intricacies of the two-narrator problem, and particularly the relationship of female curiosity to the whole of the novel, make us aware in still new ways of what any one person can know and the wider world in which we are all "curious" to someone else. When Esther first goes to describe her own curiosity, she in fact connects it with "quickening" and describes herself as precisely as if she were someone else narrating: "I had always rather a noticing way—not a quick way, O no!—a silent way of noticing what passed before me, and thinking I should like to understand it better. I have not by any means a quick understanding. When I love a person very tenderly indeed, it seems to brighten. But even that may be my vanity" (17). But as Esther notes, her curiosity, her quickness, and the form of the larger narrative in which she is a part are always entirely connected. What Esther wants to know, the things she wants to know about, and the form in which *we* receive the knowledge are all interconnected versions of curiosity: they all converge again on the form of the realist novel. And yet again, they converge around a problem of scale: "It seems so curious to me," Esther remarks, noticing her own estranged relationship to narration, "to be obliged to write all this about myself! As if this narrative were the narrative of my life! But my little body will soon fall into the back-ground now" (27).

It does not—in fact, if we connect Esther's illusory "little body" (as opposed to the normal, grown-up body she otherwise occupies) with this crisis of curiosity, the examination of identity and the strange "quickening," the coming to life as well as the moments of terrifying cleverness, then we are back to the question of the heroine as her *own* investigator, the scientist experimenting on herself. The notion of the heroine trapped in the experiment, like the child trapped in the dollhouse world, is a powerful one for feminism, as it is for the male authors. When Pip fantasizes freeing Estella from Miss Havisham's haunted house, no less than when the rogue FBI agent on Joss Whedon's *Dollhouse* tries to free the "actives" from their Cinderella trap (other identities that occupy them, or that they inhabit, only till the clock strikes), the terror of the animated doll is dual. Which is more terrifying: that the trapped heroine knows who she is, or that she doesn't? The curious heroine may seem to free herself from the prison of the copy, something else that we will return to in our discussion of *Bleak House* later in this book, but the question of how real she is, like the question of how big she is or how much she knows, remains an uncanny one.

What happens next? When Alice finally reaches the trial, as Jonathan Miller has remarked, she reaches her "majority," and the book ends;[24] before Nell can reach hers, she goes out like a candle; Esther Summerson—well, of course, Esther Summerson ends the novel by disappearing, in conventional heroine fashion, into "the Doctor's wife," and she lives in a miniature version of her own house, which just happens to share the name of her novel, Bleak House Two. By the time of *Bleak House*, curiosity has its answer from the realist novel: the heroine and her cabinet are all but indistinguishable. But the uncanniness of the heroine remains not only in the Gothic unease of the Bluebeard story and its ominous cabinet, to which we will turn next, but in the realist text's self-consciousness about representing the heroine's curiosity. "What was it you said to yourself?" says Ralph Touchett to Isabel Archer.

"I saw my wish outside myself," answers Gwendolen Harleth. In the chapters that follow, the author's entanglement with the heroine's experiments will commit writers variously to metafictional devices (Thackeray), statistics and stutterings (Dickens), and finally, to a recognizably modern feminist debate over how subjects represent themselves (Eliot). Not perhaps what Alice Lidell had in mind when she asked, "Who am I then?" but still, recognizably, the question of a curious heroine.

PART TWO

Crossing the Threshold

CHAPTER 4

❧

Was She Guilty or Not?

The Curious Heroine Meets the Wicked Novelist

A woman mask'd is like a cover'd dish that gives a man curiosity and appetite, when, it may be, uncover'd, t'would turn his stomach.
William Wycherly, A Country Wife

Under the mask satirical there walks about a sentimental gentleman who means not unkindly to any mortal person.
William Thackeray, Letters

His wit is bright, his humour attractive, but both bear the same relation to his serious genius that the mere lambent sheet-lightning playing under the edge of the summer-cloud does to the electric death-spark hid in its womb.
Charlotte Brontë, Preface, Jane Eyre

She has her enemies. Who has not? Her life is her answer to them. She busies herself in works of piety. She goes to church, and never without a footman. Her name is in all the Charity Lists. The destitute orange-girl, the neglected washerwoman, the distressed muffin-man find in her a fast and generous friend. She is always having stalls at Fancy Fairs for the benefit of these hapless beings.
William Thackeray, Vanity Fair

Look at the novel in the 1840s and '50s: a radical experimentation with form, a renewed passion for wider social representation, a fascination with point of view and narrative focus—and in the middle of it, a curious heroine, carrying a light before her and crossing the threshold into Bluebeard's chamber. In an age of expanding civic rights and endless variations of form, we have seen the way law, fairy tale, and formal realism come together to test the heroine and to make her into the great experimenter, and even more the way her body becomes the site of realism's trials. *Alice in Wonderland* and its odd sisters, *The Old Curiosity Shop* and *Bleak House*, offer us particularly knowing, even self-conscious versions of curiosity, versions that depend on a series of daring optical illusions, carefully deployed: a young woman with a tendency to shrink and grow travels a strange kingdom asking questions; and wherever she goes, she carries a telescope. Is there a corner of England into which she cannot peer—rising and shrinking, aging and diminishing, and always keeping her own secrets?

Our talisman for this progress has long been Jane Eyre, small and keychain sized, peering over the balustrades, talking to us confidentially, longing for a "power of vision" and speaking clearly of a woman's anger. That's the small woman we had in mind, not a snakey heroine with bare shoulders and a sly grin. Nothing in these novels could have prepared us for the novels of William Thackeray, a man who eschews if anyone ever did the forms of forensic curiosity we have been examining. Not for him the easy guilt and innocence of the paradisical; not for him a simple story of the fall; his sandy-haired heroine with the bare shoulders and snakelike neck offers her own challenges to our curiosity—and Thackeray's layered and sneaky fiction is the most duplicitous version of both realism and the Bluebeard story we have seen yet. The problem of belief with which we oriented ourselves at the beginning of the book, tracing Robert Newsom's probabilistic antinomy of fiction, Catherine Gallagher's pursuit of "nobody," even Ian Watt's realism of "presentation" and realism of "assessment," has met its match in Thackeray—as have the machinations of the would-be carniverous suitors of the curious heroine, for once utterly defeated by *her* manipulations of the marriage plot, for "she has no mother" and must do things for herself. What does she have? "She has her enemies. Who has not?" With *Vanity Fair*, and with Miss Rebecca Sharp, we are in a different, darker, if also more radiant world—and the realist novel, layered and doubled as it already was, just got a lot more complicated.

For what Thackeray offers us is what we used to call criminal knowledge—or, as Roger Shattuck has summed up Proust's stereoptic narration, "The science of optics forever shows the *errors* of our vision."[1] So let us stand on a street corner in Belgium, when Thackeray's wicked heroine takes us into her confidence, not for the first or the last time.

> "The women here are as amusing as those in May Fair," she told an old London friend who met her, "only, their dresses are not quite so fresh. The men wear cleaned gloves, and are sad rogues, certainly, but they are not worse than Jack This and Tom That. The mistress of the house is a little vulgar, but I don't think she is so vulgar as Lady—" and here she named the name of a great leader of fashion that I would die rather than reveal. In fact, when you saw Madame de St. Amour's rooms lighted up of a night, men with *plaques* and *cordons* at the

écarté tables, and the women at a little distance, you might fancy yourself for a while in good society, and that Madame was a real Countess. Many people did so fancy, and Becky was for a while one of the most dashing ladies of the Countess's salons.[2]

Becky Sharp is curious in every sense of the word—and having read her description of this scandalous salon, are we not curious as well? The mysterious scene is redolent of curiosity, "lighted up of a night," filled with gaming and dressing and masquerading. Becky herself has been stripped of her mask—her adultery (perhaps) revealed to her husband, her position in London society lost, herself up to no good—or, as the narrator says, shunning (or so he says) the spectacle of her disgrace, "when Becky is out of the way, be sure that she is not particularly well employed, and that the less that is said about her doings is in fact the better" (813). He warns us not to look below the surface at the mermaid's tale, to "peep down under waves that are pretty transparent and see it writhing and twirling, diabolically hideous and slimy, flapping amongst bones, or curling round corpses," for "it is labour lost to look into [the turgid water] ever so curiously" (820), but looking curiously is the key to this moment, which entices us to do exactly that—to look, as Barthes described the curiosity of Sarrasine, at "an object whose *underneath*, whose *insides* will continue to arouse his concern, his curiosity, and his aggression."[3]

We might be tempted to think that this eroticized "underneath" is what makes *Vanity Fair* the first of what Virginia Woolf called for, novels for grown-up people: that unlike Alice, Nell, or even Esther, Becky is fallen; or rather, that hers is an explicitly sexual fall. But that is not where *Vanity Fair* gets its knowledge—rather, it is from the other thing Barthes offered us, the heroine's curiosity, and the ways that we are seduced into falling with her; the ways, in the vertiginous changes of what Joseph Litvak has nicely called the "eaters and eaten" world of the novel, we cling nonetheless to what Becky sees.[4] However disgraced and shunned the little exile might be, she never ceases to survey the world around her and never ceases to entice our gaze. For look around you at Madame de Saint-Amour's party. The scene engages us not so much with spicy details, but with direct address and suspended revelation: "You might fancy yourself," it says, and "for a while" you are with Becky, "in good society," and Becky, too, "for a while," was one of the most dashing ladies of the countess's salons. And "you" walk into the room not only with Becky but also with an equally tricky narrator: through his deployment of Becky Sharp's progress through a story of curiosity, through what he repeatedly calls the "mystery" of her history, and in particular through his reworking of the story of Bluebeard, Thackeray forces readers to follow a similarly devious path through the narrative of curiosity, one that leads us at best to a darkened, hardly virtuous, and only barely revelatory form of knowledge. It was Thackeray who reinvented curiosity for the Victorian novel, and his famous little Becky puppet, with her flexible joints, who taught novel readers how much they wanted to know.

But to know what? Return to the display at the salon: it is, "for a while," "good society," but, like all shows in *Vanity Fair*, the spectacle cannot last. This is the structure of curiosity in *Vanity Fair*, and it radically changes the narrative we have been following: the narrative of the fall, the narrative of the trial, gives way to perceptual incongruity. Thackeray loves this dissolve—where Carroll shrinks and expands, Thackeray will always look backward, over his shoulder. For him, curiosity is a trick of the light, a moment of illumination, of too bright lighting fading into wavering darkness. He used this metaphor to telling effect earlier in *Vanity Fair*, in the preface, where he describes his own technologies of narration by writing that "the whole [of the novel is] accompanied by appropriate scenery and brilliantly illuminated with the Author's own candles," and when describing a ball earlier in the book, he invokes similar tricks of fancy lighting and fancy women, saying:

> Some ladies we may have seen—we who wear stars and cordons and attend the St. James's assemblies, or we, who, in muddy boots, dawdle up and down Pall Mall and peep into the coaches as they drive up with the great folks in their feathers—some ladies of fashion, I say, we may have seen, about two o'clock of the forenoon of a Levée day . . . who are by no means lovely and enticing objects at that early period of noon. A stout countess of sixty, décolletée, painted, wrinkled with rouge up to her drooping eyelids, and diamonds twinkling in her wig, is a wholesome and edifying, but not a pleasant sight. She has the faded look of a St. James's Street illumination, as it may be seen of an early morning, when half the lamps are out, and the others are blinking wanly, as if they were about to vanish like ghosts before the dawn. (601)

What is particularly brilliant here is the way our own eyes become dazzled, as we move from the bright light of the "forenoon," with its painted countess ("wholesome and edifying, but not a pleasant sight") to the "faded look of a St James Street illumination" in the early morning half light, half the lamps out, the others blinking wanly, about to vanish. Imagine a fearsome Joan Rivers, escorting Academy Award nominees down the red carpet under the harsh Los Angeles sun, before they enter the careful lighting of a festival hall—and imagine those same nominees, sunken, faded, in the dim lights of a drunken ballroom, long after the awards have gone to someone else. This is a language of "knowing" that is a form of seeing through—the critique of the "illusion" of belief we associate with other forms of enlightenment. As when Marx imagines that "the bourgeoisie has torn away from the family its sentimental veil, and has reduced the family relation to a mere money relation," or pictures "men and their circumstances appear[ing] upside-down as in a *camera obscura*," so Thackeray imagines those who "attend," those who "dawdle up and down" the boulevard, as having the ability to see through things—"as if they were about to vanish like ghosts before dawn." What Becky Sharp knows is precisely this: the difficulty of judging, the way one scene fades into another, the way knowledge itself is a question.

This is the already characteristic gaze of *Vanity Fair*: a scene turning to vanity before our eyes, the countess a garish spectacle, the long day waning, a world turned ghostly. Yet how do we know all this? Through yet another untrusworthy spectacle: the rigged technology of realist narration. We know what we know because Becky told it to "an old London friend who met her." Either that friend told the narrator, or that friend *was* the narrator, for he would "die rather than reveal" the secret of the gossip. By toying with our desire to know, Thackeray both lets us in on the secret, unreliable transmission of knowledge and reminds us how desperate we, too, are for information. We are poised here exactly where Thackeray (and Becky) want us, "at a little distance," hearing a report and leaning further in to see—or to hear—what? It is a narrative striptease; it is yet another revelation of the deception behind the illusion; it is a magic trick but also a moment of sadness, when Becky, "for a while," is dashing once more. "Which of us has his desire? or having it, is satisfied?" (878) we murmur with the narrator. It is a moment of sexual interest, of visual illumination, of disillusionment, of curiosity.

What happens when Thackeray opens the locked door is very different from anything else we (or any other heroines) have seen so far. Thackeray's greatest invention in retelling our wicked fairy tale, and in rethinking the novel, is that his Bluebeard is neither a hero nor a villain, but a heroine, and a highly ingenious one to be sure. Rather, as Kathleen Tillotson notes in *Novels of the Eighteen-Forties*, Thackeray enters what Thomas Carlyle called "the Bluebeard Chambers of the heart"—and a curious heart it is.[5] For in *Vanity Fair*, Bluebeard is called Becky Sharp. Combining the power of Bluebeard with the curiosity of Fatimah, Becky comes with a secret cabinet, magic jewels, a fatal key, and a closet of dead husbands. But Becky is not only both Bluebeard and Fatima; she is, as we have already seen, a figure for the artist as well, one who not only participates in the creation of spectacle but also raises its ultimate questions: Was she guilty or not? What did she see behind the locked door? What is the curious heroine to do *after* the acquisition of terrible knowledge? The novel dangles the possiblity of legal certainty in front of us, both with Becky's adultery and with her murder of Jos Sedley, but its heart is not in its criminal narrative—or at least not in its easy resolution. In the fullest incarnation of Thackeray's spectacular realism, tinged as it is with romance and haunted by fakery, Becky does what Thackeray does: she brings with her into the novel the possibility of a transformative optical apparatus, one that will (darkly) recast Victorian fiction and make possible a different (more terrifying, riskier, but also finally braver) performance from the curious heroine.

In 1844, Thackeray visited Bluebeard's castle. Imagine his delight—and his horror. Throughout his career, he was fascinated by Bluebeard.[6] In a fairly short literary career, he wrote no fewer than four Bluebeard parodies, all very different—a sketch book, a parody (from the perspective of Bluebeard's cranky widow), a romance, and a play, entitled "Bluebeard at Breakfast," in which Bluebeard argues that wife-murder could take place over something as simple as cold mutton—and that "there is cold mutton in every household." The story was not always so amusing for Thackeray. As the scandal associated with the second edition of *Jane Eyre* suggests (an unknowing Charlotte Bronte dedicated her story of mad wives and adulterous husbands to the author of *Vanity Fair*), Thackeray had his own Bluebeard shadow, a wife left in an asylum, a world of shadowy guilt. But comic or tragic, Thackeray's Bluebeard is no ordinary Bluebeard. He is a figure out of theatre, drawn as much from the fabulously successful musical version written by George Colman as out of folklore, and he carries with him a strong aura of spectacle. (Bluebeard is rarely mentioned by Thackeray without the possibility, for instance, of an elephant—and it will be an elephant, as we shall see at the end of this chapter, that offers Thackeray's most dizzying lightning-strike of transformation.)

The Thackeray who entered Bluebeard's castle was shaped by a variety of different kinds of spectacles. One of his persistent pseudonyms in the decades before he wrote *Vanity Fair* was Mr. Spec, a gentleman-about-town who roamed London, writing sketches and casting ironic gazes at the world. A cheerful mover, perpetually if mildly peeved at the inconveniences around him, he also seems to delight in his own private spectacle. Or, to quote Spec himself from the beginning of one of these sketches, "Child's Parties": "As every man, sir, looks at the world out of his own eyes or spectacles, or, in other words, speaks of it as he finds it himself, I will lay before you my own case, being perfectly sure that many another . . . will sympathize with me."[7] Unlike the lonely Thackeray, trying to provide for his daughters and amuse them in London, Paris, and wherever else he travelled to write (Anne Thackeray Ritchie provides a lovely account of the two girls at a Dickens Christmas party—overwhelmed by the beauty of Dickens's daughters' dresses, self-conscious and slow to join into the games, awed by Dickens's panache in running the party, and finally touched by their own father's arrival being cheered by a crowd of boys on the stairs), Mr. Spec has been provided with a wife and a family "already inconveniently large, yet constantly on the increase"—a family, we might note, more like Dickens's than Thackeray's own. Spec prepares us for Thackeray's curious gaze at the world when he travels to a party with his young daughters, "with the skirts of their stiff muslin frocks actually thrown over their heads, so that they should not crumple in the carriage!" The unwilling Peeping Tom, trapped in a world of stiff-skirted daughters, can proffer to his readers only the following desperate, touching paternal advice: "If you are not able to enter the world with your dress in its proper place, I say stay at home." If only, we might think to ourselves, Becky Sharp's first and bosom friend, Amelia Sedley, had managed to convince Becky of this maxim, how differently might *Vanity Fair* have turned out!

The world for Mr. Spec is one of a series of ocular devices and visual traps. In this sketch, he recounts all the visual spectacles children's parties present. Some feature "Dr Lens's microscope," some the Haymarket Theatre, but the particular party in this sketch, worst of all, features a magician, someone who, like Thackeray, plays games with vision.

> As for the conjuror, I am sick of him. There is one conjuror I have met so often during this year and the last, that the man looks quite guilty when the folding doors are opened and he sees my party of children, and myself amongst the seniors in the back rows.... I on my side too feel reciprocally uneasy. What right have we to be staring that creature out of his silly countenance? ... When I see him squeeze an orange or a cannon-ball right away into nothing, as it were, or multiply either into three cannon-balls or oranges, I know that the others are in his pocket somewhere. I know that he doesn't put out his eye when he sticks the penknife into it: or that after swallowing (as the miserable humbug pretends to do) a pocket-handkerchief, he cannot by any possibility convert it into a quantity of coloured wood-shavings. These flimsy articles may amuse children, but not us. I think I shall go and sit down below amongst the servants whilst this wretched man pursues his idiotic delusions before the children. (49)

The problem is not just that the antics are feeble but that Thackeray recognizes something in him—and he in Thackeray. There is something remarkable in that shared glance, the complicity of the two paid entertainers, staring each other out as Spec watches the magician at work and rejects his "idiotic delusions."

This is the secret of Thackeray's vision: to both perceive and reject delusions; to look at the world *after* seeing through it, as Becky does at Madame de St. Amour's party. As Thackeray goes on in this sketch, he recounts the magic lantern show presented for the children:

> I still sometimes get a degree of pleasure, by hearing the voices of children in the dark, and the absurd remarks which they make as the various scenes are presented—as, in the dissolving views, Cornhill changes into Grand Cairo, as Cupid comes down with a wreath, and pops it onto the head of the Duke of Wellington, as Saint Peter's at Rome suddenly becomes illuminated, and fireworks, not the least like real fireworks, begin to go off from Fort St Angelo—it

is certainly not unpleasant to hear the "o-o-o's" of the audience, and the little children chattering in the darkness. I stand in the door. But I think I used to like the "Pull devil, pull baker," and the Doctor Syntax of our youth, much better than all your new-fangled, dissolving views and pyrotechnic imitations. (49)

The magic lantern show, a Victorian technology that featured a series of glass slides shown by a gas lamp, was an apparatus most famous for the effect of the "dissolve," in which one image turns slowly (through the exchange of slides) into another. This is the technology behind the phantasmagoria, the large-scale spectacles that had Parisians screaming in the time of the Terror, but now rendered domestic, a home-sized theatre of the uncanny. (The magic lantern, of course, reappears most famously in the opening scenes of *Remembrance of Things Past*.)[8] While the lantern draws on some of the mechanical trickery of the magician (Victorian magic tricks were all about props and not about sleight of hand), it is also something that exploits the way our own optical apparatus works, our ocular habit of holding one image after it is gone, superimposing it on the next. While critics like Jonathan Crary have argued that the magic lantern, unlike a device like the stereoscope, hid the fact that it was an illusion by hiding the machinery that produced it, Thackeray stresses the mechanical apparatus, the "new-fangled" device that creates the transformation, and he is far more ambivalent about this trickery than he was about the wretched magician's "idiotic delusions."[9] The illusions of the magic lantern may be mechanical, but they are more like Thackeray's own: they work, and they work more in the ways that he thinks fiction does. It is not merely that the fireworks of the dissolve are "not the least like real fireworks," but that "real fireworks" begin to sound unalluring as well. Notice how elegantly the despair gets distributed between the wistful wonder of the children's enthusiasm and their "absurd remarks," and the writer's dismissal of "new-fangled" views in favor of his longing for his own past, some moment not so much when the games were more credible as when the viewers (himself, at least) were more credulous. But the sense of one scene turning into another, of the power of a staged spectacle to amaze, however briefly, by offering us a doubled perspective, a form of sight that hovers just beyond our own, is a hint as to what Thackeray himself was doing in his early writing: we stand in the doorway and watch the children, watch the play of fictional belief, but we watch it always with a sense that the spectacle, however delightful, remains only a fiction—and that the reality, the fireworks of St. Angelo as they "really" are, may not be all that illuminating either. Remember the glare and dazzle of light in *Vanity Fair*, the illumination of St. James, fading quietly into dingy dawn. The power of fiction is to play those two perspectives on the same object off one another in quick succession.

This is the perspective Thackeray brings to Bluebeard's castle, what he describes as "Vauxhall in the Daytime," anticipating the brilliant opening scenes of *Vanity Fair*. Thackeray had been a traveller all his life—born in India and returned to a strange and terrible England when he was a boy of five; lost in the terrors of Charterhouse, the boy's school he immortalized as "Slaughterhouse"; and then wandering through most of his twenties and thirties. After a stint in Weimar before his marriage, he lived in Paris, with his mother and stepfather, in order to escape debt and have a family for his daughters. He travelled in and wrote about Ireland, imagining a book called *A Cockney in Ireland*, and he made his London mark with *The Book of Snobs*, the most successful of his publications before *Vanity Fair*. He was, as Carlyle memorably described him after Thackeray's review of *The French Revolution*, "a half-monstrous Cornish giant, kind of painter, Cambridge man and Paris newspaper correspondent, who is now writing for his life in London."[10] (One of his pseudonyms was "the Fat Contributor," and he prided himself on not taking up offers to get into freak shows free, as a Giant.) His goal in all his rambles was to make enough money to make a life for himself and his daughters once and for all in London, but the travels were not just a means to an end; in particular, the journey he undertook at the behest of (and in the pay of) the P&O Steamship Company, which became the volume *Notes of a Journey from Cornhill to Grand Cairo*, made a significant difference in his life and in his writing. It served an important strategic purpose for the hungry author, for though he came under considerable attack for taking the journey in the first place, for him the trip represented authorial independence, giving him enough money to buy a home for himself and the girls, and finally to gather what was left of his family. But this trip also crystallized Thackeray's ideas about *novelistic* vision, a point made clearer by the association of the volume's title with the dissolving view he described in the sketch we have already identified as crucial to his perspective: the view when "Cornhill changes into Grand Cairo."

Thackeray writes in full awareness of the ephemerality of his own writing (at one point, one of his imaginary readers asks him the ultimate Thackerayan question, "you admit you have nothing to say and you own it; why do you write?"), but he is much more interested in the transience of vision—the world of illusion that lies before him, and that threatens always to disappear before his eyes. For Thackeray, the Orient is, as London was, a world of theatrical nostalgia and of theatrical illusion:

> I can't go to any more romantic place than Drury Lane to draw my similes from—Drury Lane, such as we used to see it in our youth, when to our sight, the grand last pictures of the melodrama or pantomime were as magnificent as any objects of nature we have seen with our maturer eyes. Well, the view of Constantinople is as fine as any of Stansfield's best theatrical pictures, seen at the best period of youth when fancy had all the bloom on her—when all the heroines who danced before the scene appeared as ravishing beauties. (63)[11]

Here we are again, not in Drury Lane as it is but "Drury Lane, such as we used to see it in our youth," a picture still "as magnificent as any . . . we have seen with our maturer eyes." The Fat Contributor recognizes the limitations of his metaphor, for, as he adds, "if you were never affected by the theatre, no words can work upon your fancy" and this quality of fancy (with "all the bloom on her") is central to the moments of rapture—and of all the hoped for, but alas never complete, disorientation of the traveller in the Orient.

Thackeray seems to want a mystery that is more than mystery, something that resists his curiosity. He finds that, and more, when he visits the seraglio in the palace in Constantinople. The fat contributor claims the seraglio

> has a romantic look in print; but not so in reality. Most of the marble is wood, almost all the gilding is faded, the guards are shabby, the foolish perspectives painted on the walls are half cracked off. The place looks like Vauxhall in the daytime. (77)

This is the most haunting thing that Thackeray sees in the orient—and it is haunting, of course, only because the mysteries of Vauxhall at night remain so powerful an illusion, so absolute a desire. Just as Thackeray still treasures the memory of "Drury Theatre, such as we used to see it in our youth," or, to recall the illusions of "Child's Parties," the "'Pull devil, pull baker,' and the Doctor Syntax of our youth," so he yearns for a lost Vauxhall. The seraglio not only looks like England, but it also looks like an England stripped of its wonder as well—wooden marble, faded gilding, shabby guards, and "the foolish perspectives painted on the walls [and] half cracked off." "The fatal Vauxhall look of the Seraglio," Thackeray recounts later in the volume, "has pursued me ever since I saw it," and that loss, that doubleness, pursues any reader of *Vanity Fair*, where, let me remind you, there are only foolish perspectives, and they are all half cracked.

But there is another twist to the view of the seraglio, for from the start, we know whose palace it really is. As Thackeray writes.

> From the kitchen we passed in the second court of the seraglio, beyond which is death. The guide book only hints at the dangers which would befall a stranger caught prying in the mysterious first court of the palace. I have read Bluebeard, and don't care for peeping into forbidden doors; so the second court was fine enough for me. (76)

Thackeray initially casts himself as a Fatima, standing outside the seraglio, tempted to "pry," to look in, that look "beyond which is death." He imagines himself, though, as a wise Fatima—one who has read and "doesn't care for peeping" (remember Spec and his daughters) and knows better than to look. But if Thackeray refuses to look in (or almost refuses, as we shall see), someone else is looking out. As he and his companions float by the palace, they are

> told that these were the apartments of His Highnesses's ladies, and actually heard them whispering and laughing behind the bars—a strange feeling of curiosity comes over some ill-regulated minds—just to have one peep, one look at all those wondrous beauties, singing to the dulcimers, padding in the fountains, dancing in the marble halls, or lolling on the golden cushions, as the gaudy black slaves brought pipes and coffee. (70)

As much as it conjures a faux oriental palace, indolent and redolent of mystery (was there really no peeping?), this scene does something else: it suggests that someone in the seraglio is laughing at you—that there is a world behind the bars, looking out at your world, and seeing it aslant. What, all readers must wonder, did the women of the seraglio see when they peered out—and how was Thackeray ever to know what was on their minds? Or as we might ask, who's curious now?

Thackeray brought this complicated point of view back with him from the Orient—and it is what alters his view of London, as well. Indeed, he summarizes the turn in his own vision when describing that of an unexpected fellow traveller, Henry Mayhew. In his sketch "Waiting at the Station," Thackeray describes a group of working-class women about to set sail for Australia, looking for husbands.[12] He imagines the waiting Australian farmers as sultans, walking among them, preparing to "throw the handkerchief" to the woman most attractive and alluring. But then he concedes that his readers cannot truly imagine the scene, for "they are not like you indeed," and these women ("lacking your education and refinements") would "not understand a hundred things simple to you." But this mixture of class difference and orientalist metaphors gives way to a very different vision, one which will pervade the rest of Thackeray's fiction: while we thought we could wait, complacently, at the station, while the women sailed for a new world, instead we are forced to move forward ourselves, when "some clear-sighted energetic man like the writer of the [Morning] Chronicle travels into the poor man's country for us, and comes back with his tale of terror and wonder."

> What a confession it is that we have almost all of us been obliged to make! A clever and earnest-minded writer [Henry Mayhew, of course] gets a commission from the Morning Chronicle newspaper, and reports upon the state of our poor in London; he goes amongst labouring people and poor of all kinds -and brings back what? A picture of human life so wonderful, so awful, so piteous and pathetic, so exciting and terrible, that readers of romance own they never read anything like to it; and that the griefs, struggles, strange adventures here

depicted, exceed anything that any of us could imagine. Yes; and these wonders and terrors have been lying by your door and mine ever since we had a door of our own. We had but to go a hundred yards off and see for ourselves, but we never did. (196–7)

Here at last, we have someone opening a door and crossing a threshold—and once we have this scene, we have all the elements of *Vanity Fair* awaiting assembly—we have a curious person (a man), trapped just outside the courtyard of an oriental palace, wondering what is going on inside; we have another person, inside the seraglio, peering out, and (perhaps) laughing mockingly; and we have a narrator trying to combine these antithetical views, opening the door and walking "a hundred yards off [to] see for ourselves." How is it that these pieces become the novel of the curious heroine? There is only one story that would allow Thackeray to integrate these tricks of sights, and that is, of course, the Bluebeard story.

Vanity Fair shares the structure of any Bluebeard story: "Want to know a secret?" it asks us, or more accurately, "You don't want to know a secret, do you?" It seduces us most powerfully through our curiosity about Becky Sharp, but we might pause at this threshold to notice what happens particularly to our desire to see (and hence to know) in this novel. The visual curiosity that *Vanity Fair* most particularly tempts and baffles makes itself felt not through the mere brilliance of its effects but through the constructedness of its spectacle—by the apparatus it, like the magic lantern show, all too visibly employs. As my description of the perspectival realism in Thackeray's sketch writing suggested, and as any casual reader of *Vanity Fair* knows for herself, it is hardly easy to piece together a "true history" of the adventures of Becky Sharp. It is not just the ambiguity Thackeray cultivates around the book's ending and the death of Jos Sedley: any single incident upon which we might dwell similarly offers us not only the very partial accounts of the various players involved and the narrator's often differently motivated account of the characters but also a layer of witnesses and commentators. To turn back to Thackeray's own theatrical metaphors, in this instance we are going to the play, interviewing the actors, sitting in several rows of the theatre at once, watching the spectacle from the wings, and reading multiple reviews written by hack journalists who themselves are owners either of this, or another, theatre company's stock—oh, and we might want to sleep with one of the actresses. To say Thackeray's world is "all an act" is to say very little indeed, for there is hardly a singular true show lying behind it. We cannot take the multiple perspectives of Thackeray's spectacular realism and make them converge on a single scene. Rather, Thackeray's showmanship leaves us uncertain about what we have seen, uncertain about what we know, lost in disturbed sight.

The disturbance begins with the novel's construction as a piece of writing, or at the least of storytelling, for it constantly raises the question of who is imagined to be telling and who to be listening. In this way, like the mermaid Becky, the novel both invites and rebuffs our curiosity. The narrator invents characters, invents other novelists, invents imaginary books within his book—at the same time that he reveals his own book as imaginary, as pieced together through the reports of eavesdroppers, other narrators, bits of information the characters themselves gave him, as if the characters were forced to invent the novelist to prove their *own* reality. Not only would a detective be baffled by the mystery plots of the novels (nobody cares especially who murders Jos Sedley—or rather, no one can build a case against Mrs. Crawley) but a literary detective would also be baffled by the text's provenance. Who is writing? Our narrator introduces himself repeatedly, but texts scripted by the novel's other author, Lady Emily, sister to Lady Jane Sheepshanks, also appear repeatedly: "The Sailor's True Binnacle," "The Applewoman of Finchley Common," "The Washerwoman of Wandsworth Common," and "The Washerwoman of Finchley Common," an amalgam of the two that appears no fewer than four times in the novel. With equal regularity, the text parades its eyewitnesses and hearsay-narrators, who have turned the straws of gossip into narrative gold. Some, like Mrs. Bute Crawley, are so well placed as to know what no one else can know: of one scene, the novelist records, "That was an awful and unfortunate visit, never to be thought of by the family without horror . . . and it was only through Mrs Bute herself, who still knew everything which took place at the Hall, that the circumstances of Sir Pitt's reception of his son and daughter-in-law were ever known at all." Mrs. Bute is unlikely to have spoken to the novelist, but others seem quite generously to have offered him fragments of his story: "Tom Eaves, (who was no part in this history, except that he knew all the great folks in London, and the stories and mysteries of each family) . . . had further information regarding my Lady Steyne, which may or may not be true" (599); "little Tom Eaves who knows everything . . . showed me the place" (589); he "was told by Dr Pestler (now a most flourishing lady's physician, with a sumptuous dark green carriage, a prospect of speedy knighthood, and a house in Manchester Square) that her grief at weaning the child was a sight that would have unmanned a Herod." But the narrator, for all his reliance on others, also claims that "the novelist who knows everything knows this also" and repeats this claim for emphasis: "the novelist, it has been said before, knows everything" (453). He speaks in a range of literary parodies (again, the fragmentary legacy of the sketch); he assumes the authority of the court almanac when "we are authorized to state that Mrs Rawdon Crawley's *costume du cour* on the occasion of her presentation to the Sovereign was of the most elegant and brilliant description"; he quotes the *Morning Post*; he even knows what Jones, in his club, will do upon reading this present novel, and where he will make a mark in the text. Even when he does not reveal information, he claims elision as a matter of choice: "Have we a right to repeat her prayers?" the narrator asks (replying no, for these are secrets [312]). But if it is the novelist who "knows everything" (even what is beyond his text), why is it he must depend on the likes of "Tapeworm, who of course knew all the London gossip, and was besides a relative of Lady Gaunt"? And if his informants are all (as they must be, being denizens of Vanity Fair) equally partial and prejudiced, why are they reliable sources? And what, finally, are we to make of his claim that it was "at Pumpernickel" (an imaginary place) "that I first saw Colonel Dobbin and his party," where "we saw them from the stalls," where he met Amelia, "this particular lady's [whose] memoirs . . . I was predestined to write," and met Colonel Dobbin, who "has since informed me" of Amelia's first wedding dress, an account we have had long before.

Thackeray pastiched his way into this novel from within a world of information he associated largely, though not exclusively, with women. Some of his enthusiasm for multivocality came from the experiments of eighteenth-century literature, not just the play of voices in epistolary novels such as *Clarissa*, but the intrusions and gaps of Fielding and Sterne, and the practices of Addison and Steele—the literature he extolled in his immensely popular lectures. Even more of it came from the fascinating hodgepodge of genres in the novels of the 1830s, which he immortalizes in the opening of chapter 6, where Amelia comes downstairs in five genres. But among Thackeray's favorite genres was the "Silver Fork" novel, to which not only *Vanity Fair* but *Daniel Deronda*, at the end of the tradition, owes so much. The novel of high life was dominated by women (as Eliot notes with some scorn in "Silly Novels by Lady Novelists"), but Thackeray pays homage to it and shows his own debts when he praises more authentically the sketches of the immensely popular (and rather compelling) novelist Mrs. Catherine Gore. "Little lords, lady-killers, linkmen, lady patronesses, hotel keepers, diners-out, clubmen, and a host more of male and female characters appear in these sketches," as he explains, but more than the sheer variety, "Mrs Gore's worldly lectures . . . are not a little curious as pictures of the present world, and of the author's mind."[13] "Clear, sprightly, coarse, and utterly worldly," as he puts it, "through the two volumes, she dashes and rattles on," offering a guide book of a world that is the "most hollow, heartless, vulgar, brazen world, and those are luckiest who are out of it." The final clause is, of course, pure Thackeray—or as pure as we get given his narrator's resistance to ever being pinned down—but the range, the "sheer variety," the "little curious . . . pictures of the present world" are his adoption of this method, hijacked from a female world of gossip, crime, intrigue, and reticules. Thackeray's fascination with narratorial knowledge, readerly desire, and the practice of spectacle comes together with our discussion of curiosity when it intersects with the role of Becky Sharp, whose story is pieced together through these fragments of knowledge, and who is the most powerful, if also the loneliest, of Thackeray's performance artists. Her progress, like that of many a curious heroine before her, takes a snaky path out of Eden: like Lucy Snowe in Charlotte Brontë's *Villette*, she is a "rising character," and her plot begins with a fall in a garden, interestingly for readers of Thackeray's early literature, Vauxhall Gardens "the morning after." The plot of *Vanity Fair* begins when Becky Sharp does not marry Jos Sedley—when the fatal combination of rack punch and George Osborne's snobbish machinations interferes with the marriage plot (the safe haven) she has found for herself. With that expulsion come a host of adventures and a host of genres: the epistolary chapters Becky writes from the Crawley estate, the romantic secret marriage to Rawdon Crawley, the historical novel that commences when all the characters travel to Waterloo, and the subsequent high court intrigues, upstairs chatter, and downstairs subterfuges of Becky and Rawdon's fraudulent London life. Any sense of where Becky Sharp came from, of how exactly she became that mixture of cunning minx and surprisingly levelheaded realist, is lost to readers; there are very few retrospective moments when, as the narrator says, "Rebecca thought about her own youth, and the dark secrets of those early tainted days; and of her entrance into life by yonder gates" (523). Despite the interpolation of "Francis who was fond of me . . . when I was the poor painter's daughter and wheedled the grocer round the corner for sugar and tea," we know that it all happened sometime before we lost the garden, and none of it (as that relentlessly flung volume of Johnson's Dixonary suggests) can be recaptured: our heroine depends on a steady, if sometimes obscure, progress forward.

The thing that we are most curious about in this brilliant, patchwork novel is Becky Sharp's progress—or rather, what makes her move, what makes her tick, what is *inside*. The other characters are open to us (Amelia, Jos, George, Dobbin)—we know what they want and why they want it. Becky eludes us and entices us much as she does the other characters— and of course, repels us as well—but what she repels best is our curiosity. Becky's plot is at once interrupted and constituted by scenes of spectacle, performance, and display, whether her own or her narrator's, and they both entice and defeat our curiosity. The scenes of spectacle never appear without irony in the text—but they are also, more than anything, how we know we are in Becky's presence. When she is performing, she is most (or we might even say, only then is she) herself. Becky is an accomplished actress, and most of her performances are punctuated by the narrator's irony at her expense—these scenes, skillful as they are, are not particularly hard to read. When Becky leaves the Sedley household, after failing to catch Jos Sedley in her net, the narrator says he "intend[s] to throw a veil" over the parting with Miss Amelia, yet adds, "after a scene in which one person was in earnest and the other a perfect performer—after the tenderest caresses, the most pathetic tears, the smelling-bottle, and some of the very best feelings of the heart, had been called into requisition—Rebecca and Amelia parted, the former vowing to love her friend for ever and ever and ever." The narrator has actually dipped into free indirect discourse, briefly, for the purposes of his satire against the "perfect performer," but the tone of the description itself is harder to read—"some of the very best feelings of the heart" must be Amelia's—or must they? Are they equally open to satire? And as for the veil he throws over the scene—well, it's an interesting question if Thackeray's narrator *ever* doesn't tell us what he swears he is not about to tell us, but this veil certainly doesn't cover much. When characters within the novel praise Becky's acting abilities, later in the novel, the narrator is similarly coy: "People compared her to [one great actress] or the other; and agreed with good reason, very likely, that had she been an actress none on the stage would have surpassed her" (652). Becky's performative skills are both fallen and, to use another of Thackeray's unexpected terms, efficient, as when she meets Amelia after many months, and the "two girls met, and flew into each other's arms with that impetuosity which distinguishes the behaviour of young ladies towards each other," and "Rebecca performed her part of the embrace with the most perfect briskness and energy." (168) While "poor little Amelia" blushes for she "had been guilty of feeling something very like coldness towards her," our Becky, presumably untroubled by feelings, knows how to play her part—and is she any the less genuine than Amelia, or Amelia any more sincere than she? In this way Becky may stand in an emblematic relationship to Thackeray's habits as a narrator. As the best showmen in the novel, they are also the most adept at seeing through the spectacles of others—but these perceptions leave them very few comforts; seeing sharply, it would seem, is not really a gift at all.

But seeing sharply is also what is demanded of the reader, whose curiosity forces her into an uneasy (and somewhat dangerous) alliance with Becky herself. Every time we are enticed to mock something, every time we are aligned with Becky, every time we (like the narrator) want to see behind the illusion, our curiosity links us to some wicked form of knowledge, some forbidden pursuit, some dangerous interiority. The promise of the book is that, like Mayhew's curious traveller or Thackeray's wandering eye, we will see more, but much of what we see is itself illicit. The promise of what is illicit, indeed, the performance of an illicit sexuality in particular, is the necessary weapon of Becky's survival, for Becky makes her living, quite literally (in the sense that Thackeray means it, of "how to live well on nothing a year") by the performance of the loss of her virtue—a virtue that she loses, of course, by singing and flirting and grimacing; by playing herself as the daughter of the Parisian dancing girl, by turning her defects (she is poor; she is humble; she is eager to please—all her Dickensian qualities) into stunning assets. She would "take care artlessly to apologize for her blunders"; "there was a frankness and humility in the manner in which she acknowledged her origin"—all in all, says the narrator, she was most dangerous when attacked, for "she had a knack of adopting a demure ingénue air, under which she was most dangerous." What Becky performs most and best is an utterly false, and yet credible because utterly worldly, openness: "Now you know the whole secret," she says. "I am frank and open." We might be tempted to believe these shows only work on others, but they work on us as well—and Thackeray is complicit in their effect. In one of the novel's most powerful performances of Becky's "secret" self, she reflects on the weariness of what is around her:

> Her success excited, elated, and then bored her. At first no occupation was more pleasant than to invent and procure . . . [but] the poor woman herself was yawning in spirit. "I wish I were out of it," she said to herself. "I would rather be a parson's wife and teach a Sunday school than this; or a sergeant's lady and ride in the regimental waggon; or, oh, how much gayer it would be to wear spangles and trousers and dance before a booth at a fair." (637)

This is seductive beyond belief—in this case, quite literally, for the narrator, having begun by telling us that she spoke thus to herself ("'I wish I were out of it,' she said to herself"), then interrupts himself (or rather her) with a comment—"'You would do it very well,' said the Lord Steyne, laughing. She used to tell the great man her ennuis and perplexities in her artless way—they amused him" (638). Again, we have ridden a roller coaster of perspectives and fictional positions: if the paragraph began by stating "Becky has often spoken in subsequent years of this season of her life," taking us beyond the scope of the narrative, it then moved us into the moment with its own little story of progress ("excited, elated, and then bored") and took us as deep into Becky's consciousness as we could hope—only to tell us, alas, that all the gaiety and irony is mere seduction, "artlessly" amusing the laughing Lord Steyne. There is nothing here, in short, that isn't "art."

But if what we crave is something open, artless, something that we might believe is more real, the true self about which we are most curious, the novel has a very different spectacle in mind for us. What it performs for the curious reader is not the scene of forbidden sexual adventure, but the spectacle of Becky alone. The haggard face our heroine wears when there is no one to watch her is the book's grimmest spectre as well as its deepest, and we see it in the midst of another of her most successful performances. As Rawdon grows wary of his wife's "improper exhibitions" (after scenes of what Pitt Crawley describes as "the habit of play-acting and fancy-dressing . . . highly unbecoming a British female"), he admonishes Becky not to "join in any more such amusements" and himself becomes "a very watchful and exemplary domestic character," who "never left home." The narrator enters his full ironic mode, noting that "Little Becky, to do her justice, was charmed with Rawdon's gallantry," adding:

> If he was surly, she never was. Whether friends were present or absent she had always a kind smile for him, and was attentive to his pleasure and comfort. It was the early days of their marriage over again: the same good humour, prevenances, merriment, and artless confidence and regard. "How much pleasanter it is," she would say, "to have you by my side in the carriage than that foolish old Briggs! Let us always go on so, dear Rawdon. How nice it would be, and how happy we should always be, if we had but the money!" (667)

We might easily think that this irony is all directed at Becky (Becky is artless—hah!); we might briefly amuse ourselves by thinking of her as stymied in her adulterous ways (does he really never leave home?), and we might sympathize with Rawdon, who is alas not in on the joke of his wife's fidelity—a joke in which everyone else in the novel participates. But Thackeray catches us up with the final "if we had but the money." At that moment, even Becky (so we believe) is telling (at least some of) the truth: domestic happiness is not possible, is it, dear reader, without money? But that irony is not the final twist, for Thackeray does not allow us to rest there. The next sentence reads, "He fell asleep after dinner in his chair; he did not see the face opposite to him, haggard, weary and terrible; it lighted up with fresh candid smiles when he woke. It kissed him gaily." To Becky, who knows that their fortunes depend on her attentiveness (what we might even call her availability) to Lord Steyne, this existence is torture—and the sheer effort at economic survival is what makes her "haggard, weary and terrible." But is she terrible because, unbeknownst to her husband, she has become a terrible object, or is it her own terror, her knowledge of the social abyss beneath their feet, that we are witnessing? That answer remains closed, however curious our gaze.

Instead, we are forced (not unlike our duplicitous heroine) to see doubly, and the moral implications of this kind of double vision will become increasingly clear as the novel progresses. Throughout, the magic lantern effect of the dissolve (as well as the stricken quality of the perceiver) haunts us. Thackeray's ability to turn our vision, to do in language what the phantasmagoria did with sound and light, is itself a bit terrifying—and it brings us up short every time. At the best of these moments, we share that stricken quality, as we do in the (imagined) death-struggles of Miss Crawley, unseen by any but Becky, her nurse. Thackeray's brilliant narration begins not with the show itself (which he never narrates directly) but with its effect on Becky, a witness who (at least at first) does not tell.

> She never told until long afterwards how painful that duty was; how peevish a patient was the jovial old lady; how angry; how sleepless; in what horrors

of death; during what long nights she lay moaning, and in almost delirious agonies respecting that future world which she quite ignored when she was in good health.—Picture to yourself, O fair young reader, a worldly, selfish, graceless, thankless, religionless old woman, writhing in pain and fear, and without her wig. Picture her to yourself, and ere you be old, learn to love and pray! (164)

The scene changes before our eyes, as it makes its way into direct address. At first we merely witness the spectacle of Miss Crawley; then we turn her (as the narrator encourages us to do) into a morality play, one which reminds us of our own all-too- inevitable demise; and then, suddenly, we are in the presence of the comic Gothic—an old lady without her wig. Can this spectre, indeed, teach us to pray? If so, to what kind of ironic deity? Only Thackeray, we might think, could have made that solitude into such a spectacle—and only Thackeray could so have highlighted his own stagecraft, by imagining that "worldly, selfish, graceless, thankless, religionless old woman . . . without her wig."

Or is this something unique to the author? This trompe l'oeil magic spectacle is a narrative habit he actually shares, at unexpected moments, with his curious heroine. At moments this gift is strictly comic, as when, in one of the more revealing moments of the novel, after a return from the Crawley estate, Becky turns the family's domestic scenes into her own private theatricals:

> Becky acted out the whole scene for them. She put on a nightcap and gown. She preached a great sermon in the true serious manner: she lectured on the virtue of the medicine which she pretended to administer, with a gravity of imitation so perfect that you would have thought it was the countess's own Roman nose through which she snuffled. "Give us Lady Southdown and the black dose," was a constant cry amongst the folks in Becky's little drawing-room in May Fair. And for the first time in her life the Dowager Countess of Southdown was made amusing. (528)

One can almost hear the Thackerayan narrator asking, Can we, oh fellow wearers of motley, hope for anything else, finally, for ourselves, but that we, too, briefly, might be in the show—might be made, if not genuinely, unrestrainedly, amused, at the least (and just for once) "amusing"?

But Becky also does something far different with performance, something that offers a clue to Thackeray's deliberately complicated approach to his novel. In one of the most powerful performances in the novel, one that, like Thackeray's, plays a game with time and space, Becky meets Lady Steyne, at a dinner at which the heroine has been viciously snubbed by all the ladies. Finally, "even Lady Steyne herself pitie[s] her," and goes up and asks her to sing and play. Becky, "sincerely grateful," says, "I will do anything that may give pleasure to my Lord Steyne or to you," and seats herself at the piano:

> She sang religious songs of Mozart, which had been early favourites of Lady Steyne, and with such sweetness and tenderness that the lady lingering round the piano, sat down by its side, and listened until the tears rolled down her eyes. It is true that the opposition ladies at the other end of the room kept up a loud and ceaseless buzzing and talking; but the Lady Steyne did not hear those rumours. She was a child again—and had wandered back through a forty years' wilderness to her convent garden. The chapel organ had pealed the same tones, the organist, the sister whom she loved best of the community, had taught them to her in those early happy days. She was a girl once more, and the brief period of her happiness bloomed out again for an hour. (619–20)

True, the narrator not so subtly undermines Becky's goodness, when Lord Steyne claims his wife told him she "ha[s] been singing like an angel" ("there are angels of two kinds," he says, "and both sorts, it is said, are charming in their way"), but he cannot erase the "sincerely" with which Becky thanks Lady Steyne, or the uncanny sound effect of the chapel organ pealing forty years before, or the moment of perfect pleasure—a moment that makes happiness "bloom out again." Becky's performance here works much like the narrator's sleight of hand, leaving readers unsure of their own perceptions—how, again, to make all these points of view ever line up; or need we even do so?

This is the central story of curiosity in the novel: we think there is a secret, an answer, a clue—that we can answer Thackeray's repeated question ("is she guilty or not?") and more, that we can know what the answer means: is she good, or is she wicked? More even than we have craved legal answers, we want a sexy curiosity, one that fulfills our prurient interest, one that we can share a giggle over, we and the narrator and perhaps a character or two. This is the chimera we pursue throughout the novel. We imagine curiosity as communal, as redemptive, as an opportunity to escape the essential loneliness of the self (we could, finally, "share" knowledge, if nothing else), but it turns out to be exactly the opposite: the sharpest form of loneliness is a fulfilled curiosity, which can only leave us stricken. This becomes clear in what we think will be the climactic scene, the moment when Rawdon returns home and finds Becky "singing a snatch of the song of the night before" in a private performance for Lord Steyne. Becky has performed at the charades, singing "The Rose upon My Balcony," dressed as Clytemnestra, bare white arms gliding, with "a smile so ghastly, that people quake as they look at her," and murdered her husband; she has become (before Rawdon's eyes and ours) "another Cleopatra" (646). On his way home from witnessing this terrifying success, Rawdon was taken to a spunging house for debt and waited in vain for Becky to bail him out; when he obtains the money from Jane Sheepshanks, he walks into his own brightly lighted house, absent any of the servants, and finds Becky, "in a brilliant full toilette, her arms and her fingers sparkling with bracelets and rings; and all the brilliants on her breast which Steyne had given her," and Steyne "had her hand in his, and was bowing over it to kiss it." At his appearance mid-tableau, Becky "started up with a faint scream as she caught sight of Rawdon's white face." Becky "tried a smile, a horrid smile, as if to welcome her husband: and Steyne rose up, grinding his teeth, pale, and with fury in his looks" (675). He too attempts a laugh—and at that moment, the scene shatters into multiple perspectives, as each player is convinced that a very different play is under way.

This dissolution of perspectives (up till now, we have all seen the same thing) is crucial to what follows: Rawdon assumes that he has entered into a scene of adultery and that Becky is fallen. Steyne assumes that, as with other husbands he has met in the past, Rawdon is in on the show and that a trap has been laid for him by both husband and wife. Becky sees something that she takes very seriously indeed: "I am innocent, Rawdon," she says, "before God, I am innocent." What does the narrator see? He goes on:

> She clung hold of his coat, of his hands; her own were all covered with serpents, and rings, and baubles. "I am innocent.—Say I am innocent," she said to Lord Steyne.
>
> "... You innocent! Damn you," he screamed out. "You innocent! Why, every trinket you have on your body is paid for by me. I have given you thousands of pounds which this fellow has spent, and for which he has sold you. Innocent, by—! You're as innocent as your mother, the ballet-girl, and your husband the bully." (675–76)

As the scene breaks into these perspectives, the narrator's perspective becomes slipperier as well: Rawdon grabs Lord Steyne and strikes him, and Becky "admired her husband, strong, brave, and victorious"—are we to believe this?[14] Before we can pause to think, the scene rushes on: Rawdon forces her to remove all the corrupt jewelry, and the narrator becomes a flat and affectless reporter. Steyne leaves the house, and the narrator doesn't even bother to notice it, lost in the drama between Becky and Rawdon. Our seat in the theatre, it would seem, is constantly shifting, until we are so focused on Becky and Rawdon and his search of her private closet that we lose track of time itself—until finally, in a parenthesis, the narrator informs us that "day had dawned again, and many hours had passed in this search." And yet, the narrator never answers our only question, was she guilty or not (677)?

"What *had* happened?" he finally asks, echoing the question of "the French maid." As Thackeray goes on,

> Was she guilty or not? She said not; but who could tell what was truth which came from those lips; or if that corrupt heart was in this case pure? All her lies and her schemes, all her selfishness and her wiles, all her wit and genius had come to this bankruptcy. [The maid] closed the curtains, and with some entreaty and show of kindness, persuaded her mistress to lie down on the bed. Then she went below and gathered up the trinkets which had been lying on the floor, since Rebecca dropped them there at her husband's orders, and Lord Steyne went away. (675)

At this moment when we want truth, where we might actually be craving the courtrooms other novels offer, some forensic authority, Thackeray can only give us more spectacle—he cannot tell us anything about "this case" but informs us that Becky is "corrupt"; he claims that she is both wily and selfish, and a genius; the maid, in a "show" of kindness, closes the curtains (surely both the curtains of the room and the stage curtains, ending the "scene" as decisively as if the director had called out "cut!") and then proceeds downstairs to steal the trinkets.

But the most revealing clue to the meaning of the scene and to the deeper significance of our curiosity comes a moment earlier, when Rawdon drags Becky upstairs into her closet and flings "open boxes and wardrobes, throwing the multifarious trumpery of their contents here and there," searching everywhere, not realizing that (as the narrator tells us) "Rebecca gave him all the keys but one." "She was in hopes that he would not have remarked the absence of that," for "it belonged to the little desk which Amelia had given her in early days, and which she kept in a secret place" (676). But Rawdon "at last found the desk," which "contained papers, love-letters many years old—all sorts of small trinkets and woman's memoranda." We are not allowed to slow down to wonder why the memory of Amelia is conjured at this moment; we are not even allowed to pause over that interesting question, what are a woman's memoranda? We are thrown ceaselessly forward in our search, for the narrator, like Rawdon in his quest for Becky's secrets, hastens us on: "And it contained a pocket-book with bank-notes. Some of these were dated ten years back, too, and one was quite a fresh one—a note for a thousand pounds which Lord Steyne had given her."

> "Did he give you this?" Rawdon said.
> "Yes," Rebecca answered.

"I'll send it to him to-day," Rawdon said (for day had dawned again, and many hours had passed in this search), "and I will pay Briggs, who was kind to the boy, and some of the debts. You will let me know where I shall send the rest to you. You might have spared me a hundred pounds, Becky, out of all this—I have always shared with you."

"I am innocent," said Becky. And he left her without another word. (676–77)

The "love-letters many years old" will return, powerfully, later in the novel, but there is no stronger indictment anywhere in Victorian fiction than Rawdon's of Becky at this moment—and it is not an accident that we finally get what we want, a juridical interrogation, one in which Rawdon examines his reluctant witness, and, for once, Thackeray uses Rebecca's full name. With that forensic overtone, we get a moment of unquestionable ethical judgment—one of the few the novel offers.

With the discovery of material evidence, rather than the uncertain avowal of her innocence, Rawdon can finally indict Becky—the secrets of the closet, the knowledge that she had money which she kept from him, the knowledge that she did not share or (thinking purely in terms of sex, now) that she had shared with someone else and not with him or with him alone. It is this that leaves Becky herself, finally, alone, "on the bed's edge [with t]he drawers all opened and their contents scattered about,—dresses and feathers, scarfs and trinkets, a heap of tumbled vanities lying in a wreck," thinking of "her long past life, and all the dismal incidents of it," "sitting in the midst of her miserable ruins with clasped hands and dry eyes." "Ah," she thinks, "how dreary it seemed, how miserable, lonely and profitless." Thackeray's irony insinuates itself once more (does she, vain as ever, merely mean that it is profitless because the money is gone, like the earlier "bankruptcy"—or is she capable of some more powerful, more existential loneliness, which we, as lonely readers, must share?), but he has also at this moment inserted his demonic heroine squarely into the Bluebeard plot, from the other side of the mirror, for here, at last, Rebecca is Bluebeard, the owner of the secret closet, the powerful monster with the terrifying secret, which blanches all who see it.

This is the scene that I am claiming as the Bluebeard scene, the great moment of nested curiosity in the world of *Vanity Fair*, and it runs like a thunder bolt (to borrow an adultery metaphor from *Dombey and Son* and many another Victorian novel) through this text. It raises the possibility of a sexual knowingness and a sheer sexual wickedness that the rest of the book cannot quite absorb, but it also refuses to resolve that possibility into a single, meaningful answer. The unreadable quality of Becky's character, on which Thackeray has harped so eloquently through the whole novel, has here resolved itself not into a single "character" but into the ultimate doubleness of the Bluebeard story: Becky is at once Bluebeard himself, wicked, sinning, duplicitous, drawing Rawdon into her web and destroying him, and Fatimah, the curious woman drawn deeper into a sexual knowledge (here, the knowledge embodied by the clearly Bluebeard-like Lord Steyne) that will in turn destroy her. This scene leaves us with a heroine we cannot read, and it leaves us in a fairy tale that has as its victims both the vicious husband and the curious wife, the cunning artist and the enthralled viewer, speculators all. It is not so easy to assign guilt, or even knowledge, amidst the ruins of this show—and it is not at all clear where the showman, Thackeray himself, stands—except, a little, aghast.

His response not only increases rather than reduces the narrative variables but also suggests that the real "matter" of curiosity is still to come, that not Becky's sexual transgressions but her epistemological investigations make up the heart of this novel. To do this, he thrusts us as well into epistemological confusion:

> And the late fair tenant of that poor little mansion was in the meanwhile—where? Who cared! Who asked after a day or two? Was she guilty or not? We all know how charitable the world is, and how the verdict of Vanity Fair goes when there is a doubt. Some people said she had gone to Naples in pursuit of Lord Steyne, whilst others averred that his Lordship quitted that city and fled to Palermo on hearing of Becky's arrival; some said she was living in Bierstadt, and had become a dame d'honneur to the Queen of Bulgaria; some that she was at Boulogne; and others, at a boarding-house at Cheltenham. (705–6)

Thackeray throws so many possible outcomes at us that we can only duck the question—and we all but fail to notice that in the middle of so many other possibilities, he asks again his fatal question: "Was she guilty or not?" No trial, no jury, no verdict. Instead, here, in this multiply vocalized imagining, is the same dangerous and alluring multiplicity in which he has been instructing us all along: if we find Becky guilty beyond doubt, we are like the inhabitants of Vanity Fair; if we fail to care, we are like the uncharitable world; and if we do care, we are doomed to haphazard guessing. Few rewards for the interested in Vanity Fair and fewer chances of hazarding out our Becky. No matter how many views we assemble (and they are all viciously partial), we cannot see what we want to see. Becky has gone somewhere terrible, and we cannot follow her there—nor, he seems to suggest, would we want to.

Where has she gone? Thackeray waits quite a while to answer his questions—both old Sedley and old Osborne die; Dobbin returns with Jos from India; Amelia inherits a fortune and regains her son; all while our black sheep is not only gone but also forgotten from the fold. But just when we might think her excision from the text is absolute (as well it might be—think, to follow my earlier echo, of Edith Dombey, after the thunderbolt chapter of *Dombey and Son*, *Vanity Fair* goes back to her, for no novel interested in what happens after you acquire vision can resist for long the "spectacle" of the woman who once sat, amidst the "heap of tumbled vanities lying in a wreck," "with clasped hands and dry eyes." Unlike Amelia, described by the scathing narrator as a veritable "water-works," Becky wastes no tears, but in another way she has been scared dry. Wherever it is that she winds up, the narrator assures us she is up to no good—but he does so by echoing her elision from the world of Vanity Fair with her elision from the world of *Vanity Fair*: "When Becky is out of the way, be sure that she is not particularly well employed, and that the less that is said about her doings is in fact the better." And yet, Thackeray can hardly keep quiet about the little he is telling us. He may say that "if we were to give a full account of her proceedings during a couple of years that followed after the Curzon Street catastrophe, there might be some reason for people to say this book was improper," but he in fact gives us an astonishingly rich account of her proceedings—not only a travelogue, but one interspersed with Becky's usual apt, pertinent, impertinent narration. And everything is this narration serves the admirably double purpose of making us both admire and fear the slippery Rebecca. "Her history was after all a mystery," he says, but as we know from our own reading of Bluebeard, a reader loves nothing more (and requires nothing more desperately, however much warned away) than a mystery. It would be a very dim reader indeed who did not perceive most of what was going on—and who did not dip beneath the waves (or beneath the covers) often enough to learn.

Instead of shielding us from sexual misadventures, what Thackeray seems to be tracing is the way in which his heroine slips the tracks of society—in part, out of her rightful exile from the world of high morality, but equally out of her own impatience with it, an ambition that finds its echo in Thackeray's own ambivalence, and in the constant veering away from Amelia that the double-plotted novel enacts. Like the novelist, "Becky loved society and, indeed, could no more exist without it than an opium-eater without his dram," the narrator says, but she also shares the novelist's craving for variety, the variety of the fair itself:

> Becky was very respectable and orderly at first, but the life of humdrum virtue grew utterly tedious to her before long. It was the same routine every day, the same dulness and comfort, the same drive over the same stupid Bois de Boulogne, the same company of an evening, the same Blair's Sermon of a Sunday night—the same opera always being acted over and over again; Becky was dying of weariness, when, luckily for her, young Mr. Eagles came from Cambridge, and his mother, seeing the impression which her little friend made upon him, straightway gave Becky warning. (819–20)

"Dulness and comfort" are our companions in the other half of *Vanity Fair*, where we reside with the virtuous, self-deluded, weepy Amelia Sedley; what Thackeray offers in Becky's pirate struggles on the Continent is not only a parody of the virtuous heroine's travails but also their antidote, an endless re-creation of self utterly unlike "the same stupid Bois de Boulogne." Even a small incident like this, where Becky resides with the virtuous Mrs. Hook Eagles until she threatens to snag a young eagle for herself, is a relief as much to us as it is to Becky—though we will also not be sorry she is thrown out of this "stupid" paradise, and the "vagabond chapter" takes to the road again, once again giving our curiosity (and hers) free rein. But as much as her peregrinations, it is the sheer labor of Becky's self-creation that the narrator tracks and, I am suggesting, shares: "Whenever Becky made a little circle for herself with incredible toils and labour, somebody came and swept it down rudely, and she had all her work to begin over again. It was very hard; very hard; lonely and disheartening" (818). As elsewhere in *Vanity Fair*, what we are watching is an act of self-creation, the self *behind* the curtains; the stage manager at work, forging a spectacle that will break down in the harsh light of day. Our perspective here is uneasily aligned with Becky's—in part because what she has learned is that social worlds are made, not born, and in part because like Thackeray, the laboring journalist, we admire anyone who works so hard at any kind of world-building.

At this point, Becky is more than a character: she is part of Thackeray's narrative work—and it is his sense of loneliness, of the painfulness involved in seeing through everything, of the fragility of vision, which she shares. "Becky only laughed [at being snubbed]: but I don't think she liked it. She felt she was alone, quite alone, and the far-off shining cliffs of England were impassable to her." This is not just the wandering heroine, but the wandering novelist, whose travels we traced earlier in this chapter, and which we see strangely re-created here. The chapters from which Becky is absent, those where Amelia was rescued by her brother and removes with him, Georgy, and Dobbin to Pumpernickel, are borrowed from Thackeray's youthful travels in Weimar, but Becky's travels owe more to his own slippages in and out of class, travelling as a rogue journalist. Becky is, as we already knew, a terrific writer (even if many of her epistolary arrows fall short of their mark), but she is an even better observer, and her abbreviated travel diaries, for such these chapters are, are full of Thackerayan perceptions, because it is only at this moment that her curiosity is given full sway. Only outside the seeming norms of society can she see fully—even if she sees alone.

Again, this requires us to see curiously as well. We traced at the beginning of this chapter the way Becky and Thackeray share a fascination with a certain slant of light—the "illuminations" of the party at Madame de Saint-Amour's, which echo so uncannily Thackeray's own observation of the faded St. James illuminations and the aged dames of Pall Mall. But the effects of the magic lantern bleed beyond its boundaries. When we meet up again with Becky in Pumpernickel, the whole world seems to have turned to illumination—and turned ghostly, too: after the first scene at the casino, as Becky leaves, Jos's servant leaves as well: "And Mr. Kirsch having lost all his money by this time, followed his master out into the moonlight, where the illuminations were winking out and the transparency over our mission was scarcely visible" (811). Are all the illusions gone? Has the novel become as wicked, as heartless, as incapable of feeling, as its siren adventuress—or as the terrifying Marquis de Steyne, as Becky last sees him: "Hate, or anger, or desire caused [his eyes] to brighten now and then still, but ordinarily, they gave no light, and seemed tired of looking out on a world of which almost all the pleasure and all the best beauty had palled upon the worn-out wicked old man" (828). What a terrible vision indeed—as haggard, as dry-eyed, as Becky, after she has looked into the closet.

But Becky, wondrously, is not burnt out—and that may be the greatest triumph of *Vanity Fair*—and one can't but suspect that she is redeemed, when we least expect it, by her curiosity, for Becky, more than any character, is still watching, still speculating, still playacting in the world of Vanity Fair:

> Above the second-floor apartments occupied by the etat major of the gambling firm; above the third-floor rooms, tenanted by the band of renowned Bohemian vaulters and tumblers; and so on to the little cabins of the roof, where, among students, bagmen, small tradesmen, and country-folks come in for the festival, Becky had found a little nest—as dirty a little refuge as ever beauty lay hid in. . . . Becky liked the life. She was at home with everybody in the place, pedlars, punters, tumblers, students and all. She was of a wild, roving nature, inherited from father and mother, who were both Bohemians, by taste and circumstance; if a lord was not by, she would talk to his courier with the greatest pleasure; the din, the stir, the drink, the smoke, the tattle of the Hebrew pedlars, the solemn, braggart ways of the poor tumblers, the sournois talk of the gambling-table officials, the songs and swagger of the students, and the general buzz and hum of the place had pleased and tickled the little woman, even when her luck was down and she had not wherewithal to pay her bill. How pleasant was all the bustle to her now that her purse was full of the money which little Georgy had won for her the night before! (830–31)

True, her happiness is paid for by the jingle of coins in her purse, but what a relief to all of us this pleasure is—and the narrator tells us clearly, she is "pleased and tickled" even when her luck was down—as, of course, in Vanity Fair, it so very often must be.

Becky was always, if not a "player," certainly a gambler, and it is no accident that she reenters the novel as a speculator—a word that throws us back on our Mr. Spec, with his interest in vision and creativity, but also takes us into the worlds of money and curiosity, and into the future, into the realm of "speculative fiction," ghosts, imagination, and unseen worlds. When Becky reappears, she is a little of each kind of speculator (gambler, wonderer, ghost-seer, projector), and like the speculum, the lens behind all these words, she is watching as carefully as ever:

> A woman with light hair, in a low dress by no means so fresh as it had been, and with a black mask on, through the eyelets of which her eyes twinkled strangely, was seated at one of the roulette-tables with a card and a pin and a couple of florins before her. As the croupier called out the colour and number, she pricked on the card with great care and regularity, and only ventured her money on the colours after the red or black had come up a certain number of times. It was strange to look at her. (808)

How do we recognize her? She is wearing clothes that, like herself, are no longer as fresh as they had been; she is wearing a mask, a clear sign that it is our deceptive heroine; she has a French accent, which slips in and out and which she can alter at will; she has her customary watchfulness (she identifies our other characters almost before we identify her), and she has the same sleight of hand (she is looking at Georgy while still playing) as always, matched with an ability to change from defense to offense faster than Roger Federer on Centre Court at Wimbledon. She is a figure of estrangement: even her eyes twinkle "strangely," and with the reciprocity of vision Becky always conjured (is she terrible to see, or has she seen something terrible?), it is "strange" to look at her.

But what is oddest about Becky's return to Vanity Fair is that she comes back with a sharp moral vision—one born of a sense of the foolishness of things, one born of the sense of the ephemeral brought on her by so much loss, and one that is entirely reminiscent of the world of the sketch (the Thackerayan world of transient vision) with which we began our investigation. This is Becky, when she returns to Belgium, to the scenes of the battles, of her desperate flirtations and canny manipulations of war; and to the death of the late, unlamented (certainly by us) George Osborne:

> How well she remembered the place! She grinned as she looked up at the little entresol which she had occupied, and thought of the Bareacres family, bawling for horses and flight, as their carriage stood in the porte-cochere of the hotel. She went to Waterloo and to Laeken, where George Osborne's monument much struck her. She made a little sketch of it. "That poor Cupid!" she said; "how dreadfully he was in love with me, and what a fool he was! I wonder whether little Emmy is alive. It was a good little creature; and that fat brother of hers. I have his funny fat picture still among my papers. They were kind simple people." (820–21)

Thackeray conveniently rehearses his own plot for us, laughing along with Becky, and not only revisits George's grave, but allows someone to make a sketch—and more interestingly, allows Becky to comes back into the novel as the sketch artist. After the vanities that surround the other deaths in the novel, it is surprising at the least to have this little reflective moment—and how much more so, to have Becky saying a good word about Emmy—even if she does present her as a kind of alien. In what other novel could the heroine address her counterpart by saying "it was a good little creature" (where did Thackeray find the courage for that "it"?) and yet have noticed, all these pages later, that the Sedleys were, as unlikely as it seems, kind. Her ability, like someone running a successful inventory in the curiosity shop of the novel, to know who everyone is, what everything means, and the limits of what is possible again makes her a strange double for our narrator and a monitor for us. That she laughs at this world (here on the battlefield, among the dead) is only an added fillip: her success is to make not being duped seem (however wickedly?) a moral quality.

Yet, can any knowledge, this Bluebeard-inspired novel asks, ever serve to make you good? Is there any use in knowing everything? Becky Sharp, almost uniquely in the history of the novel, finds one returning, unexpectedly, to the moment of her annihilation in Bluebeard's closet, the moment when she was finally condemned for not having "shared." After she has rejoined respectable society (as it appears in the guise of the credulous Amelia), Becky is trailed by other parasites like herself, all of them hoping to move in on Amelia, taking advantage of the absence of Dobbin, who was ordered away by Amelia in a fit of absolutely inappropriate sisterly solidarity with the poisonous Becky. The one person who seems to realize this is Becky herself, and in an astonishing moment of generosity, utterly unprompted by self-interest, Becky warns Amelia, "marching up and down the room before the other [like a little Napoleon] and surveying her with a sort of contemptuous kindness." She says:

> You must go away from here and from the impertinences of these men.... I tell you they are rascals; men fit to be sent to the hulks. *Never mind how I know them. I know everybody.* (865–66; emphasis added)

At this point, Becky sounds just like the narrator, "the novelist who knows everything," "moi," as Thackeray always says (sounding like his bilingual heroine), "qui vous parle." Becky has walked about with Amelia, knowing herself to be cut by all the respectable women, watching everything unfold, while the oblivious Amelia sees nothing. Through those scenes, "Becky never thought fit to tell her what was passing under her innocent eyes." But at this moment, for reasons that escape us except for her desire to "settle" things for "the silly little fool," Becky decides to open Amelia's eyes. What she does to "show" Amelia the truth about George Osborne, "that selfish humbug, that low-bred Cockney dandy, that padded booby, who had neither wit nor manners, nor heart" (866) is to show her the note George wrote years before, to encourage her to write to Dobbin, "your friend with the bamboo cane." Becky, behaving like a novelist herself, has written a better ending to the novel—finally, after hundreds of pages, not only punishing the already-dead George who baffled her own marriage plot all those years ago but also saying to Amelia what even the most patient reader has longed to say over and over again.

Becky is here, once again, not only the reader's surrogate but also Thackeray's, though the always tricky novelist upends her moment of triumph a little by revealing that Amelia has already written to Dobbin, already written for herself a happier ending. The note that Becky has held on to all these years need never have been delivered, though Amelia is, at the least, marrying with more open eyes. Thackeray may undercut the surprising gesture of Becky's generous spirit at this moment, but he does not do so entirely—and it is a moment that prepares us for far more heavily signalled scenes of unexpected generosity later in the Victorian novel. *Middlemarch*, which owes much of the wisdom it so showily displays to the more quiet knowledge of *Vanity Fair* (where did the scratches in the pier-glass mirror come from, if not from Thackeray's shifting perspectives?), has clearly lifted Rosamond Vincy's revelation to Dorothea ("you are thinking what is not true") from Becky's unprompted gift to Amelia. But Becky's commentary has a severity of judgment that Eliot's narrator reserves for herself: George Osborne is no more to be compared to Dobbin than "you are to Queen Elizabeth," says the sharp-tongued chit, and with that, Amelia Sedley must finally grow up.

But so, too, must the novel—and so does *Vanity Fair* in particular, even more relentlessly, I would argue, than does *Middlemarch*, which still allows the childlike Dorothea to promise, lips quivering, that "I will learn what everything costs." *Vanity Fair* keeps a harsher set of books, as we would expect from a novel that can only deliver wisdom from a wicked heroine. What costs the most in *Vanity Fair*, perversely, is learning things, not unlike Becky, who, earlier in the book, remembers a time not when she was innocent, but when she was not found out. Everything, everything in this book is about finding out (aren't you curious?) and no one is the richer for knowledge. Just as Becky leaves Amelia's house quietly after this scene, watching Dobbin return and exiling herself from the happy ending, so does everyone else in the book, after the burning moment of knowledge, come to an ashen wisdom, one in which nothing new will grow. "Grow green again, tender little parasite," says the narrator, again, anticipating *Middlemarch*, as Emmy hides her weepy eyes in Dobbin's great coat, a wounded bird unable to move beyond his sheltering, if no longer perfect love. Dobbin himself has seen all too clearly the limitations of the great love of his life: "You are not worthy of the love which I have devoted to you. I knew all along that the prize I had set my life on was not worth the winning; that I was a fool, with fond fancies, too, *bartering* away all of my truth and ardour against your little feeble remnant of love. I will bargain no more: I withdraw." "Good-bye, Amelia!" says Dobbin, as he leaves: "I have watched your struggle. Let it end. We are both weary of it" (853; emphasis added).

He comes back, of course, and reader, he marries her, the prize that was not worth the winning. Which of us in this world has his desire, and having it, is satisfied? asks the narrator. No one. Amelia, though she nestles in his arms on his return, knows better, too—knows that her husband loves their daughter better than his history of the Punjab—better even than he loves me, she says. And as for Jos Sedley, happiest perhaps when sitting amid the clinking plates and brandy-bottles on Becky Sharp's bohemian bed, he, too, faces the shrinking of his world. Becky may indeed be terrible; Jos himself may be terrified; but he stays with her, until his death, killed by her, his money wasted in "speculation." And for all we can say "vanitas vanitatum," only Becky stays on happily at the fair, last seen selling her wares. The puppet-master may claim to have "shut up the box and the puppets, for our play is played out" (878), but in the face of mortality that the end of the novel conjures, Becky merely "cast[s] down her eyes demurely and smile[s]," inscrutable once more (877).

Reader, you have not forgotten the elephant, have you? Thackeray, ever the lover of Bluebeard, did not—but, as we have learned over and over, he was never one to leave well enough alone, and the elephant is no exception. When Becky comes to live with Amelia, Jos, and Dobbin, she is waiting for her trunks to arrive, and the narrator is suitably scathing: beware the visitor, he warns his readers, who claims that her luggage, with all her possessions, is elsewhere. Becky's belongings do eventually appear, though the finery they were alleged to contain never appears to take the place of the clothes Amelia has thoughtfully purchased for her. But one thing does appear, as if by magic: the portrait of Jos Sedley sitting on an elephant, which Becky and Rawdon bought, all those years ago, at the auction of belongings from the bankrupt Sedley family. Becky promised us she still had it, in her little monologue on the battlefields of Waterloo, and have it she does—and it is soon hung, prominently, in her rooms in Amelia's house.

From London to Waterloo to Weimar—some trip for a portrait of a fat man who can never truly have mounted the elephant, who more exactly is the elephant, throughout this novel. This elephant was first conjured out of a scene in Bluebeard, as Becky imagined "array[ing] herself in an infinity of shawls, turbans, and diamond necklaces, and . . . mount[ing] upon an elephant to the sound of the march in Bluebeard, in order [or so she imagines, on having, in her mind, already married Jos Sedley] to pay a visit of ceremony to the Grand Mogul" (26–27). Becky never does pay that visit, but another transformation does occur. The picture, which was the size of a portrait when Becky and Rawdon first viewed and purchased it, has become a miniature by the time Becky unpacks it in Pumpernickel.[15]

Why does the picture get smaller? Have we turned unexpectedly back to the world of *Alice in Wonderland*? Is there no object on whose size we can rely? Or is there something in particular about the shrinking of this picture, an object that was never anything but comic? The potrait has to shrink, of course, so that Becky can travel with it, and the miniature version of the very large Jos on his elephant is just plain funny. But why doesn't Thackeray care? Thackeray was sometimes quite cavalier about such details in his art, and we might attribute the transformation to that, but I do not want to. There's something about size-shifting that is central to his art, and in particular to the sketch-artistry I am claiming for the novel and for its curious heroine.

What I'd like to propose instead is that, rather like the two views of Becky that can never quite be reconciled, Thackeray wants us to have the painting and the miniature side by side, never quite certain which picture is which. It doesn't shrink; it is always two versions of itself. This is curiously like the perspective of the novel—or like curiosity itself. Vision at every turn in this novel *is* double, not single. Just as we see the illusion, the illuminated night, the glorious spectacle, so we also see the morning after, the haggard old woman, what lies behind or beneath the spectacle. And just as we saw the brilliant Becky, the mistress of the scene, triumphant and dazzling, so we see her the next day, horrible and ruined, and perhaps utterly fallen. But these shifts of perspective offer us the two contrasting views of the realist novel as well. In one view of the miniature world, we see close up, the cunning, "curious" details, the care that gave curiosity its name, everything written small. But in another, we pull out from our singular heroine, our tightly focalized perspective, our monocular view, into the widest possible lens, in which we see not the single booth at which we last glimpse Rebecca, but the entire fair itself, as Bunyan saw it: "Therefore at this Fair are all such merchandise sold, as houses, lands, trades, places, honours, preferments, titles, countries, kingdoms, lusts, pleasures, and delights of all sorts, as whores, bawds, wives, husbands, children, masters, servants, lives, blood, bodies, souls, silver, gold, pearls, precious stones, and what not." By the time we have reached Pumpernickel and Thackeray is claiming himself to have met Amelia Sedley and heard Becky's story from his own characters, we are lost in the dizzying crowd ourselves, unsure of our own perspective. It would be a relief just to close the box and put these puppets away.

For many readers, it is precisely the self-referential qualities of *Vanity Fair* that provoke them into what we might call noncompliance: the question of the relationship between Thackeray and his "puppets," especially the Becky puppet, makes us uneasy, and the constant shifts in perspective are more dizzying, some would say, than revelatory: always to see through everything, readers from Ruskin onward have claimed, is to see nothing at all. Even I have claimed at moments that Becky sees more than her author, but how can we be certain? What would it mean if the "Becky puppet" were allowed a vision denied the "Thackeray narrator"? It might mean there was something we, too, were missing—something that our readerly vision was not allowed to penetrate. When asked, later in life, if Becky had killed Jos Sedley, he said he did not know; this is hardly a knowledge that sees through everything—perhaps our chagrin is merely that is seems to see through us. But this returns us to our initial question of the bright light ("Vauxhall in the daytime") that Thackeray shines on the world: returning to our question of "enlightenment," we might note that while the modern world depends on the world's ultimate legibility, the great book of nature (and of the human heart) opened wide, it is also true, as Foucault reminds us, that "visibility is a trap."[16] Seeing and being seen are not always benevolent conditions—and darkness, the shadow in which Thackeray repeatedly plunges his heroine in illustrations as in text, "protects."

What then happens to my initial claims for Becky Sharp as feminist icon, pushing the boundaries of individual vision, looking beyond the "sequestered field and hill, and along the dim skyline" that trapped Jane Eyre? Has she achieved something that might "overpass that limit"? Certainly, Becky Sharp knows few limits, though she does curiously absent herself from seeing the happy ending. Becky sees into things, is punished, and then sees still more; that is one kind of vision, one version of curiosity. But we might note something else powerful for feminism in Thackeray's deliberate oscillations of bright and dark, elephantine and miniature, heroine and Bluebeard. Just as Thackeray's fiction always bridges an eighteenth-century sensibility with Victorian despair, so the novel insists on remaining half in and half out of the closet; it refuses to claim an absolute knowledge. And Becky's mimetic gifts are similarly (strange to say) modest: the possibility of flinging oneself briefly into the melee, and, shockingly, managing occasionally to do the right thing: sing a song by Mozart, comfort an old woman, try to save your friend from a disastrous mistake. These are little virtues to hold aloft in this braying world—and they may not, to adapt again Thackeray's metaphor, withstand the harsher light of day. They offer, to return to the visual register, not so much disenchantment as a kind of reenchantment: Becky's "fall" is into a dubious wisdom, but one that is curiously unjudgmental; it is hard to shock a woman who has already gone so far beyond what she is supposed to know, and yet she cannot claim herself to exist in a world without illusion. No longer fresh, no longer good, she can "at a little distance" offer a world of bright lights, fancy, and something that only pretends to be real. This is the only world the curious heroine makes possible.

But this may be precisely the illumination Thackeray offers—not the bright light of perfect and prescriptive wisdom, nor the pure savage lightning of satire, but the flickering light of a beloved illusion, as we, along with the children we no longer are, can watch the magic lantern show, and the dizzying dissolves of light and shadow, and, for a moment, ooh and ahh in a magical, if only miniature, moment of wonder. What better, Thackeray seems to say, can we hope from the novel than an amusement, a pile of vanities at a fairground, an auction house ravaging our homes, a tale that can only chasten, like Bluebeard himself, as it charms? What better than for a moment, in an odd light, to see, with our singular heroine, doubly?

CHAPTER 5

Bleak House and the Curious Secrets

"Who Copied That?"

Recognizing that they might possess invisible treasures, the Dead Letter Office advertised items and held periodic auctions. . . . At an 1859 auction, for instance, a main item was jewelry, including no fewer than 504 rings, "many of them plain gold wedding rings." All the packages were sealed, however, so that participants had to wager blind. An 1875 auction boasted a sixty-page catalog of items that had accumulated since 1869. It advertised "8,600 different articles sent through the mails, but unredeemed," including jewelry, books, engravings, charms, corn-crushers and corn-huskers, glasses, needlework, asthmatic fumigators, toothpicks, baby clothes, rosaries, poker chips, crucifixes, and the wings of a bat.[1]

I can remember, when I was a very little girl indeed, I used to say to my doll when we were alone together, "Now, Dolly, I am not clever, you know very well, and you must be patient with me, like a dear!" And so she used to sit propped up in a great arm-chair, with her beautiful complexion and rosy lips, staring at me—or not so much at me, I think, as at nothing—while I busily stitched away and told her every one of my secrets.

Charles Dickens, Bleak House

"Meantime, believe me to be—Your ever affectionate and grateful Clarissa Harlowe" [Clarissa writes to Anna]. Her "meantime" of course creates a paradox: Anna cannot know what she is supposed to believe in the meantime until the letter arrives, but once the letter arrives the meantime has passed.[2]

Bluebeard's wife has no daughter. She has a sister; she has a husband; she has female friends; she has an egg and a key and a door. It is her job to cross the threshold and die; it is her job to cross the threshold and see the dead face of her predecessor. When Thackeray took up this plot, it was as a story of *seeing*: the heroine looks into darkness and sees something terrible. For Charles Dickens, it is a story of *moving*: the heroine crosses and crosses and crosses again. Dickens took Fatima from Thackeray along with an extravagance of narration—it was one of the many things he learned from the less practiced novelist, for no two writers could have been more aware of each other, and as early as the third number of *Vanity Fair*, Dickens was borrowing Thackeray's tricks for his already-underway *Dombey and Son*. If Edith Dombey's sexual sophistication is impossible without Becky's sterling example, so, too, is Esther Summerson's sleight-of-hand narration, or Dickens's, without Becky's knowing ways.

But where Thackeray made of narration a magic lantern show, always intent on dissolving our view, for Dickens it is a live wire along which information travels endlessly but not always smoothly, jumping from place to place.[3] If Thackeray's novels give the feeling of seeing more than one thing at the same time, Dickens's novels give the feeling of being in more than one place at the same time. Thackeray lingers, transforming "Cornhill into Grand Cairo," or laying the "mysteries of Mayfair" over a boarding house in Brussels like a sepia scrim, but Dickens hustles. Rather than placing scenes over each other in a bricolage of disenchantment, he pieces them together as if assembling a mosaic, gathering more and more bits until the whole social panorama is filled in. Only by moving constantly, nervously, compulsively, and unpredictably can Dickens hope to gather enough snapshots to fill in the picture of any single "moment." On a single night in *Bleak House* when Jo, the crossing-sweep, dies in George's shooting gallery and the lawyer Mr. Tulkinghorn is murdered in Lincoln's Inn Fields, half the characters of the novel are afoot—Lady Dedlock in her veil, Hortense with her gun, George on Tulkinghorn's staircase, John Jarndyce and Allan Woodcourt visiting Jo, Esther kissing Ada's "hearse-like" door.[4] In a novel in which everyone is customarily locked up at night, as the lawyers are, "like maggots in nuts," instead everyone is out and about. Only one of these characters killed Tulkinghorn and only one will be found guilty—but it is Dickens alone who can assimilate all these perspectives and put them in a single view. Never, never, will Dickens throw up his hands (as Thackeray does, repeatedly) when asked whodunit—and yet never, somehow, will a reader feel a total mastery over the play of Dickensian perspectives, any more than she does in Thackeray's world. As Thackeray's multiple perspective, his ready vocabulary of anticipatory nostalgia, becomes Dickens's equally strong compulsion of hurrying, the narrative keeps us (and keeps its narrative secrets) constantly in motion. And yet it holds out before us, tantalizingly if falsely, the possibility of finally, like the delusional Mrs. Snagsby ("always curious your delightful sex is!" [646]), seeing it all.

We might think, then, that Dickens's relentless mobility holds out the possibility of legal certainty as well—or at least of a certainty of legal identity. But there we would be equally mistaken. From the smallest legal subject who lacks even the last name requisite to testifying at the Inkwich to the bastard daughter who doesn't possess a father or a last name ("There was no Miss [Summerson] then"[242]) to an adulterous mother who does not even own her own secret ("It is my secret, in trust for Sir Leicester and the family," says Tulkinghorn [581]), female dispossession before the law translates as well into a shuffling of legal arenas. Will the plot of *Bleak House* be adjudicated in family law courts, marital dissolution through acts of parliaments, church weddings and christenings, or murder and criminal conversation trials—and under whose will can these characters find their fortunes hidden? The constant shifting of venue is particularly dangerous for the women characters, finding no traction on the slippery roads of the law, their curiosity (the questions Angela Carter raised, "In the beginning was... what?";"where was I before I was born?"; where is the curious room?) frustrated by the shimmering chimera of the law—"Not this world, O not this," as Richard Carstone is reminded at his story's end, when he seeks to begin the world (763).

If all stories take place "elsewhere," what to do, then, with Fatima—curious, sharp, questioning, intent on going beyond the door? Dickens, as always, has his own solution—where one Fatima is good, two would be even better; in fact, where one narrator is good, two might also be better; and then, and only then, can Dickens say, as one of his curious heroines does, "Without thinking myself a Fatimah, and you a Bluebeard, I am a little curious." Dickens at this moment is almost dizzy with the joys of doubling—the heroine doubled by her secret mother, the mysteriously frozen Lady Dedlock; he, himself, doubled in turn by his narrating heroine, shadowed by Esther Summerson ("little Esther Summerson") as he walks through the valley of the shadow of the law (391). With his Fatima's duplicitous statement, however, Dickens has also changed the rules of the game: for as even the most casual reader of *Bleak House* knows, by its third chapter, Dickens has handed over the reins of narration to a heroine who will hardly confess to any curiosity at all—who is only a "little" curious and who brings up Bluebeard only to disavow him. Esther Summerson is a "pattern young lady," modest, careful, reflective, and she has no mother—in fact, the only curiosity she will aver is "I felt more interested about my mama."[5] But if she is looking for her mother, she will not admit it—any more than her mother, Lady Dedlock, will admit to her curiosity, for milady is "bored to death." Not only is Lady Dedlock already dead, but she is also the mother of a dead child—though, of course, her daughter is Esther, introduced in Dickens's notes from the first as "Lady Dedlock's child." Yet, if Honoria Dedlock doesn't want to know where her dead daughter is, she certainly (and fatally) wants to know where Esther's (dead) father is. Are you dizzy yet? A mother who wants to know, a daughter who doesn't, a

Bluebeard who seems to slip into the text almost by accident, only to be instantly dismissed: Dickens's is a strange Fatimah, doubled and doubtful, walking back and forth across the threshold, always just about to open the door, trapped in what Hillel Schwartz has called the "desperate romance" of the dark twin.[6]

If this novel does Thackeray one better by having twinned Fatimas, it has even more Bluebeards—Lady Dedlock herself, frightening Esther into silence and locking her own door, is a Bluebeard figure; so are Sir Leicester Dedlock, locking up his beautiful younger wife; John Jarndyce, the silent guardian, who proposes to marry Esther and cheerfully incarcerate her in Bleak House; and Dickens, bustling around London and its environs, generating curiosity of his own, and satisfying it only on his own terms. Not that this Bluebeard stays in his castle. Everywhere and nowhere at once, he speaks to us imperiously from the beginning: "London. Michaelmas Term lately over." Fog everywhere, he says, and rightly, for knowing what he wants to know is even more difficult than with his reticent heroine-narrator or her melodramatic, questioning mother. The novel entices us to enter the fog, for if Dickens is Bluebeard, possessor of keys and habitué of locked chambers (who else knows how the bodies got there?), he is also his own version of Fatima. His narration, too, wants to know. But the tests it runs on its heroines, and those they are allowed to run for themselves, are radically constricted. Esther Summerson is allowed to walk the streets, but she is forbidden ever to ask the questions she most wants answered; her mother, Lady Dedlock, is frozen prematurely into silence and thaws out only to die. And if Esther is trapped in a perpetual bride test, one run both by John Jarndyce for his delectation and by Mrs. Woodcourt for her disapproval, how much worse is the trap for Lady Dedlock, under the watchful gaze of Tulkinghorn, always already having failed the test, and never allowed to run her own investigation, to seek out her daughter, seeking out only a place to die. And yet, both escape Dickens's watchful gaze for pages at a time. Dickens's contribution to our construction of the feminist heroine, the brilliance of his representation of the woman who wants to know and chooses to know but never quite knows, might just be to admit the limits of two things: the singularity of his own curious knowledge and the necessary and desolate doubling of hers. Like a half-opened letter in a trompe l'oeil painting, Dickens's imagination of the lost copy in the closet poses the clearest statement we have had yet of a lonely and radical subjectivity—that of the subject "better not born."[7]

What does *Bleak House* want to know? In chapter 2 of of the novel, a woman leans forward and asks a question: she says, "Who copied that?" The novel doesn't at that moment use the word *curiosity*, or the word I earlier identified with it, its curious affiliate *quicken*, for it has told us already that the lady possesses "an equanimity of fatigue not to be ruffled by interest or satisfaction." Here is all it says:

> My Lady [Dedlock], changing her position, sees the papers on the table—looks at them nearer—looks at them nearer still—asks impulsively, "Who copied that?"
> Mr. Tulkinghorn stops short, surprised by my Lady's animation and her unusual tone.
> "Is it what you people call law-hand?" she asks, looking full at him in her careless way again and toying with her screen. (16)

As she changes her position, we move forward as well.[8] We see; we look nearer; we look nearer still—what does she see? We are not told. Why does she look? We do not know. Even her surprise (unlike Mr. Tulkinghorn's) goes without saying; only when the antithesis of curiosity's cognate, care, appears and she leans back and speaks "in her careless way again," do we realize that what we have witnessed is curiosity. Without care, no curiosity, no impulse, no change; she returns from animation to her usual suspended animation until, with "a faintness onto death," she falls.

Lady Dedlock may have once been unruffled, but no more, for she will fall, again and again, until her death. Fear death by curiosity, the novelist must be saying. For Lady Dedlock's curiosity is, to a large extent, the plot of the novel. The moment when she leans forward is the moment when she recognizes in the documents of Jarndyce and Jarndyce not an anonymous copywriter of the law, but her (supposedly) dead lover, Hawdon, the father of her illegitimate and (she thinks) dead daughter. The writing is so revealing only because "the legal character which it has was acquired after the original hand was formed" (16). A fatal trace of personality remains. Fatal to her, that is, and not to him. The lawyer Tulkinghorn, passionless protector of the patrimony of the Dedlock name, sees enough to know that Lady Dedlock *cares*—it is her interest that interests him. He follows the lead—he traces the document to the stationer Snagsby, who farms out legal writing; he goes with Snagsby to the apartments of the law-writer "Nemo" ("Nemo is Latin for no one," says Tulkinghorn—"It must be English for some one, sir, I think," corrects Snagsby [121–22]) only to find Nemo (Hawdon, that is) dead. When Tulkinghorn announces that death to Lady Dedlock, she goes out, veiled, in the cruel London night; she pays a poor crossing-sweep, Jo, to lead her to the dead man's room, the shop, and finally to his pauper graveyard; she gives the boy a coin and disappears. But his story of a veiled woman and a large payment only attracts more attention to her secret. The more she veils it, the more it appears, and still more exposure follows. Threatened by Tulkinghorn with the revelation of her secret, then accused of his death, afraid of shaming her husband and unable to face her own disgrace, she abandons her position, abandons the daughter she has discovered and rejected, and finally abandons life altogether, walking in a wintry London night to her death, dying at the step outside the poor parish graveyard where her dead lover lies, amidst the rats and refuse, at rest at last. All this, because she once leaned forward and read a letter. Or, as Tulkinghorn says on the night he tells her story, pretending to tell someone else's, in an audience with her and her husband:

> The captain in the army being dead, she believed herself safe; but a train of circumstances with which I need not trouble you led to discovery. As I received the story, they began in an imprudence on her own part one day when she was taken by surprise, which shows how difficult it is for the firmest of us (she was very firm) to be always guarded. (506)

Tulkinghorn says it, so it must be true—Lady Dedlock believed herself safe, but a "train" of circumstances led to her discovery, all because one day she "was taken by surprise."[9] Her own imprudence (also known as her own "interest") leads to her exposure and death; if no one else in the novel learns this lesson, her daughter Esther certainly does: it is she, more than any character, who knows "how difficult it is for the firmest of us ... to be always guarded," and terribly guarded she is.

But Lady Dedlock was once guarded as well: why, then, does the question of the copy arouse her interest? Is it precisely her sense that she is not alone? Knowledge is curiously divided and doubled in *Bleak House*: it is the business of the novel slowly to bring its own investigators together and the business of the different narrations to seduce us by delaying that reunion. When the novel begins, Lady Dedlock does not know that her lover is still alive, or that her daughter is still alive. She thinks that, "as my cruel sister told her," the child was "dead in the first hours of her life" (364). But the novelist knows, for the first note on Esther's chapter in Dickens's working notes is "Lady Dedlock's child," and the Esther who writes the novel of course knows. We have no such knowledge, but we do know that an incurious woman follows a curious one, that the novel is getting curiouser and curiouser, and that a woman we do not know is beginning to talk to us.

So let that unexpected interruption be our second beginning: When Esther begins the novel for a second (or is it the third?) time in chapter 3, she can only do so by saying, "I have a great deal of difficulty in beginning my portion of these pages, for I know I am not clever" (17). Esther is the novel's "Dame Durden," an orphan girl who thanks everyone constantly and reflects endlessly on the goodness of others and, as we have already seen, promises us that "my little body will soon fall into the background" of the story. She directs that story to an "unknown friend," and "there is little [in it] which is not a story of goodness," and that "portion of these pages" she skips through as quickly as possible. Telling a fairly dark story of abandonment, neglect, and servitude (a fascinating mirror of Becky Sharp's story, without the irony or the erotic knowingness, but she, too, has "the dismal precocity of poverty"), she turns herself and those around her into icons of Victorian domesticity, and the only thing she does with cupboards and closets is to tidy them. That is all she knows and all she seeks to know: she seems to have no imprudence at all; she asks no dangerous questions; she never leans forward. But what does she learn of her mother's curiosity?

She learns, quite simply, that curiosity kills, and for that reason, she will have none of it, or none, at least, to which she will admit. She says, at every possible opportunity, and most pointedly when "her guardian," John Jarndyce, asks her if she has any questions, "I am quite sure that if there were anything I ought to know, or had any need to know, I should not have to ask you to tell it to me" (92). There is at least one question, as I have argued elsewhere, that the whole novel is framed to answer, and it must be Esther's: who killed my mother? But there are other questions that shape the novel: the first, the one that Honoria lets herself ask, fatally, once, "Where is my dead lover?" leads her to Esther and leads her to her death. This is Fatima's question: the question of the woman who already lives in Bluebeard's house, walks the Ghost Walk of Chesney Wold, paces the garden in London, and wonders, "Who is keeping the keys?" Esther's question is more subtle, but it is no less a Bluebeard question, for it is the question she never (quite) asks John Jarndyce: not, what is my mother's story, but what is mine? She is (not) asking, at once, "Whom shall I marry?" (the question of every heroine's plot, even one as adept at denial as little Esther Summerson, the sexless Little Old Woman of Bleak House, with her housekeeping keys always at her side) and, more dangerously, "Are you my father, my guardian, my suitor, or my husband?" This novel, even more than *Vanity Fair*, organizes its plot through the ambivalence the Bluebeard tale teaches us about curiosity: without curiosity, a woman has no plot; with too much curiosity, a woman has no head. Honoria seems to be the character associated with the trappings of Bluebeard—she both has and wants to know a secret; she wants to know what is in the locked chamber and dies just outside the locked pauper burial-ground gate; her letters travel through the novel in a dangerous casket. But if Honoria is Fatima, Esther is Fatima's daughter, holding the keys, but wondering if she dare ask, knowing what might follow from an imprudent question. When Esther first sees the rooms in Bleak House, she notes in Ada's room "a fine broad window commanding a beautiful view (we saw a great expanse of darkness lying underneath the stars), to which there was a hollow window-seat, in which, with a spring-lock, three dear Adas might have been lost at once" (62). Mr. Jarndyce's castle has many rooms and each leads secretly into another; and in how many of them could a woman be locked up "at once" with a spring-lock? But behind Esther's refusal to ask lies not only Mr. Jarndyce but also that other Bluebeard, the figure of Dickens, the true keeper of (the secrets of) the house, the man who keeps changing the locks on the doors.

Back, then, to the beginning: "London. Michaelmas term lately over." From its first chapter, *Bleak House* provides a short history of realist fiction, not just for the sheer pleasure of showing off (not that Dickens ever minds doing that), but to suggest the myriad ways information reaches readers of the novel—and what the novel always makes us long to know. That opening sentence flashily invokes the journalistic mode that marked the rise of the novel and, dateline and place once established, promptly takes us all around England. The fog is "everywhere," but "everywhere" is annotated very precisely: we move up and down the river, across Essex marshes and Kentish heights; we follow the fog in the eyes and throats of Greenwich pensioners, captains, skippers, cabin boys, and find it deepest at the heart of Chancery—"London. Michaelmas term." We have moved nowhere. Well, we do move—but not of our own volition, and not very far. Still, it is not we who are curious; someone somewhere must be curious to move us so determinedly, but we do not know who. But whoever that "newsy" chap is in the opening chapter, offering the insider's view of London and the courts, he doesn't talk to us for long. He gives way in turn to the gossipy voice of the second chapter, "In Fashion," with its view of Lady Dedlock and high society. That voice reminds us of yet another early moment in the history of realism, the moment at which the novel was about "real people" (celebrities), thinly disguised, approached through their acolytes and with a satiric reverence, curiosity here a form merely of prurience. This is the world of Lady Dedlock, a world of almost total stillness, suspended animation, knowing voices. But we will change voices yet once more, for we are skipping about in the novel's history in almost evolutionary form, as the beginning of *Bleak House* suggests that ontogeny recapitulates phylogeny, each novel reliving the life of the species. In this case we have moved from journalism to libel to, finally, the place where we seem to rest in chapter 3, "A Progress," when we are spoken to directly by what we might tentatively call a "real made-up person," that is, a character, Esther Summerson, writing not in order to bring us scandal, but almost as an epistolary novelist might.[10] The Esther narrator, who, remember, has "a great deal of difficulty in beginning my portion of these pages," begins by writing familiarly, intimately, and modestly, almost as the heroines of novels-in-letters do, to an absent, as yet-unnamed friend, that (curious) reader, who just might be one of us—but who remains, for the entirety of the novel, an "unknown friend."

The "friend" may be unknown, but "who is that speaking?" we ask, curious at last. Who is this "person"? To whom does she write? To what purpose? What is her relationship to the author of the other "pages" she joins? Is Esther, as we might initially suspect, only the first of many correspondents, sharing these pages with the first narrator? Is she, like the several narrators of *The Pickwick Papers*, offering only an interpolated tale? Is this less like shared authorship than like ventriloquism, a scene where a permanent (and soon-to-be-identified) narrator pretends, quite self-consciously, to be someone else, when he is speaking avowedly in the voice of another? Or is Esther, like that most-famous female narrator, Jane Eyre, speaking at the behest of an editor, Currer Bell, or even, as Dickens called himself in his journal *Household Words*, at the request of a "conductor"? And is she our final resting place? For once we are in the presence of a speaker with a proper name, doesn't the novel mean us to settle down, to be at home, to lose the difficulty of narration Dickens has so deliberately created?

We seem to have made some progress in our taxonomies of curiosity, but have we? The three different versions of Bluebeard in the novel—Esther's first person retrospective narration, the narrator who follows Lady Dedlock, the narrator who moves in a bustling way around the city—are all different forms of both generating and satisfying curiosity, but they are locked in uneasy relationship. Doesn't that narrator know who Lady Dedlock is? She is in his narrative. And doesn't Esther bustle? Indeed, she does. It is our desire to tell the difference between these narratives that marks our curiosity—the impulse to say that Esther is more than a plot function with a proper name; that she is also a passionate bastard daughter afraid to say that name; that Lady Dedlock is both a character out of melodrama and a wily manipulator of scenes who tricks us as well as the novel's two detectives, Esther and Bucket; and that the bustling guy always haranguing us (the one who cannot say I, but does say "you") must, oh must, be Dickens himself. Is he our Bluebeard? Or is Sir Leicester, he with the haunted house and locked cabinets; or John Jarndyce, with all his cabinets with sprung-locks? Spring us—but let us follow each of these narratives as we will, we cannot help but get tangled up again.

So begin again at the moment of our unsettling, when someone addresses us directly. The character who speaks to the reader at the beginning of chapter 3 would seem (merely by saying I, acknowledging her difficulties, and speaking to us directly) to be, at last, telling us the truth, but her mind wanders as much as that of the initial, willful narrator, and she is every bit as hard to locate. She, too, plays with our curiosity. It takes several pages for her to tell us her name, saying "they called me little Esther Summerson" (18) a locution no living child, not even Alice Liddell, can ever really have used. It takes her even longer to stammer out the story of her familial relationships and legal status—she never does say the word *bastard*, leaving it to be drawn from such sentences as "Your mother was your disgrace, and you hers." Stranger still is that attempt to describe her own character to us: "I had always rather a noticing way—not a quick way, O no!—a silent way of noticing what passed before me, and thinking I should like to understand it better. I have not by any means a quick understanding" (17). It is not exactly that she is not curious, so much as that she will not entirely satisfy our curiosity by drawing conclusions, for what Esther means by "thinking I should like to understand it better," we soon come to realize, is really much more like "thinking I understand too well and wish people were not truly so awful." In sorting out her complicated syntax (she says, "when I love a person very tenderly indeed . . . [my understanding] seems to brighten," but even "that"—meaning my idea that I'm smarter about the people I love—"may be my vanity"), we are more likely to be decoyed into repeating Esther's own oft-repeated self-diagnosis: "I know I am not clever." Esther, that is, compels us to repeat her own distance from knowledge, her sense that knowledge is a dangerous form of power and one she dare not claim. And the claims that omniscience and power depend equally on distance are familiar to us from Foucault, and from subsequent theorists of narration.[11] But things are not so simple in *Bleak House*, and for our narrator to have so duplicitous and anxious a relationship to information all but guarantees our own uneasy relationship to reading knowledge—a thought that becomes all the more troubling when, in chapter 4, Esther goes on to introduce us to even more new characters, and we realize that our ways of seeing the world depend upon a woman almost constitutionally incapable of saying what she means.

Telling at first seems to take us back to the question of moving. Initially, the novel's use of space seems the register of the difference between the largely stay-at-home Esther and the avowedly curious Dickens narrator. The Dickens narrator is perpetually in motion, relying on trips outside and back: he moves "as the crow flies" from Chancery to the world of fashion; he imagines "ma[king] a tour" of the wide world and coming to the brink of it. In chapter 10, Mr. Snagsby watches a crow flying straight across Chancery Lane and Lincoln's Inn Garden, over Lincoln's Inn Fields and into Mr. Tulkinghorn's "large house," which is where the "lawyers lie like maggots in nuts" (119). We follow the crow into Tulkinghorn's rooms, only to watch Tulkinghorn go, "as the crow came—not quite so straight but nearly," to Snagsby's shop. The entire expedition is designed to show off the narrator's power—and indeed, the near arbitrariness (or, this being *Bleak House*, the only-seeming so) of its narrative "progress." The Dickens narrator wants us to know that he can go anywhere—and go there "straighter" than any of us, even the slipperiest of counsellors, can travel.

It is that narrator, rather than Esther, who is allowed to invoke the great manifesto of curiosity that marks *Bleak House*'s narrative principle. As the Dickens narrator puts it, teasing us again,

> What connexion can there be, between the place in Lincolnshire, the house in town, the Mercury in powder, and the whereabout of Jo the outlaw with the broom, who had that distant ray of light upon him when he swept the churchyard step? What connexion can there have been between many people in the

innumerable histories of the world, who, from opposite sides of great gulfs, have, nevertheless, been very curiously brought together? (197)

This is, as Dickens would say, the keynote. But the Dickens narrator's movement is also dependent on Lady Dedlock, for within a few pages, within the same chapter, it is she who crosses the gulf, bringing together "Jo the outlaw" and "the Mercury in powder," himself a powerful emblem of messages travelling across broad distances. Lady Dedlock crisscrosses the plot repeatedly in pursuit first of Nemo, her undead lover, and then of Esther, her undead daughter, and Dickens needs that motion.

Lady Dedlock, though hardly a narratorial presence in the novel, is not only an anxious ambulator but also an inveterate storyteller—not only writing long letters (which we do not see directly) filling in back-pages of exposition but also constantly sneaking off and then telling us where she has been. We follow the veiled lady on her low-life tour of London, with almost as much distance as when she was glittering in the brief, high-life Silver Fork pages of *Bleak House*, surrounded by satellites. We cannot reach her directly, but we can retrace her steps when she tells Esther all the places she has been: she goes to the brickmaker's wife; she goes to visit Tulkinghorn; and of course, she walks her way (backward through her own footsteps as it were) when she leaves the novel to die. She has only one or two passages of real interiority and those so melodramatized as to leave us unsatisfied, but she is surprisingly mobile for a woman of her class and station, and remarkably successful in her secret investigations. Far more than Sir Leicester, constrained by gout, she is a free agent of curiosity, seemingly following its whims rather than the limits of plot—until we realize that, through Tulkinghorn's malice, Esther's silence, and Bucket's incompetence, she has actually been plotted to death.

Esther, by contrast, is constantly constraining her own progress, emphasizing the circularity of her motions and tying herself to the "relief" of home. She marks her narrative's limits by her physical "progress" into and out of her godmother's house, the complicated and obsessive routine she establishes in which she leaves the house, gathers material for her narrative, and returns to Dolly's side, recounting her day and establishing narrative order. She cannot be as incurious as she thinks, for all of her protestations of staying by her listener's side are belied by her own restless movement into the world—if only to seek stories to tell us. As essential to this account as the fantasy of her listener's presence is her own absence, the moments when she leaves her listener to prepare to speak again, moments constantly recapitulated in the split narrative. Esther makes these demands on us, unlike the other narrator's demands, as a person: the fact that she has a name, has a body, claims to have been born, and identifies herself as the not-clever-one seems to invite the intimacy a character requires from us; the fact that the other narrator does none of this means that a different set of desires (not those of identification with another but of liberation precisely from a set identity) is put in motion. Yet Esther's narrative is hardly one of exclusive interiority, and her "little body" is one of the primary ways of traversing the vast distances, the "great gulfs" the novel invokes. Esther, too, will also cross and recross the city of London, like the series of veiled women, dressed in black, following a crow-like progress across the novel's great divides; she, too, has things she wants to know.

In fact, Esther's curiosity draws her further afield than we might initially think. There are few places in the novel Esther and her narration do not go—and there are a few places Esther enters that the Dickens narrator cannot. Esther never goes (until the novel's end) to Tom All Alone's and the pauper graveyard, places her mother and the other narrator go. But if she cannot easily enter London's darkest slums (or enters them only at the end of the book, with the whole force of the novel's curiosity behind her), she is free throughout the book to enter the homes of the poor (Charley, Miss Flite, the brickmakers) as well as those of the prosperous middle class and the wealthy. Indeed, the only door that seems absolutely closed to her is Chesney Wold, the home of the Dedlocks; there, she never makes it past the front steps. But until he enters with Bucket, the Dickens narrator is similarly barred from Bleak House, just as that narrator meets John Jarndyce only in a brief aside and only views Ada from a distance, as one of the two wards-of-court the chancellor is about to meet in chapter 1. The Dickens narrator, we might conclude, cedes control over some of these spaces entirely to Esther.

If overall Esther seems to be more modest in her narratorial incursions, more constrained in her movements than either Lady Dedlock or the Dickens narrator, she is far less constrained in time, and as the novel progresses, we realize more and more that time rather than space is the vehicle of curiosity in the novel. This returns us to the original story, for whereas the ambivalent heroine, the cautious daughter, is frozen on the threshold of Bluebeard's chamber, unable to step forward or back, her narrative can move ambitiously and confidently backward and forward in time. Temporal displacement seems to allow Esther the freedom to move without volition—or, as we might think of it, to move without any admission of curiosity. In comparison with the other narrator, Esther's temporal motion is elegant and slippery. Esther tells a single story from a single place, but to tell her story, she moves backward in time these seven years—or rather, seven years plus many more, for though she marries her husband at the end of the novel, and she has "now called him husband seven years," the plot she narrates takes her back to the moment when she is nineteen and goes to Bleak House—though her narration recalls her birthday "when I was still quite a little thing," and a dim time even before that. The Dickens narrator, by contrast, assembling alternative points of views as if they were points on a map or license plates in a child's freeway game, is committed only to filling in his vast picture—his "panorama." For that narrator, space is everything—knowledge can only accrue, as Elizabeth Ermarth remarked of realism more generally, by travelling. But as we saw in *Vanity Fair*, that is not the only movement available to the novel—and Esther, as a narrator, behaves much more like the Thackeray narrator, standing, as she often does, in a single place, and seeing multiply, in particular by seeing in *time*. Esther, seemingly trapped in the past, is the narrator who has the possibility of seeing what is before her. However much she refuses to reveal to us, she knows (by the time of writing) everything; the narrator can only know "now," what is in front of him, what he assembles from the variety of perspectives he collects in his bustling way. This poses him enormous difficulty when he needs to move into the past to get out some crucial information. He finesses this with legal testimony, as when Mrs. Piper can recount what Nemo, "the plaintive," used to say, or with melodramatic soliloquy, as when Lady Dedlock utters sentences like "O my child, my child! Not dead . . . as my cruel sister told me." (364), but it is never easy for him to move backward or forward in time, however much he flies through the air.

Esther only rarely admits to looking forward, perhaps because it, like leaning forward, would trigger the snares of curiosity, but she is able to tell stories that look backward and yet feel as if they were moving forward. In fact, she can make the hyperactive narrator look as if he were stuck fast in a far distant past. Because he cannot know anything ahead of himself (as Esther, of course, always does), even his most present-tense statements are obsolete as soon as he utters them, a snapshot of a moment already past. Take the simple statement that begins chapter 7: "While Esther sleeps, and while Esther wakes." It is the only moment when the third-person narrator acknowledges Esther's presence, and it is the strongest element that brings the two narratives together, until the moment when Inspector Bucket goes upstairs in the third-person narrator's account and brings Esther down in her own. This short passage, the first sentence of a third-person chapter that comes between two of Esther's own narrations, places the two narratives in not the same space, but the same time; it seems to move Esther's narration out of the past tense, in which she speaks, and into the present tense, which the omniscient narrator speaks. However, the longer we stare at the passage, the more it seems to reverse these temporal polarities: true, the narrator is speaking of Esther in the present tense, but rather than making *her* present to us, it has the opposite effect, working to displace his "presentist" narration. If he is speaking of Esther in the present tense, and we know that she has lived on *after* the events of which she (retrospectively) speaks, then he is the one who is trapped in the past; he has the illusion of speaking in the present, but he is doomed to live in an eternal, false present, stuck in some yesteryear, which seems like "now" only to him. Only Esther can write a "now" that moves backward and forward, and her secret quest is to make that now completely full.

Curiosity in this novel is largely the work of temporal displacement, of information that over time has gone in different directions but must be brought back together, by the two heroines. But the work of filling in that "now" (making the present replete, however briefly) is as much Lady Dedlock's as Esther's. When the novel begins, Esther thinks she has no living parents—she in fact has two. Honoria thinks Hawdon and the unnamed baby are both dead—both are alive. Hawdon thinks—well, can Nemo think? But by the end of the book, two of the three are dead; this is the job of the plot. While each seeks the other, each also seeks that missing object, the waxy perfect(ly still) baby who haunts the plot, the family we imagine in the gatekeeper's lodge at the beginning of chapter 2, when My Lady Dedlock is "bored to death." After her initial journey, the search for Nemo's graveyard, Lady Dedlock does little of the digging for the plot. That work is carried out by surrogates, chief among them Guppy, who threatens to bring the past to light and the dead to life. In the scene where he tells Lady Dedlock her own story, he says:

> "On one occasion, and only one, she seems to have been confidential to my witness on a single point, and she then told her that the little girl's real name was not Esther Summerson, but Esther Hawdon."
>
> "My God!"
>
> Mr. Guppy stares. Lady Dedlock sits before him looking him through, with the same dark shade upon her face, in the same attitude even to the holding of the screen, with her lips a little apart, her brow a little contracted, but for the moment dead. He sees her consciousness return, sees a tremor pass across her frame like a ripple over water, sees her lips shake, sees her compose them by a great effort, sees her force herself back to the knowledge of his presence and of what he has said. All this, so quickly, that her exclamation and her dead condition seem to have passed away like the features of those long-preserved dead bodies sometimes opened up in tombs, which, struck by the air like lightning, vanish in a breath. (362)

This scene confirms the terrible nature of buried knowledge: as when Pip says, in meeting Miss Havisham, that "waxwork and skeleton seemed to have dark eyes that moved and looked at me," Lady Dedlock herself seems to "vanish in a breath." It is as if, in a displacement we have become familiar with, Lady Dedlock herself were being struck by lightning. Although the "deadness" always implicit in her name seems to pass over her as quickly as lightning, it turns her mysteriously into a dead body, disentombed, and soon to vanish "in a breath." Lady Dedlock's constant layering in shawls like shrouds, her shaking and pacing and terror, are all part of this Gothic armature, but also part of forcing her into curiosity. Guppy, refusing monetary compensation ("Oh!! I assure your ladyship I am not actuated by any motives of that sort"), instead wants her to confess to her own interest: he gets her to say "please": when he says, "Your ladyship is not very encouraging," she switches from "if you choose" to "if you please." To be interested is to be in the presence of something terrible, forced to admit not only to your past sins but also to your present danger. Lady Dedlock may be our surrogate, gathering information on our behalf, but she cannot take possession of her own secret—not if she wants to remain safe. This is the central difference between Esther and her mother: Esther's secret is not known to her, until it is, and then it is hers; but Lady Dedlock's secret is not hers. As Mr. Tulkinghorn says to her, "It is no longer your secret. Excuse me. That is just the mistake. It is my secret, in trust for Sir Leicester and the family. If it were your secret, Lady Dedlock, we should not be here holding this conversation." Lady Dedlock cannot own her own secret, and there are words she can never use: *begin, anew, my daughter*. She is owned by her own secret, which leads her to a solitary death on a dark and lonely road, and which holds her in the past. She will never be able to say the word *now* again.

If the true *now* belongs to Esther, but Esther has come to share her mother's distrust of the future, how is it that she can tell a story? How can you tell any story if you cannot say, without hesitation, "I am curious"—or even "What happens next?" Esther's solution is cunning but endlessly frustrating for readers: you tell as if you do not know—as if you never did, although you might now, at last, in spite of your refusal of knowledge, know. This is how all of Esther's stories "progress," if we can call it that. True, she speaks almost exclusively in the past tense, with the present tense sneaking into her narration only occasionally in the form of conversation (though there are some odd exceptions to that rule as well), but the past tense in which she speaks is hardly consistent or monovocal, and not always highly informative, as we might expect from her blighted curiosity. She interrupts herself often, tangling herself in the webs of her own contradictory self-presentation, when she attempts to distinguish between what she knew *then*, what she then realized she had thought *before then*, and what she knows *now*. This is Esther's curiosity game: sometimes it takes the form of foreshadowing (the funerals on the pavement when Ada and Esther go to see Richard), and sometimes it is a fairly conventional recognition scene, as when Esther cannot put together the knowledge of Ada's marriage to Richard and the plan her darling has formed no longer to return to Bleak House. But most often it is a repetition of that frozen Bluebeard moment: the moment when the heroine pauses outside the door of the locked chamber, always about to go in, never quite crossing the threshold.

For if it is Esther's narration that promises to carry on that work of bringing things "curiously together," her emphasis throughout remains on the *irreconcilability* of the great gulfs ("what connexion can there be?") that separate her from the story she is telling and the moment in which she is writing, that separate her from perfect and complete knowledge. In one of the many present-tense passages where she remembers "now" the pain of "then," she recounts the pain of suspense around the revelation of her mother's identity:

> It matters little now, how much I thought of my living mother who had told me evermore to consider her dead. . . . I am conscious now that I did these things [left the room if her name was mentioned, etc.] when there can have been no danger of her being spoken of. . . . It matters little now how often I recalled the tones of my mother's voice, wondered whether I should ever hear it again as I so longed to do, and thought how strange and desolate it was that it should be so new to me. It matters little that I once sat in the theatre, when my mother was there and saw me, and when we were so wide asunder, before the great company of all degrees, that any link or confidence between us seemed a dream. It is all, all over. My lot has been so blest that I can relate little of myself which is not a story of goodness and generosity in others. I may well pass that little, and go on. (521)

This is a remarkable passage. At the end, of course, it delivers a lacerating condemnation of Honoria Dedlock, letting us know that *her* behavior, unlike the rest of Esther's life, is a story of not-goodness and not-generosity. In Esther's limited emotional vocabulary that is a powerful indictment indeed. It is also a powerful demonstration of the different time schemes of the novel and of the difficulty we have in reading the book's narrative coherently. The Esther who writes this, unlike the first-time reader, already knows her mother is dead; society's cruelty, even more than her mother's willfulness, is the real reason she will never hear her mother's voice again, for her mother, cold and dead, will never again speak to her or even, as she did across the theatre's vast spaces, recognize her. But the image of Lady Dedlock seeing Esther across the gaps of space and class (there is a "great company of all degrees") sounds eerily like the third-person narrator's invocation of the novel's own narrative scheme. "What connexion can there be?" None, for my mother is dead and was as good as dead to me all along.

Throughout the novel, Esther's sense of time is more than duplicitous—it is shattered. But it enacts its own stuttering progress upon its readers as well, hobbling our curiosity, for it is only in retrospect that we can realize what shattered it: the interdiction of the Bluebeard story; the threat, precisely, of asking the wrong question, of discovering herself trapped in her mother's story, of becoming another Fatima. The strongest clue to this is the fracturing of the key terms (*now* and *never*) that occurs whenever she tries to tell the story of her relationship to John Jarndyce. In an equally dense and even shorter passage, Esther remembers sitting by the fire, after meeting her "Guardian." In her retrospective narration, she remembers how her

> fancy, made a little wild by the wind perhaps, would not consent to be all unselfish.... It wandered back to my godmother's house, and came along the intervening track, raising up shadowy speculations which had sometimes trembled there in the dark, as to what knowledge Mr Jarndyce had of my earliest history—even as to the possibility of his being my father—though that idle dream was quite gone *now*.
> *It was all gone now, I remembered*, getting up from the fire. It was not for me to muse over bygones, but to act with a cheerful spirit and a grateful heart. (75–76; emphasis added)

Within this retrospective moment, there is another retrospective moment nestled; in the past, Esther is calling that time "now," and remembering a still earlier moment when she thought Jarndyce could have been her father. This is the only time she makes that thought remotely explicit, and it adds a terrifying shadow to his erotic pursuit of her throughout the book once we know she once believed him or hoped him to be her father. And yet, as she describes what was then (in the past, before this moment of retrospective narration) a "now" moment, Esther remembers herself remembering, as if even in that (now past) present she had slipped back into the fantasy of benevolent fatherhood and had to remind herself that she had already lost that dream. It seems a slippery certainty to hold on to, and she suggests it always was—even though a few pages later, in her next chapter, Esther's guardian inquires if she has anything to ask him about the past, and she says, "Nothing! I am quite sure if there were anything I ought to know, or had any need to know, I should not have to ask you to tell it to me." She does not say she doesn't want to know, and she doesn't say, "I wonder..." but she says, "I am sure you would tell me if..." But she must forbid herself even that wandering curiosity. If she had anything to ask, Esther says, "I must have a hard heart indeed," which suggests the powerful interdiction against asking; but she goes on to ward off curiosity even more powerfully, saying, "From that hour I felt quite easy with him, quite unreserved, quite content to know no more, quite happy." But the fact that she still remembers the scene of quite powerful discontent suggests just how unstable her certainty and contentment are. Esther's fantasy life ("my fancy"), like Jarndyce's, follows a powerful wind and has some trouble staying anywhere fixed in time.

We find out why only when Esther finally does know all, in the scene where she finally utters the secret name, Bluebeard. In her final recognition scene, where she realizes John Jarndyce is not going to hold her to her heartbreaking promise to marry him but intends to release her to the man she loves, she plays constantly with the "now" of her narration, all leading up to the great *now*, when she can say, "My husband—I have called him by that name full seven happy years *now*" and bring her narration up to her present tense. But she stresses as well how often she was wrong to say "now" in the past: when Jarndyce first tells her she is to make Woodcourt's home pleasant for him, she tells her guardian she has "seen this in [his] face a long while," and she "knows *now*" what it means; but of course she is (in that "now" of the past) entirely, indeed blessedly, wrong. As she repeats to herself when recalling the trip down to Yorkshire,

> I travelled all day, wondering all day what I could be wanted for at such a distance; *now* I thought it might be for this purpose, and *now* I thought it might be for that purpose; but I was *never, never, never* near the truth. (749; emphasis added)

This is the one moment in the novel when, finally, she admits to her curiosity—only at the moment when its true horror (is the secret that my guardian is my father and my husband at the same time?) is finally set to rest: when John Jarndyce asks, when she arrives in Yorkshire, if she wasn't "full of curiosity" about why he has brought her there, she answers, "Without thinking myself a Fatima or you a Blue Beard, I am a little curious about it." Finally, finally, Esther can say the word *curious*—can, in spite of her disavowals and aversion and coyness, say, "I want to know."

And finally Jarndyce can redeem the word *now* for her, remarking, "It is for me to speak now"; "I am your guardian and your father now"; restoring time to its proper place now that he is not trying to take his improper place as Esther's husband. But like the other great time schisms of the novel ("there is a kind of parting in this too," he says, reminding us of her parting from Ada and her parting from her dead mother), it suggests a degree of anxiety and unfixity in time, which every self-conscious retrospective moment in Esther's narration calls up. In short, every time Esther says "now," meaning the moment when she is writing, she both suggests her own uncertainty and calls up one of the great "nevers" of the text, the silences (like her mother's great silence) that haunt her telling of her own "portion" of the story, truly a story only of now or never.

The curious mother, who will not speak; the curious daughter, who will not ask; and the curious novelist, anxiously bustling between them. But where does novelistic curiosity come from? Dickens is writing at a time of immense novelist experimentation but also at a moment of the professionalization of curiosity. Esther Summerson takes her name not only from the biblical Esther, savior of her people, and from Hester Prynne, but also from Esther Barton, Mary Barton's fallen aunt, who serves as a successful amateur detective in a novel that features a police detective four years before Inspector Bucket makes his appearance. Inspector Bucket is both the sign of Dickens's fascination with professional detection and a sign of its failure, for it cannot master the intricacies of Dickens's plotting: Bucket is there as a cautionary tale for us and a reminder that the Bluebeard plot always finds its victims.

There is a wide range of female detectives in the novel as well, shadowing the professionals but also shadowing Esther. Lady Dedlock shadows Esther; Hortense shadows Lady Dedlock; Mrs. Bucket pursues Hortense. It is Mrs. Bucket who pieces together the evidence (the torn papers and the gun) to convict Hortense of the murder of Tulkinghorn; Hortense, who, when she catches Mr. Snagsby's name in a conversation ("being uncommon quick"), makes inquiry and follows him until he turns to Tulkinghorn for help; and Mrs. Snagsby, who "sees it all," who presents a full-blown plot as elaborate as that of *our Bleak House*, rich with illegitimate children, women in disguise, and a plot in which "they were all in it." As Snagsby reports,

> My little woman is—not to put too fine a point upon it—inquisitive. She's inquisitive. Poor little thing, she's liable to spasms, and it's good for her to have her mind employed. In consequence of which she employs it—I should say upon every individual thing she can lay hold of, whether it concerns her or not—especially not. My little woman has a very active mind, sir. (274)

Mrs. Snagsby's active mind, which she thinks will lead to her husband's exposure and the high road of matrimonial separation, is of course a product of Mr. Snagsby's "being party to some dangerous secret without," as he puts it, "knowing what it is," and we might note that Esther manages to combine these two characteristics quite compactly in her narrative: she has a secret, but she never quite seems sure what it is. And even if she were certain, of course, we cannot be sure she would tell us.

Esther poses a different model of detection because she is reluctant equally to ask, to know, and to tell. What kind of detective is Esther Summerson? Everything I have been listing, her careful and deliberating games with time and space, her power of mobility and the moments when she claims she does not know, cannot tell, misremembers, or misnames—these are all incidents in the history of her coming into full knowledge of her identity but also part of her performance of curiosity. Esther's curiosity is fairly indirect. She rarely seems to look at anything squarely (her habit at once of noticing and not noticing is doubtless part of what she means by "not being clever"), but she certainly doesn't miss much. Critical truisms may make her the more sentimental of the two narrators, but she has a fairly dispassionate gaze, far more dispassionate than the narrator who witnesses Jo's death. In the scene in the brickmaker's cottage, she is watching Ada approach the baby, when, she coolly reports, "Ada bent down to touch its little face. As she did so, I saw what happened and drew her back. The child died." Even when she eschews the drily reportorial, she is hardly uniformly emotional. She has a positively Dickensian gift for noting eccentricities of personal appearance: when Mr. Turveydrop, "pinched in, and swelled out, and got up, and trapped down, as much as he could possibly bear . . . [bowed] to me in his tight state," she claims, "I almost believed I saw creases come into the whites of his eyes." She delights also in noting the eccentricities of domestic interiors: Mr. Grubble's best parlor contains "more plants in it than were quite convenient, a coloured print of Queen Caroline, several shells, a good many tea-trays, two stuffed and dried fish in glass cases, and either a curious egg or a curious pumpkin (but I don't know which and I doubt if many people did) hanging from the ceiling" (458). And Esther is similarly sharp on the subject of people's foibles and frequently enjoys telling us what she will not tell those around her: she "did not see the proof of Mr Skimpole's unwordliness in his having his expenses paid by Richard, but I made no remark about that" (459); it struck her that "if Mrs Jellyby had discharged her own natural duties and obligations, before she swept the horizon with a telescope in search of others, she would have taken the best precautions against becoming absurd; but I need scarcely observe that I kept this to myself" (473); after one of Mr. Turveydrop's more ridiculous speeches, "I said nothing, which I thought a suitable reply." In these moments, Esther seems to be playing a coy version of that standard narratological aide-de-camp, the "reader's friend," letting us know without knowing what she is seeing without comment.

But the detective plot also brings us back into the Bluebeard plot, for it is made up not only of curious wives and duplicitous husbands but also of caskets, jewels, letters, and veils, dead wives and locked doors, everything except the elephant. Think again of Becky Sharp on the floor of her bedroom, surrounded by "brilliants," letters, ribbons, and a tiny casket with letters and checks and banknotes—that is the curiosity cabinet of this novel as well. Lady Dedlock's rings are seen by Jo, imitated by Hortense, sought by Bucket; even her watch becomes a character in the novel, a symbol that her time is up, of course. But in true Bluebeard fashion, dead wives haunt the novel as well—the first Lady Dedlock; Ada's and Richard's mothers (never mentioned); and of course the chancellor's wife, imagined as coming in a veil to visit Jenny, the brickmaker's wife. As for keys, we have not only Esther, always shaking hers, and the keys of the prison, with which Tulkinghorn threatens Hortense, but also Lady Dedlock, letting herself in and out of the locked London garden to visit the pauper's graveyard—where she dies, locked out at last. But chief among the objects is the bundle of letters Honoria sent to Hawdon, letters that move from Nemo to Krook, are meant to move to Guppy, and are pursued by Tulkinghorn and Smallweed. This bundle is one of the primary characters of the novel.

The letters are part of that larger cultural story of curiosity and information with which I began, which makes *Bleak House* not only a novel but the world's most efficient postal system. Dickens, as we know from his running battle with James Fitzjames Stephen and the *Edinburgh Review*, was fascinated with the reform of the postal system; in an exchange published in *Household Words* a few years after *Bleak House*, he defends *Little Dorrit* against attacks on its realism by invoking the example of Rowland Hill, the great reformer of the system and a kind of Daniel Doyce figure, maligned and ignored by the Circumlocution Office until it can take credit for his success—a success it, Chancery-like, balked at every turn.[12] But Dickens's own information network is as compelling and eerie as any system of mail. Like Lady Dedlock, attempting to send her last letter to her daughter, "pencil-writing, on a crushed and torn piece of paper, blotted with wet... folded roughly, like a letter, and directed to me at my guardian's," Esther writes the much longer letter that is the novel, in portions, at different times, "particular," as Bucket says, "to a word"—but with a similar anxiety that the delivery system will fail, that human error will intervene, that the messages will not get through: the letters appear dead on arrival. We might argue, only half jokingly, that Dickens has two narrators because he fears that only one will ever manage to get a message through the maze of a less-than-wonderful delivery system. Secure communication requires redundancy; every letter yearns for its own copy.

The problems of documentation are themselves well documented in *Bleak House* criticism: from the matters in Chancery, which can only be conveyed by written and not oral testimony, to the various wills, documents, and "wiglomeration" that circulate, to the scraps of paper in Miss Flite's reticule, writing flies around the novel. Yet even in that busy world of writing, Esther is a special case. It seems no exaggeration to note that Esther is her own private post office: from the law letters of Kenge and Carboys to her mother's private missive (which we never read) to her job as personal correspondent of Bleak House, charged with writing to Richard Carstone, to the letters she sends off chirpily describing her various changes of venue, Esther writes and mails constantly, a single-minded demon of epistolarity. But she is also Dickens's chief correspondent; almost all of her chapters begin by identifying the place from which she writes, the people who accompanied her there, and any details we might have missed in between. In her illness, which occasioned in her hallucinatory dreams some of the most important of her confusions of now, then, and writing, everything is mediated by letter-writing, for she is too contagious to approach anyone in any other way. It also offers the moment when she carries out perhaps her strangest experiment in epistolarity, one that links her, and her portion of these pages, with the transformation of information at work in Victorian England and with Dickens's fascination with the dispersal of knowledge. The scene comes in between two crisis points of her narrative, the first her illness and the second her discovery that her mother is still alive but wants no further communication with her. It is further prepared for by the customary web of epistolarity Esther builds around her, like a safety net of correspondence: she begins the chapter by remarking on her removal to Lincolnshire with Charley; she announces her arrival there by writing to Boythorn to describe all his things to him; she writes long letters to Ada and receives responses in return.

In this nest of scenes, Esther writes a letter for an old lady who lives in "such a little thatched and whitewashed dwelling that when the outside shutter was turned up on its hinges, it shut up the whole housefront." This in itself is remarkable in a village where, as Esther claims, "there were faces of greeting in every cottage." But this shut-up cottage contains yet another affectionate mother, who wishes to communicate with (in this case) a distant grandson, who was a sailor.

> I wrote a letter to him for her, and drew at the top of it the chimney-corner in which she had brought him up, and where his old stool yet occupied its old place. This was considered by the whole village the most wonderful achievement in the world; but when an answer came back all the way from Plymouth, in which he mentioned that he was going to take the picture all the way to America, and from America would write again, I got all the credit that ought to have been given to the Post-office, and was invested with the merit of the whole system. (446–47)

Like every paragraph of Esther's narration, this passage does the uncanny work of reminding us of her lost home, of "the old place" that she never occupied in anyone's heart (the good grandmother taking the place of her wicked godmother), and it foreshadows the "shut up" front of Chesney Wold, where Esther will shortly walk the Ghost Walk, realizing that she is the doom of the Dedlock family, come to destroy them and carry out the curse of her spiritual grandmother, the first Lady Dedlock. Just a few pages away is a letter from her own mother, which will tell her that to her mother's knowledge she herself had been born dead, had been buried (much like poor Dolly), "had never been endowed with life—had never borne a name." But here, Esther brings life to others; with her letter, she not only brings the family back together (all the way from Plymouth) but also brings to life the whole postal system, "the most wonderful achievement in the world."

I suspect that for both Esther and Dickens, epistolarity (and its games of absence and presence) is about death; it is through a tear-spattered, barely legible letter that Esther finds her mother, "cold and dead"; it is in a remarkable series of letters, in a few months in 1851, when he began *Bleak House*, that Dickens tells of his father's death, learns (at a literary fund dinner) of his baby daughter's death, and (in an uneasy and haunting letter) writes to his absent wife, urging her to return to London and warning her that she may find what he knows to be true, that their baby is already dead. Like Esther, seeing her father's handwriting first in a letter from a law office and then again in a notice in a law-stationer's window just before she passes the threshold of the room in which he has recently died, Dickens knows that letters both commemorate and obliterate death; that the dead hand of the past, to use the language of literary wills, continues to write to us, and that we write back. Dickens's letter to Kate warning her that their child is ill is a powerful and indeed an uncanny literary performance. While I used to resent it for its paternal prerogative, the John Jarndyce–like way in which Dickens withholds the knowledge of their child's death to cushion Kate's return to London from her sickbed at Malvern, it now seems to me to offer something very different. It is a letter that screams out, without ever saying the words, that their child is already dead; it is a letter that prepares for death while being virtually written in the presence of the dead baby; and that dead little girl (Dora Annie, named, as Dickens was to note, rather inauspiciously for the already-dead heroine of *David Copperfield* and hence for the dead-image of the young Catherine Dickens herself) haunts the dead children of *Bleak House*. In Dickens's account he had been playing, like Esther and Ada, with his daughter before his departure that evening. Only a letter sent (and withheld) while he was giving a speech tells him that the child he last saw "well and gay" was now, to borrow a phrase, "cold and dead." As he says to Catherine in his letter,

> Mind! I will not deceive you. I think her *very* ill.
> There is nothing in her appearance but perfect rest. You would suppose her quietly asleep. But I am sure she is very ill, and I cannot encourage myself to much hope of her recovery. I do not—why should I say I do, to you my dear!—I do not think her recovery at all likely.[13]

But of course, for a novelist like Dickens, at least within the world of *Bleak House*, what could be more likely? A baby, left cold and dead, buried without a name, grows up to be a narrator, one who can animate the postal system and send chimney-corners to America. Business as usual for the Dickens novel; is there anything curious here?

Think more, though, about the way Dickens both tells and doesn't tell the story of his baby's death, and you are closer not only to the novel's games of telling and knowing but also to the Bluebeard story. What's in the closet? The anecdote depends on the idea that the husband knows and the wife does not. If it isn't his secret he is protecting, why keep the wife out of the bloody chamber? But that depends on the idea that what is in the closet is Bluebeard's first wife—and all his subsequent wives—and that he put them there. In *Bleak House*, of course, there is no wife in the closet: Jarndyce may own a spring-chest, and Sir Leicester a picture-gallery, but (as far as we know, at least) they have yet to kill any wives. What is in the closet? Lady Dedlock believes that it is her dead baby—the Esther Hawdon who "never drew breath." Not so. Esther believes it's her mother—but of course, that's not true either. And both assume (as do readers) that someone, somewhere knows—that there is a secret in the closet. There isn't—or at least not yet. Only when Lady Dedlock dies and is placed in the mausoleum (near the first Lady Dedlock, dead of her husband's political ambitions) is there finally a woman in the closet. Until then, there are only signs of deadness—jewels, letters, caskets—all in motion around the novel.

What, then, does Bluebeard know? The Dickens who writes the letter to Catherine performs knowing-and-not-knowing, but he does, after all, know something: "The baby died." The secrets are not so clear in this novel. John Jarndyce does not know Esther's secret—and the secret he is keeping is the one of his own desire, not hers. Sir Leicester knows nothing; Tulkinghorn knows enough to get himself murdered; Bucket knows too late. This is the radical solution to the problem Dickens will propose in *Hard Times* and the one that George Eliot will pursue in *Middlemarch* and *Daniel Deronda*: that the father in fact does not know more than the daughter, that there is no secret knowledge, that the secret is that Bluebeard doesn't know. Louisa asks her father for erotic guidance—he utters statistics instead; Dorothea believes Causabon has the key to all mythologies and he doesn't even speak German; Gwendolen Harleth, in her half of *Daniel Deronda*, believes that Daniel will be the perfect father/confessor/guide and give her the secrets to a moral life—we, who read his half of the novel as well, know that he is haunted by his own empty closet, a space that he cannot fill until he finds his mother, marries Mira, and abandons Gwendolen to go to the Holy Land. Empty fathers, empty closets; where should the daughters/wives go for knowledge?

Esther gets one letter that holds an answer, and that is the long letter from her mother that tells her the story we have already heard in chapter 29, that "my child" was "not dead in the first hours of her life, as my cruel sister told me." That story is told again, by Lady Dedlock, to Esther herself, in a letter we do not see: as Esther narrates it, "I clearly derived from it—and that was much then—that I had not been abandoned by my mother." "Her elder and only sister . . . discovering signs of life in me when I had been laid aside as dead, had . . . reared me in rigid secrecy." "I had never," she goes on, "to my own mother's knowledge, breathed—had been buried—had never been endowed with life—had never borne a name" (452). This is Esther's retelling of her mother's retelling of her story—the darkest version of Esther's own sense of her life, that she had no claim to her own name, that she was buried (alive), that she had never (and what a verb it is) been "endowed" with life.

But Esther doesn't end her story there; rather she promises us future revelations. "What more the letter told me needs not to be repeated here. It has its own times and places in my story" (453). Esther, at the moment of telling us her entire story, instead promises us another secret and promises to tell it to us later—but she does not. Instead, she moves on to her burning of the letter, the thing that finally shuts the door on Lady Dedlock's story—Esther's own Bluebeard moment, when she locks Fatima in the closet. What was that missing narrative link? What piece of the story was going to be connected? What else did Lady Dedlock say?

At this moment, we are back in Bluebeard: who owns the closet and who has the keys? Is it Lady Dedlock's secret or Esther's? To my mind, this is linked again to the larger question of form, and my suggestion that this is finally an epistolary novel, but that one of its correspondents, Lady Dedlock, has (to borrow a Pip locution) had her part in it hammered off. We are back in the world of *Clarissa*, and despite all the advancements (not least of them the postal system itself), we are as haunted and lonely as ever. Our curiosity seems as doomed here as it did there, and our powerlessness as complete. What does it mean to be in this or any epistolary novel and cut off from one of the letter-writers? Esther talks and talks and talks—or rather, she writes and writes and writes, promising to be our friend. But she is not necessarily a friend to all her "characters," and in her continued hoarding of her secrets, she may not finally be our friend after all. The letter she does end with, Lady Dedlock's final letter, tear-stained and pencil written, is an unfinished text, a death knell, a misdirected will—it cannot finish the story; and Esther will not, breaking off, even supposing.

Where does all the writing lead? In this novel, of course, it is supposed to lead back to Chancery, to the will plot, to a trial that will prove decisive. For if epistolarity provides one version of curiosity for the novel, the legal system (with its equally endless stream of writing and writers and copywriters) provides another—and another of the trials of Bluebeard. Much of the novel is constructed like an inquisition, as characters turn on and interrogate one another. Again, Esther's seeming refusal to interrogate is one response, but her mother's far savvier jousting with the likes of Tulkinghorn and Guppy is another. It is Lady Dedlock's interest in the suit that brings the texts copied by Nemo into her house and her desire to follow the "inkwich" and its investigations that takes her into the streets. Even Tulkinghorn is in awe of her lawyerly skills—"That's a home question," he says in admiration as she grills him about the time of her unmasking—and the threat of yet another trial, a murder trial, propels her into her escape and toward her death. Maria Manning's trial for murder hangs over the novel (and certainly over Hortense's death), but the idea of a woman unmasked on the stand, a woman testifying and a woman hanged for sexual misconduct as much as for murder, provides the erotic charge of the detective plot—no one is as interested in Hawdon's death as in Lady Dedlock's fall.

The courts of Chancery have more than a little of *Alice in Wonderland* in them, of course, but the law is taken more seriously as an instrument for women than we might suspect. Both Honoria and Esther engage with its "mysteries" and sustain hope for its outcomes. Esther until the end of the novel at least pretends to believe Richard and Ada will find an answer to their inheritance conundrum, and perhaps she wishes the same for herself, as she resides in bastardy, outside the law. But she also hopes that the law can disentangle curiosity: while she follows Jarndyce's other interdiction, never to go to law or "wiglomeration," she does not disavow it, and in fact is in the courtroom for Richard's final "hearing," though she arrives a moment too late. Not for nothing is she the daughter of a law-writer, for she, too, is a law-writer, writing an alternative legal story.

But what it means to be a law-writer is of course not to be an author but to be a copyist—and remember, everything in Chancery must be copied, for there is only (as in the novel) written testimony. The question here isn't just what a copy means, but how does a copy know itself—is Esther her mother? Is she merely a copy? The curiosity everyone feels for her is precisely *because* she's a copy. Her face (we are told) can "harm" the original (she must disguise her relationship to her mother), but it is also how she and her mother find each other—"When she had first seen me in the church, she had been startled; and had thought of what would have been like me, if it had ever lived, and had lived on, but that was all, then" (453). Another of Esther's "thens" marks the spot, in which she is an "it" (a dead baby) and a mere copy—what would have been like me? She doesn't think "I am like her," but "my dead baby would have been like her." All the efforts at finding your "original" produce only this—the idea that, finally, you are only a curiosity, a copy, a forgery (for what else is a bastard but an illicit copy?) and you are only a relic of something that never lived at all. Does anyone care for a copy? Is there any stuff of curiosity left after the original is gone? Is each Fatima the same as the last, merely another object of Bluebeard's dispassionate and judgmental gaze? In this novel, maybe so—no one, it would seem, is an object of a loving gaze, all on her own; all, it would seem, are doubles, and no one, finally, can be loved for herself alone.

Thus the final question of curiosity in the novel: what if "curiosity" could express not only morbid interest or erotic play but also an ethic of "care"—one of concern strangely absent from the world of *Bleak House*? The universe makes but an indifferent parent, says Mr. Jarndyce (himself a rather self-interested parent) —but is it too much to ask for a mother who might watch over one, so that one is not, as we shall see, a pickled baby? What would it mean to "care" for a copy?

Lady Dedlock dies knowing everything, and knowing that her baby did not die, but she is alone. Esther, the dead baby, seems to survive and seems to live to tell the tale—but does she? The genius of *Bleak House*, we might argue, is precisely not to tell all, but rather to make Esther Summerson's disavowal of curiosity the object of our curiosity. Never can a heroine have worked so hard to know so little. And certainly Esther is rewarded for her refusal to be curious: like an unimaginably successful Fatima, she acquires not one but two houses, for at the end of the novel she is bustling out of Bleak House Two and Bleak House One with equal enthusiasm. She has her own two little daughters ("my dearest little pets"), and she also calls Ada's son Richard "my Richard." She has her husband and her guardian; she has all the rewards of self-abnegation and modesty, and she even has her old face back—even supposing. Does she still have a secret?

We can't be sure. What were Esther Summerson's secrets, before the end? She was not dead. She was not born dead, nor did her mother die while giving her life. She loved Allan Woodcourt and she did not love John Jarndyce, but she never told anyone those things. She was furious at her mother for dying, and she was furious at her mother for not dying, and she was furious at her mother for abandoning her, and finally, again, she was furious at her mother for dying, this time for real, whatever that means in a novel, and whatever that means for a woman who has been dead since the beginning of the novel. She gave up her own face to keep her mother alive, and it did not work—even supposing. I have argued elsewhere that Esther's greatest secret is that she was curious, after all—she never gave up wanting to know, and she never asked, and instead she wrote her mother's story night after night in her room, unable to ask anyone anything for fear of giving away the secret of her existence, the secret of her mother's sin, the secret that she was, somehow, not loved enough. But if that is true, then Esther's secret is that she was a dead baby, after all.

Dead baby, dead mother—curiosity is a peculiar state in *Bleak House*. Become curious, come to life, die—this is the story of Lady Dedlock. It is not quite the story of Esther Summerson, but it could be. Esther's story suggests something else terrifying about curiosity—its odd and predatory relationship to the copy itself, the other point with which we began. A "curio" is precious, always, because it is unique; if it were easily duplicated, it would not, to be obvious about things, be curious at all. A curio can reflect care, can reflect miracles of size or execution, but it cannot be mass produced. The portrait of Lady Dedlock that Guppy sees at Chesney Wold in his late-night tour is precisely the one that Sir Leicester does not allow to be reproduced; the scary thing about Esther herself is, of course, that she *is* Lady Dedlock, reproduced. Not only is she the too-perfect copy, but she is the copy that longs for the original—it is the force of her desire, we somehow believe, that brings her mother to life and to death; her own footsteps at Chesney Wold that pronounce her mother's doom; her interest, however stifled and mummified, that propels the plot. Or rather, at the least, the curiosity that we, as readers, feel for her, even if she cannot express it. We want to know—and our quest for information is the breath that strikes Lady Dedlock like lightning, striking her down.

Go back to the first copy, the dead baby, that strange object repeatedly imagined in the course of *Bleak House,* and throughout Dickens's career. For all that Esther imagines herself "better not born," it is Ada who mourns the dead baby, not she; it is her mother who collects the handkerchief that cradled that baby and gives it up only at the moment of her own death. Dead babies are grim curios for the (perhaps too) dispassionate Esther, as they are a little bit for the writer as well—by the time of *Our Mutual Friend,* Dickens is multiplying them for brilliant comic effect. In Mr. Venus's shop, as he watches Wegg peruse it, dead babies are simply part of the merchandise:

> You're casting your eye round the shop, Mr Wegg. Let me show you a light. My working bench. My young man's bench. A Wice. Tools. Bones, warious. Skulls, warious. Preserved Indian baby. African ditto. Bottled preparations, warious. Everything within reach of your hand, in good preservation. The mouldy ones a-top. What's in those hampers over them again, I don't quite remember. Say, human warious. Cats. Articulated English baby. Dogs. Ducks. Glass eyes, warious. Mummied bird. Dried cuticle, warious. Oh, dear me! That's the general panoramic view.[14]

Preserved Indian baby. African ditto. Articulated English baby. Wegg's leg, or so he comes to believe, rests next to yet another: "Mr Wegg gradually acquires an imperfect notion that over against him on the chimney-piece is a Hindoo baby in a bottle, curved up with his big head tucked under him, as he would instantly throw a summersault if the bottle were large enough." Dead babies turning summersaults—for Dickens, we might think, the very stuff of curiosity.

That is so, if we think of the novel as just another curiosity shop, as our opening meditations might encourage us to do. The novel becomes either Nell's grandfather's shop, or Venus's workbench, or Grubble's inn ("more plants in it than were quite convenient, a coloured print of Queen Caroline, several shells, a good many tea-trays, two stuffed and dried fish in glass cases, and either a curious egg or a curious pumpkin (but I don't know which and I doubt if many people did) hanging from the ceiling"[458]) or worse yet, Mrs. Jellyby's closets, with "such wonderful things ... tumbling out ... when they were opened—bits of mouldy pie, sour bottles, Mrs. Jellyby's caps, letters, tea, forks, odd boots and shoes of children, firewood, wafers, saucepan-lids, damp sugar in odds and ends of paper bags, footstools, black-lead brushes, bread, Mrs. Jellyby's bonnets, books with butter sticking to the binding, guttered candle ends put out by being turned upside down in broken candlesticks, nutshells, heads and tails of shrimps, dinner-mats, gloves, coffee-grounds, umbrellas" (373). That's the lost property office of the novel as well (shall we restore the umbrella to Mrs. Bagnet?), but it is also meaningless, a helpless bundle of curious objects that once were interesting, of value, unique, and are now just so many dreadful odds and ends.

But remember, Esther is not just a collector—or rather, she is an accidental collector. All the collecting in the world cannot make her a person now. True, by the end of the novel she has husbands, fathers, babies, "pets" galore, and she lives in two overstuffed houses. But we do not believe her story ends there: in some important way, her story ended long before, at the foot of her mother's unexpected grave, where the original lay, "cold and dead." In the eerie alternations of *Bleak House*, we are able to bring to life all sorts of fantastical things, each more curious than the last. We meet three dark young men, and for many pages we know three surgeons, until we realize they are all Allan Woodcourt. We meet a young man who greets Esther in London with the news of a "London particular"; a young London man visits Chesney Wold and sees a portrait of Lady Dedlock and is astonished; the two young men come together and are presented to Esther, as they later will be to Lady Dedlock, as a young man by the name of Guppy—but that shadowy, unnamed young man of the first chapter is never quite resolved into the "name of Guppy," for how could he be? The split narrative, with its constant sense of multiple letters flying at us from different senders, in slightly different and never quite reconcilable time frames, with different tenses and with different metaphors, keeps information travelling and documents circulating, but can all of its restlessness, all of Esther's loving correspondence bring back the dead? As Hortense boasts to Bucket, in words that echo the book's compulsive praise of Esther, "Listen then, my angel, You are very spiritual. But can you re-store [Sir Leicester] back to life? Can you make a honourable lady of Her? Or a haughty gentleman of Him? You cannot do these things? Then you can do as you please with me. It is but the death, it is all the same" (653). And it is all the same: the unnamed dead baby in the brick-maker's house becomes one with the imaginary Esther, the one her mother thought "had never borne a name," just as Richard Carstone, dead with blood in his mouth, becomes one with his infant son, who never knows his father, but has two mothers; as John Durham Peters memorably put the conundrum of failed correspondence, "What is the meaning of the letter burned in the Dead Letter Office whose writer does not know it is lost and whose recipient does not know it was ever sent?" (172). It was my mother, cold and dead; as far as she knew, I had never borne a name; "it is but the death, it is all the same."

As his career continued, Dickens turned repeatedly to the dead letter office, to the fatal separation of the original and the copy, and the even more deadly encounter between them: when Miss Havisham creates the heartless Estella in her image, or Magwitch creates Pip in his, what else are they doing, but imagining themselves again, imagining sending a letter of themselves, to themselves, preserving themselves. Even the bully of humility, Bounderby, will attempt the same thing in comic form in Dickens's very next novel, when he leaves behind a will that creates twenty-six Josiah Bounderbys out of twenty-six aged pensioners, only to have the will be tangled up, in Jarndyce & Jarndyce fashion, in endless Chancery lawsuits, after his death. The law is useless here, and the twenty-six Bounderbys will no doubt die without ever coming into their inheritance, and they die unnamed by our novel as well. Such is the fate of the copy—or, at least, of the desire to copy, to continue on beyond death, to keep writing after you are gone, even supposing. In Kazuo Ishiguro's *Never Let Me Go*, a revision of both *Bleak House* and *Great Expectations*, he imagines clones seeking out their human-born original, seeking a birthday, a place of origin, seeking, we might imagine, not to be curious, to be singular, any longer. And perhaps that is the most powerful motive we can conjure, finally, for the writing of *Bleak House* itself; perhaps it is there, in imagining a Fatima who does not open the door but instead pushes a letter under it, that we can locate Dickens's final version of female curiosity, as well as his own. And what a strange answer that would be—that Dickens wrote the novel, invented the split narrative, created Esther Summerson, the curious woman unable to ask, unable to speak, sitting up all night writing to her unknown friend, so that he, too, might not wander, might not be singular, might not be curious, alone.

CHAPTER 6

The Bluebeard of the Classroom

Bad Marriages, General Laws, and the Daughter's Curiosity

On what table, according to what grid of identities, similitudes, analogies, have we become accustomed to sort out so many different and similar things? What is this coherence?

                    Michel Foucault, *The Order of Things*

Statistics plays a greater role in topics that have variability, giving rise to uncertainty, as an essential ingredient, than in more precise subjects. Agriculture, for example, enjoys a close association with statistics, whereas physics does not. Notice that it is only the manipulation of uncertainty that interests us. We are not concerned with the matter that is uncertain. Thus we do not study the mechanism of rain; only whether it will rain. This places statistics in a curious situation in that we are, as practitioners, dependent on others.[1]

    For it was not knowledge but unity that she desired, not inscriptions on tablets, nothing that could be written in any language known to men, but intimacy itself, which is knowledge.

                    Virginia Woolf, *To the Lighthouse*

However bleak the end of *Bleak House*, we are still in the business of writing novels, or Dickens was. And we are still in the grip of the great legal conundrum of the Victorian period. If a woman signs away her story when she signs the marriage contract, if she gains her identity only after passing the test and crossing the threshold of the bloody chamber, how is she to write herself into law? Even if the curious heroine is doomed to singularity, nonetheless, we must find a way for her to be able to form a more perfect union, to continue to move between the domestic and the public sphere, to be more than "the doctor's wife." The heroine who found herself alone at the end of *Bleak House* ("it was my mother, cold and dead") needs to find her way back into the social order. She needs to move from her loneliness to general laws, from the evacuation of identity in marriage into an active, choosing, writing self. Answering these challenges takes us back not only into the marriage plot but also back to legal reform—a move Dickens, surprisingly enough, anticipated for us. For at the end of *Bleak House*, Mrs. Jellyby, a woman with a mission, abandons Africa for women's rights, and specifically for the franchise. "She has been disappointed in Borrioboola-Gha, which turned out a failure in consequence of the king of Borrioboola wanting to sell everybody—who survived the climate—for rum, but she has taken up with the rights of women to sit in Parliament, and Caddy tells me it is a mission involving more correspondence than the old one."[2] The most active letter-writer of the novel has changed her topic, but she continues to use the language she aimed at her apolitical, "nonsensical . . . degenerate child," Caddy, to "devote [herself] to the great public measure." How are we to make sense of this? Dickens, we assure ourselves, cannot be serious—and as if to prove us right, winking at us across the century, at the end of *Hard Times*, Jem Harthouse, the young man who has joined "the party of Fact" in the hopes of entering Parliament, abandons politics altogether, deciding instead to "go in for Camels."[3] And so Mrs. Jellyby, too, must once again be nothing but a joke.

Such a conclusion would be wrong, however, and so would our assumption that a novelist who "devotes" such characters as Mrs. Jellyby and Miss Wisk to the cause of women's representation in Parliament has no interest in feminism and the public sphere. For what Dickens goes on to do in *Hard Times*, following the harrowing end of *Bleak House*, is to connect women's rights to the two other things that concern us most here: female curiosity and the form of the realist novel. He does so by playing not only on that pun of "unions" but also on the nature of marriage and divorce laws, the rise of statistics, and the counting of persons. In this surprisingly complicated political fable, he returns to the problems of *Bleak House* with a difference. He takes on not only female curiosity but also female knowledge, not only sentiment but also statistics, and not only female adultery but also the question of how a woman gets to be a "person" in the eyes of the law. But in doing so, he does not leave Bluebeard behind. For Louisa Bounderby, the heroine who comes after both Lady Dedlock and Esther Summerson, the "something-ological" daughter of the utilitarian parliamentarian Thomas Gradgrind, the question of personality is one of social and fictional representations—and for Louisa, Bluebeard's castle is an unexpected path to her own form of (parliamentary) representation.

For this reason, when Bluebeard does appear in *Hard Times*, he appears in a nest of statistics. *Hard Times* is a novel that consistently takes social representation as its theme,[4] but it also participates in the same information revolution that shaped *Bleak House*'s formal innovation, asking how are we to know a larger society, and how small can a person be and still count? This is a version of the "little Esther Summerson" question I raised in chapter 3 ("how big is anything in a novel?"), but here the question returns as an interest in general laws: the attempt to create a just society by aggregate.[5] Statistics are in a sense the ultimate curiosity cabinet, the single table that renders an account of every single thing. It is no accident that statistics came into being at the same moment as *Paradise Lost*: Milton, Malthus, the numbered world. But the enormous revolution in statistical thinking came in the 1830s and '40s. As Theodore Porter puts it, "That all generations previous to the 1820s managed to get by without [the term *statistics*] reveals dimly how different was the world they lived in—a world without suicide rates, unemployment figures, and intelligence quotients." As Porter notes, liberal thinkers were "impressed by the power and dynamism of that complex entity, society, and . . . delighted by the unifomity from year to year which was found to characterize not only natural events like births and deaths, but also voluntary acts such as marriages." But the rise of statistical thinking is a rise of probability, of "mere regularities," of (to cite the origins of the infamous bell curve) "astronomical error." No mean coincidence for a novel like *Hard Times*, obsessed with the astronomer trapped in a room with no windows. For Dickens, refusing the fascination of what was by the 1840s known as the "average man," the rise of the unstatistical heroine was equally compelling. Like its predecessor, *Bleak House*, *Hard Times* is fascinated by the copying of the heroine, her progress from singularity to doubleness and back again, and particularly the "cultivation" of her curiosity—a story we have here associated with the Bluebeard plot and the heroine's willingness to cross the threshold, to do Dickens's work of crossing the social divide. But *Hard Times*, like both *Bleak House* and *Paradise Lost*, needs its heroine to become curious; it needs her to make a bad marriage that defies the statistics; it needs her to go out in the world and look around, opening doors and windows, reporting back to the novelist and to us.

Dickens's interest in the statistics of the marriage plot suggests why when Bluebeard appears in *Hard Times* he is not immediately recognizable. He appears in a joke: the chatty, almost breezy narrator assures us that "although Mr. Gradgrind did not take after Blue Beard, his room was quite a blue chamber in its abundance of [parliamentary] blue books" (75). This Bluebeard belongs to the father; his realm is Parliament and the classroom; the heroine is, once again, locked out of knowledge. But yet, not so—for the heroine of *Hard Times* is unexpectedly bombarded with knowledge all the time. Louisa Gradgrind is diligently trained in experimentation, trained to test hypotheses, trained to ask questions. She is not, of course, trained especially well—that, rather than the premise of experimentation itself, is Dickens's complaint—but her (flawed) education and her finding out of its limits are the heart of the novel. Bluebeard's bloody chamber is no longer the bedroom but the classroom, and in that room, Dickens himself is a Bluebeard figure, as are the patriarch Thomas Gradgrind, Louisa's experimenting father, and the dark husband, Josiah Bounderby, utilitarian businessman, blowhard, and fraud, mad scientists all. Their laboratories are not only classrooms but also factories and breakfast tables (instruction everywhere), as if the best teacher were a paternalistic, spousal demon, and Dickens were taking on the nature of social knowledge itself.

James Mill and Jeremy Bentham, the fathers of modern social thought, appear here as Bluebeard at the breakfast table, which is surprising in itself.[6] But here is where Dickens makes the world even more interesting—and where sexuality reenters the social. For if the subject of the great experiment, John Stuart Mill, appears in this novel, he does so as a curious woman, as Fatima herself—which is to say, as Louisa Gradgrind. Dickens uses the figure of Louisa explicitly to challenge the "party of fact," but he is equally curious about the realm of feeling, and John Stuart Mill's account of growing up "a calculating machine" gave him the plot through which to explore the possibility of social transformation. More than that, he can use Louisa to return to the issues at the heart of this book: what do women want to know and how are they to act on their knowledge? The odd familial and marital relations of *Hard Times* allow Dickens to test the limits of curiosity, to extend curiosity into the world by at once disaggregating it and personalizing it, using it to imagine what other forms of individuality might be. If the daughter is an experimental subject and the wife a legal nonperson, then the novel takes on the erotic and epistemological problem of proof, asking what makes the the heroine's curiosity count.

From the beginning of the novel Louisa Gradgrind is a curious girl, in our doubled sense of the word—she is an object of curiosity to others, both as the subject of her father's child-rearing experiments and as a possible rebel, and she is curious about the world. But what is most remarkable about her is that something in her seems to fire Dickens's curiosity as well. Whereas in other novels he warns his heroines explicitly, "Read Bluebeard, pet, and don't be curious," and in fact seems to find nothing so seductive as a woman who resists curiosity (think again of Esther Summerson refusing to ask her guardian any questions about herself, or of Amy Dorrit's unwillingness to disentangle the complicated will plot of *Little Dorrit*), here Dickens not only is on Fatima's side but also seems literally to stand beside her, curious to know what it is that she wants to know. Even the other characters seem to catch her curiosity. Her interest in the forbidden travelling circus, the place where we first meet her, not only leads her brother to stand gawking with her at the fence, where they are discovered by their father, but also leads Mr. Gradgrind himself, on his return home, to suffer an entirely uncharacteristic moment of wonder. "'Then comes the question,' said the eminently practical father, with his eyes on the fire, 'in what has this vulgar curiosity its rise?'" (18).

It doesn't come from him, that's for sure. He asks the question with such astonishment because everything he has done for his children was designed precisely to destroy curiosity—though the very presence of his daughter at the circus (the circus!) would suggest that he is asking it too late, for his daughter is already fallen. Until this moment the Gradgrind household has been utterly, and intentionally, devoid of wonder, and this taboo is the key to Louisa's education as Dickens presents it:

> No little Gradgrind had ever seen a face in the moon; it was up in the moon before it could speak distinctly. No little Gradgrind had ever learnt the silly jingle, Twinkle, twinkle, little star; how I wonder what you are! No little Gradgrind had ever known wonder on the subject, each little Gradgrind having at five years old dissected the Great Bear like a Professor Owen, and driven Charles's Wain like a locomotive engine-driver. (11)

As the novel begins, the Gradgrind pedagogy is primarily limited to the dissemination of incontrovertible facts about the world, in what is at once a terrible and a comic exercise. As the boy called Bitzer and the girl called Jupe (who begins as "girl number twenty," resolves into Sissy Jupe, and then becomes a heroine all on her own) are quizzed, the world is reduced to Carrollian nonsense. When M'Choakumchild asks Sissy Jupe to "give me your definition of a horse," Sissy cannot answer, perhaps because the required answer is: "Quadruped. Graminivorous. Forty teeth, namely twenty-four grinders, four eye-teeth, and twelve incisive. Sheds coat in the spring; in marshy countries, sheds hoofs, too. . . . Thus (and much more) Bitzer" (7–8). As Mr. Gradgrind says, shutting the book on knowledge of horses, in dismissal of the circus child who has lived among them all her life, "Now girl number twenty. . . . You know what a horse is." To "know what a horse is" is to absorb the lesson that Dickens initially means to be both the homeschooling of the Gradgrinds and the larger social-schooling of the working class: always "know," never wonder. This education is designed to negate the world, to end curiosity before it can even quite begin, and Gradgrind would have it be of a piece across society.

In Dickens's initial critique, Louisa Gradgrind is like the workers, and they are like her.[7]

> When she was half a dozen years younger, Louisa had been overheard to begin a conversation with her brother one day, by saying "Tom, I wonder"—upon which Mr Gradgrind, who was the person overhearing, stepped forth into the light and said, "Louisa, never wonder!" (41)

The image of the stern father stepping into the light, darkening the world for his child, becomes the image of class difference in industrial Coketown, in which "there happened to be . . . a considerable population of babies who had been walking against time towards the infinite world, twenty, thirty, forty, fifty years and more." The "never wonder" education is all mathematical "settlements": "By means of addition, subtraction, multiplication, and division, settle everything somehow, and never wonder. Bring to me . . . yonder baby just able to walk, and I will engage that it shall never wonder" (41). Thus is, and much more, we might say, the mission of Thomas Gradgrind, that eminently practical man.

And yet, all recipients of paternal wisdom (or, as we might think of it, paternal darkening) are not created equal. The workers in their "baby" form are counseled endlessly against wonder by political economists of all stripes; they are offered libraries with volumes of useful information; and yet, the narrator remarks in faux-outrage, "even these readers persisted in wondering. They wondered about human nature, human passions, human hopes and fears, the struggles, triumphs and defeats, the cares and joys and sorrows, the lives and deaths of common men and women! They sometimes, after fifteen hours' work, sat down to read mere fables about men and women, more or less like themselves, and about children, more or less like their own. They took DeFoe to their bosoms, instead of Euclid, and seemed to be on the whole more comforted by Goldsmith than by Cocker" (42). Somehow, the workers have the materials to resist the lessons of the political economists—they still wonder; they still care; they still read—they might even still become Dickens readers. Louisa, as we first encounter her, will not, and not only because there are no novels in the Gradgrind library.

Instead, it is because Louisa's education is something different: Dickens, despite his initial analogy, differentiates very clearly between the "general" education the students in the Gradgrind classroom receive and the one that Mr. Gradgrind's children receive in that other, most dread classroom, his family home, the aptly named "Stone Lodge." True, Louisa's education also comes to us first in comic form, but it isn't as funny as chapter 1. As her mother unintentionally parodies it: "The lectures you have attended, and the experiments you have seen! . . . I have heard you myself, when the whole of my right side has been benumbed, going on with your master about combustion, and calcination, and calorification, and I may say every kind of ation that could drive a poor invalid distracted" (45). Like the workers, the Gradgrind children are "benumbed": the "five little Gradgrinds . . . had been lectured at, from their tenderest years; coursed, like little hares. . . . The first object with which they had an association, or of which they had a remembrance, was a large black board with a dry Ogre chalking ghastly white figures on it" (11). The "Ogre" at the chalkboard is the same father who darkened the sun, and in some ways he is very much like the ogre-teacher, M'Choakumchild, of the opening chapter. He is more particularly a version of James Mill. The echo of the utilitarians in the two next-younger children, "Adam Smith Gradgrind" and "Malthus Gradgrind," confirms that connection—but no connection exists between Thomas Gradgrind's devotion to his "most beloved child" and the far colder James Mill. One cannot imagine James Mill addressing John Stuart Mill as his "favorite child," nor can one imagine a teenaged John at a circus. Dickens has brilliantly picked up the utilitarian commitment to women's education (that is why Sissy is at the school, because Thomas Gradgrind cares about the education of girls—"he wanted girls at his school"—and little Jane Gradgrind has "manufactur[ed] a good deal of moist pipe-clay on her face with slate-pencil and tears, . . . [and] fallen asleep over vulgar fractions"), but Dickens is interested more precisely in the education of daughters, and beloved daughters at that. It is Louisa's father's love for her that is central to his experiments, but he needs not only to make her want to know but also to make her want to know only "enough."

For that reason, Louisa's education has an edge to it. Without this education, as her father suggests, she "would have been self-willed." The aim of education is not just (as the narrator later remarks) to "harden her," but to prepare her for a wider, and hence (or so Gradgrind, like James Mill, believes) impersonal point of view. Like any good utilitarian, she is to know the whole of society through statistical gatherings and scientific method: "dragged to a statistical den," she is to dwell only in "general laws"; she is to be hardened out of desire altogether. But Louisa is not only the perfect model of a person created out of the general; she has also been formed as a test case, a prototype, a model—a curiosity.

And that she is. She is a paragon of knowledge, for all the "little Gradgrinds had cabinets in various departments of science, too. They had a little conchological cabinet, and a little metallurgical cabinet, and a little mineralogical cabinet; and the specimens were all arranged and labelled, and the bits of stone and ore looked as though they might have been broken from the parent substances by those tremendously hard instruments their own names" (12). Her education takes the form of a curiosity cabinet, in which all knowledge can be labelled, and Louisa herself bears such a label, "broken" as she is from "the parent substances." When the gentleman-dandy James Harthouse comes to town to "go in for" parliamentary questions, joining Mr. Gradgrind in the Blue Chamber, the first curious object he visits, in lieu of a museum of curiosities, is Louisa. He asks Mrs. Sparsit if Mr. Bounderby married "Gradgrind's daughter," and then goes on:

> "The lady is quite a philosopher, I am told?" "Indeed, sir," said Mrs Sparsit. "Is she?" "Excuse my impertinent curiosity," pursued the stranger, fluttering over Mrs Sparsit's eyebrows, with a propitiatory air, "but you know the family, and know the world. I am about to know the family, and may have much to do with

them. Is the lady so very alarming? Her father gives her such a portentously hard-headed reputation, that I have a burning desire to know. Is she absolutely unapproachable? Repellently and stunningly clever?" (94–95)

Louisa is of course stunning, though not in the way Harthouse imagined: she enters his correspondence along with other sights of the neighborhood, as he announces that "the female Bounderby, instead of being the Gorgon he had expected, was young, and remarkably pretty" (127).

The image of the Gorgon gives us a version of what Louisa's education was designed to do: to make her someone who will turn others to stone at the sheer spectacle of her knowledge, as she has been rendered "hard-headed" by her father's erudition. If Gradgrind is a "dry Ogre" at the board, and the reader is first introduced to him as a man with "a voice, which was inflexible, dry, and dictatorial," we are not surprised to hear Louisa speaking with "dry reserve." And yet, something surprising remains. When that reserve comes up in a conversation with Sissy Jupe, "girl number twenty," it resonates differently. Sissy, now part of the Gradgrind family, is describing her difficulties at the hands of M'Choakumchild's pedagogical mill, and of course Dickens means us to believe her—but also to watch Louisa's response:

> "Then Mr. M'Choakumchild said he would try me once more. And he said, Here are the stutterings—"
>
> "Statistics," said Louisa.
>
> "Yes, Miss Louisa—they always remind me of stutterings, and that's another of my mistakes—of accidents upon the sea. And I find (Mr. M'Choakumchild said) that in a given time a hundred thousand persons went to sea on long voyages, and only five hundred of them were drowned or burnt to death. What is the percentage? And I said, Miss;" here Sissy fairly sobbed as confessing with extreme contrition to her greatest error; "I said it was nothing."
>
> "Nothing, Sissy?"
>
> "Nothing, Miss—to the relations and friends of the people who were killed." (48)

What Sissy counts as "nothing" is the comfort of statistics, the law, the stutterings, everything the system prides itself on conveying. As she recounts the lesson, M'Choakumchild is "explaining to us about Natural Prosperity." "'National, I think it must have been,' observed Louisa. 'Yes, it was.—But isn't it the same?' she timidly observed. 'You had better say, National, as he said so,' returned Louisa, with her dry reserve" (47). The dryness is her father's—the reserve, however, suggests something else: some pool of feeling; something that, despite all the stoniness she can muster, suggests she is trying not to laugh and trying not to cry; something her brother does *not* have; something that suggests why the hero of this novel is a daughter and not a worker, a child, or a boy.

This gives us another answer to why her father has worked so hard on his prototype, why he has attempted to create this hardheaded woman. The key to her education, remember, is to at once satisfy and kill her curiosity: never wonder, only reason; no fancy, just facts; an observatory without windows. Without curiosity, without wonder, there will be no errant desire, and hence, we would think, no errant women—or, to change the letter of the law, no wandering. If the point of her education was to educate desire out of her, then that point is made most clearly in the scene where Louisa, as it were, completes her education and graduates: the scene where she is asked to choose. As her father imagines her education, it will end with a single test, and that is a marriage proposal, and after that, she will never need to learn anything again. This education, we might note, comes with an expiry date, and its expiry date is (can it really be that obvious?) a proper marriage.

At this point, startlingly, we reenter the Bluebeard story; for it is at this moment that we are told that "although Mr Gradgrind did not take after Blue Beard, his room was quite a blue chamber in its abundance of blue books." In part, this is an ironic joke: the full weight of parliamentary knowledge, via the blue books, is to be brought to bear on Louisa and her choice. These books, we are told, can be used to "prove" anything—and the word *prove* retains its sense of both "test" and "defend." But what the intrusion of Bluebeard also suggests is that, once again, a true education for an intelligent woman is not any formal education at all, but the marriage plot and romantic choice. This is true in *Hard Times* even though what follows is a decidedly unromantic scene—so much so that it unnerves even the dry father, who finds himself "not so collected at the moment as his daughter." When he poses the test, saying that Bounderby has made an offer of marriage, Louisa does not respond; when he queries her silence, she says, "I hear you, father. I am attending, I assure you." When she asks her father if Bounderby asks her to love him, her father says, "Mr. Bounderby does not do you the injustice, and does not do himself the injustice, of pretending to anything fanciful, fantastic, or (I am using synonymous terms) sentimental" (76–77). The expression, he says, is "misplaced," and when his daughter asks him, "What would you advise me to use in its stead, father?" her father replies, with a sense of deep comfort, "as you have been accustomed to consider every other question, simply as one of tangible Fact" (77).

This is the response Louisa's education has trained her to expect—and yet, it is not clear how her education has prepared her to identify the relevant facts, to answer the question, to pass her father's test. Her father, too, seems baffled. He answers her questions with more and more stutterings—I mean, statistics—specifically with disparities of age in marriage in England and

Wales, and "among the natives of the British possessions in India, also in a considerable part of China, and among the Calmucks of Tartary." Louisa, for the first time in her life, asks her father for something more: looking out at the factories that lie outside her window in the harsh light, she has "one wavering moment in her, when she was impelled to throw herself upon his breast, and give him the pent-up confidences of her heart." We think the reserve might melt; we sense more is going on—and so, oddly, does he, for he asks,

> "Are you consulting the chimneys of the Coketown works, Louisa?"
>
> "There seems to be nothing there but languid and monotonous smoke. Yet when the night comes, Fire bursts out, father!" she answered, turning quickly.
>
> "Of course I know that, Louisa. I do not see the application of the remark." To do him justice he did not, at all.
>
> She passed it away with a slight motion of her hand, and concentrating her attention upon him again, said, "Father, I have often thought that life is very short."—This was so distinctly one of his subjects that he interposed.
>
> "It is short, no doubt, my dear. Still, the average duration of human life is proved to have increased of late years. The calculations of various life assurance and annuity offices, among other figures which cannot go wrong, have established the fact."
>
> "I speak of my own life, father."
>
> "O indeed? Still," said Mr. Gradgrind, "I need not point out to you, Louisa, that it is governed by the laws which govern lives in the aggregate." (78)

"Stunned," as Dickens elsewhere describes another character, with a "weighty piece of fact," Louisa subsides into stoniness, to her father's relief. The language her father invokes, the "laws which govern lives in the aggregate," is the only language available to her as well, and she retreats into it. "Mr. Bounderby asks me to marry him. . . . The question I have to ask myself is, shall I marry him?" Her answer is, "what does it matter?" Even her stony father worries a little at this. He asks if she has any other romantic fancy. When she reminds him that such a thing is impossible given her education and her home for "what escape have I had from problems that could be demonstrated, and realities that could be grasped?" she "unconsciously close[s] her hand, as if upon a solid object, and slowly open[s] it as though she were releasing dust or ash" (79). Her reproach of him, when she reminds him that "you have been so careful of me that I have never had a child's heart," leads him only to say, "My dear Louisa . . . you abundantly repay my care. Kiss me, my dear girl" (79–80). And here we ask again: if the goal of his education was, as he reports, "so to educate you, as that you might, while still in your early youth, be (if I may so express myself) almost any age," a fact here confirmed by the Calmucks of Tartary, has he in fact been able to raise her as if she might be any gender, or is Dickens suggesting something particularly female about this quality of fire, of fancy, of realities that "can[not] be grasped," this quality of, shall we say, curiosity?

She might have answered her father differently, within even his own terms, and this is what the novel goes on to do, for as Ian Hacking pointed out in his book on the rise of probability, law (not least of all marriage law) is as much the home of probability as mathematics. In his brilliant chapter on Leibniz, probability, and law, Hacking reminds us that law is the primary place where questions of evidence emerge, precisely as probabilities where there is only testimony—the relationship between demonstration and testimony, between "what causes things to happen and what tells us that they happen."[8] As Hacking quotes Leibniz, "The whole of judicial procedure is nothing but a kind of logic applied to questions of law." "Mathematics is the model of reasoning about necessary truths," in Hacking's elegant summary, "but jurisprudence must be our model when we deliberate about contingencies." Mr. Gradgrind, of course, has the wrong kind of evidence, but he is not wrong to clutch at it—the delight of statistics with which we began, the realization that you can find patterns everywhere, can actually be of help in predicting what will happen when, and his reply about age differentials suggests he understands that something (something!) is wrong. But Dickens is pointing out the central point that Hacking makes about law, which he might make about novels as well: that "proof is a formal matter, attaching to the form of sentences, not their content" (137). The fact that you can "prove" it doesn't in any way make a proposition true.

The invocation of Bluebeard at this pivotal moment reminds us not only of the limits of statistics but also of a certain kind of realism: Gothic fairy tales will resurface; exceptions will plague the general, in fiction as in life; and however much Gradgrind thinks his education in ologies will triumph, a different project is under way in this novel. When Louisa fails either to point out her father's absurdity or examine her own heart, instead releasing the dust or ash from her hands, she is lost in the world of dry matter, and her father takes her silence to mean her education was a success. Such a girl, he thinks, will be a good wife. She will not wander; she will stay out of Bluebeard's chamber; she will never ask for his secret nor have secrets of her own. For Gradgrind, the end of the daughter's education is to make her not just free of gender, or at least of the whimsy he associates with femininity, but generalizable: he can marry her to any man, any Bluebeard, and have him never disappointed, her never wonder. But Louisa, as we know, already has a secret. She does not love Bounderby; she in fact despises him; she is marrying against a strong sense of personal revulsion. Earlier when he kissed her, she rubbed at the spot on her cheek as if she would rub it off and told her brother he could cut it out with a knife and she wouldn't cry out. In fact, she is marrying only to protect her brother, to give him the freedom, the leap into the "wild visionary," that she cannot imagine taking herself. So Dickens has already alerted us that Louisa will be no docile wife, no open book, no wonderless creature—she is her own little bundle of resistance and prepared to wander far: the "robber fancy," remember, is not killed but maimed and will strike back.

We might think ourselves awfully clever at this moment. We know, because we are canny Dickens readers, that this maimed, wandering, searching curiosity always held in reserve ("she answered with the old, quick, searching look of the night when she was found at the Circus; then cast down her eyes") will somehow make its way to the surface, like the fire of factories. "When night comes," Louisa reminds her father, "the fires burst out," and so, we think, with our keen grasp of metaphor, will she. We think Dickens has chosen Louisa for his education to carry out the same revolutionary message he instilled in the workers' bad education: without a proper goal for workers, there will be revolution; without a proper expression of desire for women, adultery; Louisa will, like the workers, "rebel." We think he has chosen a daughter to make her a wife, so that he can run an adultery plot to its bitter end and show that without emotional expression, without a visionary leap, all of life is mere materiality, mere sexuality, mere dust and ash.

The plot Dickens writes proves no such thing. The analogy works for Tom, who quite literally becomes a thief, as the *Arabian Nights* fable predicted, but not for Louisa. Daughters may be more impressionable than sons, but being her father's favorite also appears to have given Louisa some capacity for love, however much it is held in reserve. Louisa is clearly more capable of love than her brother, as she will later be more capable of taking on the "impressions" of someone else's love. Making Louisa, in the words of *Dombey and Son*, "a daughter after all" does not make Louisa an adulteress. But it does something far more important: it allows Dickens to pull us forward through the erotic draw of an adultery plot; it allows him to present his own version of the Bluebeard plot, as Louisa, at the end of book 1, turns her back on Stone Lodge, on Sissy's yearning look and loving eyes, and enters the violence of Bounderby's embrace, only to become a very different kind of Fatima. Dickens wants to write a plot not of sexual awakening but of both emotional and social curiosity—something we might loosely call novelistic curiosity—and for that, it would seem, he needs a curious woman and he needs her to make a bad marriage.

Dickens is brilliant in his misdirection, toying with our misreading constantly, knowing that we are reading for adultery, watching Louisa Bounderby walk down Mrs. Sparsit's staircase, waiting for a fall.[9] Book 1, the book in which Louisa chooses, ends with Louisa's disappearance into marriage, without another look at the loving Sissy and only a last clinging to her heartless brother. Book 2, the story of her marriage, begins not with her husband but with the introduction of her would-be seducer, James Harthouse, who is watching Louisa to see what makes her "brighten," what, to be vulgar, turns her on; it is his interest in the "stunning" woman that will draw him, and us, on. As Louisa starts to come to life, particularly given how strong our identification with her grew to be in book 1 (the portion of the book where we saw her struggling toward the light and failing), the experience of reading becomes terrifying for readers; it is as if we, too, were losing her. Hypnotized by Harthouse's interest in her brother, she seems to be indifferent to her fate, drawn not to some true affection, but to a darkness in him that mirrors her own. It seems that she can break out only by breaking down, breaking the law, breaking her vows. We, like Harthouse, think it will be a sexual awakening, but instead, Dickens gives us a story of coming to enlightenment, the story of her becoming a person.

Louisa has seen something terrible in the marriage chamber—and marriage is, as John Stuart Mill reminded us, a brilliant device for the opening up of persons to curiosity, requiring, as it does, the subsuming of the girl's identity into the wife's, the terrible forced intimacy of what Louisa calls the "tie" of marriage. But unlike other Fatimas, Louisa has no interest in her husband's locked chamber. As she remarks when he is pouting over her presumed indifference to him, "You are incomprehensible this morning.... Pray take no further trouble to explain yourself. I am not curious to know your meaning" (148) Again, she says, "What does it matter?" Far from entering her husband's locked chambers, she is a locked chamber herself—and not only for her husband and her would-be seducer. For Mrs. Sparsit, Bounderby's super-elegant, attenuated household companion, herself the image of Bluebeard's first, and still angry, wife, "[Louisa's] curious reserve did baffle, while it stimulated," while for her brother, "her thoughtfulness baffled his cunning scrutiny," but it is Harthouse who puts it best: "She baffled all penetration" (156, 74, 99).

And yet, if Louisa herself is the locked chamber ("Her features were handsome, but their natural play was so locked up, that it seemed impossible to guess their genuine expression" [99]), she is locked even for herself: the key rests outside of her, in her learning something that is not in her father's "general laws," "something genuine." The tragedy of the novel is that she doesn't know what that is, either—there is little "natural" or "genuine" in her. The usual travail of the realist novel, the question, what is life outside my sphere of existence? is here a highly personal question: what is it like to be a real person? Because of who Louisa is, raised as she was in the library of Blue Books, her personal curiosity takes on her father's social charge: how can we craft laws for other persons, until we know what a person is? Louisa's story, her "rise" into a better form of personhood, is made possible by the adultery plot, but not only by it. In fact, the changes that matter the most, those that open her up to a wider world of understanding and a world of feeling, began earlier—that trajectory, as we trace it, is not independent of her marriage (without the violence of Bounderby's household, would she have come to it at all?), but it is not necessarily contiguous with it. Louisa's progress into feeling subsumes her marriage plot—the marriage is an episode in a broader transformation; Bounderby is incidental to her growing awareness; and it is instead a series of departures from her marital abode (into the homes of the factory workers; into the garden of the adultery plot; and back into her father's house) that forms the map of her education. For all of Louisa's passion, not sexual wickedness but a different version of curiosity, the curiosity that comes (as it does for all Bluebeard's wives, after the marriage ceremony) with both a sense of justice and a sense of novelistic inquisitiveness, is what will save her—inasmuch as she can, after the initial violence of her father's darkening shadow, be saved at all.

The transformation begins when Louisa returns to Stone Lodge to see her mother, who is dying, and Dickens's sense of novelistic depth begins fully to emerge as well.[10] When Louisa returns to her father's house, the home of the "grim statistical clock," the Sphinx of enlightenment is not, as most readers assume, her Bluebeard father or Sissy of the "sweet face with the trusting eyes," but her mother, the world's least likely oracle. Readers heretofore delighted by the baroque comedy of Mrs. Gradgrind may be surprised as she slips into meaningfulness: how did Mrs. Gradgrind get wise? Dickens has been subtly preparing us for this, for she has performed the oracular once before, with her brilliant pronouncement on Louisa's engagement:

> "Oh!" said Mrs. Gradgrind, "so you have settled it! Well, I'm sure I hope your health may be good, Louisa; for if your head begins to split as soon as you are married, which was the case with mine, I cannot consider that you are to be envied, though I have no doubt you think you are, as all girls do. However, I give you joy, my dear—and I hope you may now turn all your ological studies to good account, I am sure I do! I must give you a kiss of congratulation, Louisa; but don't touch my right shoulder, for there's something running down it all day long." (80)

To readers as skeptical as Mrs. Gradgrind (or Sissy) of the impending bliss of this couple, the account of marriage as your head beginning to split is astonishingly accurate—and reminds us that that wherever Louisa goes, she is still following the tracks of the Bluebeard plot. The verbal play also allows us a moment of Dickensian delight in the precision of the "right shoulder" with "something running down it all day long," but the sudden moment of depth also offers an alternative account of Mrs. Gradgrind's own blighted state. She may not always have been "a transparency without enough light behind it"; she, too, may have been stunned into idiocy by the constant shower of fact.

But this whimsical moment does not entirely prepare us or Louisa for what we see in the scene in which, as Dickens puts it, "the light that had always been feeble and dim behind the weak transparency, went out." The mother who first named the "ologies" now attempts to supplement them by something she cannot name:

> You learnt a great deal, Louisa, and so did your brother. Ologies of all kinds from morning to night. If there is any Ology left, of any description, that has not been worn to rags in this house, all I can say is, I hope I shall never hear its name. . . . But there is something—not an Ology at all—that your father has missed, or forgotten, Louisa. I don't know what it is. I have often sat with Sissy near me, and thought about it. I shall never get its name now. But your father may. It makes me restless. I want to write to him, to find out for God's sake, what it is. Give me a pen, give me a pen. (151–52)

"It makes me restless"; I want him "to find out for God's sake"; "give me a pen"—this is powerful stuff. The missing knowledge must somehow be conveyed to the father—but alas, it cannot, and she cannot hold a pen. Yet she "fancies that her request had been complied with." "It matters little what figures of wonderful no-meaning she began to trace upon her wrappers . . . [for] the hand soon stopped in the midst of them," but that impulse to find some other form of knowledge, "something not an Ology at all," pervades the rest of the book.

Mrs. Gradgrind's sense that Louisa's father has missed or forgotten something tallies interestingly with Louisa's growing sense that her husband is, shall we say, "missing" something—that there is something she must "find out" that her husband cannot see, as well as something that he does not want her to see. Louisa sees much more of her husband's closeted life (at least, his life apart from her) when she is forced to sit through his humiliation of the one worker we get to know well in the novel, Stephen Blackpool. He has first come to Bounderby's house to inquire about the possibility of divorcing his drunken, errant wife (he cannot, of course, without an act of Parliament), but the divorce is only part of how he enters the novel: the rest is as a worker who refuses to join the union, refuses to articulate a clear position for the workers ("It's a' a muddle," he says repeatedly), and is eventually captured in a plot by the whelp-like Tom Gradgrind. Blackpool then falls into an empty mine shaft (shafted) only to die a poignant and still muddled death. But his interactions with Bounderby, and hence with Louisa, are far more interesting than that maudlin plot suggests. Bounderby first interrogates him about his reasons for not joining the workers' strike and then fires him (bizarrely) for remaining loyal to the firm while still having opinions of his own. Interestingly, throughout the interview scene in the Bounderby home, Stephen has found himself watching Louisa—and her eyes guide him to the door, after the first of his passionate speeches. Louisa, having been stunned herself, knows and cares enough to tell him not to speak—not to be that "representative" worker Bounderby longs to have him be. But in defiance of her warning not to challenge her husband further, he stays to speak again—and it is at that moment that her husband gives Stephen notice, in effect (since, having been "turned out" at Bounderby's, he will not be hired anywhere else) dooming him to starvation. And here our attention switches back to the wife, for Louisa has just watched her husband sentence a man (a man currently in Coventry, a form of social death, for loyalty to Bounderby's own works) to death.

What drives Louisa to want to see more, to seek out Stephen's home, is more than pity. Rather, Louisa feels a curiosity born out of her sense of justice—one, we might note, nurtured in her father's, not her husband's home—as well as a sense of personal outrage at her husband. Not only does she recognize in the tale of Stephen's miserable marriage her own misery, but she also measures again her husband's misunderstanding of her own sense of ethics. In his injustice toward his workers, and his confidence that she will share his contempt for them, she feels his deeper injustice toward her, his assumption (one that anticipates Casaubon's condescension toward Dorothea Brooke) that she will see things only through his eyes, the ultimate Bluebeard crime, that of subsuming his wife's ability to choose.

And here for the first time she is truly a Fatima, choosing to know, for this is what leads her to open the closet door, to follow her newfound interest and sympathy not into her husband's secrets but into Stephen Blackpool's rooms. Her first impulse seems to be a sociological curiosity—the same desire that led her to the circus, to see what something is like. "For the first time in her life," the narrator tells us, "Louisa, had come into one of the dwellings of the Coketown Hands; for the first time in her life she was face to face with anything like individuality in connection with them" (120). She retains briefly the sociological detachment her education imparted ("She stood for some moments looking round the room. From the few chairs, the few books, the common prints, and the bed, she glanced to the two women, and to Stephen") but that education is precisely what is challenged at this moment:

> She knew of their existence by hundreds and by thousands. She knew what results in work a given number of them would produce in a given space of time. She knew them in crowds passing to and from their nests, like ants or beetles. But she knew from her reading infinitely more of the ways of toiling insects than of these toiling men and women. (120)

One mark of the cleverness of Dickens's Bluebeard revision is that in no other novel could the mere recitation of social statistics ("workers are like ants or beetles") remind us that we are in the marriage plot! But the reminder that Louisa knows the world only through large numbers reminds us also of the failures of *imagination* that led to her disastrous marriage. We are suddenly back in the same war of reading methods that we saw in her father's study, reminded that her reading has not been imaginative, not novelistic or metaphorical, but statistical. It produces, as Sissy pointed out long ago, not individuals but "crowds," or, as we learn again in the next paragraph, "laws":

> Something to be worked so much and paid so much, and there ended; something to be infallibly settled by laws of supply and demand; something that blundered against those laws, and floundered into difficulty; something that was a little pinched when wheat was dear, and over-ate itself when wheat was cheap; something that increased at such a rate of percentage, and yielded such another percentage of crime, and such another percentage of pauperism; something wholesale, of which vast fortunes were made; something that occasionally rose like a sea, and did some harm and waste (chiefly to itself), and fell again; this she knew the Coketown Hands to be. But, she had scarcely thought more of separating them into units, than of separating the sea itself into its component drops. (121)

This is the language that Sissy implicitly criticized long ago: the laws of supply and demand, something "a little pinched," "something that increased at such a rate of percentage." Rates, percentage, units, blunder. In the past, we thought this was bad language because it didn't incorporate the depths of individual character, and in this way, too, Sissy was there as the disproving as well as disapproving exception, a separate unit, a dark-haired, warm-eyed singularity. Even Mr. Gradgrind, noting regretfully Sissy's "very limited acquaintance with figures," has second thoughts. "Somehow or other, he had become possessed by an idea that there was something in this girl which could hardly be set forth in a tabular form. Her capacity of definition might be easily stated at a very low figure, her mathematical knowledge at nothing; yet he was not sure that if he had been required, for example, to tick her off into columns in a parliamentary return, he would have quite known how to divide her" (73). This idea of Sissy as having something that couldn't be "set forth in tabular form" does double duty, though: it is like Dickens's idea that a fictional person must be more; it is also akin to Louisa's idea here, in Stephen's room, that she must do what she never did before and "separate [the Hands] into units." But where for Mr. Gradgrind this is an idea of a self that cannot be divided ("ticked ... off into columns"), a self that cannot be accounted for in his well-meaning but blundering social system, a failure, for Louisa, this moment of "separating" the sea into "component drops," finding an individual unit, is the beginning of feeling, of understanding a different form of representation.

Dickens here connects the very machinery of realism, the "sympathy" it conjures, with the flatness of character for which his own fiction was so often, and particularly after the play of *Bleak House*, chided. He is unflattening Louisa before our eyes, giving her emotional depth—but he is also marking, much as John Stuart Mill does in his autobiography, the near impossibility of generating feeling out of nothingness, out of ash, out of statistics. For Louisa, trying that sympathy on for the first time (remember, she is not a reader of fiction), this is a sympathy that confuses itself as it grows, and the narrator tracks its growth. We list her failings: she "redden[ed] at her mistake" after addressing Rachael as Stephen's wife; "her manner was short and abrupt, yet faltering and timid"; she "turned her head to him, and bent it with a deference that was new in her. She looked from him to Rachael, and her features softened. 'What will you do?' she asked him. And her voice had softened too." We are watching her at the scene's climax, as she tries to perform a compassion she has always wanted to feel: we watch her literally reach out to express her new understanding and fail to cross the gap:

> Louisa looked, in part incredulous, in part frightened, in part overcome with quick sympathy, when this man of so much self-command, who had been so plain and steady through the late interview, lost his composure in a moment, and now stood with his hand before his face. She stretched out hers, as if she would have touched him; then checked herself, and remained still. (122)

Louisa's sudden "stillness" marks her response to her own feeling, a "quick[ening of] sympathy" that threatens to "overcome" her but also frightens her, in which she cannot quite believe. She is watching someone else be overcome, but she is not quite overcome herself. It is a *curiosity* about feeling, rather than a feeling entirely free to express itself. Louisa is again testing, "proving," to use Gradgrind's word. She must determine for herself those abstractions, how it is we come to feel, how we recognize another person, how we become persons ourselves.

This is the story of marital separation—the legal debate that frames the novel—for both Louisa and (wistfully) for Dickens himself, lonely in his own marriage. But it is even more powerfully the idea of "separating" people into individual "drops"—it is the story of disaggregation rather than adultery. Louisa's emotional transformation, her sentimental education, reaches a climax in the scene that we think will bring the revelation of her fall into adultery but instead marks the collapse of her father's system of education, her final return to the first Bluebeard's castle, and her fall into insensibility. After being followed by Mrs. Sparsit into what seems to be an adulterous tryst, Louisa instead appears at her father's door, wet and shaking and terrified, and offers not a confession of adultery but her own savage indictment of both her father and herself:

> Yet, father, if I had been stone blind; if I had groped my way by my sense of touch, and had been free, while I knew the shapes and surfaces of things, to exercise my fancy somewhat, in regard to them; I should have been a million times wiser, happier, more loving, more contented, more innocent and human in all good respects, than I am with the eyes I have. (164)

At this moment Louisa imagines herself outside the realm of the human, merely a curiosity, not just "stone blind" but turned to stone, unwise, unhappy, and, even if she is not guilty, she is certainly not innocent. Her misery is the clearest indictment of her father's "system" of education, and what she needs is a new lesson, one essentially in personhood:

> "All that I know is, your philosophy and your teaching will not save me. Now, father, you have brought me to this. Save me by some other means!" He tightened his hold in time to prevent her sinking on the floor, but she cried out in a terrible voice, "I shall die if you hold me! Let me fall upon the ground!" And he laid her down there, and saw the pride of his heart and the triumph of his system, lying, an insensible heap, at his feet. (165)

That moment, when he sees the daughter he loved best of his children lying at his feet, fallen, is the moment when his pride (as well as his defiance of a world of curiosity and wonder) must give way to something else—but Dickens registers this not as enlightenment, but as sheer Gothic horror. Louisa's voice, as she prepares to fall, is "terrible" and so is her fall.

The fall here, as the initial fall into "idle curiosity" suggested, is a fall into personhood, a fall that undoes the general and makes one an individual—both in the early sense of "part of something bigger" and our modern sense of "uniquely alone." In much the same way that Sissy represents a unit that cannot be "divided," and Stephen Blackpool becomes more than an "insect" or a "wave," so Louisa wants to be a person. And this is what the marriage plot, with its Bluebeard violence and its sense of dark secrets, has unexpectedly accomplished. Louisa has come up against the law—in the sense of the "general laws" her father has expressed, and that of Victorian laws of marriage, but also in the deeper sense in which every marriage is a testing of individual persons against the statistical norm, the other version of what Mill called "doing what everyone does." The language of political economy and industrial relations here meets up in an entirely unexpected way with the language of romantic love and marriage, much as the unexpected confluence of Stephen's and Louisa's plots entangled the two characters with each other. The repression of the workers seems to shadow forth the constraints against wives, but the two do not form a real equivalency: once again, Dickens tries out an abstract social language only to turn instead to the language of an almost perverse singularity, the language of character. It is only by trying to join a union, one might joke, that Louisa has realized she was an individual after all—although the ferocity with which she expresses this is no laughing matter. As she says to her father, explaining the failure of her marriage, "[Something in me] rose up into rebellion against the tie, the old strife, made fiercer by all those causes of disparity which arise out of our two individual natures, and which no general laws shall ever rule or state for me, father, until they shall be able to direct the anatomist where to strike his knife into the secrets of my soul."

Louisa does not desire a more perfect union: instead, what she has sought all along are the "secrets of her soul." This was the locked chamber to which she (again, both Bluebeard and Fatima) wanted the key. What she has always wanted—what her mysterious "passion," her "idle curiosity," the self held in "reserve" sought all along—was to escape, finally, the general: the laws her father expressed, the laws she now turns against. No law can know the secret self; no law can "state [it] for me." We might say, in fact, that what Louisa wants is precisely to *have* a secret. The plot offers her several (that Sissy is waiting for her father's letter, that Tom has robbed a bank, that she herself is contemplating adultery), but they are not enough: they are not a secret about her inner self. Nothing in her story has provided one—and Dickens is looking at her, analytically, from the position of the novelist himself often mocked for his flat characters, wondering what he can put inside her.

This is where Fatima's curiosity is not only pedagogical ("what shall we teach?") or epistemological ("what do I know? I am a secret to myself") but representational: "how can I tell?" Representation here poses two problems—both Dickens's question of how to represent Louisa's transformation and her question of how to account for what she has learned in Stephen's chambers. The novelistic version is a complexity we have hitherto associated with Thackeray: there is no single answer to "is she guilty or not?" for even Louisa cannot "state" the secrets of her soul. But surprisingly, the social version is equally complex: Gradgrind's statistical tables might have begun with the idea that aggregates of suffering tell us where a society must be mended, but the brokenness of Louisa reminds us that individual selves are less easily repaired—less easily rendered (in every sense of that word) whole. How then is Louisa to master the arts of representation? How to "tell" what she has seen—and what has been done to her? Louisa's exclamation of her own failures is offered by Louisa herself and by Dickens not as an excuse but as a plea for true understanding: that there might in fact be secrets that do not fit in tables or in curiosity cabinets; there might be some fragments of self (and there should be) that escape the social. But in what way would that be sufficient?

This is the moment to return to the problem of general laws, probabilities, and realisms with which we began this chapter: in what way is Louisa's marriage expressed, and in which ways obliterated, by national statistics of unequal marriages? What is the relationship between the general and specific not only as a system of justice but also as a novelistic system, something integral not just to realism but to curiosity as a way of knowing? This is where precisely the question of law as form, as a problem of evidence and probabilities, started us going in the Bluebeard plot, when Louisa asked her father about her marriage: What are the laws that should tell us how to conduct ourselves? What are the probabilities of comfort and understanding, of sympathy and curiosity, which might govern realism? Or as Ian Hacking puts it, what do we do when "the stories of witnesses may go against the common run of things?"[11]

The Whelp, Tom Gradgrind, by far the worst probabilist as well as the worst person in the novel, invokes general laws in defense of his guilt, grumbling, "I don't see why," when his father expresses horror at the robbery he has committed. "So many people are employed in situations of trust; so many people, out of so many, will be dishonest. I have heard you talk, a hundred times, of its being a law. How can I help laws? You have comforted others with such things, father. Comfort yourself!"[12] But Louisa and her father cannot be comforted by this kind of formalism; there is no comfort at all in the general in this novel—as, indeed, is there ever any in life? "I had proved my—my system to myself, and I have rigidly administered it, and I must bear the responsibility of its failures. I only entreat you to believe, my favourite child, that I have meant to do right," says Louisa's father, as he turns to her in despair, as he sees her collapsed at his feet. As the broken-down Mr. Gradgrind reports to his truly brokenhearted daughter, "There is a wisdom of the Head, and . . . there is a wisdom of the Heart" (168) but he cannot instruct her in the latter. For that, Mr. Gradgrind proposes that they turn to Sissy, seeking a way out of the law of the head, wanting against all their experience of testing a way of proving themselves exceptional, individual, singular; of saying, as Louisa did on the night her father gave her away in marriage, "I speak of my own life."

Critics have scorned these answers, believing that Dickens, like Gradgrind, wants us to turn to Sissy, to the wisdom of circus clowns, abandoned children, and the dogs who love them; they believe that Sissy ("girl number twenty") can teach us what a person is ("give me your definition of a person."). But they have misunderstood deeply, I think, the sophistication of this novel. They are right that Sissy is put into the novel to embody feeling naïvely, purely, endlessly.[13] Sissy's heart is constantly on parade as an agent of change in the novel, as if she were a walking pamphlet whose singular mission were to teach others how to love. Gradgrind himself, no mush-head he, must finally concede that it is the "stroller's child" who rescues his daughter, saves his family, and keeps his son from certain disgrace and imprisonment. This is entirely unlike the talking, reasoning, hardheaded system he has propelled, but as he says, sitting by his daughter's bedside, playing with her hair, "I have a misgiving that some change may have been slowly working about me in this house, by mere love and gratitude: that what the Head had left undone and could not do, the Heart may have been doing silently" (168). Oh wondrous, silent, slow Sissy, we are meant to remark.

But no one, least of all Dickens, can want Louisa Bounderby to turn into Sissy. There's simply no novel there. Furthermore, even if we wanted such a thing, Louisa can't be Sissy, nor can Mr. Gradgrind—if nothing else, they lack a drunken-clown father and a dog named Merrylegs, and they didn't have the benefit of being raised in a circus. And they wouldn't be much use to Dickens if they had, for Sissy is neither a novelist nor a member of Parliament, and she cannot answer any of the deeper questions Dickens is asking, about his own or about the heroine's curiosity. The answers to these questions (What are we to do in the world? What are our relations with other people to be? What is the secret of the self?) are far beyond Sissy's experience.

For these things, you need a form of representation that gives you the social knowledge implicit in statistics but that also allows you the power of law—something that returns erotic, connective, curious energy to individuals while allowing them some larger vista. This is Louisa's quest but it is the novel's as well: the novel wants to figure out what a person is, to fulfill the anxiety we have seen since *Clarissa*: what is a form of redress or justice that allows for self-representation? In some ways, *Hard Times* says there ain't no such thing: any system of justice will involve a set of "general laws," statistics, stuttering, all of which of necessity inflict a violence against an individual person. Forms of organized power want us to believe we are persons, have secrets, are stronger than mere metaphor, at the same time that they make us all the same, subjects, part of a system. Bentham, for all of his humanity, is the figure for that erasure, and Gradgrind's Blue Books stand in his stead; this is why the empty Harthouse, who feels that "nothing matters," can be their boy. But Louisa Bounderby, trapped in Bluebeard's closet, draws a different picture of a person: a violent and desperate attempt to insert a soul, to make a person more than a statistical variant. Her sympathy for Stephen Blackpool, for remaindered people, is very different: What if Louisa were in a position to speak for the people left out by the stuttering tables? And what if Dickens were, similarly, to imagine different kinds of persons?

In part, this is what he has been doing throughout his career: depicting the parts of Victorian society that no one else saw, so much so that his novels become their own register, their own tables, their own collections of ordinary life. As Trollope described it,

> No other writer of English language except Shakespeare has left so many types of character as Dickens has done.—characters which are known by their names familiarly as household words, and which bring to our minds vividly and at once, a certain well-understood set of ideas, habits, phrases and costumes, making together a man, or woman, or child, whom we know at glance and recognize at a sound,—as we do our intimate friends. . . . [These characters, including Pickwick and Sam Weller, Mrs. Gamp, Bucket the Detective] are persons so well known to us that we think that they, who are in any way of the professions of these worthies, are untrue to themselves if they depart in aught from their recognised and understood portraits. Pickwick can never be repeated. . . . But a "boots" at an hotel is more of a boots the closer he resembles Sam Weller.[14]

Dickens's ability to recount the people around him is so intense that he is his own geography and directory: "We have heard,—we do not know whether correctly or incorrectly,—that he can go down a crowded street and tell you all that is in it, what shop each was, what the grocer's name was, how many scraps of orange-peel there were on the pavement."[15] But this ability to fill a canvas with types of people is precisely what filled critics with rage, and nowhere was this clearer than in the criticism of *Bleak House*, where critics fumed about "the whole Dedlock set, [which] might be eliminated from the book without damage to the great Chancery suit, or perceptible effect upon the remaining characters. We should then have less crowd, and no story; and the book might be called 'Bleak House, or the Odd Folks that have to do with a long Chancery Suit.' This would give an exact notion of the contents of a collection of portraits embracing suitors, solicitors, law-writers, law-stationers, money-lenders, law-clerks, articled and not-articled, with their chance friends and visitors, and various members of their respective families. Even then, a comprehensive etcetera would be needed for supernumeraries."[16]

Dickens, of course, loved his supernumeraries (Really? Would *Bleak House* exist without the whole Dedlock set?), and he has his own little joke about this when Louisa Bounderby finally goes to the circus. When she does, at the end of the novel, among the characters she meets is "the Emperor of Japan, on a steady old white horse stencilled with black spots, [who] was twirling five wash-hand basins at once, as it is the favourite recreation of that monarch to do. Sissy, though well acquainted with his Royal line, had no personal knowledge of the present Emperor, and his reign was peaceful" (208). The Emperor is of course not a person; he is a role played by a juggler in the circus, and in the time the novel has lasted (the time that Sissy has been away from the circus) one Emperor/juggler has died and another (or several others?) taken his place in turn. He is like a parody of a fictional character—and he is both a wry comment on Dickens's critics ("So crowded is the canvas which Mr Dickens has stretched, and so casual the connexion that give to his composition whatever unity it has, that a daguerreotype of Fleet Street at noon-day would be the aptest symbol to be found for it")[17] and Dickens's attempt to reimagine Gradgrind's "drops of water in the sea."

So the Emperor of Japan is no joke. His representation is instead the experiment of Dickens's fiction—what Dickens and Louisa Bounderby learned from Bluebeard. It is a story at once of social individuation and character eccentricity, carried out with a stunning minimalism—here, a stroller's child; there, a man going in for camels; and, in the novel's climax, a young man balancing five washbasins at once. Think again of the problem posed by statistics, which we need to take seriously as the attempt of the party of fact to imagine a whole society. Statistical tables, much like a curiosity cabinet or a novel, are not only an attempt to measure suffering but also an attempt to give us the whole world in a single box, to "represent" everything. Is that not exactly what *Hard Times* is doing? It is its own "copy" of the world, its own mimetic experiment, and it has to move from representation to identification to justice—the thing we imagine a truly political form of fiction would offer. Critics have argued that England has no political fiction because of the failure of Chartism, the great working-class movement of the 1840s, but *Hard Times* is clearly a novel shaped by and yet aloof from Chartism, trying to imagine some different relationship to alienated labor of both workers and wives. Stephen Blackpool can describe maimed workers and noble characters, but he cannot articulate a political platform, any more than the damaged Gradgrind can—but Dickens can, and it would be a political program in which strollers' children and failed dandies and young men with five washbasins would still *count*.

But Gradgrind and Blackpool don't get to speak. It is Louisa who speaks, and behind her the figure of John Stuart Mill, about to introduce into Parliament a motion for the inclusion of women as legal persons in the suffrage in England. It is they who can pose the question, how is it that I get to be a person, too? John Stuart Mill, at the end of his "mental crisis," learned that all the reform in the world would not make him happy; Louisa has faced her own collapse as "the collapse of the system"—how, out of these two systems, the one political and the other romantic, are we to create the possibility of reformation of people or of the world? Dickens's brilliant and unexpected answer is to do so through that legal nonperson, that statistical nonentity, a wife. More particularly, a woman separated from her husband, a double-ghost, if you will, ghosted in the first place by her disappearance into the coverture of marriage; in the second by her loss of even that legal status, someone absolutely without place—and perhaps, for that reason, without anything chaining her to convention.

Dickens wants to be a better Gradgrind, a better Bluebeard, and in creating his prototype of the heroine, he wants to build a better Bluebeard's wife. He not only wants the daughter to be seduced by wonder; he also wants her to retain her curiosity, stay skeptical, to fall (as he wants us to fall) in more interesting ways. The cultivation of curiosity, even more than "figures of wonderful no-meaning," is the business of the realist novel—not only "general laws" but also eccentric examples, proving a system only by testing it, testing and tricking and battering readers, as Dickens tests and tricks and baffles his heroine. This does not, however, make for happy endings. Realism, though it can teach us new ways of counting as well as being people, though it can expand the gaze of the skeptical heroine, though it can break and remake hearts, cannot do everything. Undoing Gradgrind's calculations, undoing self-interest and the general laws, offering the living texts of sentimental characters, seems to undo the harsher lessons of the Bluebeard plot, but it cannot. As Louisa stares into the fire at the end of the novel and is allowed prophetic wisdom, she is allowed to see "Happy Sissy's happy children loving her; all children loving her; she, grown learned in childish lore; thinking no innocent and pretty fancy ever to be despised; trying hard to know her humbler fellow-creatures, and to beautify their lives of machinery and reality with those imaginative graces and delights." She learns the value of "a childhood of the mind no less than a childhood of the body, . . . knowing it to be even a more beautiful thing, and a possession, any hoarded scrap of which, is a blessing and happiness to the wisest." But she does not see "herself again a wife—a mother—ever watchful of her children." *Hard Times* offers no new birth to its heroine and is in fact one of the bleakest postmarriage epics of the Victorian period.[18] The fairy tale ends with no weddings and no christenings: Sissy marries without our knowing whom; if little Jane marries (not to mention little Adam Smith and little Malthus Gradgrind), we do not hear of it. Tom dies trying to return to his sister's side, penitent at last but failing still, again, always, and Louisa (who loved him both erotically and maternally) has no children to take his place. But this is the final sign, is it not? of the disaster of the marriage to Bounderby for, as with so many miserable unions in the Victorian novel (Grandcourt and Gwendolen, Dorothea and Casaubon, Edith and Dombey), this one will bear no fruit. And so to the extent that being a person in the Victorian novel always means re-creating yourself in the form of children, the most powerful version of the copy, Louisa is entirely exiled from the realm of the personal. We might be forgiven for doubting that there are any new beginnings here– why should any Gradgrind escape the wintry blight of Fact and generate a new Fiction?

There might, though, be a promise of hope in a different future—that wild escape into something visionary that Louisa Bounderby imagined. Her father claimed that there was "a wisdom of the heart" as well as a "wisdom of the head." What if there were also a "law of the heart"? That is the Sissy Jupe version of the novel speaking, of course—but is it only that? What if someone who had entered Bluebeard's chamber, someone who had learned the painful lessons of individuation, were subsequently in a position to create a new law? What if, now that Jem Harthouse is abandoning Coketown and going in for camels, Louisa Bounderby could stand for Parliament in his place? If she is not going to be a novelist, why not a member of Parliament? We might imagine her as that ultimate paradox, the woman who understands statistics and understands broken hearts as well—for, as a contemporary theorist of statistics has argued, "I keep saying the sexy job in the next ten years will be statisticians. People think I'm joking, but who would've guessed that computer engineers would've been the sexy job of the 1990s?"[19] With her interest in unlocking doors, her curiosity about the human soul, and her wide statistical grasp of the entire population of England (and, of course, of the Calmucks of Tartary), wouldn't Louisa be exactly the "representative" we all crave? Only, of course, if Mrs. Jellyby and Miss Wisk have their way, and only at the neglect of Louisa's "domestic mission." But in a world that was differently ordered, perhaps "when George the Fourth was still reigning over the privacies of Windsor, when the Duke of Wellington was Prime Minister, and Mr. Vincy was mayor of the old corporation in Middlemarch, and Mrs. Casaubon, born Dorothea Brooke, had taken her wedding journey to Rome,"[20] the singular heroine might in fact find another way of being "representative." Then the curious daughter might find her own way into the Blue Books and find yet another threshold to cross. She might, ghostlike and curious, find out the thing that Dorothea Brooke wants to know, "how to lead a grand life here—now—in England" (27) but that question will have to wait for another decade, a second reform bill, and another novelist.

CHAPTER 7

George Eliot and the Curious Bride

Ghosts in the Daylight

In Chinese tradition, a *ghost marriage* (also known as a 冥婚*Minghun* or *spirit marriage*) is a marriage in which one or both parties are deceased. Other forms of ghost marriage are practiced worldwide, from Sudan, to India, to France since 1959. The origins of Chinese ghost marriage are largely unknown, and reports of it being practiced today can still be found.[1]

But she should be dressed as a nun; I think she looks almost what you call a Quaker; I would dress her as a nun in my picture. However, she is married; I saw her wedding-ring on that wonderful left hand, otherwise I should have thought the sallow *Geistlicher* was her father.

George Eliot, *Middlemarch*

Here came the terror. Quick, quick, like pictures in a book beaten open.
George Eliot, *Daniel Deronda*

In my chapter on *Hard Times*, I argued that Louisa Bounderby is "really" John Stuart Mill, and that Dickens, to the extent that he is engaged with an essentially utilitarian project of deciding what a legal person is and if a woman can be one, wants simply to be a better Gradgrind. But if I were to write that novel again, in 1871, I would have to write it differently. I would call my curious heroine Dorothea Brooke; I would make my novelist a brilliant woman who writes under a male pseudonym; and I would make the whole novel a weird tribute to John Stuart Mill, one that answers not only the explicit question it asks, "how to lead a grand life here—now—in England?"[2] but also an implicit question: what is a curious woman to do with her life? If I did write that novel, and if I called it *Middlemarch*, I would have to do something else that never occurred to Dickens—I would have had to make it a ghost story. And then I would have to follow it with another, even darker novel, in which a passionate and angry woman stands before a not-yet-curious-enough heroine and says, "I am a woman's life,"[3] and makes it a curse. By then, of course, I would have written *Daniel Deronda* and I would have reached the end of a certain tradition of the curious heroine, but I would have done something else: I would have imagined the curious woman as not only a (sometimes fearless, sometimes fearful) investigator, I would have reimagined her as a force for justice, and I would have made my alternative tradition of the novel matter. But for that, I, myself, would have to be a ghostwriter.

And so was George Eliot.[4] She began her career as a translator and editor, writing the words of others, and she went on to write fiction under an assumed name. But she did more than write as someone else—she lived as someone else, adopting a series of fictional (legal) identities. She had, by the late 1860s when she started *Middlemarch*, been living with George Henry Lewes for more than fifteen years, their relationship a victim of divorce laws that stated that because Lewes had been on the birth certificate for one of the children his wife bore to another man (and hence, had "accepted" her adultery), he was unable to sue for divorce. Nevertheless, Eliot considered herself married to Lewes in much the kind of marriage Mill imagined, one of freedom and perfect sympathy. She dedicated books to him as her husband, signed herself Mrs. Lewes, and asked that her friends and publisher write to her as Mrs. Lewes, in spite of the fact that, as Gordon Haight wryly notes, "Mrs Lewes lived at 26 Bedford Place with four young children." But as for "Miss Marian Evans," as Haight tersely but elegantly put it, "except on legal documents, Miss Evans had ceased to exist."[5] At the same time, of course, she wrote under yet another name, George Eliot, in a kind of parody of the marketplace's invisible hand, shaping the lives of other imaginary people. So, we might note, Marian Evans, publishing fiction as someone else, was a made-up person in a made-up marriage making up other lives, many of them, of course, the lives of fabulists living under assumed names, with secret pasts, and inheritances and debts as yet unknown to them, which only the invisible hand of the author will reveal through time and plot. It is no wonder, then, that George Eliot came to be considerably more skeptical of that legal fiction, marriage, than John Stuart Mill, and commensurately somewhat more skeptical of legal reform.

Even if you agreed with me that George Eliot was a professional ghostwriter, you still might argue that none of the identities she assumed was that of John Stuart Mill, but that would have been less clear if you were a Victorian reader. An 1875 volume called *Men of the Time* purveyed the following story about George Eliot:

> She is the daughter of a poor clergyman, but in early life was adopted by a wealthy clergyman who gave her a first-class education when she left school, which happened when she was very young.... [When she joined the *Westminster Review*,] by her intimacy with Mr John Stuart Mill and others, she became confirmed in their peculiar religious and philosophical view.[6]

Playing Athena to John Stuart Mill's Zeus was clearly no fantasy of George Eliot, who snapped the following reply to Elizabeth Stuart Phelps, when the latter questioned her about this account:

> I never—to answer one of your questions directly—I never had any personal acquaintance with J.S. Mill—never saw him to my knowledge, except in the House of Commons; and though I have studied his books, especially his Logic and Political Economy, with much benefit, I have no consciousness of their having made any marked epoch in my life.[7]

Strong words, and very much the language of Eliot's novels: the "marked epoch" is precisely what the spiritual transformations of *Middlemarch* and *Daniel Deronda* encourage us to look for, and the author is telling us there is none of that going on here. But with all respect to George Eliot, she and Mill do share a "peculiar religious and philosophical view," and it is a remarkable cocktail of curiosity, marriage, law, and mystery, and like all the best mysteries, it requires a ghost.

Though his mentor, Jeremy Bentham, believed in ghosts, John Stuart Mill (not surprisingly) did not—but he was not above telling a good ghost story when it served his polemical purposes, and so he does in "On Liberty." There, he tells the story of a man who attempts to do with his property what others do not like—for, as Mill reminds us, "The man, and still more the woman, who can be accused either of doing 'what nobody does,' or of not doing 'what everybody does' is the subject of as much depreciatory remark as if he or she had committed some grave moral delinquency."[8] As Mill puts it, "Originality is the one thing which unoriginal minds cannot feel the use of.... They cannot see what it is to do for them; how should they? If they could see what it would do for them, it would not be originality" (65). And Mill further reminds us of what is political, what is dangerous, and what is ghastly in this singularity. Those people who "allow themselves much of that indulgence" of "doing as they like" incur the risk of "something worse than disparaging speeches—they are in peril," he says, of "a *commission de lunatico*, and of having their property taken from them and given to their relations" (68). In an astonishing footnote, Mill remarks on the ease with which "any person can be judicially declared unfit for the management of his affairs and after his death, his disposal of his property can be set aside." "So far from setting any value on individuality—so far from respecting the right of each individual to act, in things indifferent as seems good to his own judgment and inclination, judges and juries cannot even conceive that a person in a state of sanity can desire such freedom." Yet Mill's description of the dead person still haunting the house, unable to dispose of his affairs, to manage his *story* after his own death, is also the legal status of every wife under the law, every woman who cannot dispose of her property or manage her affairs once married; who in essence has no freedom to act at all. Mill stunningly anticipates the way Eliot will put her heroines within the tangle of inheritance law, unable to control their own fortunes, let alone those of their husbands—but what he notes most clearly are the limits of female experimentation. If in the "Subjection of Women," he will try to imagine the "consciousness a woman would have [after the franchise] of being a human being like any other, entitled to choose her pursuits, urged or invited by the same inducements as any one else to interest herself in whatever is interesting to human beings" (200), here he meets up with the limitations not just of society but of law: "On women this sentence . . . of passing their lives in doing one thing reluctantly and ill, when there are other things which they could have done well and happily . . . is imposed by actual law, and by customs equivalent to law" (216). Law, custom, *commissions de lunatico*: everywhere, women are told they are free to choose, are expected to choose wisely for they will choose only once, and instead, everywhere, they are (as Mill puts it) "compelled" or (as we might put it) "ghosted."

This is the language of liberty with which we began this study ("if ever a woman chose freely, she did," said Isabel Archer), but here we are, in England in the 1870s, in the midst of feminist agitations for the vote and debates over property laws for women, and here we find George Eliot invoking John Stuart Mill's vision to reinflect the curious heroine and bring a ghost story to life. But Eliot has been reading the same books we have, and her "novelization" of John Stuart Mill blends his politics with a generous borrowing from the Bluebeard tale, that other mixture of curiosity, marriage, law, and mystery. For Mill, remember, the dominant language is one of contract, even when dealing with that strangest of legal contracts, the marriage bond. Mill's story goes like this: we know; we choose; we contract; we achieve full legal subjecthood. The question is how to move a woman (as a legal subject, a someone who imagines herself part of the political realm) to a state in which she is ready to perform this conscious, knowing choice. In the novel, as we have seen, things are not quite so simple, if for no other reason than that the novel, and particularly the fiction of George Eliot, scrambles the pieces of Mill's puzzle. For the curious heroine, choosing often comes before knowledge, yet only by choosing to move forward, by choosing to know, can she acquire the forbidden knowledge that is the promise and threat of the marriage plot, and only such acts of curiosity can bring about the change in moral vision that Eliot's novels seek. The problem (or is it the possibility) of knowledge for the curious heroine in the Bluebeard story is that though curiosity may move the heroine of any novel to cross what the narrator of Middlemarch calls the "doorsill of marriage" (183), Bluebeard's wife crosses another threshold after that when she enters the locked room. The political language of knowledge, choosing, and contract returns in Eliot's language as a problem of plot—or, as she will call it, hallucination, romance, and vision. Eliot tells stories of choice in language uncannily reminiscent of Mill's; she nowhere renounces absolutely the possibility of independence, of the individual self everywhere so important to Mill and necessary to any liberal regime of contract and willed self-alienation (or what we familiarly know as marriage). And yet, her novels, through their tangled path to sympathy and renunciation, and their almost vicious immersion in the constraints on free choice for their curious heroines, cannot hold up the same possibility Mill imagines, that of a practiced self free to choose, knowingly and forever. Instead, the marriage plot Eliot offers is darker, the road to self-awareness more rocky, and the opportunities for choice far more limited. For Eliot, that path through error and unhappiness is the only way to the full subjectivity, and the passion for justice, that Mill was able far more blithely to conceive.

The trace of this compulsion is the ghost story—one that suggests at once the invisible hand of (female) authorship and the dead hand of the inheritance plot, both central to Eliot's narrative and moral framework. From the moment Dorothea Brooke asks for something to do "here— now— in England," when she commits herself to crossing the threshold and going beyond the "toy-box history of the world adapted to young ladies which had made the chief part of her education" (MM:79). Eliot has committed herself to what Virginia Woolf referred to tellingly as the heroines' "demand": they "utter a demand for something—they scarcely know for what—for something that is perhaps incompatible with the facts of human existence."[9] That demand, like Louisa Bounderby's "leap into something visionary," makes Eliot's corpus into an extended ghost story—a flight into something visionary, something terrible and Gothic. The flight into personhood doesn't begin with the Gothic: Eliot instead starts with Mill's problem of originality, how we are to choose that which seems impossible, but moves from there to the impossible choice of femininity within liberalism, of the heroine within the marriage plot, of singularity (or what Mill would call "originality" or "eccentricity") under English law as it presently exists. Eliot calls this haunting something else: as her most feminist heroine says, it comes upon her in the form of the law, like "ghosts [in]the daylight" (DD:545). If this is the return of the law onto the subject, her ultimate alienation, it is also a form of self-possession. "I saw my wish outside me" says Gwendolen Harleth in Daniel Deronda (596), and this is the curious woman's unexpected prize: to perceive herself, fully, as both subject and object before the law.

The heroine's haunted perception is at the heart of both the political emancipation and the formal innovations that make these novels matter so much to us, still. Both *Middlemarch* and *Daniel Deronda* place female curiosity within novels of legal reform: *Middlemarch* explicitly so, for the novel takes place between the initial failure and the ultimate success of the Reform Act of 1832; *Daniel Deronda* more covertly, for its plot depends not only on the repeal of the Jewish Disabilities Act but also on the less transparent, more halting progress toward female emancipation that shadowed Jewish emancipation in the nineteenth century.[10] But in both novels, the heroine's curiosity and the political reformations around her call out for formal transformations as well. Eliot began *Middlemarch* as a novel of provincial life without Dorothea Brooke; when that novel faltered, she began a novella she called *Miss Brooke*, which she described as one of her first ideas for fiction. When that novella neared its end with the wedding of Dorothea Brooke to the sickly and pedantic Edward Casaubon, a moment of astonishing if endearing quixotism on the part of its idealistic heroine, Eliot suddenly realized that her two novels were one—that the heroine's quest for a wider sphere of action and the provincial village's resistance to any real ideas of change would come together in a story of damaged ideals and confused heroism.[11] *Daniel Deronda*'s doubled plot, the complex fictional arrangement that Eliot calls "Meeting Streams," similarly highlights the constraints on female experimentation. Gwendolen Harleth is increasingly enmeshed in *Daniel Deronda*'s plot but, lost as she is in her own marital and epistemological doubts, she cannot know until the end that she has been, all along, in a story that imagines not her happiness but the liberation of the Jews. In these novels, women who marry in a quest (however benighted) to know more, will end with a (legal) portion that seems to us as well as to them all too little, and the forms of the novels work to make readers participate in that exclusion. The way our readerly hopefulness is stymied as well might be the novel's strongest argument for social change.

What does the heroine want?[12] In both novels, to some extent, Eliot begins where Mill did: with a curious heroine making an eccentric choice. But Dorothea's choice, with which we shall begin, seems designed to boggle the sympathies of even the most liberal readers. The citizens of Middlemarch helpfully provide an elegant if somewhat inexact account of the plot, repeating "the tradition concerning it in Middlemarch, where [Dorothea] was spoken of to a younger generation as a fine girl who married a sickly clergyman, old enough to be her father, and in little more than a year after his death gave up her estate to marry his cousin—young enough to have been his son, with no property, and not well-born. Those who had not seen anything of Dorothea usually observed that she could not have been 'a nice woman,' else she would not have married either the one or the other" (784). That voice places us directly back in the world of John Stuart Mill and convention, and indeed, the sentence I quoted earlier describing "the man, and still more the woman, who can be accused either of doing 'what nobody does' or of not doing 'what everybody does'" could have come as easily from *Middlemarch* as from *On Liberty*. It is but a short step from Mill's sentence to the passage that begins, "In Middlemarch a wife could not long remain ignorant that the town held a bad opinion of her husband" (698) or to Celia Brooke's comment, when her sister Dorothea reminds her, "I never could do anything that I liked. I never carried out any plan yet," that she has been stymied only "because you always wanted things that wouldn't do" (770).

Should Dorothea get her choice? Eliot brilliantly anticipates the reader who might wonder if anyone so mis-judgeful as to marry Edward Casaubon *should* be allowed to vote, when she notes of Dorothea's first marriage, "certainly, the mistakes that we male and female mortals make when we have our own way might fairly raise some wonder that we are so fond of it" (67), and it would be easy enough to share this dismissal—a view in which Dorothea really is nothing more than a fine girl who has married a sickly old man, and her "mistake" is only an error, a "misjudgment," at which we, too, must smile. But the novelist does not allow us to be quite so certain. *Middlemarch* begins, again, as a story of reform, and it is no accident that Dorothea's uncle, Mr. Brooke, the "reform candidate," says (alas, with customary clarity) that "people should have their own way in marriage, and that sort of thing—up to a certain point, you know. I have always said that, up to a certain point" (42). Even more than "her own way," he says, Dorothea is to be free to do "what she likes": "You shall do as you like, my dear," he insists. Sir James says, quite to the contrary, "She is too young to know what she likes" (63). "It was wicked," he reflected, "to let a young girl blindly decide her fate in that way, without any effort to save her." The nearest he can come to conceding the point is, finally, to feel "with some sadness, that she was to have perfect liberty of misjudgment" (66). Characters are repeatedly torn between "reform" positions of choice and "sensible" positions of ridicule: Mrs. Cadwallader says James is well spared having a wife who would always require him "to see the stars by daylight" (54), but "she has her notions, you know," says her uncle, "She likes to go into things—property, land, that kind of thing. . . . Dorothea would want to act" (454) The longer she talks, the more we are magically impelled to the other position, until it would seem certain which side we should be on. When finally, after her husband's death, Lydgate pronounces that "in my opinion Mrs Casaubon should do what would give her the most repose of mind. That repose will not always come from being forbidden to act," he seems to be speaking for the novelist, and for us: "Let Mrs Casaubon do as she likes," he says to Sir James: "She wants perfect freedom, I think, more than any other prescription" (462).

But Eliot reminds us of something else about women's choices, starting with an idea that Mill would surely endorse, and then going even further into the realms of curiosity. Even accepting a more liberal idea of choice, there really wasn't much to choose from, was there? In a rigged game, Eliot seems to say, a woman has very few *real* choices. As she points out in the opening chapter, when the sisters divide their dead mother's jewels and Dorothea is torn painfully between her love of the beautiful gems and her desire always to renounce, in a situation as narrow as the two-suitor plot of the conventional novel, the two available unconventional positions (choose the unexpected in a fit of passion; refuse all desire, in a fit of pique) may be equally unsatisfying. What Eliot imagines instead, however, is not simply "more choice" but a different view of choice—or rather, of what choosing in marriage means.

As Eliot insists, Dorothea in fact tried to choose otherly: she did have "an original romance" in marrying Casaubon, that of living a "grand life here— now— in England." Dorothea's marriage is less a mistaken impulse of an uneducated heart (to borrow *David Copperfield*'s language) than her own form of experiment, the desire for a new and more "useful" self. "After that toy-box history of the world," says the narrator, "Mr Casaubon's talk about his great book was full of new vistas" (79). She marries him wanting a transformation, believing he will "give her a binding theory which could bring her own life and doctrine into strict connection with that amazing past, and give the remotest sources of knowledge some bearing on her actions" (79) something that will "joyously illuminate [the world] for her" (185). She imagines that Mr. Casaubon is that guide, that teacher (like Milton or Hooker, "father and teacher in one," clearly the perfect husband for an ardent girl!) who will lead her into the light. But as the narrator says with savage and merciless pseudo-pity,

> Poor Mr Casaubon himself was lost among small closets and winding stairs, and in an agitated dimness about the Cabeiri, or in an exposure of other mythologists' ill-considered parallels, easily lost sight of any purpose which had prompted him to these labors. With his taper stuck before him he forgot the absence of windows, and in bitter manuscript remarks on other men's notions about the solar deities, he had become indifferent to the sunlight. (185)

For Dorothea, asking as she does repeatedly about the wonders of Rome, "but do you care about them?" his indifference, his lack of care, his lack of *curiosity*, feels like cruelty: "There is hardly any contact more depressing to a young ardent creature than that of a mind in which years full of knowledge seem to have issued in a blank absence of interest or sympathy" (185). This blankness, this absence, this lack of sympathy, are all Dorothea finds in her marriage, where "these characteristics [are as] fixed and unchangeable as bone in

Mr Casaubon," not living, not quick; or, to borrow Eliot's metaphor, they are the place Dorothea is trapped, a "small closet"

But in the ghastly dimness of Mr. Casaubon's closet, Eliot traces brilliantly the transformations in Dorothea, which are very different from the Bluebeard story we might expect. Dorothea is hardly a rebellious Fatimah: her "bent" is to have "pour[ed] forth her girlish and womanly feeling," the bent "of every sweet woman, who has begun by showering kisses on the hard pate of her bald doll, creating a happy soul within that woodenness from the wealth of her own love" (186) And far from having a passel of dead wives, Mr. Casaubon is all politeness. He "pronounce[s] her, with his unfailing propriety, to be of a most affectionate and truly feminine nature, indicating at the same time by politely reaching a chair for her that he regarded these manifestations as rather crude and startling" (186). There has surely been no more devastating critique of a bad marriage—and yet, despite this relentless opposition of terms (Dorothea is full of feeling, tender, understanding, intimate, affectionate, sweet, childlike, happy, benignant, ardent, and yearning; Casaubon is, like the imaginary bald doll, hard, wooden, soulless, careful, stiff, and, worst of all, unpublished), the marriage is not a simple story of Dorothea's wonderful sympathy and Casaubon's unredeemed hardness.

For the hardness of Dorothea's marriage (bony, wooden, and bald) is the prelude to two more important things: first, to the suffering that will deepen her; second, the quickening of Dorothea's curiosity, in which she realizes, as the narrator says with devastating clarity, that "the lights and shadows fall differently" in another person's life. The suffering comes quickly, but it is followed almost as quickly by the understanding of Mr. Casaubon's separate identity. When it comes to his own fears, inadequacies and self-doubts, the narrator tells us, "Mr Casaubon had a sensitiveness to match Dorothea's, and an equal quickness to imagine more than the fact" (188) Indeed, her questioning of him (When will he be ready to write his great book, "The Key to All Mythologies"? When can she be a true helpmeet?) so exactly matches the voices of doubt that follow him each day to the Vatican Library that he meets her questions with a "quick, angry flush upon his [face]": Mr. Casaubon's mind may be a catacomb, but his spirit fights as fiercely as Dorothea's to be seen as he would be seen.[13] It is all too easy to see Casaubon as his young cousin Will, already falling in love with Dorothea, sees him: "a Bat of erudition," a "dried-up pedant, this elaborator of small explanations about as important as the surplus stock of false antiquities kept in a vendor's back chamber, [who] having first got this adorable young creature to marry him, then pass[ed] his honeymoon away from her, groping after his mouldy futilities" (192). As the narrator interrupts this passage, "Will was given to hyperbole," and this is not what Dorothea sees. Indeed, as soon as Will explains, in his own resentment of his cousin, that Casaubon's studies will come to nothing, for he does not know German, Dorothea comes to a new illumination: her eyes "brighter than usual with excited feeling," she seeks another way to be of use, and when her husband reenters the room ("rayless," unlike the sunny and coruscated Will), she is only "conscious of that new alarm on his behalf which was the first stirring of a pitying tenderness fed by the realities of his lot and not by her own dreams."

This is the transformation of curiosity into true sympathy that Eliot struggles for throughout the novel, as suddenly, someone else's life is as vivid to you as your own. As the narrator puts it most powerfully, at the end of this devastating set of chapters detailing the truly miserable story of a most unpleasant honeymoon,

> Dorothea remembered [that day] to the last with the vividness with which we all remember epochs in our experience when some dear expectation dies, or some new motive is born. Today she had begun to see that she had been under a wild illusion in expecting a response to her feeling from Mr Casaubon, and she had felt the waking of a presentiment that there might be a sad consciousness in his life which made as great a need on his side as on her own. (197)

What wakes us from moral stupidity is precisely that shock of running up against the desires of others, their woodenness, their absence—which is merely the reminder that they are not ourselves, but that they have a separate self.[14] All of Rome, all of her honeymoon, is a shock to Dorothea—the city itself is stupendous (that is, it renders her stupefied); the statues hold the "monotonous light of an alien world"; the "vast wreck of ambitious ideals . . . at first jarred her as with an electric shock, and then urged themselves on her with that ache belonging to a glut of confused ideas which check the flow of emotion" (181) Rome, in words that bring us back to Thackeray's vision of the traveller's imagination, is "like the magic-lantern pictures of a doze," and "the red drapery which was being hung for Christmas spread[s] itself everywhere like a disease of the retina" (182).[15] Rome hurts; Rome stuns; Rome changes her vision; her marriage changes her vision; nothing short of this barrage, this pain, this disease of the retina, will expand her capacity for sympathy; it will give her a new curiosity. Dorothea has done what Mill would imagine, then, and has grown in sympathy and moral wisdom; what she has yet to do, however, is to use that in the way Mill and Eliot both imagine: to *choose* to know more; to *choose* to do the right thing; to *choose*, that is, an alternative vision of the self. But that is what happens when she returns from Rome and enters Bluebeard's chamber—or rather, when she reenters it as her own ghost, as that legal nonperson, a wife.

Dorothea learns about the law through a ghost story. She first saw this ghost when she visited Bluebeard's castle before her marriage, and she did not know (as is usually true of the theoretic Miss Brooke) what she was seeing. Unlike the more conventionally minded Celia, Dorothea is charmed by her first view of Lowick. This is nowhere more true than in the blue bow-windowed room upstairs, where "the furniture was all of a faded blue, and there were miniatures of ladies and gentlemen with powdered hair hanging in a group" (69). But when she returns from Rome, returning to the Blue Chamber as a bride, everything looks different: "the shrunken furniture, the never-read books, and the ghastly stag" are "in a pale fantastic world that seemed to be vanishing from the daylight," as "each remembered thing in the room was disenchanted, was deadened as an unlit transparency" (258). Dorothea, having crossed that doorsill of marriage, must see everything with different eyes, the eyes of Bluebeard's wife, the eyes of a woman who has married that "geistlicher," Casaubon. What she sees in the room is not her own picture, but "the miniature of Mr Casaubon's aunt Julia, who had made the unfortunate marriage—of Will Ladislaw's grandmother." Her curiosity about Will and about the mysterious Julia is what leads Dorothea to cross the final threshold, for the more she learns of Julia's marriage and disinheritance, and of Will's excision from Casaubon's family property, the more indignant, and yet the more visionary, she becomes.

For the novelist, Dorothea's thinking about Julia is explicitly a moment of both vision and curiosity, and one that brings about a transformation that demands action, demands choice:

> The vision of all this as what ought to be done seemed to Dorothea like a *sudden letting in of daylight*, waking her from her previous stupidity and *incurious* self-absorbed ignorance about her husband's relation to others. Will Ladislaw had refused Mr Casaubon's future aid on a ground that no *longer appeared right to her;* and Mr Casaubon had never himself *seen fully* what was the claim upon him. "But he will!" said Dorothea. "The great strength of his character lies here. And what are we doing with our money? We make no use of half of our income. My own money buys me nothing but an uneasy conscience." (350; emphasis added)

These are the terms we have seen throughout this book: a sudden shift in perception (like Maggie Verver's telescope) forces us to see differently; we cannot see what we once saw—or rather, the sight of what lies beyond the chamber door will make us certain, will give us certainty, will make us, or so Dorothea imagines, powerful. Repeatedly, Dorothea speaks to her husband, she tries to impose her vision on his, to make him see what she sees. But Dorothea is of course wrong about Casaubon's character, and, as Reva Stump notes, it is Dorothea's insistence on the correctness of answering Will Ladislaw's "claim" upon him that leads Casaubon to draft a vicious codicil, trying to bar Dorothea at once from marrying again and from interfering with the patrimony he wishes to protect.[16] Casaubon writes with a "dead hand," and the patriarchal authority speaks from beyond the grave—this Bluebeard, we might suggest, is even more powerful dead.

This is because, of course, contra John Stuart Mill, mere contract law alone cannot save the heroine. Dorothea has learned too late what her marriage means—it has been a path to a larger sympathy but also an end to a certain freedom of action in the world. Her husband's refusal to take seriously her assertion of his obligation to his cousin, Will Ladislaw, has frustrated the fantasy that Dorothea (not unlike John Stuart Mill) continues to hold, that female influence can overcome the wife's lack of legal authority, moral suasion coming to her aid. Only the narrator's invisible hand striking Casaubon dead frees Dorothea from Casaubon's clutches, but interestingly, even after his death, she remains superstitious. Refusing his last request, that she immerse herself for the rest of her life in his tomb, committing herself to finishing his vast and useless tome, the "Key to all Mythologies," she takes up the notes he has left for her, "the Synoptical Tabulation for the use of Mrs Casaubon," and "carefully enclose[s] and seal[s] [it], writing within the envelope, 'I could not use it. Do you not see now that I could not submit my soul to yours, by working hopelessly at what I have no belief in?—Dorothea'" (506–7). Dorothea says she might have promised it to him when he was alive—but even Dorothea's sympathy balks at signing a contract with a ghost.

But interestingly, she balked at making promises while he was still alive as well. Casaubon, after she asks him if she may use her money for Lydgate's hospital, suddenly begins to call on her labor for his book, and it is at this moment precisely that he asks her to "let me know, deliberately, whether, in case of my death, you will carry out my wishes: whether you will avoid doing what I should deprecate, and apply yourself to do what I should desire." Dorothea is "not taken by surprise," for she has been led to "the conjecture of intention on her husband's part which might make a new yoke for her" (449). When she doesn't answer, he grows belligerent (he questions her "with more edge in her tone,"), and she says, "I do not yet refuse," but she does refuse "to make a promise when I am ignorant what it will bind me to." And she goes on, interestingly, to say, "Whatever affection prompted I would do without promising." Dorothea, as always, thinks she is being obedient—what more could he ask than affection?—but she is also rejecting a certain contractual view of marriage, imagining it rather as a covenant, something that already binds and does not need still more promising. In fact, she interestingly anticipates contemporary theorists of contract (and, implicitly, of marriage) who point out that to have signed a contract is already to admit the possibility of failure: to need a contract is to imagine a will (a desire) separate from your own. Yet what is it Casaubon is asking? Is he asking that Dorothea agree to complete his manuscript, such as it is (a hopeless and in fact impossible task, giving its fragmentary nature and obsolete assumptions) or is he instead asking the thing that he will in fact place in the codicil, the interdiction that she not marry Will Ladislaw? Our instinct might be to choose the latter—for, quoting Mrs. Cadwallader, the great theorist of marriage, "There was no safety in anything else. Mr Casaubon had prepared all this as beautifully as possible. He made himself disagreeable—or it pleased God to make him so—and then he dared her to contradict him" (767). The codicil is what generates the plot, a plot of romantic forbidding and compelling, but the promise to subsume herself in his work is equally terrifying: sealing herself up in a catacomb, and, more, renouncing her own will. As Casaubon perceptively notes, "But you would use your own judgement: I ask you to obey mine; you refuse" (449). But Dorothea, as well, cannot (as he puts it) "confide in the nature of my wishes"; the mere thought that she might have a wish of her own is, to him, the end of their marriage.

We might think that the manuscript is the intellectual, the second marriage the erotic, version of the wife's continuing (separate) desire, but they are fascinatingly commingled through the inheritance plot. It is hard to know where Dorothea's legal interest in Will's property (and distrust of her own marital settlement) turns into her physical desire for him, but both prompt the unfolding of the plot. It occurs to Dorothea that Casaubon might "mean to demand something more from her than she had been able to imagine" (451), and in that shadow of hesitation is the sign as well that she recognizes her own love for Will, but she is not wrong that they are the same promise. Just as Mr. Casaubon imagined (wrongly) that sonneteers were beseeching him to leave a "copy" of himself in the form of a son and observed "with pleasure that Miss Brooke showed an ardent submissive affection which promised to fulfil his most agreeable previsions of marriage" (58) so he imagines that Dorothea's every thought should be a copy of his. Mr. Casaubon, if no one else, has solved the problem of separate minds, for his "confidence" in Dorothea is that she will be purely his copy, carrying out not his dead hand but his (still) living will.[17]

The novel gives us two versions of compulsion here—and both connect for forms of literary plot as well. The one proposed by Casaubon is explicitly rejected by Dorothea: she foresees "that she must bind herself to a fellowship from which she shrank," but she is clear: "neither law nor the world's opinion compelled her to do this—only her husband's nature and her own compassion, only the ideal and not the real yoke of marriage." "She saw clearly enough the whole situation, yet she was fettered: she could not smite the stricken soul that entreated hers" (452). Casaubon, believing in the fetter of the marriage union (with his terrible talons intact) does not see himself as stricken—and yet Dorothea does. To her, the dreadfulness of her union is precisely that it compels her through compassion, not through force or fear. But this sense of compulsion, of union to another soul, is what leads her to take on that other "yoke," the dreadful burden of Lydgate's marriage, and (by going to Rosamond out of sympathy and a sense of her own failures) offers her the knowledge that Will loves her, that her marriage to him can take place.

One of the fascinating things about *Middlemarch* is that its final Bluebeard scene takes place not in Casaubon's closet (his final scene, remember, is his own unexpected death, outside in the wintry garden) but in Rosamond Lydgate's drawing room. That is where Dorothea finally crosses the threshold of curiosity and learns what she needs to know to be free. When she first goes to visit Rosamond, she unexpectedly comes upon Mrs. Lydgate and Will Ladislaw—and the encounter is a shock to us as well. Ladislaw has returned unexpectedly; the servant does not know he is in the house, and she and Dorothea

> crossed the broader part of the entrance-hall, and turned up the passage which led to the garden. The drawing-room door was unlatched, and Martha, pushing it without looking into the room, waited for Mrs Casaubon to enter and then turned away, the door having swung open and swung back again without noise.
>
> Dorothea had less of outward vision than usual this morning, being filled with images of things as they had been and were going to be. She found herself *on the other side of the door* without seeing anything remarkable, but immediately she heard a voice speaking in low tones which startled her as with a sense of *dreaming in daylight, and advancing unconsciously* a step or two beyond the projecting slab of a bookcase, she saw, in *the terrible illumination of a certainty which filled up all outlines,* something which made her pause motionless without self-possession enough to speak. (729; emphasis added)

"Dreaming in daylight" is one of a series of ghostly elements in the encounter and in her subsequent meetings with Will and Rosamond. Will has already said that "it could not be fairly called wooing a woman to tell her that he would never woo her. It must be admitted to be a ghostly kind of wooing" (595). Rosamond is only "the lovely ghost of herself" (745). "Her face had become of a deathlier paleness" (749). The "great shock that had shattered her dream-world in which she had been easily confident of herself and critical of others" increased by "this strange, unexpected manifestation of feeling in a woman whom she had approached with a shrinking aversion and dread, as one who must necessarily have a jealous hatred towards her, [which] made her soul totter all the more with a sense that she had been *walking in an unknown world* which had just broken in upon her" (748–49). But this scene in the closet, the "other side of the door" through which they all seem to step, is simply a recognition of the always-ghostly quality of marriage, of which the narrator quite early spoke in the book, when she compared Lydgate's love of his work with romantic love, wondering why troubadours are only interested in the latter, and then noted that "perhaps their ardor in generous unpaid toil cooled as imperceptibly as the ardor of other youthful loves, till one day their earlier self walked like a ghost in its old home and made the new furniture ghastly. Nothing in the world more subtle than the process of their gradual change!" (135). Or, as Dorothea says in her final generous confrontation with Rosamond, describing what happens when a married person loves someone else, "Marriage drinks up all our power of giving or getting any blessedness in that sort of love." "I know it may be very dear—but it murders our marriage—and then the marriage stays with us like a murder—and everything else is gone" (749).

"A smothering instead of a marriage" is how Affery describes her wedding in *Little Dorrit*, and *Middlemarch* is not far from that. But Dorothea's revelation of her own terrible marriage ("he knows that I had much trial in my marriage, from my husband's illness, which hindered his plans and saddened him, and he knows that I have felt how hard it is to walk always in fear of hurting another who is tied to us") is what makes it possible for Rosamond to confess that it is Dorothea and not she whom Ladislaw loves: "You are thinking what is not true." Dorothea's actions came out of another law: "What sort of crisis might not this be in three lives whose contact with hers laid an obligation on her as if they had been suppliants bearing the sacred branch? . . . 'What should I do, how should I act now, this very day if I could clutch my own pain, and compel it to silence, and think of those three?'" (741). Dorothea's compulsion (the compulsion to her own silence, her own smothering) is certainly another "heroic hallucination," but it comes out of that same sense of revelation: that having crossed the threshold and seen something different from what she expected, she is compelled to follow that vision, to answer it sympathetically, to respond ethically. This is the moment when "all this sympathetic experience returned to her now as a power: it asserted itself as acquired knowledge asserts itself and will not let us see as we say in the day of our ignorance" (741), when the ghastly vision returns as a strength, not as a murder—but it is what makes possible the novel's happy ending.

That happy ending is, of course, another contract. "They were bound to each other by a love stronger than any impulses which could have marred it" (782) says the narrator—or, as Dorothea says to Celia at the end of *Middlemarch*, "It is quite true that I might be a wiser person, Celia, . . . and that I might have done something better, if I had been better. But this is what I am going to do. I have promised to marry Mr Ladislaw; and I am going to marry him" (771). In signing another contract, making another promise, becoming someone else's (ghost) wife, the novel might not seem to have brought us very far. Yet it has. The first contract, the first marriage, was made in a hopeful burst of ignorance, a brilliant if finally futile error, which the novel was never really taken in by. As the narrator poignantly said, "Having once embarked on your marital voyage, it is impossible not to be aware that you make no way and that the sea is not within sight—that, in fact, you are exploring an enclosed basin" (184). Yet the novel (like Dorothea) never entirely rejects that first mistaken impulse, for it knows that only that mistaken choice could lead her to the second choice, the choice to know, to refuse to see as she did when she was ignorant. But the novel remains ambivalent about Dorothea's second contract, her choice of Will Ladislaw, for that second choice can never be entirely free of the web of circumstances, the compulsion of law, the haunting of other "impulses." Where *Middlemarch* is most prescient is in its understanding that even knowledge will not, of itself, lead to better choices—it is, as we would say, necessary but not sufficient; a woman still needs something else, be it luck or coincidence or simply a more benevolent novelist, willing to knock her husband over the head in the nick of time; willing to grant her another choice.

With her second choice, Dorothea gains a wider form of personhood: both the capacity to promise and the freedom to marry a man she loves. She does not gain social acceptance, of course. To the other Middlemarchers, this freedom remains a mistake—Will Ladislaw is simply another bad choice, an "Italian with white mice" (460), "the grafting of a Jew pawnbroker" (676), a wastrel and a dilettante and, worst of all, a writer. (They have not yet even imagined his parliamentary career.) But Dorothea sees something else, and her right to choose eccentrically and choose for herself is all the more precious. As she says to Mrs. Cadwallader, when the latter insists that "we have all got to exert ourselves a little to keep sane, and call things by the same names as other people call them by," "I never called everything by the same name that all the people about me did." Mrs. Cadwallader retorts, "I suppose you have found out your mistake, my dear, and that is a proof of sanity," but Dorothea has the last word: "'No,' she said, 'I still think that the greater part of the world is mistaken about many things. Surely one may be sane and yet think so, since the greater part of the world has often had to come round from its opinion'" (505). This is a particularly apt comment for a novel written in the time between the first and second (successful) reform bills, but Dorothea's faith in her own judgment is not the sign that the world has "come round from its opinion," for that is something she has learned not to expect. It is instead her confidence in the knowledge she has gained, the growth in sympathy she experienced, by having been through the crucible of her first marriage; the knowledge and sympathy that allowed her to save Lydgate and Rosamond's marriage; the freedom to hurtle herself toward Will, saying, "Oh, I cannot bear it; I will learn what everything costs." All this now gives her the courage to make and *keep* her final promise.

To the extent that we think that this is a happy ending, we are joining George Eliot in perpetrating a fiction, for Eliot imagines Dorothea and

Will's marriage as that (legally) impossible thing—a marriage without Bluebeard. She imagines they are entering into the binding (and, at least for women, self-destructive) marriage contract, and emerging with their sense of self intact, something that is truly a visionary leap. This is something not yet possible under Victorian law, as John Stuart Mill found when he married Harriet Taylor and wrote that separate contract renouncing his (legal) rights. Had he died first, leaving so "eccentric" a will, Harriet Taylor might have found out the limits of her rights under law, as both Dorothea and in time Gwendolen Harleth do—and remember, although Dorothea Brooke retains not only her original inheritance but also her rights to her uncle's estate when she renounces Casaubon's fortune and marries Will Ladislaw, those rights to Tipton Grange will pass, on Mr. Brooke's death, to her son. Even the most benevolent marriage is still performed under the despotic shadow of the law—and as we have learned in this novel, law does not disappear because the heart wills it to do so. *Middlemarch* somehow believes in the possibility of marital happiness within the strictures of that law: Eliot imagines for Dorothea what she and Lewes had, a marriage undertaken in full knowledge, one governed by a law of heart, ruled by attachment and what she describes as "longing and constancy." Faithfulness is everything in *Middlemarch*, and private contract is imagined as true union.

But this is not realism, it is witchcraft; it is precisely the kind of reenchantment Thackeray imagined at the end of *Vanity Fair*, when we should know better but chose not to. Eliot even echoes his language: when Dorothea conjures her longing for Will she thinks: "If a princess in the days of enchantment had seen a four-footed creature from among those which live in herds come to her once and again with a human gaze which rested upon her with choice and beseeching, what would she think of in her journeying, what would she look for when the herds passed her? Surely for the gaze which had found her, and which she would know again" (507). "Life would be no better than candlelight tinsel and daylight rubbish," Eliot says, without this union of true minds, and that is what she is promulgating, as if she had found a back door in Bluebeard's chamber, as if we could escape the image she has beautifully echoed from our earlier chapter, "Vauxhall in the daytime." Eliot loves this marriage—but she knows that, like her own fictional union, it will not survive a harsh light.

In *Deronda*, by dreadful contrast, marriage is not merely "candlelight tinsel and daylight rubbish"; it is something far more terrifying. In *that* book, all forms of contract (at least between men and women) seem to take place within the desperate violence of law; every husband is a Bluebeard, and a woman who seeks a contract of her own, as Gwendolen Harleth bitterly and repentantly announces, "shall be punished." In this universe, marriage is still a progress toward enlightenment and a necessary journey for the curious heroine—but it is also, as Eliot reworks Mill's language yet once more, the most dangerous "venture" of all.

Enter Gwendolen, gambling. Gwendolen Harleth, unlike Dorothea Brooke, does not see courtship as a progress toward enlightenment. All she wants is to "do what she likes," and the novel depicts that desire in so bleak a form that even John Stuart Mill might not recognize it. What Gwendolen demands (and, we would have to concede, what she receives) is simply "the liberty ... to risk breaking my neck" (111). She is a "spoiled child," with a misplaced sense of adventure and a powerful sense that women's lives are only disappointments. Gwendolen begins in fact as the embodiment of Matthew Arnold's sharpest critique of Mill, that while we are told to do as we like, no one tells us what we are to like; that liberalism represents only a kind of anarchy of thought. For Mill, of course, that is precisely the point, but Gwendolen might bring an end to his notions. She begins as a person whose choices are made entirely for her own pleasure. Much like Rosamond Vincy at the beginning of *Middlemarch*, who feels that other people should not eat food whose cooking odors offend her delicate senses, Gwendolen has grown up in a world that has revolved around her sensitivities—though the novel does hint at the darker shadow of that history, the death of the heroine's father and something questionable about her stepfather, who stole her mother's jewelry and sold it, abandoned the family routinely, and has somehow left his stepdaughter with a near-pathological aversion to male intimacy. But Gwendolen's aversions, her superstitions, her "dread," suggest from the beginning that she is no Rosamond Vincy. Her independence, meted out over a trivial realm, also grows out of a more genuine sense that the world should hold more, a sense we associate with Dorothea rather than Rosamond, with Mill rather than Arnold, with the struggle Gwendolen herself does not recognize, the struggle into personhood.

Not that Gwendolen is a heroine in quest of deeper meaning. She is "inwardly rebellious,"

> as if she had been sustained by the boldest speculations; but she really had no such speculation, and would at once have marked herself off from any sort of theoretical or practically reforming women by satirising them. She rejoiced to feel herself exceptional; but her horizon was that of the genteel romance where the heroine's soul poured out in her journal is full of vague power, originality, and general rebellion, while her life moves strictly in the sphere of fashion; and if she wanders into a swamp, the pathos lies partly, so to speak, in her having on her satin shoes. (43)

Gwendolen has that spark of rebellion, of liveliness and cleverness, which sounds like critique, but as Eliot's irony makes clear, it is a cleverness as yet unable to read the real darkness of the world around her, or the Bluebeard plot coming toward her. While she begins by refusing marriage and traditional girlhood ("Girls' lives are so stupid," she says; "they never do what they like"[56]) and adds that she will never marry, and if she does, "when I married, I should not do as other women do" (57). she cannot find anything else to do, either. "We women can't go in search of adventures—to find out the North-West passage, or the source of the Nile, or to hunt tigers in the East," she says: "We must stay where we grow" (113).

Gwendolen is seeking adventure, but she little suspects just what an adventure (as in risk, as in heart of darkness, as in haunted house) marriage in Victorian England can be. And yet, the darkness begins to gather quickly, far more quickly than it does around Dorothea Brooke, as early as Gwendolen's courtship. At first confident of her ability to manage Henleigh Grandcourt, "Gwendolen had no sense that these men were dark enigmas to her, or that she needed any help in drawing conclusions about them" (102). This changes in a fantastic Bluebeard moment, one whose prophetic qualities are not in the least lost on Gwendolen. Gwendolen receives a written note that reads, in part, "If Miss Harleth is in doubt whether she should accept Mr Grandcourt, let her break from her party after they have passed the Whispering Stones and return to that spot. She will then hear something to decide her, but she can only hear it by keeping this letter a strict secret from every one" (125-26). A rebellious Fatima from the start, Gwendolen gives in to her curiosity, and she learns. A dark and beautiful woman, Lydia Glasher, stands in the glade with two of her illegitimate children, including her beautiful son, and explains that just as she should be Grandcourt's wife, so this boy should be his heir—and Gwendolen believes her. Terrified and outraged, pale and drawn, Gwendolen has courage enough only to say, "I will not interfere with your wishes" (128). Gwendolen sees Lydia as if "some ghastly vision had come to her in a dream and said, 'I am a woman's life.'" She acts immediately upon that vision, and she flees—and the book should end there.

It doesn't—and in fact, it doesn't begin there, either, though this is a scene that happens long before the first chapter of the novel, when a beautiful woman is gambling in a mysterious European watering spot. The fact that the novel "begins" after this scene means, however, that *Daniel Deronda*, unlike every other book in our study, begins with a heroine who has already opened the door, who has already seen the ghost of her predecessor, who already knows the secret. She knows the secret because she was curious, and knowing it, she has tried to evade Fatima's doom: she will, it seems, do anything rather than set foot again in Grandcourt's bloody chamber. Gwendolen initially seems to refuse marriage altogether, choosing instead a life of gambling, adventures abroad, speculations other than marital, we might posit—for that is the heroine we meet (serpentine, lovely, careless, and fraught) in chapter 1, when we first see her through the gaze of the equally speculative Daniel Deronda. It will be many chapters, though, before the novel tells us the story of how our speculative heroine got herself here, trapping us as it traps her in a fatal choice. We can piece together the story only when we move forward and fall backward in time: the underfunded heroine, spoiled daughter of a widow with four other, less alluring daughters, finds herself in a beautiful old English house, being watched over with a speculative interest of his own by her benevolent (if slightly too worldly) uncle, the reverend Mr. Gascoigne, and a host of interested neighbors. Just as her plot threatens to pall, a wealthy man appears, lizard-like and silent and watchful, but as he is about to propose (pulled a little off the marital path by his own "freaks" of temperament), the heroine receives a letter from a woman with a secret. That is the story as the book eventually tells it, making Gwendolen's great moment of curiosity seem decisive, seem to offer the kind of knowledge we wish other heroines (Dorothea Brooke not least among them) had in advance. And yet this knowledge, however transformative, neither begins nor ends her plot. "It is come in time," she thinks, after she meets Lydia and as she crosses from the seemingly inevitable marriage plot into knowledge, and yet it comes to us, as I am arguing it does to her, strangely out of time.

It's hard to know what John Stuart Mill would make of this. The novel plays almost defiantly with time, with beginnings and endings and "marked epochs," offering neither his rational narrative, in which we learn, we know, we choose, nor even *Middlemarch*'s organic evolutionary progress toward enlightenment. Instead, Eliot is playing with us as much as she is with Gwendolen, teasing us, playing with our curiosity, seducing us into believing (to borrow Rosamond Vincy's phrase) "what is not true." Gwendolen does learn before she chooses, but we do not learn what she has learned for quite a while, for the scene with Lydia comes well into our reading of the novel (chapter 14), even though it was the precipitating event for the scene that begins the book. The opening episode in Leubronn, which encouraged us, like Gwendolen, to see Deronda as her destined lover, ended with Gwendolen's hurried departure for Offendene, but rather than following her to her mother's side, takes us rather to her first arrival at Offendene, a year earlier. Only after a narration covering several months, and including her introduction to Grandcourt, do we learn of the meeting with Lydia that startled Gwendolen into flight, reading the scene I have already recounted. But even then we do not return to Offendene in "the present" to see what Gwendolen will do "next," but instead we rejoin Deronda in Leubronn where he has just learned of Gwendolen's departure, and where he encounters Grandcourt, who has (too late) followed Gwendolen there. After many chapters of Daniel's prior history (childhood till "now"), we at last find Gwendolen returning (again, it feels, although it is really for the first time) to Offendene, where she will (and is it by now inevitable?) break her promise to Lydia Glasher, her promise "not to interfere with your wishes," by agreeing to marry Grandcourt. We, like Gwendolen, already know a secret, but we don't always know what we know—the novelist, we can only suggest, is Gaslighting us.

But perhaps it suggests something different. The novel is here playing self-consciously with our knowledge in order to raise an unusual possibility: that it is a plot entirely about the period after curiosity, after Fatima has been in the bloody chamber, a plot that aims to suggest just what a small difference knowledge might make after all. For the novel begins with a heroine who already "knows," and rather than merely asking what she knows, asks what she will *do* with that knowledge. If, by the time Grandcourt finally proposes to Gwendolen, she knows what Dorothea will learn only after her wedding (that her marriage has stolen another woman's fortune, that her husband has a guilty plot, that she should not marry him), the problem is not that she doesn't know better; the problem is that she has exactly enough knowledge to make the promise not to marry him and not enough to keep it. The plot comes not from her learning Grandcourt's secrets (though it does teach her more and more) but from learning her own—from realizing that she has something after all, call it dread, call it doubt, call it conscience, or call it curiosity, that makes her more than a spoiled girl, something that moves her toward a moral choice.

Why this difference between Dorothea and Gwendolen's Bluebeard plots? I think it is that Gwendolen not only knows different things than Dorothea, she wants different things, and this difference marks her entrance into Bluebeard's castle. Gwendolen has a fierce desire for independence, which the novel does not entirely mock, and yet which it shows to be utterly useless to her in her quest for true freedom of choice. Eliot deliberately situates Gwendolen's quest for independence in legal terms that remind us fiercely of the constraints on "maidens choosing." At the crucial moment when Gwendolen returns to Offendene, having learned of her mother's bankruptcy, the narrator observes her as if from afar:

> Deposited as a feme sole with her large trunks and having to wait, Gwendolen ... felt the dirty plant in the waiting-room, the dusty decanter of flat water, and the texts in large letters calling on her to repent and be converted, were part of the dreary prospect opened by her family trouble. ... Contemptible details these, to make part of a history; yet the turn of most lives is hardly to be accounted for without them. . . . Even philosophy is not quite free from such determining influences; and to be dropt solitary at an ugly irrelevant-looking spot with a sense of no income on the mind, might well prompt a man to discouraging speculation on the origin of things and the reason of a world where a subtle thinker might find himself so badly off. How much more might such trifles tell on a young lady equipped for society with a fastidious taste, an indian shawl over her arm, some twenty cubic feet of trunks by her side, and a

mortal dislike to the new consciousness of poverty which was stimulating her imagination of disagreeables? (194–95)

The narrator does all she can to make us see Gwendolen's troubles as puny in the face of larger social changes ("Could there be a slenderer, more insignificant thread in human history than this consciousness of a girl, busy with her small inferences of the way in which she could make her life pleasant?" she asks [102]), but the language of the "feme sole" reminds us of the married women's property debates swirling around Eliot: Gwendolen's return to Grandcourt, her doomed choice, her limited vision of freedom, are all part of the realization that in the realm of property, she has, and will continue to have, nothing she can legally call her own.

She does try, fiercely, to regain some independence, but she fails. In an attempt to save her family from poverty and herself from the servitude of being a governess, she sends for the brilliant musician Klesmer—who has himself just contracted a marriage with the heiress Catherine Arrowpoint, who is in the middle of yet another plot Gwendolen barely suspects. To her mortification, her request that he guide her to a life as an actress meets not with instant promises of success nor even with scorn, but with a gentle condescension that both scalds her narcissistic confidence and reminds her again of the larger world she cannot control. Yet what Gwendolen reveals at that moment is more complicated than mere wounded narcissism: it is that desire for larger knowledge that we see frustrated at every turn:

> I desire to be independent. . . . That was my reason for asking whether I could not get an immediate engagement. Of course I cannot know how things go on about theatres. But I thought that I could have made myself independent. I have no money, and I will not accept help from anyone. (221)

That plea, "of course I cannot know how things go on about theatres," might be the larger cry of (all) female desire for knowledge: "I cannot know how things go on." For a moment, in the midst of excoriating the spoiled child, Eliot suggests that Gwendolen's tragedy is not a failure of curiosity, or even of imagination, but quite simply of experience. There is no way that a woman, trying to see beyond the scope of her narrowed and proscribed existence, can ever know enough about how things go on to make herself independent; Gwendolen, like Dorothea, though for very different reasons, cannot emancipate herself on her own.

The fact that she already knows something she does not want to know, the fact that she has had other doors slammed so sharply in her face, leaves Gwendolen in a very different position from Dorothea when she finally "gets her choice," but strangely, despite what she has known and what she wanted, the marriage plot is still the only place where she can truly learn "how things go on," and it remains the place where she will acquire far more terrible knowledge. That is to say, we are not quite done with the Bluebeard plot, as the scene where Gwendolen "chooses" Grandcourt makes clear. The novel frames this (second) choice in a highly literary way, reminding us, too, of our status as readers of women's curiosity, of the terror and mystery behind the door, of the way we are always trying to look down a dim corridor at a woman's receding back. What does it mean to choose freely? After hearing Grandcourt's proposal, which she entirely expects and yet dimly hopes she can refuse, Gwendolen asks herself, "What was the good of choice coming again?" At the moment when she makes the choice, she is given an image of shuffling through a book, much as we do:

> Again she seemed to get a sort of empire over her own life. But how to use it? Here came the terror. Quick, quick, like pictures in a book beaten open with a sense of hurry, came back vividly, yet in fragments, all that she had gone through in relation to Grandcourt . . . her own pledge (was it a pledge not to marry him?). (247)

Gwendolen tries to do what we do, look backward and gauge exactly the extent of her promise to Lydia—which was, simply, "I will not interfere with your wishes." The words she dreads, "I will not marry him," are never said, but they are what she means, and she (and we) know it; this is the broken promise that haunts the remainder of the book, the words that give her a conscience.

One would expect, then, that Gwendolen's honeymoon cannot be a Bluebeard moment, for her Bluebeard moment has come and gone, and yet, that is precisely what happens: knowledge comes (back) again. Eliot offers us one more fascinating scene of open caskets and locked doors: the scene when Gwendolen is dressing for dinner after the wedding and opens the package with Grandcourt's mother's diamonds, diamonds Lydia had promised to return to his bride on his wedding night. Gwendolen, previously brittle and nervous and chattering, is alone when she opens the "packet." She is sure that it contains the diamonds, but it comes with a letter: "She knew the handwriting of the address. It was as if an adder had lain on them," for of course it is Lydia's handwriting. The letter says:

> These diamonds, which were once given with ardent love to Lydia Glasher, she passes on to you. You have broken your word to her, that you might possess what was hers. Perhaps you think of being happy, as she once was, and of having beautiful children such as hers, who will thrust hers aside. God is too just for that. The man you have married has a withered heart. His best young love was mine: you could not take that from me when you took the

rest. It is dead: but I am the grave in which your chance of happiness is buried as well as mine. You had your warning. You have chosen to injure me and my children. He had meant to marry me. He would have married me at last, if you had not broken your word. You will have your punishment. I desire it with all my soul. (303)

Lydia's uncanny ability to speak of herself in the third person is not the least remarkable thing about the passage, in the course of which she "buries" herself to resurrect the "I," but the most remarkable thing is its effect on Gwendolen. Her eyes are "spell-bound"; she feels "spasm[s] of terror"; the casket falls; the diamonds roll out; and though "she could not see the reflections of herself then; they were like so many women petrified white; but coming near herself you might have seen the tremor in her lips and hands." This is Gwendolen's great moment of alienation less from her husband than from herself, for she is "poisoned," and when her husband enters, she "scream[s] again and again with hysterical violence," in what he thinks is "a fit of madness." As Grandcourt instantly thinks, "In some form or other the furies had crossed his threshold," but it is Gwendolen herself, facing the "doubleness" in herself that Deronda and everyone else notes from then on, who has crossed the threshold, Gwendolen who has walked into Bluebeard's chamber, into the knowledge that, suddenly, she is less Fatima than another guilty, pale, dead wife, already buried alive.

But of what is she guilty? At times it seems that Gwendolen is punished for nothing so much as her lack of curiosity about other people, for her ignorance of anything except their ability to make her happy, to admire her, to do for her what she wants—or more accurately, what she thinks she wants. Not unlike Esther Lyon, and very much as Mill promised, she has chosen mean things because only mean things are offered to her, and she doesn't know what she might desire until too late. This in a sense is a sign of incuriosity, but many people in *Daniel Deronda* are far more incurious, and few are punished as greatly as Gwendolen. The brilliance of the novel, the way it posits the relationship between its own form and its heroine's quest, is the way it alternately encourages us and discourages us from sharing her lack of knowledge; reminds us of what she does not know, that in the book called *Daniel Deronda*, the story of "Gwendolen Harleth" is a shrinking tale; leads us, repeatedly, alternatively, both to scorn and pity her.[18] What else could she do, she (like us) asks over and over? This book acknowledges far more powerfully than *Middlemarch* the limits of what women *can* do in polite society (a world it makes at once more trifling and more cruel than almost any novel in the tradition, *Bleak House* excepted); it also, and here is its greatness, makes the alienation of Gwendolen from that trifling world, her slow evolution into a choosing subject, a powerful moment of female emancipation, one that even John Stuart Mill might recognize, a conclusion less eccentric than fully individual, as tragic as it is utterly comprehensible, at the last, to us.

In a perverse way, Gwendolen's hands are tied precisely by her knowledge: whenever her husband returns to challenge her, Gwendolen can only remember that she knew (not everything, but enough) what she was getting in for. "She had broken her word," the narrator reminds us, and all her easy fantasies, like Dorothea Brooke's, that she might "influence" her husband to change his will, to include Lydia, were in vain. "For the reasons by which she had justified herself when the marriage tempted her, and all her easy arrangement of her future power over her husband to make him do better than he might be inclined to do, were now as futile as the burnt-out lights which set off a child's pageant.... With the reading of that letter had begun her husband's empire of fear" (364). Her husband's will does get altered, but in a way designed to punish her further for her earlier shows of independence and resistance. When Grandcourt's servant Lush appears with the will that leaves the bulk of Grandcourt's estate and his property to Lydia's children, Gwendolen understands that "the conditions were what she had accepted with her eyes open," that she has prepared her humiliation for herself in marrying him. Even worse, she learns that Grandcourt knew all along that she had accepted him unwillingly, for money, to save herself from a life of slavery as a governess.

The worse slavery she has chosen, however, has surprisingly, an ethical dimension, one that aligns with the pedagogical function we earlier imagined for curiosity. Having chosen this slavery, having learned the limits of her freedom, Gwendolen nonetheless retains some ability to choose, and, not unlike Dorothea Brooke, some ability to renounce, to choose not to profit further from someone's else misery:

> At first it was not easy to take in the meaning of the words. When she had succeeded, she found that in the case of there being no son as issue of her marriage, Grandcourt had made the small Henleigh his heir; that was all she cared to extract from the paper with any distinctness. The other statement as to what provision would be made for her in the same case, she hurried over, getting only a confused perception of thousands and Gadsmere. It was enough. She could dismiss the man in the next room with the defiant energy which had revived in her at the idea that this question of property and inheritance was meant as a finish to her humiliations and her thraldom. She thrust the paper between the leaves of her book, which she took in her hand, and walked with her stateliest air into the next room, where Lush immediately arose, awaiting her approach. When she was four yards from him, it was hardly an instant that she paused to say in a high tone, while she swept him with her eyelashes—
>
> "Tell Mr Grandcourt that his arrangements are just what I desired." (513–14)

When she embraces her own elision from the inheritance plot into which she has stumbled, tangled and lost, Gwendolen reclaims some modicum of choice for herself. As Eliot says later, "Her capability of rectitude told her again and again that she had no right to complain of her contract or to withdraw from it" (515), and she does not. This is a dignity even Lush, if not her husband, will respect—although Lush, however struck with admiration for her he might be, nonetheless turns immediately to the thought of a lobster salad for lunch.

Lush may dream of delicacies, but Gwendolen, we might imagine, is not a morsel that her Bluebeard husband can swallow all that easily. True, she renounces desire, and along with it one form of curiosity:

> She would not look a second time at the paper Lush had given her; and before ringing for her maid she locked it up in a traveling-desk which was at hand, proudly resolved against curiosity about what was allotted to herself in connection with Gadsmere—feeling herself branded in the minds of her husband and his confidant with the meanness that would accept marriage and wealth on any conditions, however dishonorable and humiliating. (516)

She refuses to pursue the property, and she refuses to seek a legal separation from Grandcourt, which she also sees as impossible, for a woman who went into the darkest of marriages with her eyes wide open—or as wide as her education and worldly knowledge allowed. But she allows herself two other forms of wondering—one, whether she can use her "dread" and the instruction Daniel offers to nurture the conscience she tried to murder with her marriage; the other, which is its own source of dread, if she can murder Grandcourt. She imagines plunging a knife into him: "quick, quick, came images, plans of evil that would come again and seize her in the night, like furies preparing the deed that they would straightway avenge" (583). The "quick, quick" is the sign both of the disjointed time and of a guilty conscience, for the word *quick* in this book suggests always its opposite, that we are frozen in time, and that we cannot undo what we have done. But though to Gwendolen "the strife within her seemed like her own effort to escape herself," all of this "strife" is in fact an effort not to escape but to become herself, to follow this other form of (moral) curiosity to the unexpected end of an enduring singularity.

Gwendolen's ghost story does not end particularly well. Grandcourt does die, and she is set free by his death, but she does not get Daniel, and she does not get a conventional happy ending, or even what we might think of as a new beginning. She does get some capacity to promise ("It should be better . . . better with me . . . for having known you," she says, sobbingly, to Daniel, and it is a promise[691]), but she does not get to write her own contract, make her own law, capture the stage she dreamed of. But Gwendolen's marriage, as her involvement with Grandcourt's rewritten will suggests, has already pulled her into the world of law in ways Dorothea's did not, and it pushes her toward some new form of subjectivity, even if it is not quite what Mill had in mind. Her acceptance of Grandcourt's second proposal already pushed her toward becoming a legal subject in Mill's sense, for that eventual "'Yes' came as gravely from Gwendolen's lips as if she had been answering to her name in a court of justice" (257). But the novel pushes her further, toward something else, even after she loses her name and becomes a wife. When she confesses to Daniel her desires for Grandcourt's death, she is allowed a scene of testimony as much as religious confession, and what she confesses is a moment of total self-alienation that is a form of self-knowledge. "I saw my wish outside me," says Gwendolen, in an uncanny echo of the scene where she opened the poisoned jewels and was reflected endlessly in the shivering glass, but this moment of alienation is a moment of self-recognition as the other was not. If being married to Grandcourt gave her, as in any Bluebeard tale, a sense of her own disappearance, his death seems to liberate her into another identity. Even the otherwise conventional Daniel says to Sir Hugo, "Is it absolutely necessary that Mrs Grandcourt should marry again?" (685). Gwendolen might wish that she "had never known" the secret (248); she might have the feeling of being pulled into "backwards secrets" (253), but "she could not go backwards now" (262). Instead, she is being pulled forward, however reluctantly, into the independence she dreamed of and a legal personhood (that was open to widows, even those who strive only to renounce their inheritance) that Dorothea Casaubon did not maintain. For Gwendolen, having no second marriage may be less narratorial punishment and more an open future of promising and contracting otherwise closed off to her, a future in which *not* marrying might make her wiser.

That is not to say that the novel entirely abandons Mill's fantasy of a woman who is free to choose and choose again—but when it conjures her, it does so in the form a woman seemingly buried in the past, come to life briefly to tell her story and disappear again. Daniel's mother, the singer, the Alcharisi, only appears for two chapters, late in the novel, and her mysterious appearance coincides with what seems to be Gwendolen's rebellion, her decision to murder (or at least, not to save) her husband. In the novel's most unexpected twist, Gwendolen, Daniel, and Daniel's mother are all in Genoa, and Daniel is on the scene when the near-drowned Gwendolen appears on the docks; but more, he has come from hearing his mother's fierce confession (more of an accusation, really) and goes on to hear Gwendolen's, as she returns from the boat trip, broken and battered and self-loathing. The Alcharisi is none of these things. For a rebel angel, she is remarkably fierce still, though punished by the novelist with a cruel cancer and with the loss of her greatest power, her captivating appearances on a world stage. Like the singer Mirah refused to be, and Gwendolen longed to be, the Alcharisi has had Europe at her feet—now, she has a son kneeling before her, yearning for something she still refuses to give, a gentle answer and a warm touch. Relentlessly incurious about his mother throughout his life (though he first seeks out Mirah because he believes his mother might be "such a one like her," he shies away even from his own realization that his fortune almost certainly comes from his mother), he realizes that he has become her secret, for, as his mother says to him, "I have a husband and five children. None of them know of your existence" (547). The Alcharisi appears bearing caskets, jewels, secrets, keys—and rather than providing him with the gentle mother's touch he had so long fantasized about and tried to embody in himself, she instructs him, reluctant as he is, in both the father's law and the daughter's contract.

For the Alcharisi, alone of the women in this book, has written her own marriage contract and lived it to the letter. Like Gwendolen, in chapters too long passed for us really to remember, she sees marriage as a way of escaping the world of fathers and stepfathers and uncles, of "doing what she likes"—and so it is for her, for a time. (One of the reasons Eliot resists legal change, it occurs to me occasionally, is that her sense of time is not too short but too long—the changes that to Mill are the new Eden are to her already another paradise lost.) The Alcharisi is there to deliver to Daniel the news of his patrimony, that he is a Jew of a learned and distinguished line, and that the law is on his side. She makes very clear that the law was never really on hers, and now it is "beginning to make ghosts upon the daylight," that haunting metaphor for the return of patriarchy with which we began our investigations. But for a time, she wrote her own law, in defiance of her father, who "only thought of fettering me into obedience" (540). The Alcharisi wanted "to live a larger life, with freedom to do what everyone else did, and be carried along in a great current, not obliged to care" about the Jewish law that was everything to her father: "I cared for the wide world," she says, in almost a parody of Mill's hopefulness, and refused to care for "the shadow of my father's strictness ... which was a thunder without meaning in my ears" (540). But like a Millian individual, the Alcharisi believes the way out of "bondage" is in fact through another, a better bond, through the contract she crafts. Daniel's father, "unlike me [was] all lovingness and affection." "I knew I could rule him, and I made him secretly promise me, before I married him, that he would put no hindrance in the way of my being an artist" (540). "When a woman's will is as strong as the man's who wants to govern her, half her strength must be in concealment" (541), she says, and the secret promise she extracts from the loving man is her freedom to carry her voice into the world.

The Alcharisi is defeated, of course—her gift deserts her at a moment of crisis; she retires from the stage and cannot go back; her first husband dies; her second knows none of her secrets; and she is in the grip again of her father's law, the dead hand that reaches from beyond the grave: "Some other right forces itself upon me like iron in an inexorable hand; ... even when I am at ease" (545). A ghost imprisoned by the hand of another ghost, she has been fettered by what the narrator at least at moments suggests is a higher law. She comes into the novel to carry a word from beyond the grave. "My father ... wished I had been a son; he cared for me as a makeshift link" (541), and she has been a link indeed—his wish, his law, his documents, all come to Daniel, who will fulfill the promise his mother failed to make, evading it through a promise of her own. But the Alcharisi has her own theory of law. "If that is the right law for the world," she says, "I will not say I love it,"—or as she says in explicit echo of John Stuart Mill, "I don't consent. We only consent to what we love" (567). What is life otherwise, she asks, but "the slavery of being a girl?"

The Alcharisi's idea of consent is Gwendolen Harcourt's native tongue, a resistance to the binding of will, a desire for freedom, for something wider—everything that briefly leads Gwendolen to hope that she can separate from Grandcourt, only to realize she cannot. The Alcharisi, freed by fame if finally bound by fate, imagines a separateness that to Daniel is abhorrent in every way: the current of Judaism, the bondage to the will of the father, is everything he has sought in his amiable aimless life. But her vision of separateness, what we might call alienation, is a powerful one; her second marriage, no less than her first, is imagined as one that serves her purposes, and however much she is punished, she is no Fatima. Instead, she instantiates some more modern vision of marriage without a bloody chamber, marriage that does not lead to sympathy or moral choice, marriage that is just another choice along the path to independence. And when she utters the words *consent*, *choose*, and *law* in a sentence, she is uttering the cry that leads to what not just Gwendolen but many others (and Mill, in some telling parentheses) recognized as the road to divorce—that, as Lydgate says, "the certainty, 'She will never love me much,' is easier to bear than the fear, 'I shall love her no more'" (MM:613) and what does a promise mean, what does consent mean, when there is no love? The rational side of Marian Evans, trapped in an illicit relationship with George Henry Lewes, her "husband," because of the idiocies of English divorce law, cannot help but assent, but the fiction (at least explicitly) never does; the Alcharisi will die a painful death, and she will leave no daughters, or leave them no freer than she was herself. Unless the invisible hand of the author alters the script of the contract (striking, as it does, both Grandcourt and Casaubon dead in timely and elegant fashion), heroines stay bound, returning and renouncing and choosing not to choose again. Or rather, they are forced to choose again their first benighted choice, for no better reason than that they once assented to it; even if they did not love it (as we know Gwendolen did not), they pretended to do so, and they dare not reveal the barenness of the harlot-like contract they signed.

Gwendolen Harleth, however, does sign something else. At the end of *Daniel Deronda* she writes a letter to Daniel, which, the narrator tells us, is "something more precious than gold and gems." That letter, she says, "contain[s] these word:—'Do not think of me sorrowfully on your wedding-day.'" In it, of course, Gwendolen renounces what she never had; she renounces any claim to Daniel, and she says, "It shall be better with me for having known you" (694–95). Readers tricked by the novel's chronology may never have recovered from their sense that Daniel and Gwendolen should be together, that he has instead married a woman whose tiny slippers echo the Alcharisi's father's wish that women should be made following a "receipt," their will "pressed small, like Chinese feet" (541). "Do not think of me . . . on your wedding day," she says, and, undoing the curse that Lydia Glasher put on the novel, she is, we might imagine, undoing the marriage plot as well. Let others dwell in the room of the dead wife; let others sign the self-binding contract of a marriage they only think they can control; Gwendolen, at the end, steps off the moving sidewalk.

Or does she? Is there any trick more powerful than that which begins, "Do not think of me"? How better to see that your ghost remains alive for all time, than to exile her to oblivion? Let others dwell on Mordecai's beautiful death, on Mirah's devotion, on Daniel's ability to count the gifts after the reception (tellingly, a watch from Sir Hugo and Lady Mallinger, the better to count their dwindling days with). I choose to notice only that last signature, Gwendolen Grandcourt, that imaginary being, inscribing her name in full at the end of the novel that in every other way seems to bear someone else's. At that moment, two ghostwriters, we might think, are, on their way out of our lives, saluting each other.

John Stuart Mill, in the sweetness that marks him as a political thinker, imagines a husband who is not a Bluebeard, a contract that would bind one's spirit only in the true liberty of choosing another, creating a higher, a larger freedom. At times Eliot believes this as well—and those readers who do not object fiercely to Will Ladislaw (and I am one, though most Victorian critics remained, like Sir James, adamant) believe she went some ways to imagining a marriage without a bloody chamber. But her fiction also suggests something different, something that we would lose if we lost the Bluebeard plot. Without curiosity, no plot; without Bluebeard, no treacherous, alluring, pedagogical transformation. "Doubtless a vigorous error vigorously pursued has kept the embryos of truth a-breathing: the quest of gold being at the same time a questioning of substances, the body of chemistry is prepared for its soul, and Lavoisier is born" (450). Or so says the narrator of *Middlemarch*: in Dorothea's mistakes, in Gwendolen's terrible struggles against her fate, we can see a different view of progress: one in which alchemy can become chemistry; and what is illusion, romance, error, can become the higher reality, invisible, always, to those trapped in a clogged and darkened medium, but visible to the curious heroine, and to us.

That "medium," to return to George Eliot's figure, is no more—and in fact, to an extent few scholars have noticed, the rigidity of Victorian marriage was already a-crumbling as these novelists were writing. But where would any of these books have been without error? Every Victorian novel in this study was produced by a novelist trapped in a bad marriage. Thackeray, notoriously, was married to a lovely, vulnerable woman who gave way to postpartum depression, and he could never marry again; she outlived him and all but one of their children in an asylum. Dickens, even more notoriously, separated acrimoniously from his wife Catherine and (before leaving) had the door between their bedrooms bricked over. Marian Evans was, as we have seen, unable to marry George Henry Lewes, trapped as he was in his own unhappy marriage. We might have expected that she, rather than the prescient Dickens, would have written the exchange between Stephen Blackpool and Mr. Bounderby, where the former, having piteously determined that "there's a law to punish me" if he leaves his wife, if he beats her, if he lives with his true love, Rachael, in sin, says, in the simple appeal of the period, "Now, a' God's name, show me the law to help me!"[19] In the absence of significant reform to the law of divorce, marriage hobbled along, accompanied always by its other form of alienation, "separation." Even Rosamond Vincy, that paragon of social correctness ("In fact there was but one person in Rosamond's world whom she did not regard as blameworthy, and that was the graceful creature with blond plaits and with little hands crossed before her, who had never expressed herself unbecomingly, and had always acted for the best—the best naturally being what she best liked" [625–26]) imagines leaving her husband: "It came into her mind once that she would ask her father to let her go home again; but dwelling on that prospect made it seem utter dreariness to her; a married woman gone back to live with her parents—life seemed to have no meaning for her in such a position: she could not contemplate herself in it" (712). Mrs. Bulstrode's friends similarly imagine that she might leave her husband in his disgrace. Mrs. Hackbutt, we are told, "longed to say, 'if you take my advice you will part from your husband,' but it seemed clear to her that the poor woman knew nothing of the thunder ready to bolt on her head, and she herself could do no more than prepare her a little" (704), and Harriet's brother Walter Vincy (who thinks that Rosamond, as well, ought to come back and live with them), says, "But you must bear up as well as you can, Harriet. People don't blame you. and I'll stand by you whatever you make up your mind to do" (706). That "whatever" is what Mrs. Snagsby would refer to as "the high road of marital separation," and we need to remember that Harriet Bulstrode's heroic gesture of renouncing her clothes and hat, with its perfectly dyed-to-match feather, for a "Puritan bonnet," is also renouncing the opportunity to live in material comfort and marital alienation with her brother and sister-in-law.

Alienation will have its day, and it might seem that the proper end to the marriage plot is divorce law, pure and simple. Fix the law, we might think, and the lovers will follow. That solution is hovering in Anna Karenina's adultery, in the Princess Casamassima's wandering the continent alone, and most powerfully in Ellen Olenska's visit to New York in *The Age of Innocence*. That novel enters thoroughly into the language of curiosity. When Newland Archer and Ellen meet alone it is in the Metropolitan Museum ("someday it will be a great museum," they muse) in front of the Cesnola antiquities: "its glass shelves . . . crowded with small broken objects—hardly recognizable domestic utensils, ornaments and personal trifles—made of glass, of clay, of discloloured bronze and other timeblurred substances."[20] "It seems cruel," says Ellen, "that after a while nothing matters . . . any more than these little things, that used to be necessary and important to forgotten people, and now have to be guessed at under a magnifying glass and labelled: 'Use unknown.'" But so, too, does the novelist look: cruelly, curiously, guessing "under a magnifying glass." Newland and Ellen are surrounded by cabinets of curiosity, and the social relations that bind them in their roles are merely another artifact, just as they are in *Middlemarch*, that "study of provincial life." Wharton's hero and heroine are subjects of an equally clinical observation, as hemmed in by carriages at the beginning of the novel as they are by convention at its end. And when May Archer lies to Ellen, telling her she is already pregnant, prompting her to leave New York without Newland, she is merely (as we learn at the end of the novel) a wiser Fatima—not holding on to the key, but allowing her husband to believe he holds it; waiting her time, waiting for the conventions of (neo)Victorian law to catch him up, as he senses all of society closing in on him at the book's final dinner party, preparing to sacrifice him and Ellen to social duty, as powerfully as Dorothea Brooke was prepared to sacrifice herself. Like an angry Savonarola in the middle of *Romola*, "an arresting voice," forcing the heroine to return to Florence and her disastrous marriage ("you chose the bond," he says, in familiar language), the novelist insists, once more, that she and only she will grant a divorce—anything else, she suggests, is just cheating.

With that much disapproval hanging over our heads, the novel had to get George Eliot out of the way. Leslie Stephen had no sympathy with Dorothea's remarriage to Will Ladislaw—a "dabbler," he says, "a small journalist" with a "liking to lie on a rug in the houses of his friends and flirt with their pretty wives," an "amiable Bohemian," but no solution to the problems of a modern Saint Theresa, unless "a Theresa of our days has to be content with suckling fools and chronicling small beer."[21] Similarly, his daughter, Virginia Woolf, had to dispose of *Middlemarch* to commence her own career. *To the Lighthouse*, when it imagines a woman artist who does not need to get married ("Then her eye caught the salt shaker which she had placed there to remind her that tomorrow she would move the tree further towards the middle of the painting ... for at any rate, she need not marry, thank heaven ... she would move the tree rather more to the middle") and when it undoes the Rayleys' marriage, the act that triumphantly concludes part 1 ("Things had worked loose after the first year or so; that marriage had turned out rather badly"), signals its greatest rebellion when Minta Rayley leaves volume 3 of *Middlemarch* on a train "and she never knew what happened at the end." A wise woman, Minta Rayley, refusing to finish *Middlemarch*, and last seen handing tools to her (alienated) husband, "businesslike, straightforward, friendly," laughing. As Virginia Woolf knew better than anyone, the novelist is harsher than even the law; the novel has its own laws to enforce.

After such rebellions, after divorce law and the vote and married women's separate property, is Bluebeard even necessary? "On or about December 1910 human character changed," Virginia Woolf tells us—but if that is so, why does Bluebeard appear at the beginning of her first novel? Is it merely that a ghastly hallucination is briefly interrupting our voyage out, a quaint memory of a previous age, banished along with the angel in the house and mother's best china? Or can curiosity, Bluebeard, and the marriage plot still matter? My suggestion here, following the unexpected lead of Sir Leslie Stephen, is that the novel goes on trying to rewrite *Middlemarch* long after we might expect it to do so, and that the Bluebeard plot shows up everywhere from contemporary fiction and graphic novels to science fiction and modernist poetry. The curious heroine, in short, outlived the legal framework that gave her form, but she continues to suggest some of the limits of patriarchal knowledge.

What accounts for this uncanny half-life? Jeffrey Eugenides has elegantly summed up my difficulty in his novel of the same name: the heroine of *The Marriage Plot* has taken that subject for her senior thesis and begins with great confidence. "Her plan was to begin with Jane Austen. After a brief examination of *Pride and Prejudice*, *Persuasion*, and *Sense and Sensibility*, all comedies, essentially, that ended with weddings, Madeleine was going to move on to the Victorian novel, where things got more complicated and considerably darker. *Middlemarch* and *The Portrait of a Lady* didn't end with weddings. They began with the traditional moves of the marriage plot—the suitors, the proposals, the misunderstandings—but after the wedding ceremony they kept on going. These novels followed their spirited, intelligent heroines, Dorothea Brooke and Isabel Archer, into their disappointing married lives, and it was there that the marriage plot reached its greatest artistic expression."[22] A splendid summary so far—but, she plans to conclude, "By 1900 the marriage plot was no more." And, despite her research into "the rise of industrialism and the nuclear family, the formation of the middle class, and the Matrimonial

Causes Act of 1857," Madeleine grows bored; doubts about the originality of her work nag at her; she moves on to Barthes's *A Lover's Discourse*, where "waiting is an enchantment." If she finishes her thesis, she thinks, she will end it with John Updike, and with wife-swapping, what she calls "the last vestige of the marriage plot," for there is no "husband-swapping."

This makes an uneasy end to the Bluebeard story (does the wife no longer want to know?) but it is not quite Madeleine's end: instead, her own progress through the marriage plot is surprisingly conventional. She has two suitors: she marries the unsuitable one; she sleeps once with the suitable one; finally, in a heartbreaking scene, the unsuitable one divorces her, and she moves on to studying the works of Elizabeth Gaskell. Undone by Barthes and poststructuralism, Madeleine instead reinvents the marriage plot with utopian open-endedness. A happy ending all around—but is she then right about the twentieth century? If she were, Eugenides suggests, then Dorothea Brooke and Isabel Archer would matter to no one, for there would be other ways for women to know, with or without the experimentations of the marriage plot, with or without divorce.

This does not seem to be true. If anything, Dorothea Brooke and Isabel Archer continue to be emblems of some quest for knowledge, some quest even for happiness, which the novel blithely refuses to resolve. In P. D. James's *Children of Men*, the narrator, Theo Faron, a historian of Victorian England, is asked to cover a friend's extension school course: "*Middlemarch, Portrait of a Lady, Vanity Fair, Cranford*. Only fourteen in the class, fifty-year-old women mainly. They should be fussing round their grandchildren, so they've time on their hands, you know how it is. Charming ladies, if a little conventional in their taste."[23] The class goes as planned "until a large woman in the front row began extravagantly praising Isabel Archer's moral qualities and sentimentally lamenting her undeserved fate," and one woman, a younger woman, bursts out:

> "I don't see why you should particularly pity someone who was given so much and made such poor use of it. She could have married Lord Warburton and done a great deal of good to his tenants, to the poor. All right, she didn't love him, so there was an excuse and she had higher ambitions for herself than marriage to Lord Warburton. But what? She had no creative talent, no job, no training. When her cousin made her rich, what did she do? Gad round the world with Madame Merle, of all people. And then she marries that conceited hypocrite and goes in for Thursday salons gorgeously dressed. What happened to all the idealism? I've got more time for Henrietta Stackpole." The woman had protested: "Oh, but she's so vulgar!" "That's what Mrs. Touchett thinks, so does the author. But at least she has talent, which Isabel hasn't, and she uses it to earn her living, and support her widowed sister." She added: "Isabel Archer and Dorothea both discard eligible suitors to marry self-important fools, but

one sympathizes more with Dorothea. Perhaps this is because George Eliot respects her heroine and, at heart, Henry James despises his." She might, Theo had suspected, have been relieving boredom by deliberate provocation. But, whatever her motive, the ensuing argument had been noisy and lively and for once the remaining thirty minutes had passed quickly and agreeably. He had been sorry and a little aggrieved when, the following Thursday, watched for, she had failed to appear. (46–47)

But this alternative, rebellious heroine does reappear, in his life if not his course—and when she does, it is as the figure of renewal, the mother of the first child born in England in over twenty years; from the womb of Dorothea Brooke, we might imagine, a new world is born.

The eerie conjunction of Dorothea Brooke, Isabel Archer, and a promise of female power betrayed occurs in all sorts of strange places in contemporary fiction, and it always carries with it a strange wistfulness. In Alison Bechdel's *Fun Home*, Isabel Archer (shadowed unexpectedly by Oscar Wilde) represents the heroine's mother's lost youth, her dream of independence and creativity, stamped out even more fiercely than the "Icarus Games," the Joycean recollections that haunt Bechdel after her father's suicide. In a powerful if brief sequence, she conjures her mother's beauty and spark, as the latter poses for her passport picture, preparing to fly to Germany to marry her (unknown to her gay) husband. Bechdel frames the Jamesian moment with her parents' meeting in a production of *The Taming of the Shrew*, adding that "if the Taming of the Shrew was a harbinger of my parents' marriage, Henry James's The Portrait of a Lady runs more than a little parallel to their early days together."[24] Then she interrupts her parents' courtship to recount the plot of the novel: "Isabel Archer, the heroine, leaves America for Europe. She's filled with heady notions about living her life free from provincial convention and constraint." Those words appear over Bechdel's drawing of her mother's passport photo; then, as her mother descends the stairway from an airplane at the Stuttgart airport, the caption reads "Isabel turns down a number of worthy suitors, but perversely accepts Gilbert Osmond, a cultured, dissipated, and penniless European art collector." A series of smaller frames enacts her parents' drive to Paris to visit "an army friend of my father's," and, as her mother leaves the car in stunned fury at her husband's attack in a "terrible fight" in the car, the caption reads above the frame: "Later, my mother would learn that Dad and his friends had been lovers." And in a box within the frame, Bechdel adds, "Much like Isabel Archer learns that Gilbert had been having an affair all along with the woman who had introduced them" (70–71). Then there is a single, long frame in which the only caption bubble says, "Get back in here!" as her mother, attempting to flee, hesitates and turns back, and then two smaller frames in which the father says, "Now!" and (in the next frame), "Crazy bitch," while the commentary above them reads "But too good for her own good, Isabel remains with Gilbert . . . [next frame] and despite all her youthful hopes to the contrary, ends up 'ground in the very mill of the conventional.'" The James quotation hovers over the drawing of their receding backs, as the car continues to drive into curved Paris streets, the bubble saying "Crazy bitch" lurching similarly between the father's contempt for his wife and Bechdel's sympathy for her mother *and* Isabel. The next frame, the length of the page, shows a picture of a young Bechdel with her parents and older brother, and the caption above reads "In a passport photo taken eight years later, my mother's luminous face has gone dull."

This interests me precisely because Bechdel is breaking the frame of the narrative, toying with realism and intertextuality, words and pictures, past and present. In the middle of a graphic novel of a lesbian artist's coming of age, Isabel Archer crashes the party, and Henry James speaks in a bubble, like a palimpsest of realism. This "writing over" of the heroine's plot allows us to hazard some less expected claims about the future both of realist fiction and the curious heroine, to make the story something new. Like Madeleine's blending of "a lover's discourse" and the "enchantments" of the marriage plot, Bechdel's odyssey suggests something very different from the orthodox exclusion of the curious heroine and her marriage plot from high modernism and postmodernism, the critical account that traps her in a version of realism linked to the readerly, the materialist, the "woman's picture." Always a governess, always in love, always checking the weather report (to borrow Barthes's barometer)—that is hardly our story.

If the conventional critique of realism echoes Virginia Woolf's attack on *Jane Eyre*, we can nonetheless locate a similarly heterodox equation of modernism and the curious heroine in the works of Woolf herself. For the allure of Isabel Archer, Dorothea Brooke, and the unlived lives of the lost mother haunts Virginia Woolf as surely as it does Bechdel, the fictional Madeleine, or my book. And when, at the end of *A Room of One's Own*, Woolf imagines Shakespeare's sister, resting in an unvisited grave, she imagines her precisely as a Victorian heroine "ground in the mill of the conventional":

> Now my belief is that this poet who never wrote a word and was buried at the crossroads still lives. She lives in you and in me, and in many other women who are not here tonight, for they are washing up the dishes and putting the children to bed. But she lives; for great poets do not die; they are continuing presences; they need only the opportunity to walk among us in the flesh. This opportunity, as I think, it is now coming within your power to give her. . . . If we have the habit of freedom and the courage to write exactly what we think; if we escape a little from the common sitting-room and see human beings not always in their relation to each other but in relation to reality, . . . then the

opportunity will come and the dead poet who was Shakespeare's sister will put on the body which she has so often laid down. Drawing her life from the lives of the unknown who were her forerunners, . . . she will be born. I maintain that she would come if we worked for her, and that so to work, even in poverty and obscurity, is worth while.[25]

In Woolf's ecstatic prose, we might hear more than an echo of Eliot's conclusion to *Middlemarch*: "Many who knew her, thought it a pity that so substantive and rare a creature should have been absorbed into the life of another, and be only known in a certain circle as a wife and mother. But no one stated exactly what else that was in her power she ought rather to have done—not even Sir James Chettam, who went no further than the negative prescription that she ought not to have married Will Ladislaw" (783). But Eliot goes on: "The effect of her being on those around her was incalculably diffusive: for the growing good of the world is dependent on unhistoric acts and that things are not so ill with you and me as they might have been, is half owing to the number who lived faithfully a hidden life, and rest in unvisited tombs" (785).

Not so unvisited as all that, perhaps. The inheritance of female curiosity, and no less of Victorian feminism, is a complicated one for all the modernists, but most especially for Virginia Woolf, who recounts humorously but with a touch of horror an encounter with Henry James. "Well then, we went and had tea with Henry James today . . . and Henry James fixed me with his staring blank eye—it is like a childs marble—and said 'My dear Virginia, they tell me—they tell me—they tell me—that you—as indeed being your fathers daughter nay your grandfathers grandchild—the descendant I may say of a century—of a century—of quill pens and ink—ink—ink pots, yes, yes, yes, they tell me—ahm m m—that you, that you, that you write in short.' This went on in the public street, while we all waited, as farmers wait for the hen to lay an egg—do they?—nervous, polite, and now on this foot now on that."[26] The sense of Virginia Woolf, while writing her own sentences, shifting nervously "now on this foot now on that," is our sense of her Victorian inheritance, the one that she marked most vividly in *Night and Day*, with her brilliant parody of her beloved (step)aunt Anne Thackeray Ritchie, daughter of the novelist and sister of Leslie Stephen's first wife, Minny. There is a powerful element of nostalgia in *Night and Day* and throughout Woolf's work for the world of the Victorians, the world, as she put it in "Mr. Bennett and Mrs. Brown," before "the smashing and the crashing began," the world of Shakespeare and Milton and Keats, and "even of Jane Austen and Thackeray and Dickens, if you think of the language, and the heights to which it can soar when free."[27] (It is, remember, a Thackeray manuscript Woolf longs to see when she crosses the grass in *A Room of One's Own*—did Thackeray alter his manuscript "for style or sense?") Anne Thackeray's double, the heroine's mother, Mrs. Hilbery, is particular aghast at seeing a portrait under cracked glass, for "I know how it would hurt me to see my father in a broken glass."[28] The novel reflects Woolf's own doubled reflection, her movement between the two worlds of curiosity we have been following, the doubled consciousness of a material life, a life, she says, "lived unconsciously," "the broken vacuum cleaner; ordering dinner; bookbinding," that goes alongside a life more deeply felt, things "more memorable," "separate," "all plumy and soft green and purple and blue." In her memoirs, she locates that double life (being alongside nonbeing) in two places, in what she "tried" in *Night and Day*, and in the Victorian novel—"The real novelist can convey both sorts of being. I think Jane Austen can; and Trollope; perhaps Thackeray and Dickens and Tolstoy. . . . I have never been able to do both."[29]

If we take that seriously, then *Night and Day* is a bridge from Victorian to modern, from one form of feminism to another, from curiosity to curiosity. And it lets us see the depiction of ordinary life as itself more "luminous." Mary Datchet's life, spent in an office, alternately getting tea and getting votes, suggests a world of Victorian improvement elsewhere invisible in Woolf's work—the world in which Woolf, like other members of her family, taught at Morley College, the institute for working men and women, and was the only member of her family to persist in doing so. Politics exist in the novel partly as a world in flight from romance (after another disappointment, "Happily for Mary Datchet she returned to the office to find that by some obscure Parliamentary manoeuvre the vote had once more slipped beyond the attainment of women"[268]) and partly as a world of independence: it is in her life as a political woman that Mary claims that most remarkable thing, a room of her own; by the end of the novel Katharine Hilbery also claims, "I went back to my room by myself and I did—what I liked."

The reality Woolf offers in this world is very close to the doubling of curiosity we have seen throughout this book and its attendant *unreality*. By the end of the novel, the realist view is available only through reflections and imagination: "[Katharine] saw the forms of Ralph, William, Cassandra and herself as if they were all equally unsubstantial, and, in putting off reality, had gained a kind of dignity which rested upon each impartially"; "each person possessed in Cassandra's mind some fragment of what privately she called reality"; "while the drive lasted, no one was real, nothing was ordinary: the crowds, Government buildings, the tide of men and women washing the base of the great glass windows, were all generalized, and affected her as if she saw them on the stage"; "the indecent spectacle was her own action beheld for the first time from the outside" (424). As in *Alice,* as in *Bleak House,* as elsewhere in the Victorian novel, the very attempt to locate a fixed reality turns the novel itself into a broken glass, in which figures waver and disappear. In the novel's most powerful scene of looking, just as the lovers are changing partners for the final time, Cassandra and Katharine come together to dress for a party: Cassandra saw

> the reflection of her cousin's face in the looking-glass. The face in the looking glass was serious and intent, apparently occupied with other things besides the straightness of the parting which, however, was being driven as straight as a Roman road through the dark hair. Cassandra was impressed again by Katharine's maturity; and, as she enveloped herself in the blue dress which filled almost the whole of the long looking-glass with blue light and made it the frame of a picture, holding not only the slightly moving effigy of the beautiful woman, but shapes and colours of objects reflected from the background, Cassandra thought that no sight had ever been quite so romantic. (364–65)

We are back once more to the romantic side of familiar things—but we are also back to a moving effigy, something haunted, doubled, as the two women (in the pivotal "she" of the quotation) come together, in the blue dress, another tiny Alice.

But not exactly another Bluebeard's wife. It was Woolf's aunt, Anne Thackeray, who in "Bluebeard's Keys" (a story in which a young girl finally does not marry Bluebeard) first asked, how did the first Mrs. Bluebeard get in the bloody chamber? For Woolf, Bluebeard is a bit of a joke. When he appears on the second page of *The Voyage Out*, the Ambroses walk along the embankment, and Mr. Ambrose appears such a picture of eccentricity that young boys call out "Bluebeard." But in their later appearance as (perhaps) the Ramsays, when Mr. Ramsay has exhausted Mrs. Ramsay and (perhaps) done her to death, we might think Victorian visions of patriarchy are not quite so far from Woolf's mind—nor Victorian mysteries, either.

For modernism also could not entirely elide female curiosity. The disillusioned heroines of Jean Rhys; the Jamesian wistfulness of Elizabeth Bowen's; Marianne Moore's "The Pangolin": "To explain grace requires / a curious hand." But oddly, some of the most intriguing impulses of curiosity and the novel go more directly into genre fiction, first into detective fiction in the hands of women like Dorothy Sayers and Margery Allingham, then into speculative fiction, in the writing of women like Ursula Le Guin and Octavia Butler. Writers who begin as passionate post-Victorian realists— Margaret Atwood, who takes on Lewis Carroll in *The Edible Woman*; Doris Lessing, drawing on Tolstoy and George Eliot to write *The Golden Notebook*— find themselves lured increasingly into subjective realism, then into science fiction. A. S. Byatt may not turn *Possession* directly into a ghost story, but she ends on a beautiful note of romance, just as *Angels and Insects* ends with a husband returned from the dead and a séance that concludes with the embrace of a waterlogged corpse. Even Margot Livesey, in the eerie and comical *Eva Moves the Furniture*, suggests that Milton's Eve has returned, and she wants to remodel the house of fiction.

But what of our third term—curiosity, realism, the law? This kind of haunted lyricism, Woolf's activism notwithstanding, would suggest that curiosity has pulled further and further away from the law, perhaps, as I have suggested, because of the granting of political rights in Anglo-American law; or perhaps perversely because these rights (especially the right to vote) did not offer the new world feminists imagined. In *Possession*, certainly, feminists are not only not the answer, they are also not in the know. The wistful, happy ending of the novel is kept carefully both from the Victorian and the modern heroine: "There are things that happen and leave no discernible trace, are not spoken or written of, though it would be very wrong to say that subsequent events go on indifferently, all the same, as though such things had never been. Two people met, on a hot May day, and never later mentioned their meeting. This is how it was."[30]

Not for Byatt, it would seem, either the Gothic or the law; rather, she offers the ultimate words of realism, however shrouded in mystery : "This is how it was." E. M. Forster might approve—this is certainly not the world of "and then . . . and then . . . " But the law finds its way back in nonetheless: : poetry, letters, gossip, desire, are all mediated by inheritance, and it is through a complicated will plot that the feminist scholar Maud Baillie comes to "possess" as many secrets as anyone in the book. It is Maud, in the end, who inherits the secrets of the locked room.

And so it remains in much of contemporary fiction, despite the trappings of a more sophisticated metafictional world. For as Margaret Drabble puts it in *A Natural Curiosity*,

> Secrets, pigeon-holes, little plots. As a solicitor, Clive Enderby is aware that there are far more family secrets in the world than most people know of—well, if they knew of them, they wouldn't be secrets, would they? People don't want to think about these things. So they don't. People want to believe in an ordered, regular world, of faithful married couples, legitimate children, normal sex, legal behaviour, decent continuity, and they will go to almost any lengths to preserve this faith. Any suggestion that "real life" is otherwise tends to be greeted as "melodramatic" or "implausible."
>
> Solicitors know better. . . . The subplots fester, break out, infect strangers. Dark blotches spread. Life is more like an old-fashioned, melodramatic novel than we care to know. Clive knows more about the Ablewhite girls than they know about themselves.[31]

"Wills, legacies, inheritance tax, capital gains tax. A real old nineteenth-century property plot," says a character in another Drabble novel. "This is a real old-fashioned nineteenth-century country," murmurs his friend.[32] Is it too much to imagine that the world of secrets, of "old-fashioned, melodramatic novel[s]," is still the world of female curiosity?

Drabble herself mocks this vision, and so should we, but not too much. At the beginning of *A Natural Curiosity*, Liz Headleand's friend Alix reports that "I've got to go to prison in the afternoon. . . . I'm off to see P. Whitmore [the murderer in whom she has, unlikely as it seems, taken an interest]. But yes, I'll be in in the evening. Brian's out, teaching his evening class on the Victorian novel. But Sam and I will be in." Is anyone really still teaching the Victorian novel? Are these trappings of female curiosity (wills, murderers, capital gains taxes) really all that is left? Of course not—and this is far from the only interesting strand of feminist fiction at the present moment. But for that, we must a little slip the bonds of realism and let the fiction itself be more curious.

CONCLUSION

The Clockwork Princess, or Justice for the Dolls

The word, however, pleases me. To me it suggests something altogether different: it evokes "concern"; it evokes the care one takes for what exists and could exist; a readiness to find strange and singular what surrounds us; a certain relentlessness to break up our familiarities and to regard otherwise the same things; a fervor to grasp what is happening and what passes; a casualness in regard to the traditional hierarchies of the important and the essential. I dream of a new age of curiosity.

      Michel Foucault, "The Masked Philosopher"

. . . My prime request
(Which I do last pronounce) is (O you wonder)
If you be Mayd, or no?
Mir. No wonder Sir,
But certainly a Mayd.

      Shakespeare, *The Tempest*

The cyborg is a matter of fiction and lived experience that changes what counts as women's experience in the late twentieth century. This is a struggle over life and death, but the boundary between science fiction and social reality is an optical illusion.

      Donna Haraway, "A Cyborg Manifesto"

What is there in "Farewell," "Door," "Gift"?

      Roland Barthes, *S/Z*

After the vote, after modernism, after Bluebeard's castle has been emptied, does realism have anything new to teach us, and if so, what can we learn? How can we follow Foucault in asking of curiosity that it "find strange and singular what surrounds us," that it teach us to "regard otherwise the same things"? My argument throughout this book has been that this is actually the task of realism, to borrow from the forms of the familiar only to make it in turn "strange and singular," that the more we think critically about the realist novel, the more we realize that, in Haraway's terms, "the boundary between science fiction and social reality is an optical illusion," and furthermore, that it is a struggle over life and death.

We might return to Kate Atkinson, the novelist whose works have been threaded through this volume: the writer who goes "behind the scenes at the museum," whose narrator imagines her mother's life (the curious room) before she was born; the novelist of the dollhouse, the dead twin, the lost sister, the curious heroine ("Reggie Chase, orphan of the parish"), and the end of the world. In her most recent novel, *Started Early, Took My Dog*, she comes to ground in this world and offers a dialogue that could be spun from the pages of my book and that can help us to begin to find an answer:

> Before he had taken on the task of investigating her past [Jackson] had felt obliged to remind Hope McMaster how curiosity had worked out for the cat.
>
> "Pandora's box," Julia said, already reaching for a second scone before finishing the first. "Although the word *pithos* actually translates as 'large jar.' Pandora released evil into the world and—"
>
> "I know," Jackson interrupted. "I know what she did."
>
> "People have a need to find the truth," Julia said. "Human nature can't abide a mystery."
>
> In Jackson's experience, finding the truth—whatever that was—only deepened the mystery of what had really happened in the past. And perhaps Hope's little Aaron and the squid would discover a family history that they would rather had stayed securely locked away, well out of pesky Pandora's reach.
>
> "Yes, but it's not about *liking* what you find out, it's about *knowing*," Julia said.
>
> Any time he spent with Julia always degenerated in the end into a mixture of comforting familiarity and irritable argument. Rather like marriage but without the divorce. Or the wedding for that matter.[1]

Just how did curiosity "work out" for the cat? Not very well, Atkinson might answer, but that never stopped the cat before.

What strikes the most familiar chord for us in Atkinson's lethal irony is the ambiguity of all narrative pedagogy, the failures (in every sense) of curiosity. Finding the truth, says the detective Jackson Brodie, "only deepened the mystery of what had really happened," a story that might better have "stayed securely locked away, well out of pesky Pandora's reach." To the extent that this book has followed pesky Pandora, this has always been a book about knowing—and certainly not always about liking what you find out. It began with a series of curious heroines drawn from myth and the novel; it unlocked many a door, but it ends, as so many contemporary books on the novel do, with "marriage but without the divorce. Or the wedding for that matter." My question in concluding this study is in part Kate Atkinson's: in the modern world, that is, the world after the Victorians, what difference does knowing make—and is there any hope for knowledge beyond, or even without, the wedding?

This is where speculative fiction enters, for there is another history of curiosity and the novel that runs parallel to this one, the tradition of wonder that finds meaning precisely in a dehumanizing of gender and femininity. In a pivotal scene in Joss Whedon's film *Serenity*, a young girl walks into a bar called The Maidenhead. She is entranced by everything she sees; it is unlike any place she has ever been. She wears an oriental wrap and an expression of wonder—and as she nears the bar, an electronic display of small doll-like figures begins to sing about the "fruity oaty bar." She looks at them, outlined in the eerie light of overexposed film, and utters a single word: "Miranda." At that moment, she drops her kimono, reveals a slender body and the ability to wrap her leg backward around a bar, and precedes to drop-kick everybody in the joint. As the film explodes into color and movement and sound, that single word echoes in our ears: "O brave new world!" we say.

This vision of female curiosity to my mind answers Foucault's dream of another form of curiosity in a very different way than Woolf and her literary progeny did, and it does so by going back to curiosity's roots in the cabinets and in the automaton. In 1835, in a waxwork museum in London, Madame Tussaud, having started her curious collection with heads taken from the victims of the guillotine, settles into Baker Street. Her star exhibition is a special creation crafted by her mentor Philippe Curtius: the Sleeping Beauty, whose chest rises and falls with "real" breath, a mechanism run by clockwork.[2] In a world in which the pornographic possibility of wax dolls was first exploited by private connoisseurs, this is an object closed to us: a princess on display dreaming her own secret dreams, "within within within." Now, here, in the beginning of the twenty-first century, the curious heroine once again becomes a doll, with secrets tucked inside.

This is the claim that postmodernism makes on us and makes in the name of both feminism and curiosity. Donna Haraway's plea in the "Cyborg Manifesto" offers us a sense of these different metrics: "The nimble fingers of 'Oriental' women, the old fascination of little Anglo-Saxon Victorian girls with doll's houses, women's enforced attention to the small take on quite new dimensions in this world. There might be a cyborg Alice taking account of these new dimensions" (154). Hints of the cyborg Alice have returned throughout this book (Alice returning underground, the curious princess rebelling against her inheritance, the clever heroine refusing the test; Galatea 2.2, the heroine in the machine), but other examples abound in contemporary culture. Joss Whedon's *Buffy the Vampire Slayer*, *Firefly*, and *Dollhouse*; Tim Burton's *Alice in Wonderland* (in which a proper Victorian heroine resists the marriage plot by becoming a warrior); and Krzysztof Kieslowski's *The Double Life of Veronique*, the heroine doubled by a photograph and haunted by a puppeteer, all reanimate our Persephone, bringing her back from underground ("I've died twice," sings Buffy). And this same powerful impulse is at work in the novel: the curious heroine pushes not just its thematic but its formal limits. Where is realism going? Where the curious heroine no longer fears to tread—beyond the human.

What is the soul of the cyborg Alice, and does she get to be curious about it? Like Alice's fall, Katharine Hilbery's mirror, or Esther Summerson's face in a broken glass, the cyborg heroine finds herself trapped in that "optical struggle" Haraway described, attempting once more to cross the limits the realist novel imposes on the curious heroine. Which is to say, that only rarely, and only with difficulty, and without even the slender margin of choice we have been hunting throughout this book, can the contemporary curious heroine choose her fate. "There wasn't a lot of choice but there was some, and this is what I chose," says Offred, the heroine of Margaret Atwood's *The Handmaid's Tale* (1986), and she might speak for any of these clockwork heroines: Joan Foster, the former fat girl turned closet writer of romance novels, faux-terrorist and Gothic poet, author of the eponymous *Lady Oracle* (1976); Kathy H., the clone narrator of Kazuo Ishiguro's *Never Let Me Go* (2005), the dystopian love story / story of origins with which we seem to have come full circle, back to Eve herself, forced out of the garden. The terms of the contract with which we began, where the reader's curiosity follows that of the heroine, where the novelist teases and seduces, and where our education leads us to enfranchisement, might seem radically to have changed, but they have not. That beginning, the first seduction, was the contract of "Sarrasine": sex for story, the passage over the threshold, the cold maiden's refusal, the pensive text. Or, as we first heard Barthes ask, "By what division is this exchange established? What is there in farewell, door, gift?"[3]

Perhaps nothing marks our placement within the postmodern more than beginning with "farewell." All three of my texts are in a sense valedictory, but only one of them, *Lady Oracle*, is actually posthumous. Its opening sentence reads "I planned my death carefully; unlike my life, which meandered along from one thing to another, despite my feeble attempts to control it," and then proceeds along two different time frames but also through a set of alternative texts, written by the heroine, Joan Delacourt Foster.[4] *Lady Oracle* embraces, however warily, an almost universally denigrated form of female curiosity, romance fiction, for Joan is the secret author not only of such works as *The Lord of Chesney Chase*, *The Secret of Morgrave Manor*, and *Escape from Love* but also of a novel she is currently writing and that forms a large part of *Lady Oracle*, a work tentatively titled *The Lord of Redmond Grange* or *Terror at Redmond Grange* or *Love and Terror at Redmond Grange* (32). (This, she rejects as "too long, and it sounded too much like The Bobbsey Twins at Sunset Beach.... My Love Was Terror ... too Mickey Spillane. Stalked by Love, that would do in a pinch," she concludes.) Both Joan's costume Gothics and her poetry, written under the influence of spirit writing performed with an equally Gothic set (mirrors, heavy drapes, candles, straight out of *Jane Eyre*), rely on the conventions of Victorian fiction and the poetry of Tennyson—particularly, as a young and sarcastic Joan notes, "the lady of the small onion" (141). But more importantly, both play with the logic of fictional form—the suspended question, the interrupted plot, the husband behind the door. They ask the question rather than deliver the answer: what is the mystery? they say.

Joan carries out her own postmodernist experiment, for she has a natural gift (or is it natural, cultivated as it is by her miserable teenage years and her exclusion from the conventional world of female romance?) for costume novels. She imagines explaining to her husband and his tediously revolutionary friends that this is her form of oppressed labor; it is "what she's good at." Joan's fiction comes out of her love affair with the past, one that she imagines as both dangerous and more real than her own, precisely because of its elaborate constructedness. It is a place where violence knows the rules and where she can control it, at least initially. She comes to write novels while living with a Polish count, who writes nurse novels under the name "Mavis Quilp"—Mavis because it is "archetypally English," Quilp after Dickens's dwarf in *The Old Curiosity Shop*, an inside joke against a man who insists that in moving to England he has "lost his stature" (153). (He means status, of course, but already Joan says she is learning not to correct him.) The Victorians themselves offer more than just status. They stand in some way as both ideal and rebuke. The rebuke is clear: their lives are the "tidy" ones Joan imitates, though they produce heroines whom Joan longs to force to "burp, fart." But they also offer a world of necessary rather than merely dangerous allure: Joan spends hours in the costume department of the Victoria and Albert Museum in South Kensington, for "if I could only get the clothes right, all the rest would fall in line." *Fichu, paletot, pelisse*, she says, and indeed "it did: the hero, a handsome, well-bred, slightly balding man, dressed in an immaculately tailored tweed cloak, like Sherlock Holmes's, pursued the heroine, crushing his lips to hers in a hansom cab and rumpling her *pelisse*. The villain, equally well-bred and similarly clad, did just about the same thing, except that in addition he thrust his hand inside her *fichu*. The rival female had a lithe body like that of a jungle animal beneath her exquisitely stitched corset, and like all such women, she came to a bad end. I wasn't as good at bad ends as I later became; I think she merely tripped on her *paletot*, going downstairs. But she deserved this, as she'd attempted to reduce the heroine to a life of shame by tying her up and leaving her in a brothel, under the supervision of a madam to whom I gave the features of Miss Flegg" (162).

Joan's anger here finds the perfect target, as well as the perfect outfit. Miss Flegg is Joan's vicious dance teacher, seemingly left behind in the earlier chapters of this novel of childhood embarrassment, and the reader feels a powerful joy coming across her at this moment, as Miss Flegg is finally punished for her misrecognition of Joan's love of dancing. But our joy is equally at the verbal flair of Atwood's integration of the exotic costuming terms, her resurrection of the far-too-curious heroine, and her fluid rounding of the bases on the baseball diamond of Gothic fiction: hero, villain, evil woman, HOME. These icons, however, are also the markers of the Bluebeard board game, and of novels as far removed from *Love and Terror at Redmond Grange* as *Clarissa*, Mrs. Sin-clair (Clarissa's sin) reentering our narrative as the comically vile Miss Flegg. The first time is tragedy; the second time, when we pass through the castle gates again, through the eyes of mass culture, are we only visiting in farce?

But that is only superficially the case: the novel's relationship to its past and to the tradition of the curious heroine is far more complicated. We see that in the middle of *Love and Terror at Redmond Grange*, when the heroine walks into the castle's maze to confront the secret of the grange, and particularly of its owner. What will she find there, the killer, the lover, the husband, the past, her past, the answer? Charlotte's journey into the maze is a reminder of curiosity as clockwork mechanism, a journey into the heart of narrative convention. Despite the ferocity of the character's desire for the suspended answer, the author/narrator is more ambivalent. "She'd wanted to go in ever since reaching Redmond Grange, and nothing anyone could say, not all the hair-raising tales of the servants, not all the sneering hints of Felicia had been able to deter her. But her feelings were ambiguous: did the maze mean certain death, or did it contain the answer to a riddle, an answer she must learn in order to live? More important: would she marry Redmond only if she stayed out of the maze, or only if she went in?" And her author speaks to her, and a little to us: "Don't go into the maze, Charlotte, you'll be entering at your own risk, I told her. I've always got you out of it before but now I'm no longer dependable. She paid no attention to me, she never did; she stood up, put down her embroidery, and prepared to go outside" (365). Once inside the maze, however, things are not as Charlotte expected: the first time, she finds Felicia, the vixen-like rival, waiting to kill her, only to have Lord Redmond rescue her, but that ending does not work. The second time, she finds herself "in the central plot" where there is a bench with four women. "Two of them looked a lot like her, with red hair and green eyes and small white teeth." The third is Joan's aunt Louisa, though Charlotte doesn't of course recognize her since they are in different parts of the novel and different orders of fictionality (aunt Louisa is "real," Charlotte a creation of that fictional creation Joan Delacourt); the third is the fat lady—and then suddenly we realize that Atwood has tricked us: the clockwork is a jack-in-the-box; this is not an ending for Charlotte, but for Felicia, the first (or rather, the most recent) Lady Redmond, who has instead walked herself out of her husband's life. It is she who must confront the secret at the heart of the maze, not the virginal girl with her inability to burp or fart. "Who are you?" Felicia asks the others. "We are Lady Redmond," says the middle-aged woman sadly. "All of us," the fat woman with the wings adds. "There must be some mistake," Felicia protests. "I myself am Lady Redmond." "Oh, yes, we know," says the first woman. "But every man has more than one wife. Sometimes all at once, sometimes one at a time, sometimes ones he doesn't even know about." And as she looks around, Felicia sees that the other women are turning ghostly, that "she could see the dimensions of the bench through their tenuous bodies." Then she sees Redmond, who turns into the killer in disguise ("he wanted to murder her as he had murdered his other wives"); then he turns into a masked man, then into Joan's lover, and then finally into Arthur, Joan's husband, "wearing a turtle-neck sweater." And at that moment, the two stories collide. There is a knock on the door of Joan's apartment, and when she opens the door, unsure yet again who is on the other side, she knocks out the waiting journalist, hitting him over the head with a Cinzano bottle and sending him to the hospital.

It is to that person that Joan finally tells this story—or at least most of it. But despite her promises, despite the contract, she never answers the central question—not only who is that man (husband, lover, father, killer, sexual predator, fool) but who is she—the fat lady; her own aunt; the first, the second, the third wife, or the last. That plot matters less than we might think—what we have instead is Joan's repetition of her mother's warning: "I keep thinking I should learn some lesson from all this, as my mother would have said." Has she? She has dispensed with the good heroine, the Jane Eyre figure, the "tidy" second wife, the mirror of innocence, but she is not terribly interested in the male figure, either. As in the novels of Virginia Woolf, Bluebeard isn't the point; the point now is entirely the story between women, the heroine, and her fictional (clockwork) double. We might see it as merely playful feminism, the comic version of that old story, "is my husband trying to kill me?" imagined in its modern, most anxious form: Is my marriage going to make me disappear? Is there any self left after the love story? What if I enter the maze and wander, clueless, forever? The Victorians, we might think, would never have let that happen. But there is something beyond the love story, something captured in the formal innovation and the generic play that tugs at the rest of our tradition. Joan's final act of telling us the story, of telling it without lies ("Well, not very many. Some of the names and a few other things, but nothing major"), suggests the essential loneliness of all our heroines—to whom can she tell this story, if not to a total stranger whom she has just clocked with a bottle of Cinzano? Joan promises to stop telling stories: "I won't write any more Costume Gothics, though; I think they were bad for me." But she goes on: "But maybe I'll try some science fiction. The future doesn't appeal to me as much as the past, but I'm sure it's better for you."

Is it? Not so easy a question to answer in *The Handmaid's Tale*. The goal of the society of Gilead, in which Offred is a sexual prisoner of the state renamed as a "handmaiden," is to empty women up entirely, to render them nothing but "vessels." In the wake of an imagined threat from an Iranian theocracy, the United States has turned to its own religious makeover, banning Jews, shipping off blacks, and reorganizing society around a nuclear family, with father, mother, children, and servants constituting a household. But the truly nuclear twist here is that due to persistent levels of radiation, syphilis, and (we are meant to think) sheer exhaustion, the men are sterile. Since the patriarchal order cannot admit this impotence, in place of "natural" reproduction it has reinstated the biblical habit of "lying with" the wife's handmaidens, and each household above a certain class (where the husbands are known as "Commanders") has its own handmaid. Policing this improved state requires a world of "eyes" (the secret police), barbed wire fences, dogs, informers, but more than that, involves transforming the still-fertile women into willing participants in socially organized rape: it involves winning their consent.

Well, sort of, and here marital law undergoes much the same twist as the fiction. As Offred explains her own presence in the Commander's household: "Nothing is going on here that I haven't signed up for."[5] This is when she asserts, "There wasn't a lot of choice but there was some, and this is what I chose." In another parody of the bourgeois marriage plot we have been tracking, the plot that needs to romanticize the wife's legal disappearance into marriage by congratulating itself on requiring her consent, this is the last choice she will make. But to make any further choice not only irrelevant but also dangerous requires a more radical break with the traditions of romantic love. Not only are the handmaids moved from household to household like players in an NFL draft, stripped of their individual names ("of-Fred," "of-Glen"), rendered invisible by robes and "wings," which frame their faces and in turn make it impossible for them to see around them, but *all* women are kept from reading. Even the stores no longer have signs, and the servants doing the shopping, rather than being handed lists or money, neither of which they are allowed, are handed tokens in the shapes of the things they are to buy: chicken, cow, eggs, the same icons displayed in shop windows. The only book in the house, at least the only book the women see, is the Bible, around which the household gathers on the ritual night, before the Commander mounts the Handmaid, lying in her mistress's lap, clutching her hands, in the ritual that binds the household, and presumably this society, together.

The joy of any dystopian novel is always "how did things get like this?" and *The Handmaid's Tale* has a chilling and convincing account: as dissent gradually mounted in the face of excess liberalism, the porno-marts, the rapes, the increasing violence (perhaps staged deliberately by the religious right?) in the streets, a new right-wing army arose. Feminism itself is seen as part of the repressive force: Offred remembers a jubilant book-burning held by her mother and her friends, tossing girlie magazines and pornography on the flames and watching naked women burn. But the crackown the right-wing army carries out is immediate and touches more precisely on the roots of the liberal subjectivity we have been tracing: in a single day all working women lose their jobs, and the army shows up to make them leave work. Simultaneously, their bank accounts are cut off or transferred to their husbands, if they are married; and the airports and the borders are closed. With a push of a button, all the ID numbers and bank accounts and tokens of identity that made women people disappear; divorces are undone; children are confiscated and reassigned; the modern arrangements people have taken for granted disappear, and a woman becomes either a sex slave or an un-woman, sent off to clean nuclear waste in some un-world, never seen again, left there until her body begins to fall off, in parts.

This partitioning of women is the mark of the new society: Offred is her womb, and there is nothing else about her that the state needs. Her memories, her ideas, even her eyes and skin and hair are unnecessary. She has a limited number of chances to bear a child (to bear "fruit," as the rhetoric has it), and if she fails, then she, too, will be an unwoman. It would seem that the sole aim of this regime is to reduce sex to anything but a mystery—in fact, to eliminate all mystery, all romance, all curiosity entirely. In a world where the only question is, will there be oranges at the market, where is curiosity to arise? It arises precisely where we would expect: behind a closed door, at the moment when Offred is invited to enter the Commander's (private) study, where not even the servants are allowed to dust—but what she finds there, however conventional the setup, is not the punch line we would predict.

That is because "what is on the other side is normal life. I should say: what is on the other side looks like normal life. There is a desk, of course, with a Computalk on it, and a black leather chair behind it" (137). And Atwood goes on to list items: potted plant, penholder set, papers, an oriental rug on the floor and a fireplace without a fire in it; a small sofa, a television set, an end table. But that is not what draws Offred's eyes: "All around the walls there are bookcases. They're filled with books. Books and books and books, right out in plain view, no locks, no boxes. No wonder we can't come in here. It's an oasis of the forbidden."

This is the most brilliant thing in the novel: that where we expect sex toys and erotica and forbidden pleasure, instead we find ordinary life from before the revolution—and particularly, a life of words. And the strangest request of all is that the Commander would like Offred to play Scrabble with him. Not that Scrabble is Scrabble anymore—"Now of course it's something different. Now it's forbidden, for us. Now it's dangerous. Now it's indecent. Now it's something he can't do with his Wife. Now it's desirable. Now he's compromised himself. It's as if he's offered me drugs" (138–39). And he has—as Offred begins to spell ("larynx, I spell. Valance. Quince. Zygote"), she wants to put the counters in her mouth; she wants to eat the letters; she wants to take them in because "this is freedom, an eyeblink of it. Limp, I spell. Gorge. What a luxury." The words have the same quality as the costume terms in *Lady Oracle*—*pelisse*; *paletot, fichu*. They are erotic because they are what she cannot have, and because the constraints of the Scrabble game have come to be a form of freedom—the freedom, the magic, of spells.

The mystery is the old question of the Bluebeard tales: not what does the wife want, but what does the husband desire? What does the Commander really want? It isn't sex, or not exactly. He wants to talk, to get to know her, to listen to her, to know what she thinks "about all this"—and he offers her rewards, chief among them, a fashion magazine from the time before. "It's an old one, he said, a curio of sorts. From the seventies, I think. A *Vogue*. This is like a wine connoisseur dropping a name. I thought you might like to look at it" (157). And she does—looking with "a force that made the ends of [her] fingers ache" at what she'd "taken . . . lightly enough once," when they were "infinitely discardable." She would leaf through them, throw them away, and "a day or two later [she] wouldn't be able to remember what had been in them." She continues:

> Though I remembered now. What was in them was promise. They dealt in transformations; they suggested an endless series of possibilities, extending like the reflections in two mirrors set facing one another, stretching on, replica after replica, to the vanishing point. They suggested one adventure after another, one wardrobe after another, one improvement after another, one man after another. They suggested rejuvenation, pain overcome and transcended, endless love. The real promise in them was immortality. (157)

The language here draws deep in the history of curiosity we have been tracing: not only the transformative possibilities of romance, something that ran from Milton to Eliot with hardly a break, but also the promise of endless self-transformation, makeovers, "two mirrors set facing one another," the perfect replica of the self, something yearned for since Eve first looked at her own reflection in the pool. But the infinite sadness that limns the infinite possibilities here is the sadness of another paradise lost, the loss of what was truly ordinary, a self that one could call one's own, that is not rendered freakish by the transformations of history. The Commander looks at the model in the magazine clinically, "a look you'd give to an almost extinct animal, at the zoo," but she is extinct; Offred herself is extinct; she is the last woman who will have the memory of freedom. "For the ones who come after you, it will be easier," one of the Aunts at the retraining center says. "They will accept their duties with willing hearts." Offred goes on: "She did not say: because they will have no memories, of any other way. She said: Because they won't want things they can't have" (117). Offred is a curiosity not only because she is a curious woman, the thing the State didn't imagine, but because she is the last curious woman—what is in the Commander's closet is her lost sense of herself.

Offred seems always to be opening doors, always to be crossing thresholds. She goes to an illegal sex club with the Commander, one held in a hotel from the old days, and behind a locked bathroom door, she finds her best friend, Moira, now employed as a prostitute and wearing what we recognize as an old Playboy bunny costume. She meets her lover Nick behind another closed door, in what may or may not be a romantic scene (the narrative is too ironic to give us these scenes straight.) Perhaps most movingly, she meets her predecessor—or rather, *becomes* her, finding a scribbled note from her in schoolboy Latin written in the closet—and then, on falling asleep on the floor and scaring the Martha half to death, realizing that the earlier Offred had killed herself, hung herself in the closet. It is a dead woman with her own name that the heroine finds in the closet, along with, of course, the traces of her own "real name," the name no one will ever use again.

These meetings with other women are the most powerful thing in the text, far more so than the scenes of sex with Nick. Despite Atwood's habitual scorn of female culture, with its petty jealousies and intrinsic, maternally gifted hostility, the sweetness of the novel rests in the heroine's memories of her mother and her mother's freedom ("You were a wanted child if there ever was one," her mother says, conjuring a world of all kinds of choice now gone), the flood of pleasure when she sees Moira again, and the sadness of her twinned walks with her companion handmaid, Ofglen. There is the ghost of an earlier Offred, but astonishingly, there are three Ofglens in the novel. The first is gone before the book opens, and we do not know where she is; the second becomes the heroine's friend, guide to the underground, confidante, and fellow rebel—she is the one who provides information about the resistance and who kills a man with a swift kick during the "Salvaging," when he would otherwise die by being torn apart by Handmaids as others look on. But the third Ofglen comes on us unexpectedly, bearing the news that the previous Ofglen killed herself after the Salvaging, when she realized the police were on their way to arrest her. The scene where Offred recognizes that she is meeting a different Ofglen is absolutely haunting and suggests again how easy it is to remove all singularity from a person, or at least from a woman:

> I wait at the corner for Ofglen. She's late. At last I see her coming, a red and white shape of cloth, like a kite, walking at the steady pace we've all learned to keep. I see her and notice nothing at first. Then, as she comes nearer, I think that there must be something wrong with her. She looks wrong. She is altered in some indefinable way; she's not injured, she's not limping. It's as if she has shrunk.
>
> Then when she's nearer still I see what it is. She isn't Ofglen. She's the same height, but thinner, and her face is beige, not pink. She comes up to me, stops.
>
> "Blessed be the fruit," she says. . . .
>
> "Has Ofglen been transferred, so soon?" I ask. But I know she hasn't. I saw her only this morning. She would have said.
>
> "I am Ofglen," the woman says. Word perfect. And of course she is, the new one, and Ofglen, wherever she is, is no longer Ofglen. I never did know her real name. That is how you can get lost, in a sea of names. It wouldn't be easy to find her, now. (282–83)

She looks wrong. Wherever Ofglen is, she isn't Ofglen because she isn't in the household—and the Ofglen we knew, we suddenly realize, wasn't a person, but was property. "It wouldn't be easy to find her"? All that she was, even more, all that she *knew*, is gone with her—and of course that is why she has killed herself, to stop herself from revealing whatever she knew of the rebellion and the cracks in the official regime.

That is what Offred wants—her mother, a friend, her daughter, her husband, yes. But given that she will never again have those things, she wants the one thing that will make her a person: she wants to know. And that is what is in the closet: forbidden knowledge. "What do you want?" the Commander asks her. "To know." "To know what?" Whatever there is to know. That is what she thinks at the beginning: later, of course, as she does come to know more, she says, "I would like to be ignorant. Then I wouldn't know how ignorant I was," but that isn't true. To know where you are is to *be* somewhere; to be somewhere is to be someone. Ofglen says to her, "Don't be stupid" and of course that is the trick—that is the refrain we have heard from Eve on.

"For the ones who come after you, it will be easier." "Ordinary is what you are used to," say the Aunts. In the face of the terror, doors keep opening and heroines keep walking through them, as Offred does at the end, going into the arms of the revolution, entering the female railroad, leaving her taped memories behind for history to decipher and mangle. In a world without choice, without ownership, without rights and contract and all the ephemera of personhood we have been tracking—without even a change of clothes, for goodness' sake!—there is one trace of a person left, scribbled on the wall of the closet, and that is, the person who, whatever the cost, still wants to know—and who still, Pandora-like, leaves Hope at the bottom of the box, for the next Offred to find.

Pesky Pandora! What did she leave us with? What would Roland Barthes say? Final question: what is the gift? What is it that the curious heroine, the dispossessed shadow of a person left under nineteenth-century law, has to give—and to whom can she give it freely, when her every move is constrained? Not surprisingly, none of the novels I am turning to in my conclusion has much to give any of us, and certainly not much in the way of hope. But it is fascinating to me that the one thing they all want to offer is a history lesson, and Kazuo Ishiguro's in *Never Let Me Go* is that of a terrible gift.

In this world, roughly contemporaneous with ours, a technology has been available since the 1950s to generate clones who would exist only as organ donors for ordinary people. With these spare parts, doctors were able to cure cancer, extend life, give the gift of more. Once the technology was available, it became impossible to refuse to use it, and centers grew up, terrible places, where the clones were housed and raised until physical maturity, when they could be harvested. A few places ("schools") were created attempting to prove to a reluctant society that the clones were people: that they had souls, could learn, could feel, could love, and could even create. But in the light of a greater scandal, when one man goes too far with the experiments and breeds superior clones, all the kinder, gentler training centers are closed, and the nightmare remains where most people want it, in the shadows. The invisible nonpresent, nonhuman clones are raised not as "students" but as if they were mere clusters of organs, as if they were body parts grown on trees and temporarily housed in temporary people, nestled like clockwork, waiting to be removed.

We receive this fractured history in bits, and only because one character, Kathy H., is a woman who wants to understand. She is asking the generic fictional questions that mark a human subject: Who am I? Where did I come from? What does my life mean and what will I leave behind? But she is asking them in a parallel world where words no longer mean what we expect them to mean, and this gives her story a terrifying slant. The very first and most powerful thing that Kathy H.'s story teaches us is how easy it is to change society, without the cattle prods, forced rape, and torture centers of *The Handmaid's Tale*. Ishiguro brings a brave new world into existence by changing the meaning of only four words: students, carers, donors, complete. In the shadow of those four words, Kathy H.'s story of her curiosity is the nightmare we've been waiting for since Eve.

Understanding the world for Kathy H., Tommy, and Ruth, the "children" of Hailsham, the Edenic school to which they all hope to return, means understanding what they do not have, the way they have shed the paraphernalia of the realist novel. They do not have parents; they do not have birthdays; they have no connection to an outside world. The "guardians" (as their beloved teachers are called) are a legal fiction, for there is no property waiting for them, and the only things that the guardians are truly guarding are the organs, which are imagined as already the property of someone else. The children go through the world looking for their "originals," those from whom they were cloned—and they will die without ever, as the saying goes, meeting their makers.

But that is not their tragedy—nor, exactly, is it their unnaturally short lives. Their tragedy is in the way their curiosity is mangled, in the way, as Tommy explains it, they are told everything just before they are able to understand it, so they can never claim they do not know, but they can also never fully understand their own stories. This makes their relationship to the closed door significantly different than our other novels. Whereas in other novels what the heroine found behind the door were other wives, husbands, and mysterious strangers, in this novel, what is behind the door is the secret of themselves. For Ishiguro, all the doors in the characters' quest—whether it be to understand the past, to find another future, or to look for their "possible," the place where they were forged—lead only to a single image: a young girl, dancing by herself, holding a pillow and imagining it is a child, someone she is terrified of losing, to whom she sings "Never let me go."

In the absence of any fuller narrative, Kathy and Tommy construct their own account, their own answer to the question, where did I come from?: the "curious room." Madame, a visitor to the school when they were young, collected the students' paintings and artwork to exhibit, so that years later she would know what is inside them, would be able to read their souls. Kathy and Tommy come to believe that with that evidence of their "souls," they would be able to prove their love and win extra years of life, a deferral of "donations" and "completion." (It is typical of the modest hopes of any Ishiguro character that these two do not imagine living a full life; they ask for only a few more years.) They go in quest of that promise—their own lives, more life, true love. But when they find Madame, she is living with Miss Emily, the principal of their school, and the two together offer an alternative narrative of the children's lives. In this story, the students were not students; caring is just what you do until your organs mature; donation is not volitional; completion is only death. And the clones, our "characters," themselves are not real; they are made *things*. Only in the minds of the school were they people; the rest of society (like Madame herself) feared them. The sentence is fierce: "All clones—or *students*, as we preferred to call you—existed only to supply medical science."[6]

Miss Emily tells a story of knowing and not knowing—which is also a story of being half in and half out of the closet. "In the early days," Miss Emily says, "after the war, that's all you were to most people. Shadowy objects in test tubes. . . . That was why we collected your art" (261). The art was a shout, a challenge to the rest of the world: "There, look!" we could say. "Look at this art! How dare you claim these children are anything less than fully human." But the shout was into an echo chamber, and there was no answering voice: the children quite literally have no reflection in the world, for since people prefer to believe these "organs appeared from nowhere, or at most that they were in a kind of vacuum," even at the moment "they came to consider just how you were reared, whether you should have been brought into existence at all, by then it was too late. There was no way to reverse the process."

The terrifying aspect is not that the process can't be reversed, that history cannot be undone, that the donations must continue—it is that the students' presence at the limits of the human, a presence as terrifying and uncanny as a spider, cannot be reversed. Even to their beloved guardians, the children are alien, living in a perpetual not-quite of persons. As she says good-bye to them, Madame, who has always feared them the most, admits that "your stories this evening, they touched me too," and she says, "Poor creatures. I wish I could help you. But now you're by yourselves." And then she touches them physically, like Louisa Bounderby experimenting with what it means to be a person:

> She reached out her hand, all the while staring into my face, and placed it on my cheek. I could feel a trembling go all through her body, but she kept her hand where it was, and I could see again tears appearing in her eyes.
> "You poor creatures," she repeated, almost in a whisper. Then she turned and went back into her house. (272)

At that moment, our own quest as readers, the curiosity we want to have answered, turns viciously against us. We have been on Kathy H.'s side; we have wanted her to find out the truth; we have wanted her to be saved. But here, Ishiguro is slamming the door in *our* face, telling us we cannot walk through it with her. Is it too much to imagine that at that point Kathy gives up being a carer (and a very good one, as she tells us) and, rather than tending to those "donating" organs, becomes a "donor" herself? Truly, at that moment, more than any woman in any marriage plot, she is giving herself away—but to what end?

It has something to do with being a creature—with seeing that, in the absence of any recognition of your own shared humanity, your humanity will come only from *choosing* where there is no choice, choosing to give yourself away. What else does Kathy have? In the reproductive bleakness that has increasingly haunted my own study, nothing can be born from Kathy's curiosity, or from her care. We might have thought that the heart of the story, the secret, was the work of memory, was the lost pop song, was a girl, writing, as Miss Lucy, the angriest of the teachers, does, for hours, laboriously rubbing out everything she has written in her rage at the ways the children are being misled. But that is not the heart—nor is it even, exactly, the young Kathy H., clutching a pillow, dancing by herself, imagining a child she will never have, the child she never was. What does it mean to be a creature? If this, like both *Lady Oracle* and *The Handmaid's Tale*, is a doubled story of curiosity and reproduction, the story of the copy, the story of the lost (m)other, it does not offer the story of finding what was lost, writing her story along with yours, completing the circle. Rather, it offers the darker version of curiosity, in which you discover that you are the puzzle not because you are the measure of all things, but because you are, finally, a curiosity: uniquely your own, singular, wonderful, but also hideous, the lone survivor of a brave new world, and all you can do is accept your own death, accept it as a gift ("donation") and move toward a lonely completion.

But the novel leaves us, nonetheless, with a vision of care in spite of everything—a world of compassion in the face of loss, rather than revolution in the face of violence, rather than anything as simple as despair. For during that final drive, Kathy takes a detour to Norfolk, where, as children, the students believed all lost things were to be found. There, in the face of all that says she is not and never was a person, she reassembles, or recollects, the pieces of herself:

> I was thinking about the rubbish, the flapping plastic in the branches, the shore-line of odd stuff caught along the fencing, and I half-closed my eyes and imagined this was the spot where everything I'd ever lost since my childhood had washed up, and I was now standing here in front of it, and if I waited long enough, a tiny figure would appear on the horizon across the field, and gradually get larger until I'd see it was Tommy, and he'd wave, maybe even call. The fantasy never got beyond that—I didn't let it—and though the tears rolled down my face, I wasn't sobbing or out of control. I just waited a bit, then turned back to the car, to drive off to wherever I was supposed to be. (287–88)

That final image of "everything I'd ever lost since my childhood" brings the novel back into the realm of the curiosity shop, just as the figure of Tommy, "a tiny figure . . . on the horizon . . . gradually get [ting] larger" brings up the shrinking heroine of our Alice meditations. "If I waited long enough," Kathy says, and again she introduces delay, the suspended answer, the enigma of desire, everything that curiosity has promised throughout this study, when I first promised you that I would, by the end of the project, deliver the modern (feminist) subject, intact and agentive and alive.

What would that subject look like, we can now ask? Haraway was right, of course, that any "self" is an optical illusion, but she is also right that any difference between science fiction (or, as I argued in the beginning of this chapter, any realist fiction) and lived experience is also an optical illusion. Throughout this last chapter, fragmented selves have confronted other, fragmented versions of themselves—a Handmaid sees herself in a mirror, both the same and different; Joan Foster writes herself into a maze, stares at herself in the mirror long enough that her three-headed mother stares back, and then writes herself into another story; Kathy H., in spite of everything else, cries real tears—or whatever passes for real tears in a novel. "Cold, artifice, death (the eyes of a doll)," as Roland Barthes sums it up (60). To confront the possibility of an empty life, one with no meaning, one precisely with no "humanity," has been the gift of fiction since at least *Clarissa*, when the heroine confronted the utter, terrifying emptiness of Lovelace, of whom, as Linda Kauffman wrote, "If only Lovelace could feel something for himself, Clarissa could feel something for him too; it is in this sense that her letters are an elegy of desire. . . . What she recognizes is not only that he can feel nothing for her but that he is so self-alienated that he feels nothing at all."[7] The opposite of the curious heroine, it turns out, isn't someone who doesn't want to know; it is someone, as Foucault could have told us, who doesn't *care*. Fiction is at the end only a made thing, an optical device, a device for feeling—but it is also a curiosity cabinet in the oldest sense, a place where everything that once had meaning can have meaning again, can be cared for, can even be loved. Perhaps it is only through artifice that we can find love at all, suggest all three of these novels, with their curious assemblages, which seem almost to challenge us: Go ahead. Do you care? What do you see? Imagine that it is absurd; imagine that it is a collection of broken things; now *care anyway*. I dare you. Or so Margaret Atwood seems to say, similarly, when, at the end of *Lady Oracle*, she imagines everyone her heroine has ever loved or lost standing on a beach ("I'd seen a lot of Fellini movies") with the wind rippling their hair: Arthur, the Royal Porcupine, Leda Sprott and Fraser Buchanan and Sam and Marlene (the evil Brownie) and Aunt Lou, striding "towards a distant hot-dog and orangeade stand that beckoned to her from the horizon like a tacky mirage."

A hot-dog and orangeade stand. And why ever not? I played with so many final images for this book: John Fowles in a train compartment at the end of *The French Lieutenant's Woman*, meeting his main character; Kate Atkinson's Ruby, asleep in the dollhouse in *Behind the Scenes at the Museum*; Ellen and Newland in the dark rooms of a museum yet to be born; Rachel Vinrace, on the ship's deck in *The Voyage Out*, playing cards with the Lady Eve; the great woman poet who did *not* die; "secrets, pigeon-holes, little plots"; some perfect image of realism and the dream of the other; some *Wunderkammer*; some final words of profundity. I wanted to make you care; I wanted to find a Ruby fast asleep, doll-like and at rest, in these pages. But like Joan Foster, I am not a tidy person. If I did write a scene for the end of the book, some companion piece to my princess, some answer for the sadness of the clone, some sentence that would find justice at last for the dolls, I would fail. I would rather have the tacky mirage; I, too, want to set the characters and the objects free to reassemble themselves as they wish, outside the law, dancing in unexpected combinations: Esther Summerson waltzing with the mad hatter; Isabel Archer playing shuffleboard with Ellen Olenska; the two shattered couples, the Prince and Maggie and Charlotte and Adam Verver, doing the lobster quadrille; Clarissa with Anna Howe, chattering wildly once more, holding hands. In my curious room, Clarissa's coffin, covered with cyphers, rests in a corner next to Dickens's Hindoo Baby; Mr. Gradgrind's Blue Books lean sloppily against Dorothea Brooke's book of maps and Eve's pruning shears, while Eve tries desperately to pin back her wanton tresses. Do you still want to know more? Good. That we can never quite be curious enough was the one thing our tradition taught us; but that curiosity is a spark of life, a lightning strike, a match to the heart, is something we forget at our peril. It is in that spirit, that of continuing to ask questions and finding no final answer to the great question, what does it mean for a curious heroine to become a person? that I can at last, for the moment and in this one place, if not complete, at least break off.

NOTES

INTRODUCTION

1. Charles Dickens, *Hard Times* (New York: Norton, 2001), p. 41; Charles Dickens, *Bleak House* (New York: Norton, 1977), p. 749; Charlotte Brontë, *Jane Eyre* (New York: Norton, 2001), p. 243.
2. Charles Dodgson took the boat trip with the Liddell sisters in 1862, finished "Alice's Adventures Underground" in 1864, and published *Alice in Wonderland* in 1865; the Oxford lecture "The Function of Criticism at the Present Time" was delivered in 1864; "A Woman's Last Word" was published in *Men and Women* in 1863.
3. See *Tradescant's Rarities: Essays on the Foundation of the Ashmolean Museum, 1683*, edited by Arthur MacGregor (Oxford: Clarendon Press, 1983), as well as *The Culture of Collecting*, edited by John Elsner and Roger Cardinal (London: Reaktion Books, 1994).
4. George Steiner, Review of "John Murray and the Web of Words," *New Yorker*, November 21, 1977; reprinted in *George Steiner at the New Yorker* (New York: New Directions, 2009), pp. 306–15.
5. *Ruth* (Oxford:Oxford University Press, 1985), p. 392.
6. Virginia Woolf, *Mrs. Dalloway* (San Diego, CA: Harcourt and Brace, 1925), p. 125.
7. Ian P. Watt, *The Rise of the Novel* (Berkeley: University of California Press, 1959), pp. 10–11; Elizabeth Ermarth, *Realism and Consensus in the English Novel* (Princeton, NJ: Princeton University Press, 1983), p. 78; George Levine, *The Realistic Imagination: English Fiction from Frankenstein to Lady Chatterly* (Chicago: University of Chicago Press, 1981).
8. Charles Dickens, *Little Dorrit* (Oxford: Oxford University Press, 1979), p. 163.
9. See Peter Brooks, *Reading for the Plot: Desire and Intention in Narrative* (Cambridge, MA: Harvard University Press, 1984) and Leo Bersani, "Realism and the Fear of Desire," in *A Future for Astyanax: Character and Desire in Literature* (New York: Columbia University Press, 1984), pp. 51–88. Bersani notes, along lines very much like my own, that in the novels of Henry James and others, "the resistance to potentially disruptive characters itself disrupts the conditions of realistic fiction" (81). I think of this as in part the *text's* curiosity.
10. See Nancy K. Miller, "Emphasis Added: Plots and Plausibilities in Women's Fiction,"*PMLA* 96, no. 1 (January 1981), pp. 36–48; see my discussion of Teresa de Lauretis, "Desire in Narrative," in *Alice Doesn't* and of Nancy Armstrong, *Desire and Domestic Fiction* in chapter 1.

11. "Preface," *The Portrait of a Lady* (Boston: Riverside, Houghton Mifflin, 1963), p. 8.
12. "Into the Woods," quoted from Stephen Sondheim, *Look, I Made a Hat* (New York: Knopf, 2011), p. 70.
13. See Helena Michie's marvelous *Victorian Honeymoons: Journeys to the Conjugal* (Cambridge: Cambridge University Press, 2007) for a similar analysis of why the marriage plot extends far beyond the marriage night and its sexual revelations.
14. *Middlemarch* (Oxford: Oxford University Press, 1996), p. 27; p. 450.
15. Angela Carter, *The Sadeian Woman and the Ideology of Pornography* (New York: Harper Colophon Books, 1980), p. 62.
16. For treatments of the Gothic and realism, see in particular Judith Wilt, *Ghosts of the Gothic* (Princeton, NJ: Princeton, 1980). My sense of the Gothic as the realm of both the psychoanalytic and the pornographic owes much to Terry Castle, *The Female Thermometer: Eighteenth Century Culture and the Invention of the Uncanny* (New York: Oxford University Press, 1995).
17. Franco Moretti, *The Way of the World: The Bilungsroman in European Culture* (London: Verso, 2000), p. 189.
18. See Q. D. Leavis, "Introduction," *Jane Eyre* (Harmondsworth, UK: Penguin Books, 1966), p. 21 and Virginia Woolf, "*Jane Eyre* and *Wuthering Heights*," in *The Common Reader* (New York: Harcourt, Brace and Company, 1925), p. 221.
19. Stanley Cavell, *Pursuits of Happiness: The Hollywood Comedy of Remarriage* (Cambridge, MA: Harvard University Press, 1984), pp. 4–5.
20. Jane Rendall, "Who Was Lily Maxwell? Women's Suffrage and Manchester Politics, 1866–67," in *Votes for Women*, edited by June Purvis and Sandra Stanley Holton (London: Routledge, 2000), pp. 57–83.
21. Margaret Atwood, *The Handmaid's Tale* (New York: Anchor, 1998), p. 188.
22. Caroline Levine, *The Serious Pleasures of Suspense: Victorian Realism and NarrativeDoubt* (Charlottesville: University of Virginia Press, 2003).
23. Donna Haraway, "A Cyborg Manifesto: Science, Technology, and Socialist-Feminism in the Late Twentieth Century," reprinted in *Simians, Cyborgs, and Women: The Reinvention of Nature* (New York: Routledge, 1991), p. 151.
24. Roland Barthes, *S/Z* (New York: Hill & Wang, 1974), p. 75. As Barthes adds, "Expectation is a disorder."
25. Jane Austen, *Sense and Sensibility* (Oxford: Oxford University Press, 1990), p. 229; the power of this moment was particularly brought home to me by Emma Thompson's emphasis (as screenwriter and actress) in Ang Lee's film adaptation of *Sense and Sensibility*; see *The Sense and Sensibility Screenplay & Diaries: Bringing Jane Austen's Novel to Film* by Emma Thompson and Lindsay Doran (New York: Newmarket Press, 2002).
26. George E. Toles, *A House Made of Light: Essays on the Art of Film* (Detroit: Wayne State Press, 2001), p. 210.

CHAPTER 1

1. James Van Horn Melton, *The Rise of the Public in Enlightenment Europe* (Cambridge: Cambridge University Press, 2001), p. 8.
2. 1 Bulst 6 Edward Bulstrode King's Bench. *Burton's Legal Thesaurus*, 4th ed., under "construction," edited by William C. Burton (New York: McGraw Hill, 2007).
3. Jane Austen, *Pride and Prejudice*. (London: Penguin, 1996), p. 106.

4. Max Horkheimer and Theodor W. Adorno, *The Dialectic of Enlightenment* (New York: Continuum, 1989).
5. Roy Porter, *Enlightenment: Britain and the Creation of the Modern World* (London: Penguin, 2000), p. xxiii.
6. Among other guides to electricity in the modern world, see Iwan Rhys Morus, *Frankenstein's Children: Electricity, Exhibition, and Experiment in Early-Nineteenth-Century London* (Princeton, NJ: Princeton University Press, 1998) and Linda Simon, *Dark Light: Electricity and Anxiety from the Telegraph to the X-Ray* (Harcourt, 2004).
7. Angela Carter, *The Sadeian Woman and the Ideology of Pornography* (New York: Harper Colophon Books, 1980), p. 127.
8. Teresa de Lauretis, *Alice Doesn't: Feminism, Semiotics, Cinema* (Bloomington: Indiana University Press, 1984), p. 157.
9. See Timothy Gantz, *Early Greek Myth: A Guide to Literary and Artistic Sources* (Baltimore: Johns Hopkins University Press, 1993), p. 496. Gantz cites another tale from Pausanias, "who cites in account in which the Sphinx was actually a bastard daughter of Laios to whom he had confided the oracle given to Kadmos by Delphi; when she ruled after her father's death she used this secret as a test to discourage claimants, until Oidopous came, having learned the prophecy in a dream" (498).
10. "The Theme of the Three Caskets" (1913) in Freud, *On Creativity and Culture*, edited by Benjamin Nelson (New York: Harper & Row, 1958). See also D. A. Miller's observation, that in this essay, as in Victorian fiction, "perversely, inward choices have turned out to coincide with externally imposed necessity"; or as Freud puts it, "a choice is made where in reality there is compulsion." Miller, *Narrative and Its Discontents: Problems of Closure in the Traditional Novel* (Princeton, NJ: Princeton University Press, 1981), p. 119.
11. Angela Carter, *The Bloody Chamber* (London: Penguin, 1979), p. 38.
12. Paradise Lost, in John Milton, *Complete Poems and Major Prose*, edited by Merritt Hughes (New York: The Odyssey Press, 1957).
13. Hans Blumenberg, *The Legitimacy of the Modern Age*, translated by Robert M. Wallace (Cambridge, MA: MIT Press, 1983). For an illuminating review of the volume, see Martin Jay, "Review of *The Legitimacy of the Modern Age*," *History and Theory*, 24, no. 2. (May 1985), reprinted in *Fin- de-Siecle Socialism* (New York: Routledge, 1988), pp. 149–164.
14. There are several fine recent histories of curiosity: the most productive for me has been Lorraine Daston and Katherine Park's *Wonders and the Order of Nature, 1150–750* (Cambridge, MA: Zone Books, 2001), pp. 303–28 in particular. R. J. W. Evans and Alexander Marr's wonderful collection of essays *Curiosity and Wonder from the Renaissance to the Enlightenment* (Aldershot, UK: Ashgate, 2006) is especially fruitful, in particular its brilliant introduction, which does more than summarize recent work in the field: it offers the best structural understanding of the different meanings of curiosity in the modern world. For similarly helpful analysis, see Neil Kenny's *Curiosity in Early Modern Europe Word Histories* (Wiesbaden, Germany: Harrassowitz Verlag, 1998). Other recent accounts include Barbara Benedict's remarkably thorough *Curiosity: A Cultural History of Early Modern Inquiry* (Chicago: University of Chicago Press, 2001); for other classic studies, see Krzysztof Pomian, *Collectors and Curiosities* (Oxford: Polity, 1991) and Paula Findlen's *Possessing Nature: Museums, Collecting, and Scientific Culture in Early Modern Italy* (Berkeley: University of California Press, 1994). For

reflections on curiosity and collecting, see John Elsner and Roger Cardinal, *The Cultures of Collecting* (Cambridge, MA: Harvard University Press, 1994).

15. Christian Zacher, *Curiosity and Pilgrimage: The Literature of Discovery in Fourteenth-Century England* (Baltimore: Johns Hopkins University Press, 1976). It is worth remembering, in this context, that such later sketch books of "curious" culture as Gustave Doré's London bear the subtitle of "a pilgrimage." Donald Howard, however, notes that for Chaucer, traveling for "curiosity" or "fun" was the very opposite of a true "pilgrimage." *Writers and Pilgrims: Medieval Accounts of the Jerusalem Pilgrimage* (Berkeley: University of California Press, 1980), p. 89.

16. The history of closets, and the idea of privacy, goes back to economic models of subjectivity as well: see Stephanie Jed's brilliant treatment of mercantilism and the rise of private (humanist) writing in *Chaste Thinking: The Rape of Lucretia and the Birth of Humanism* (Bloomington: Indiana University Press, 1989), pp. 74–120; see also Julie Sanders, "The Closet Opened: A Reconstruction of Private Space in the Writings of Margaret Cavendish," in *A Princely Brave Woman: Essays on Margaret Cavendish, Duchess of Newcastle*, edited by Stephen Clucas (Aldershot, UK: Ashgate, 2003). The idea of a woman who counts or sorts in order to become a self (the mercantilist wife) will become important when Bluebeard's last wife begins to enumerate the bodies of her predecessors.

17. See in particular *The Origins of the Museum: The Cabinet of Curiosities in Sixteenth- and Seventeenth-Century Europe*, edited by Oliver Impey and Arthur MacGregor (Oxford: Clarendon Press, 1985) and Tony Bennet, *The Birth of the Museum: History, Theory, Politics* (London: Routledge, 1995).

18. Julie Peakman, in *Mighty Lewd Books: The Development of Pornography in Eighteenth-Century England* (New York: Palgrave Macmillan, 2003), cites such titles as "Venus in the Cloister: Or, the Nun in her Smock" (cited in Fielding's *Shamela* as one of her possessions) and "The Cabinet of Venus Unlocked and Her Secrets Laid Open." George Rousseau, in a brilliant essay, "Curiosity and the Lusus Naturae: 'Proteus' Hill," also notes the centrality of optical curiosity for women, in such unexpected places as *Tristram Shandy*, where Mrs. Shandy, who speaks only four times during the course of Sterne's epic novel, claims in chapter 8 that she would like "to look through the key-hole out of curiosity." He links this interest to the pinhole curiosa of Victorian erotic and pornographic books.

19. On the woman who is all hole, see Carter, *Sadeian Woman*, p. 4: "In the stylisation of graffiti, the prick is always presented erect, in an alert attitude of enquiry or curiosity or affirmation; it points upwards, it asserts. The hole is open, an inert space, like a mouth waiting to be filled. From this elementary iconography may be derived the whole metaphysics of sexual difference—man aspires; woman has no other function but to exist, waiting.... Between her legs lies nothing but zero."

20. See the British Museum Gallery Guide "Enlightenment Gallery: Discovering the World in the Eighteenth Gallery," © 2004 The Trustees of the British Museum. Among other wonderful examples, see the cabinet rooms at the National Gallery in Washington, D.C., and the redesign of the Walters Museum of Art in Baltimore, where the Flemish collection features a beautifully designed "Chamber of Wonders" (I am particularly grateful to Frances Ferguson for taking me there). The most engaging curiosity rooms I have seen are in the Rembrandt House in Amsterdam, where the artist's shelves are full of skulls,

shells, beautiful objects. The room, off the chamber that serves as bed and living room, suggests an artist fully at work in nature and artifice.
21. Daston and Park, *Wonders and the Order of Nature*, p. 273.
22. W. M. Thackeray, "Prize Novels," published in *Punch*, 3 April–9 October 1847. Reprinted in *Miscellanies*, Vol. 2, 1856, under the title *Novels by Eminent Hands*.
23. Amazingly, Thackeray himself wrote a parody of an illustrated novel called [*Specimen-Extracts from the New Novel*] *The Orphan of Pimlico: A Moral Tale of Belgravian Life* by Miss M. T. Wigglesworth, many years governess in the nobility's families, and authoress of "Posies of Poesy," "Thoughts on the Use of Globes," &c., London, 1851. (The volume was published in 1876 in his original handwriting and hand drawings by Smith & Elder.) In this marvelous text, the narrator says that "in vain I pointed out in my visits to my noble pupil, the danger likely to result from the society of this ill-regulated young man. It was not because in his vulgar insolence and odious contempt of the poor, Mr Mordant (as I heard through the open door) called me a 'toothless old she dragon' and 'a twaddling old catamarn'—that I disliked him, but from his general levity and daring licence of language." The text notes ironically that "keyhole" has been cancelled before "through the open door."
24. See http://www.commercialalert.org/issues/culture/books/authors-ask-editors-to-treat-fay-weldons-new-work-as-an-ad-not-a-book.
25. Burke, *A Philosophical Inquiry into the Origin of Our Ideas of the Sublime and Beautiful with an Introductory Discourse concerning Taste, and Several Other Additions* [1756] reprinted in *The Portable Enlightenment Reader*, edited by Isaac Kramnick (London: Penguin, 1995), pp. 329–33.
26. E. M. Forster, *Aspects of the Novel* (Harcourt, Brace and World, 1927), pp. 86–87.
27. Doris Lessing, *The Golden Notebook* (New York: Bantam, 1973 [1962]), p. 58.
28. John Stuart Mill, "On the Subjection of Women," in *On Liberty and Other Writings*, edited by Stefan Collini (Cambridge: Cambridge University Press, 1989), p. 185.
29. From James's essay on "Mrs. Humphry Ward," *Essays in London* (London 1893), p. 265, quoted in Ian Watt, *The Rise of the Novel: Studies in Defoe, Richardson, and Fielding* (Harmondsworth, UK: Penguin Books, 1957), p. 311.
30. Nancy Armstrong, *Desire and Domestic Fiction: A Political History of the Novel* (New York: Oxford University Press, 1987).
31. Peter Brooks, *Reading for the Plot: Design and Intention in Narrative* (Cambridge, MA: Harvard University Press, 1984), p. 225: "Something yet more active and dynamic than contract is being played out." This flattening of contract seems inexact to me.
32. Although my work echoes some of the concerns of recent critics such as Elaine Hadley and Lauren Goodlad, the exclusion of women from the business of "practical politics" means that my liberalism sounds very different from theirs; it also, however, licenses me to take more seriously the concerns of novelistic form as a commentary on the process of becoming a (liberal) subject. See Elaine Hadley, *Living Liberalism: Practical Citizenship in Mid-Victorian Britain* (Chicago: University of Chicago Press, 2010) and Lauren Goodlad, *Victorian Literature and the Victorian State: Character and Governance in a Liberal Society* (Baltimore: Johns Hopkins University Press, 2003). The book which, interestingly, most shares my concern with liberalism and knowledge (though not, alas, with novels) is Chris Otter's *The Victorian Eye: A Political History of Light and Vision in Britain, 1800–1910* (Chicago: University of Chicago Press, 2008).

33. Mill, "The Admission of Women to the Electoral Franchise," speech delivered 20 May 1867 to the House of Commons.
34. Eliot, *Felix Holt the Radical* (Harmondsworth: Penguin, 1995), p. 263, p. 262.
35. One need not be biographically obsessed to think that for John Stuart Mill, in love with Harriet Taylor, an already-married woman, this narrative had a particular appeal.
36. Angela Carter, *The Fairy Tales of Perrault* (London: Penguin Books, 1977), p. 10. There is a fascinating contemporary interest in Bluebeard by feminists: Shuli Barzalai locates in it a female curiosity divided between "curiosity as self-preservation as opposed to curiosity as epistemophilia"; Maria Tatar was fascinated equally by "the crimes of Bluebeard and the curiosity of his wife ... across different cultures" (3). Shuli Barzalai, *Tales of Bluebeard and His Wives from Late Antiquity to Postmodern Times* (New York: Routledge, 2009); Maria Tatar, *Secrets beyond the Door: The Story of Bluebeard and His Wives* (Princeton, NJ: Princeton University Press, 2004). Both are interested in wide historical sweep—Barzali usefully connects to Eve and Midrash texts; Tatar, in ways I do not, turns to contemporary versions, including, most productively, Bartok's. I will have opportunities to engage their discussions later in this volume, but I am grateful to their work. For more historical analysis, see Graham Anderson in *Fairytale in the Ancient World* (London: Routledge, 2000) who, going back to ancient mythography, argues that "the story of this serial wife-killer has a number of significant connections with the legends about King Minos of Crete, including the curse of his being fatal to women with whom he has had sexual relations, his labyrinthine (and now excavated) palace at Knossos, which may well have contained a secret chamber or two, and the purple lock of hair he obtains during the course of one of his adventures" (quoted in Barzilai, 4). In my own field, among the most interesting work is John Sutherland, "Can Jane Eyre Be Happy?" in the book of the same name (Oxford, 2007) and Juliet McMaster, in " 'Bluebeard at Breakfast': An Unpublished Thackeray Manuscript," *Dickens Studies Annual: Essays on Victorian Fiction* 8 (1980), pp. 197–230, who shares my obsession with Thackeray's obsessions.
37. Henry James, *The Portrait of a Lady* (Boston: Riverside, Houghton Mifflin, 1963), p. 8.
38. Sade, *Justine* (New York: Grove Press, 1990), p. 741.
39. George Eliot, *Middlemarch* (Oxford: Oxford University Press, 1996), p. 761.

CHAPTER 2

1. I owe this quotation, as so much in this chapter, to Stanley Fish, *Surprised by Sin: The Reader in Paradise Lost* (Cambridge, MA: Harvard University Press, 1998), p. 46; the original is Empson, *Milton's God* (London: Chatto & Windus, 1961), p. 94.
2. For a fine discussion of realism, probability and fictional belief, see Robert Newsom, *A Likely Story: Probability and Play in Fiction* (New Brunswick, NJ: Rutgers University Press, 1988); his comments on the antinomy of fictional probability are on p. 159.
3. For the classic statement of the rules of formal realism, see Ian Watt, *The Rise of the Novel* (Berkeley: University of California Press, 1957).
4. As Williams puts it, "*limits* meaning *hard facts*, often of power or money in their existing and established form," rather than "let's be realistic" meaning " 'let us look at the whole truth of this situation' (which can allow that an existing **reality** is changeable or is changing)." *Key Words* (New York: Oxford University Press: 1976, 1983), p. 259.

5. George Eliot, *Middlemarch: A Novel of Provincial life* (Harmondsworth: Penguin, 1994), p. 537.
6. Adam Phillips, *The Beast in the Nursery: On Curiosity and Other Appetites* (New York: Pantheon, 1998), p. 17.
7. See Prendergast, *The Order of Mimesis* (Cambridge: Cambridge University Press: 1986), p. 85. The classic and still brilliant exegesis of contract and its fictions is Clare Dalton, "An Essay in the Deconstruction of Contract Doctrine," *Yale Law Journal* 94 (April 1985), pp. 997.
8. Jonathan Grossman, *The Art of Alibi: English Law Courts and the Novel* (Baltimore: Johns Hopkins University Press, 2002); Alexander Welsh, *Strong Representations: Narrative and Circumstantial Evidence in England* (Baltimore: Johns Hopkins University Press, 1995).
9. John Milton, *Complete Poems and Major Prose*, ed. Merrit Hughes (New York: Odyssey Press, 1937), *Paradise Lost*, Book 9, ll. 366–71. All subsequent references included in the text.
10. Milton himself is one of the great early theorists not only of marriage but of divorce—of the emptiness of marriage without intellectual companionship. See "The Doctrine and Discipline of Divorce" in Hughes, pp. 696–715; for companionate marriage more generally, see Lawrence Stone, *The Family, Sex and Marriage in England 1500–1800* (New York: Harper & Row, 1977).
11. Among discussions of Milton and Richardson, see in particular Gillian Beer, "Richardson, Milton and the Status of Evil" in *Review of English Studies* 19 (1968), pp. 26–70, reprinted in *Arguing with the Past: Essays in Narrative from Woolf to Sidney* (Routledge, Kegan & Paul, 1989).
12. Samuel Richardson, *Clarissa, or the History of a Young Lady* (Hardmondsworth, UK: Penguin Books, 1985).
13. George Rousseau, "Curiosity and the Lusus naturae: 'Proteus' Hill," in *Curiosity and Wonder from the Renaissance to the Enlightenment*, edited by R. J. W. Evans and Alexander Marr (Aldershot, UK: Ashgate, 2006), p. 219.
14. My discussion of maxims generally is shaped by Catherine Gallagher's in "George Eliot: Immanent Victorian," in *Proceedings of the British Academy* 94 (1997), pp. 157–72, particularly on the circularity of all maxims: "Of all Dorothea Brookes, she is the most Dorothea Brooke," to summarize Gallagher's wonderful argument.
15. On the complexity of character-hunting in eighteenth-century fiction and realism more generally, see Deidre Lynch, *The Economy of Character: Novels, Market Culture, and the Business of Inner Meaning* (Chicago: University of Chicago Press, 1998).
16. Linda S. Kaufmann is particularly persuasive on Clarissa's faith that she can constitute her own moral universe—and the sadness when this fails. *Discourses of Desire: Gender, Genre, and Epistolary Fictions* (Ithaca, NY: Cornell University Press, 1988).
17. Many critics, among them Terry Eagleton, have written well about the relationship between Clarissa's pain and her triumph; for another brilliant approach, see Jayne Elizabeth Lewis, "*Clarissa*'s Cruelty: Modern Fables of Moral Authority in *The History of a Young Lady*," in *Clarissa and Her Readers: New Essays for the Clarissa Project* (New York: AMS, 1999).
18. Schantz, *Gossip, Letters, Phones: The Scandal of Female Networks in Novels and Film* (New York: Oxford University Press, 2008).

19. One of the more interesting paradoxes of *Clarissa* scholarship to my mind is that William B. Warner, Clarissa's great enemy, actually sees her as far more active and inquisitorial herself than his deconstructive hero, Lovelace; even more interesting, in their later essays on the novel, Castle and Warner seem to have, more than a little, adapted each other's perspectives. See Castle, "Lovelace's Dream," in *The Female Thermometer: 18th Century Culture and the Invention of the Uncanny* (New York: Oxford University Press, 1985) and Warner, "Reading Rape: Marxist-Feminist Figurations of the Literal," *Diacritics*, Winter 1983, pp. 12–32.
20. For an essay that raises similar questions about *Pamela*, see Vivasvan Soni, "The Trial Narrative in Richardson's *Pamela*: Suspending the Hermeneutic of Happiness," *Novel*, Fall 2007, pp. 5–28.
21. Jed, *Chaste Thinking: The Rape of Lucretia and the Birth of Humanism* (Bloomington: Indiana University Press, 1989), pp. 6–7.
22. Sandra Macpherson, *Harm's Way: Tragic Responsibility and the Novel Form* (Baltimore: Johns Hopkins University Press, 2010).
23. See again Newsom, *A Likely Story*, and Catherine Gallagher, *Nobody's Story: The Vanishing Acts of Women Writers in the Marketplace, 1670–1920* (Berkeley: University of California Press, 1995).
24. Wilt, "He Could Go No Farther: A Modest Proposal about Lovelace and Clarissa," *PMLA* 42 (1977), pp. 19–32.
25. Wilkie Collins, *The Law and the Lady* (Oxford: Oxford University Press, 1992) p.9 3. Miss Hoighty accompanies the heroine on her search through a cabinet of curiosity, only to land on a book, and that an account of her husband's trial and semi-acquittal (a "Scotch verdict") for his wife's murder. But no Fatima, Mrs. Woodville never believes in her husband's guilt, searching for evidence of his innocence literally through the trash ("a midden") to assert her right to be Bluebeard's second wife.
26. Anthony Trollope, *An Autobiography* (London: Penguin: 1996), p. 165.
27. "Miss Braddon," *Nation* 1 (9 November 1865), pp. 593–95. Quoted in *Wilkie Collins: The Critical Heritage*, edited by Norman Page (Routledge, 1974), pp. 122–23.
28. Henry James, *The Golden Bowl* (Harmondsworth, UK: Penguin Books, 1966), p. 333.
29. Peter Brooks, *The Melodramatic Imagination: Balzac, Henry James, Melodrama, and the Mode of Excess* (New York: Columbia University Press, 1985 [1976]), p. 164.
30. As we saw, Henry James refered to the novelist, in his preface to the New York edition of *The Portrait of a Lady*, as "a wary dealer in precious odds and ends" placing things "in the dusky, crowded, heterogeneous back-shop of the mind," but forced to keep "the precious object locked up indefinitely." Henry James, *The Portrait of a Lady* (Boston: Riverside, Houghton Mifflin, 1963), p. 8.
31. Freud, *Civilization and Its Discontents* (New York: Norton: 1961), p. 85.

CHAPTER 3

1. Angela Carter, "Alice in Prague: The Curious Room," in *Burning Your Boats: Collected Stories* (New York: Vintage, 2006), pp. 397–408. Originally published in *American Ghosts and Old World Wonders* (1993).
2. Freud, "The Uncanny," in *Freud: On Creativity and the* Unconscious (New York: Harper, 1958), p. 130.

3. Lewis Carroll, *Alice in Wonderland*, edited by Donald J. Gray (New York: Norton, 1992), p. 28–29.
4. This school of criticism would be nowhere without a brilliant essay by James R. Kincaid, "Alice's Invasion of Wonderland," *PMLA* 88 (1973), pp. 92–99, which escapes the flaws of the later criticism by brilliantly illuminating the sadness underneath the comic Alice—essays like mine, as well as Donald Rackin's and Nina Auerbach's (see notes 6 and 7), would be unimaginable without it.
5. Susan Stewart, *On Longing: Narratives of the Miniature, the Gigantic, the Souvenir, the Collection* (Balimore: Johns Hopkins University Press, 1984), p. 61.
6. The person who has written most persuasively about this question is Nina Auerbach, in her wonderful chapter, "Alice and Wonderland: A Curious Child," first published in *Victorian Studies* 17, no. 1 (September 1973), pp. 31–47, reprinted in *Romantic Imprisonment: Women and Other Glorified Outcasts* (New York: Columbia University Press, 1985).
7. "Laughing and Grief: What's So Funny about Alice in Wonderland," in *Lewis Carroll Observed: A Collection of Unpublished Photographs, Drawings, Poetry, and New Essays*, edited by Edward Guiliano (New York: Clarkson N. Potter, 1976), pp. 1–18.
8. For a wonderful recent account of John Snow's endless curiosity, see Steven Johnson, *The Ghost Map: The Story of London's Most Terrifying Epidemic—and How It Changed Science, Cities, and the Modern World* (New York: Riverhead, 2007).
9. "Lewis Carroll: *Alice in Wonderland*," in *New Invitations to Learning*, edited by Mark Van Doren (New York: Random House, 1942), p. 208.
10. A. S. Byatt, *The Children's Book* (New York: Vintage, 2010), p. 438.
11. Kate Atkinson, *Behind the Scenes at the Museum* (New York: Picador, 1997), p. 114.
12. Peter Goodrich, *Oedipus Lex: Psychoanalysis, History, Law* (Berkeley: University of California Press, 1995), p. 135.
13. Sharon Marcus has a fascinating discussion of dolls and gender (particularly dolls as emblems and tokens of desire and violence between women) in her recent study of lesbianism in the Victorian novel; I am less likely to assume that there are any gendered roles to the doll-status of characters and the playing-status of readers—for that aspect of doll theory, it doesn't really matter whom Barbie wants to marry, it just matters that she doesn't know she's a doll. Marcus, *Between Women: Friendship, Desire, and Marriage in Victorian England* (Princeton, NJ: Princeton University Press, 2007), pp. 109–84.
14. *The Nutshell Studies of Unexplained Death*, essay and photography by Corinne May Botz (New York: The Monacelli Press, 2004). Botz further notes the coincidence of Glessner creating her murder rooms at the same moment that Mrs. James Wood Thorne was creating the Thorne miniature Rooms at the Art Institute of Chicago.
15. For a brilliant discussion of the genre, see Deidre Lynch, *The Economy of Character: Novels, Market Culture, and the Business of Inner Meaning* (Chicago: University of Chicago Press, 1998).
16. Harry Davis and Jay Paul, *Tasha Tudor's Dollhouse: A Lifetime in Miniature* (New York: Little Brown, 1999).
17. Rosemary Folliot, *De Bever Hall—The Story of a Stately Dolls House* (London: Duckworth, 1976).

18. Mrs. James Ward Thorne, *American Rooms in Miniature* (Chicago: The Art Institute of Chicago, 1941), p. 1.
19. Tim Burton does, of course, indulge in enormous dresses on tiny Alice and short skirts on giant Alice, but that comedy is unusual in the world of "Alice alternatives." Perhaps it is a function precisely of an older Alice. The child Alice can maintain the fiction of always being properly (and tidily) dressed, but the older Alice, more anxious about such things, cannot. Her near nakedness is a sign of the increasing closeness (as soon as she leaves the hole, in fact) of the marriage plot. (She does not, of course, marry, for her heart belongs to Daddy—or at least, to Daddy's business, which she plans to expand around the globe. Alice in the China Seas, perhaps?)
20. Dickens, *The Old Curiosity Shop* (London: Penguin, 1972), p. 56.
21. Walter Bagehot, "Charles Dickens" (1858), reprinted in *The Works and Life of Walter Bagehot*, Vol. 3, *Historical and Literary Essays* (Longman, 1915); also in *Charles Dickens: The Critical Heritage*, edited by Philip Collins (Routledge, 1995), p. 391.
22. See the many articles discussing Dickens and books of "eccentric characters," including my own chapter in *Dickens and the Daughter of the House* (Cambridge: Cambridge University Press, 1999); David Musselwhite, *Partings Welded Together* (Routledge, 1987); and Paul Schlicke, *Dickens and Popular Entertainment* (Unwin, 1988). All these discussions owe a great deal to Richard Altick, *The Shows of London* (Cambridge, MA: Harvard University Press, 1978) and his brilliant examination of popular collections and exhibitions. See again Stewart for the study of these contrasts.
23. Dickens, *Bleak House* (New York: Norton, 1977), p. 17.
24. In DVD commentary, "Alice in Wonderland," 1966, DVD released 2003.

CHAPTER 4

1. Roger Shattuck, *Proust's Binoculars: A Study of Memory, Time and Recognition in A la Recherche du Temps Perdu* (Princeton, NJ: Princeton University Press, 1983), p. 18.
2. *Vanity Fair: A Novel without a Hero*, edited by John Sutherland (Oxford: Oxford University Press, 1999), p. 820.
3. Barthes, *S/Z* (New York: Hill & Wang, 1974), p. 112.
4. Joseph Litvak has beautifully captured what he calls the "blurring of the line" between the two in *Strange Gourmets: Sophistication, Theory, and the Novel* (Durham, NC: Duke University Press, 1997), p. 59.
5. Tillotson, *Novels of the Eighteen-Forties* (London: Oxford University Press, 1961), p. 73; Tillotson notes that this phrase was reported by Caroline Fox from "The Hero as Man of Letters" in her journal for 1840, *Memoirs of Old Friends* (2 vols. 1882), 1: 186. This phrase, interestingly, as Tillotson notes, does not appear in the published version of the lecture. Curious!
6. For the best account of this, see Juliet McMaster, " 'Bluebeard at Breakfast:' An Unpublished Thackeray Manuscript," *Dickens Studies Annual: Essays on Victorian Fiction* 8 (1980), pp. 197–230. Shuli Barzilai also discusses Thackeray but primarily through his biographical interest in Bluebeard; she doesn't discuss Becky Sharp at any length. *Tales of Bluebeard and His Wives from Late Antiquity to Postmodern Times* (New York: Routledge, 2009).
7. "Child's Parties," from *Sketches and Travels in London* (Newcastle-on-Tyne: Cambridge Scholarly Publishing, 2008), pp. 46–49.

8. For a brilliant reading of phantasmagoria, see Terry Castle, "Phantasmagoria and the Metaphysics of Modern reverie," in *The Female Thermometer: Eighteenth-Century Culture and the Invention of the Uncanny* (New York: Oxford University Press, 1995), pp. 140–67. See further, Marina Warner, *Phantasmagoria: Spirit Visions, Metaphors, and Media into the Twenty-First Century* (New York: Oxford University Press, 2008). The critic who has best illuminated Thackeray's sense of spectacle is Andrew Miller in *Novels behind Glass: Commodity Culture and Victorian Narrative* (Cambridge: Cambridge University Press, 1995).
9. Crary, *Techniques of the Observer: On Vision and Modernity in the 19th Century* (Cambridge, MA: MIT Press, 1992).
10. Quoted in *Anne Thackeray Ritchie: Journals and Letters*, edited by Lillian Shankman (Columbus, OH: Ohio State University Press, 1994), p. 296; originally Charles Townsend Copeland, *Letters of Thomas Carlyle to His Youngest Sister* (Boston, 1899), p. 96.
11. I am indebted to a fine contemporary edition of this amazing book, *Notes of a Journey from Cornhill to Grand Cairo*, with an introduction by Sarah Searight and illustrations compiled by Briony Llewellyn (London: Cockbird Press, 1991).
12. Thackeray, "Waiting at the Station," from *Punch*, 9 March 1850, republished in *Punch's Prize Novelists, The Fat Contributor and Travels in London* (New York, 1853).
13. Thackeray, *Contributions to the Morning Chronicle*, edited by Gordon N. Ray (Urbana: University of Illinois Press, 1955), pp. 139–42.
14. Thackeray himself said that when he wrote that, when instead of fainting or protesting Becky "admired her husband, strong, brave, and victorious," he slapped his fist on the table and exclaimed "that is a touch of genius."
15. As Sutherland elegantly notes, when the narrator says, on p. 859, "Mrs Becky . . . had got a miniature too hanging up in her room," a pencil drawing of "a gentleman . . . his face having the advantage of being painted up in pink . . . riding on an elephant, away from some coco-nut trees, and a pagoda," "it has shrunk; see p. 203" (948; footnote). We can almost hear Virginia Woolf adding, ironically, at some fifty years distance, "Are there two lighthouses then?"
16. Foucault, *Discipline and Punish*, translated by Alan Sheridan (New York: Vintage, 1995), p. 200.

CHAPTER 5

1. John Durham Peters, *Speaking into the Air: A History of the Idea of Communication* (Chicago: University of Chicago, 199), pp. 165–71.
2. Ned Schantz, *Gossip, Letters, Phones: The Scandal of Female Networks in Film and Literature* (New York: Oxford University Press, 2008), p. 40.
3. For the best recent discussion of Victorian media and information technology, see Richard Menke, *Telegraphic Realism: Victorian Fiction and Other Information Systems* (Stanford, CA: Stanford University Press, 2007).
4. Charles Dickens, *Bleak House* (New York: Norton, 1977), p. 615.
5. See Marcia Renee Goodman's " 'I'll Follow the Other': Tracing the (M)other in Bleak House," *Dickens Studies Annual* 19 (1990), pp.147–67. Among the many fine studies of Esther's narration, see in particular William Axton, "The Trouble with Esther," *Modern Language Quarterly* 26 (1965), pp. 545–57.

Robert Newsom, *Dickens on the Romantic Side of Familiar Things: Bleak House and the Novel Tradition* (New York: Columbia University Press, 1977) and Alex Zwerdling, "Esther Summerson Rehabilitated," *PMLA* 8, no. 33 (1973), pp. 429–39. The most thorough and inventive of these is John O. Jordan, *Supposing Bleak House* (University of Virginia Press, 2011). The primary emphasis of this chapter, however, is to view Esther less as a character with interiority than as a plot function with a proper name—as a narrating mechanism for the curious novelist. My approach to narrative might most closely echo Steven Connor, *Dumbstruck: A Cultural History of Ventriloquism* (New York: Oxford University Press, 2001).

6. Hillel Schwartz, *The Culture of the Copy: Striking Likenesses, Unreasonable Facsimiles* (Cambridge, MA: Zone, 1998), p. 27.

7. Hillel Schwartz makes the point that surely curiosity cabinets should have unique copies (215); instead, he notes, they are "stocked with fabrications purporting to be ones-of-a-kind"; in another moment of copying-a-copy, he notes the incredible popularity of trompe l'oeil paintings with "half-opened letters" (179), a point to which I will return later in this chapter. The paradox of the "unique copy" is at the heart of my chapter—who doesn't want to believe however much she knows she "resembles" another, that she herself is the "unique" copy? (Anyone who has ever fought to be the best-loved daughter knows the pain of too many duplicates running around the house.)

8. Ned Schantz has pointed out to me that Lady Dedlock's posture is straight out of a book of poker "tells"—and Tulkinghorn would make a great poker player.

9. Given the anxiety about mobility in this novel, the play on "train," in a novel set before the railway, is no accident; this set of puns began in *Dombey and Son*, a novel that of course has the train to end all trains—both in terms of locomotives and plots.

10. My history of the novel draws on Ian Watt, *The Rise of the Novel* (Berkeley: University of California Press, 1957); Michael McKeon, *The Origins of the English Novel* (New Brunswick, NJ: Rutgers University Press, 2002); Lennard Davis, *Factual Fictions: The Origins of the English Novel* (New York: Columbia University Press, 1983); J. Paul Hunter, *Before Novels* (New York: Norton, 1990); and Catherine Gallagher, *Nobody's Story: The Vanishing Acts of Women Writers in the Marketplace, 1670–1820* (Berkeley: University of California Press, 1996).

11. See Michel Foucault, *Discipline and Punish*, as well as the provocative opening to *The Order of Things*, which has haunted so many new historicist readings. For narration, I am thinking of Jonathan Arac, *Commissioned Spirits: The Shaping of Social Motion in Dickens, Carlyle, Melville, and Hawthorne* (New York: Columbia University Press, 1989) and Audrey Jaffe's *Vanishing Points: Dickens, Narrative, and the Subject of Omniscience* (Berkeley: University of California Press, 1991). For a reading similarly inflected but less interested in techniques of narration, see Amanda Anderson, *The Powers of Distance: Cosmopolitanism and the Cultivation of Detachment* (Princeton, NJ: Princeton University Press, 2001).

12. See in particular Dickens's "Curious Misprint in the 'Edinburgh Review'" in *Household Words* (August 1, 1857) in which he challenges Stephen's assertion that novelists knew nothing (and could do less) about politics and where he correctly identifies the government's persistent mistreatment of Hill as an example of what the (fictional) Circumlocution Office performs on the hapless and inventive Doyce.

13. Letter to Mrs. Charles Dickens, 15 April 1851, in *The Letters of Charles Dickens*, Vol. 6, edited by Graham Storey, Kathleen Tillotson, and Nina Burgis (Oxford: Clarendon Press, 1988), p. 353.
14. *Our Mutual Friend* (London: Penguin Books, 1997), pp. 86–87.

CHAPTER 6

1. Dennis V. Lindley, "The Philosophy of Statistics," *Journal of the Royal Statistical Society*, Series D (The Statistician), 49, no. 3 (2000), pp. 293–337 (at 294).
2. *Bleak House* (New York: Norton, 1977), p. 768.
3. *Hard Times* (New York: Norton, 2001), p. 177.
4. Readings of *Hard Times'* considerable literary sophistication have been frustrated by the social criticism of George Bernard Shaw or F. R. Leavis, who read the novel as close to reportage. The critical literature on *Hard Times* is focused largely on the novel as social text; among the most important examples are those which complicate this singular reading. See Raymond Williams, *Culture and Society, 1780–1950* (New York: Columbia University Press, 1983); Catherine Gallagher, *The Industrial Reformation of English Fiction: Social Discourse and Narrative Form, 1832–1867* (Chicago: University of Chicago Press, 1988); and Rosemarie Bodenheimer, *The Politics of Story in Victorian Social Fiction* (Ithaca, NY: Cornell University Press, 1988). For one essay that takes the novel's quality of imagination seriously, see Robert Newsom, "To Scatter Dust: Fancy and Authenticity in *Our Mutual Friend*," *Dickens Studies Annual* 8 (1980), pp. 39–60, which begins with a fine reading of the powers and limits of the imagination in *Hard Times*; and Steven Connor's *Charles Dickens* (London: Blackwell, 1985) for another reading of the limits of "fact and fancy."
5. As David Lindley ends his essay on "the philosophy of statistics":

    The philosophy of statistics presented here has three fundamental tenets: first, that uncertainty should be described by probabilities; second, that consequences should have their merits described by utilities; third, that the optimum decision combines the probabilities and utilities by calculating expected utility and then maximizing that. If these are accepted, then the first task of a statistician is to develop a (probability) model to embrace the client's interests and uncertainties. It will include the data and any parameters that are judged necessary. Once accomplished, the mechanics of the calculus take over and the required inference is made. If decisions are involved, the model needs to be extended to include utilities, followed by another mechanical operation of maximizing expected utility. One attractive feature is that the whole procedure is well defined and there is little need for ad hoc assumptions. There is, however, a considerable need for approximation. To carry out this scheme for the large world is impossible.

    Or, as he continues and my chapter will argue, "Where a real difficulty arises is in the construction of the model." This is the dilemma the curious heroine proposes in realism. For two other fine histories, see Stephen M. Stigler, *The History of Statistics: The Measurement of Uncertainty Before 1900* (Cambridge, MA: Harvard University Press, 1990) and Theodore M. Porter, *The Rise of Statistical Thinking, 1820–1900* (Princeton, NJ: Princeton University Press, 1986), which I discuss at greater length below; for a literary critical text engaged with these questions, see Mary Poovey, *A History of the Modern Fact:*

Problems of Knowledge in the Sciences of Wealth and Society (Chicago: University of Chicago Press, 1998). The work of Ian Hacking on probability is central to this analysis; see in particular *The Emergence of Probability: A Philosophical Study of Early Ideas about Probability, Induction and Statistical Inference* (Cambridge University Press, 1984); see my discussion below. See also Robert Newsom's *A Likely Story: Probability and Play in the Novel* (New Brunswick, NJ: Rutgers University Press, 1988), which I discussed in chapter 2.

6. The best and most sympathetic critic of Dickens and the utilitarians is Robert Newsom; see his *Dickens Revisited* (New York: Twayne, 2000) among other discussions. His reading of Pickwick as Bentham is particularly captivating. Humphry House first raised these questions in *The Dickens World* (Oxford: Oxford University Press, 1941), and his discussion remains particularly trenchant. My reading of the utilitarians in general is indebted to Frances Ferguson's inventive discussion in *Pornography, the Theory: What Utilitarianism Did to Action* (Chicago: University of Chicago Press, 2004).

7. See Catherine Gallagher's reading of these parallels in *The Industrial Reformation of English Fiction*.

8. Hacking, *The Emergence of Probability*, p. 86; the quotation from Leibniz is from "Nouveaux essaies sur l'entendement humaine," in *Die philosophischen Schriften von G. W. Leibniz*, Vol. 4, pp. xvi, 9.

9. See my reading of the adultery plot in *Dickens and the Daughter of House* (Cambridge: Cambridge University Press, 1999).

10. For other readings that focus on Mrs. Gradgrind and Dickens's "no-meaning," see Jean Ferguson Carr, "Writing as a Woman: Dickens, *Hard Times*, and Feminine Discourses," in *Dickens Studies Annual* 18 (1989), pp. 161–78. Anne Humpherys's "Louisa Gradgrind's Secret: Marriage and Divorce in *Hard Times*," *Dickens Studies Annual* 25 (1996), pp. 177–96, focuses on the relationship between Stephen and Louisa as well.

11. Hacking, *The Emergence of Probability*, p. 87.

12. James Harthouse makes the point, when he says, "The side that can prove anything in a line of units, tens, hundreds, and thousands, Mrs. Bounderby, seems to me to afford the most fun, and to give a man the best chance. I am quite as much attached to it as if I believed it. I am quite ready to go in for it, to the same extent as if I believed it. And what more could I possibly do, if I did believe it!" (100). But he is echoing not only Mr. Gradgrind but also the narrator's parody of the "party of Fact" when discussing workers: "So many hundred Hands in this Mill; so many hundred horse Steam Power. It is known, to the force of a single pound weight, what the engine will do; but, not all the calculators of the National Debt can tell me the capacity for good or evil, for love or hatred, for patriotism or discontent, for the decomposition of virtue into vice, or the reverse, at any single moment in the soul of one of these its quiet servants, with the composed faces and the regulated actions. There is no mystery in it; there is an unfathomable mystery in the meanest of them, for ever.—Supposing we were to reverse our arithmetic for material objects, and to govern these awful unknown quantities by other means!" (56). To its credit, the novel doesn't really worry too much about the "unfathomable mystery" in the workers. As I have tried to suggest above, unlike Thackeray, Dickens doesn't really find many things unfathomable after all. A fathom, after all, is a fairly precise measure, and Dickens sounds people out all the time.

13. Martha Nussbaum's essay, "The Literary Imagination in Public Life," offers one of the most compelling, if also commensurately dangerous, of these readings. *New Literary History* 22, no. 4, Papers from the Commonwealth Center for Literary and Cultural Change (Fall 1991), pp. 877–910.
14. Reprinted from *St. Paul's Magazine* (July 1870) in *Dickens: The Critical Heritage* edited by Philip Collins (New York: Routledge, 1986), pp. 338–39.
15. Walter Bagehot, "Charles Dickens," *National Review*, October 1858, reprinted in Collins, p. 405.
16. George Brimley, from an unsigned review, *Spectator*, October 1853, reprinted in Collins, p. 296.
17. Brimley, in Collins, p. 296.
18. The critic who most deeply shares my sense of the unhappiness of this ending is Catherine Gallagher in *The Body Economic: Life, Death, and Sensation in Political Economy and the Victorian Novel* (Princeton, NJ: Princeton University Press, 2008); she, too, finds neither the plot of the dog nor the plot of the heroine redemptive.
19. Hal Varian, "On How the Web Challenges Managers," *The McKinsey Quarterly*, January 2009, http://www.mckinseyquarterly.com/Hal_Varian_on_how_the_Web_challenges_managers_2286. Varian then goes on to say: "The ability to take data—to be able to understand it, to process it, to extract value from it, to visualize it, to communicate, it's going to be a hugely important skill in the next decades, not only at the professional level but even at the educational level for elementary school kids, for high school kids, for college kids. Because now we really do have essentially free and ubiquitous data. So the complimentary [sic] scarce factor is the ability to understand that data and extract value from it."
20. George Eliot, *Middlemarch* (Oxford: Oxford University Press, 1996), p. 176.

CHAPTER 7

1. I have borrowed this nifty definition from Wikipedia; for a more thorough and engaging discussion of the practice, see Janice E. Stockard, *Daughters of the Canton Delta: Marriage Patterns and Economic Strategies in South China, 1860–1930* (Stanford, CA: Stanford University Press, 1989), who makes clear the ways that this "strategy" worked to gain autonomy for single women who could marry ghosts and retain their freedom. If only such structures had been more widely available in Victorian England, my own book need not have been written.
2. George Eliot, *Middlemarch* (Oxford: Oxford University Press, 1996), p. 27.
3. George Eliot, *Daniel Deronda* (Oxford: Oxford University Press, 1984), p. 128
4. For a characteristically brilliant reading of George Eliot and the Gothic, see Judith Wilt, *Ghosts of the Gothic, Austen, Eliot and Lawrence* (Princeton, NJ: Princeton University Press,1980). For a broader reading of the Gothic and property relations, see Walter Benn Michaels, "Romance and Real Estate," in *The Gold Standard and the Logic of Naturalism* (Berkeley: University of California Press, 1988).
5. *George Eliot: A Biography* (Oxford: Clarendon, 1968). The best account of Eliot's fiction and its relationship to her life is Rosemarie Bodenheimer, *The Real Life of Mary Ann Evans: George Eliot, Her Letters and Fiction* (Ithaca, NY: Cornell University Press, 1994); a fascinating account that also consider Eliot's changing relationship to law is Alexander Welsh's *George Eliot and Blackmail* (Cambridge, MA: Harvard University Press, 1985).

6. *The Men of the Time*, 9th ed., 1875, pp. 383–84.
7. 13 August 1875, *The Letters of George Eliot*, Vol. 9, edited by Gordon Haight (New Haven, CT: Yale University Press, 1954), p. 163; for more on Eliot's relationship to John Stuart Mill, see Bernard Paris, *Experiments in Life: George Eliot's Quest for Values* (Detroit: Wayne State University Press, 1965).
8. John Stuart Mill, *On Liberty and Other Writings*, edited by Stefan Collini (Cambridge: Cambridge University Press, 1989), p. 68.
9. "George Eliot," in Virginia Woolf, *The Common Reader* (New York: Harcourt, Brace, 1925), p. 241.
10. *Middlemarch* was first published in 1871–72; *Daniel Deronda* in 1876. There is a vast literature on reform in *Middlemarch* and the Jews in *Deronda*; on the Jewish question, see in particular Edward Said, "Zionism from the Standpoint of Its Victims," *Social Text* 1 (Winter 1979), pp. 7–58. Said's essay has dominated recent criticism of the novel, to the exclusion of almost every other question. An unusually well-informed response, dwelling on the ambivalence of Eliot's depiction of the Jews in the novel, and on the absence of a British, Jewish Zionist movement within history, is Susan Meyer's "'Safely to Their Own Borders': Proto-Zionism, Feminism, and Nationalism in *Daniel Deronda*," *ELH* 60, (Autumn 1993), pp. 733–58. As Meyers notes, Zionism as a political movement came to life in the 1880s following the pogroms in Russia and Eastern Europe; it is hardly on the minds of British Jews in 1871, when Eliot wrote the novel. Among the best readings of Jewish questions in the novel are Catherine Gallagher, "George Eliot and Daniel Deronda: The Prostitute and the Jewish Question," in *Sex, Politics and Science in the Nineteenth Century Novel*, edited by Ruth Bernard Yeazell (Baltimore: Johns Hopkins University Press, 1986); Michael Ragussis, *Figures of Conversion: "The Jewish Question" & English National Identity* (Durham, NC: Duke University Press, 1995); and Irene Tucker, *A Probable State: The Novel, the Contract and the Jews* (Chicago: University of Chicago Press, 2000). On reform, see Jerome Buckley, "History by Indirection: Reform in *Middlemarch*," *Victorian Studies* 1, no. 2 (1957), pp. 173–79.
11. For an incredibly helpful discussion of the transformation of the novel, see Jerome Beaty, *Middlemarch from Notebook to Novel: A Study of George Eliot's Creative Method* (Illinois Studies in Language and Literature) (Urbana: University of Illinois Press, 1960) and for subsequent debates, in particular Stanton Milet, "The Union of 'Miss Brooke' and *Middlemarch*: A Study of the Manuscript" *JEPG* 79, no. 1 (January 1980), pp. 32–57.
12. Gillian Beer's volume, *George Eliot* (Bloomington: Indiana University Press, 1986), remains the best study of Eliot and feminism; for the most wide-ranging and acute reading of the general movement toward transcendence in *Middlemarch*, see D. A. Miller, *Narrative and Its Discontents: Problems of Closure in the Traditional Novel* (Princeton, NJ: Princeton University Press, 1981). Among other feminist readings, see particularly Zelda Austen, "Why Are Feminist Critics Angry with George Eliot?" *College English* 37 (1976), pp. 549–61.
13. It is moments like this that remind us that when George Eliot was asked for the origins of Mr. Casaubon, she was silent, and then tapped her own breast.
14. We might think of this as part of what Stanley Cavell has called "the problem of other minds"; for a brilliant account of this "problem" as the ethical center of Victorian fiction, see Andrew H. Miller, *The Burdens of Perfection: On Ethics and Reading in NineteenthCentury British Literature* (Ithaca, NY: Cornell University Press, 2008).

15. For a wonderful story of the transformation of honeymoons, that crossing of the threshold, see Helena Michie, *Victorian Honeymoons: Journeys to the Conjugal* (Cambridge: Cambridge University Press, 2006). Michie very much shares my sense that sex is only one of the forms of knowledge women were imagined to gain from the jounrey into marriage; she also shares my obsession with Dorothea Brooke's honeymoon in Rome.
16. Reva Stump, *Movement and Vision in George Eliot's Novels* (Seattle: University of Washington Press, 1959). See also Bernard Paris, *Experiments in Life: George Eliot's Quest for Values* (Detroit: Wayne State University Press, 1965) and Barbara Hardy, *The Novels of George Eliot* (London: The Athlone Press, 1959), who make similar (and fascinatingly historically contiguous) arguments about the relationship between movement, sight, and morality in Eliot's fiction; they form a fascinating triumvirate of early scholarship in the Victorian novel.
17. The narrator suggests that the change Casaubon has in mind is the codicil: "She [Dorothea] had no presentiment that the power which her husband wishes to establish over her future action had relation to anything else than his work." But the narrator goes on to agree with Dorothea, saying, "But it was clear enough to her that he would expect her to devote herself to sifting those mixed heaps of material, which were to be the doubtful illustration of principles still more doubtful." The shifting nature of Eliot's sympathies even for Dorothea makes this a hard one to call: the narrator goes on, "The poor child had become altogether unbelieving as to the trustworthiness of that Key which had made the ambition and the labour of her husband's life," and then notes that "it was not wonderful that, in spite of her small instruction, her judgement in that matter was truer than his." But the narrator never clearly states what was in Casaubon's mind in that night in the bedroom: almost as if the novel were endorsing the law's rejection of a wife's testimony against her husband, she seems reluctant to pull apart the threads of that particular web, his sexual and his intellectual jealousy.
18. To cite only the most obvious examples of incuriosity (apart from his much-discussed habit of never looking down, for which see Steven Marcus, *Representations: Essays on Literature and Society* [New York: Random House, 1975], p. 212 and Cynthia Chase, "The Decomposition of the Elephants: Double-Reading *Daniel Deronda*," PMLA 93, no. 2 [March 1978], pp. 215–27), Daniel Deronda refuses to ask questions about his mother through the entire novel. He never asks Sir Hugo, "Are you my father?" and, we are told, "his imagination was as much astray about Grandcourt as it would have been about an unexplored continent where all the species were peculiar" (353). He may be a titular hero, but Daniel's ignorance is as willful and large as Gwendolen's—the difference is, clearly, only in the degree of punishment.
19. Charles Dickens, *Hard Times* (New York: Norton, 2001), p.60
20. Edith Wharton, *The Age of Innocence* (Oxford: Oxford University Press, 2006), p. 217.
21. Leslie Stephen, *George Eliot* (New York: Macmillan, 1902), p. 179.
22. Jeffrey Eugenides, *The Marriage Plot* (New York: Farrar, Straus & Giroux, 2011), p. 22.
23. P. D. James, *The Children of Men* (New York: Vintage, 2006), p. 46.
24. Alison Bechdel, *Fun Home: A Family Tragicomic* (New York: Mariner Books, 2007) p. 70.
25. Woolf, *A Room of One's Own* (Orlando, FL: Harcourt Brace, 2005), p. 112.

26. 25 August 1907; to Violet Dickinson; *The Letters of Virginia Woolf*, edited by Nigel Nicolson and Joanne Trautmann, Vol. 1 (New York: Harcourt Brace Jovanovich, 1975), p. 306.
27. Woolf, *Mr. Bennett and Mrs. Brown* (London: Hogarth Press, 1924), p. 20
28. Woolf, *Night and Day* (London: Hogarth Press, 1919), p. 15.
29. Woolf, *Moments of Being* (Orlando, FL: Harcourt Brace, 1985), p. 70.
30. Byatt, *Possession* (New York: Vintage, 1991), p. 552.
31. Drabble, *A Natural Curiosity* (New York: Random House, 1992), p. 141.
32. *The Witch of Exmoor* (New York: Harcourt, 1997), p. 215.

CONCLUSION

1. Kate Atkinson, *Started Early, Took My Dog* (New York: Reagan Arthur Book/Back Bay Books, 2011), p. 75.
2. Richard Altick, *The Shows of London:* (Cambridge, MA: Harvard University Press, 1978), p. 335. The original of the Sleeping Beauty was "Mlle. de Ste. Aramanthe, who had fallen a victim to Robespierre because, as it was explained, 'she indignantly refused to become a victim of his lust.'" This doubling of the fairy tale figure with the historical victim (and the de Ste. Aramanthe family did fall victim to the guillotine, if not other forms of Robespierre's violence) suggests the contained violence of the heroine of the realist novel as well. Contemporary versions of mechanical dolls also play with the erotic and violent potential within them (as well as the futurist possibility of a figure like Thomas Edison's "Tomorrow's Eve," in Villiers de L'Isle Adam's novel of the same name) but also suggest their poignancy. Among the most compelling is the film *Lars and the Real Girl* (Nancy Oliver/Craig Gillespie, 2007), in which a desperately shy young man buys an anatomically correct doll, practices (as it were) loving her, and then moves on to a "real girl," a co-worker named Margo. But in Ryan Gosling's delicate performance, and in the responses of all the townspeople to "Bianca," we are left uncertain which is the "real girl," or if both Margo and Bianca become real only by being loved. The climax of the film comes when Lars screams that Bianca has stopped breathing, and his sister-in-law cries out to her husband, "Call 911!" The power of fiction to animate has never been more breathtakingly displayed.
3. Roland Barthes, *S/Z* (New York: Hill & Wang, 1974), p. 82.
4. *Lady Oracle* (New York: Anchor, 1998) p. 3.
5. *The Handmaid's Tale* (New York: Anchor, 1998), p. 94.
6. Kazuo Ishiguro, *Never Let Me Go* (New York: Vintage, 2005), p. 261.
7. Linda S. Kauffman, *Discourses of Desire: Gender, Genre, and Epistolary Fictions* (Ithaca, NY: Cornell University Press, 1986), p. 153.

INDEX

Adam, Villiers de L'Isle, *Tomorrrow's Eve*, 266 n. 2
Addison, Joseph and Richard Steele, *The Spectator*, 112
The Age of Innocence, 220, 246, 247
Alice in Wonderland, 2, 20, 69–78, 82, 87, 89, 90, 94, 100, 101, 157, 226, 227, 245
    cyborg Alice, 232
    film versions, 70, 233, 258 n. 19
Allingham, Margery, 227
Altick, Richard, 258 n. 22
Anderson, Amanda, 260 n. 11
Anderson, Graham, 254 n. 36
Aquinas, Thomas, 18
Arac, Jonathan, 260 n. 11
Aristotle, 18
Armstrong, Nancy, 25, 249 n. 10
Arnold, Matthew, 2, 206, 249 n. 2
Ashmolean Museum, 3
Atkinson, Kate
    Behind the Scenes at the Museum, 79, 246
    Started Early, Took My Dog, 231–232
Atwood, Margaret. See also *The Handmaid's Tale*; *Lady Oracle*
    The Edible Woman, 227
Auerbach, Nina, 257 n. 4, n. 5
Augustine, 18–19, 20
Austen, Jane, 24, 51, 225, 226
    Emma, 1, 59
    Persuasion, 221
    Pride and Prejudice, 5, 15, 25, 42–43, 44, 57, 67, 221
    Sense and Sensibility, 11–12, 221

Bagehot, Walter, 85, 86
Barthes, Roland, 11, 15, 17, 26, 30, 56, 101, 222, 224, 230–231, 233, 246, 250 n. 24
Barzalai, Shuli, 254 n. 36, 258 n. 6
Beaty, Jerome, 264 n. 11
Bechdel, Alison, *Fun Home*, 223–224
Beer, Gillian, 255 n. 11, 264 n. 12
Benedict, Barbara, 215 n. 14
Bentham, Jeremy, 166, 184, 191
Bersani, Leo, 249 n. 9
Blade Runner, 80
Bleak House, 2, 7, 70, 73, 78, 81, 84, 92–95, 100, 101, 133, 134–162, 163–164, 185, 212, 219, 226, 233, 247
Bluebeard, 2, 8, 9, 12, 18, 30–33, 36, 64, 66–67, 94, 99–100, 103, 104, 108, 133–134, 164, 192, 227, 235–236, 239, 254 n. 36
    and *Bleak House*, 135–136, 139–140, 141, 147–150, 151, 152, 155–158
    and *Daniel Deronda*, 206–219
    and *Hard Times* 165–166, 171, 173, 175–176, 182–183, 187, 188
    and *Middlemarch* 193, 197–200, 202, 205, 209
    and modernism, 221
    and *Vanity Fair* 110, 121–122, 127, 129–130, 132, 136
Blumenberg, Hans, 18–19
Bodenheimer, Rosemarie, 261 n. 4, 263 n. 5
Bowen, Elizabeth, 227
British Museum, 20–22, 252 n. 20

Bronte, Charlotte, 104. See also *Jane Eyre*
  Villette, 112
Brooks, Peter, 6, 25, 58, 60, 253 n. 31
Browning, Robert, "A Woman's Last Word," 2, 249 n. 2
Buckley, Jerome, 264 n. 10
Bunyan, John, *Pilgrim's Progress*, 130
Burke, Edmund, 22
Burton, Tim, 70, 72, 233, 258 n. 19
Butler, Octavia, 227
Byatt, A. S.
  Angels and Insects, 227
  The Children's Book, 78–79
  Possession, 227, 228

Campion, Jane, *The Piano*, 66
Carlyle, Thomas, 103, 107
Carr, Jean Ferguson, 262 n. 10
Carroll, Lewis, 73, 76, 102, 227, 242 n. 2. See also *Alice in Wonderland*
  Through the Looking Glass, 69
Carter, Angela, 7, 10, 16, 36, 37, 73, 252 n. 19
  "Alice in Prague: The Curious Room," 69–71, 135
  "The Bloody Chamber," 18, 31–32, 254 n. 36
Castle, Terry, 45, 250 n. 16, 255 n. 19, 259 n. 8
Cavell, Stanley, 10
Cavendish, Margaret, 252 n. 16
Chase, Cynthia, 265 n. 18
Clarissa, 7, 10, 44, 48–57, 59, 133, 157, 184, 235, 246, 247
Collins, Wilkie, 58, 60
  The Law and the Lady, 57, 256 n. 25
Connor, Steven, 260 n. 5, 261 n. 4
Contract law, 6, 7, 8, 9, 26–30, 163–164, 192, 200–201, 203–206, 214–217, 228, 241
Crary, Jonathan, 106
Curiosity
  cabinets and museums, 5, 20–22, 23, 59, 75, 90, 186, 246. See also *Bluebeard*
  definitions of, 4, 19–20
  history of 18–22, 251 n. 14
  and pilgrimage, 152 n. 15

Dalton, Clare, 255 n. 7
Daniel Deronda, 6, 10, 35–36, 67, 94, 156, 187, 193, 194, 206–218

Daston, Lorraine, 20, 251 n. 14
Dead babies, 151, 154–156, 158, 159–160, 247
DeBever Hall: The Story of a Stately Dolls House, 82
Defoe, Daniel, *Robinson Crusoe*, 5, 25
DeLauretis, Teresa, 16–17, 249 n. 10
The Dialectic of Enlightenment, 16, 107
Dickens, Charles, 71, 85, 90, 95, 225, 226. See also *Bleak House*; *Great Expectations*; *Hard Times*; *Little Dorrit*; *The Old Curiosity Shop*; *Sketches by Boz*
  and daughters, 104
  David Copperfield 155, 196
  Dombey and Son 123, 134, 174, 187
  and *Household Words* 141
  Our Mutual Friend, 160
  Pickwick Papers, 85, 141
  Sketches by Boz (Dickens), 85
Dickinson, Emily, 58
Divorce, 151, 180, 186, 219–221, 255 n. 10
Dodgson, Charles. See Lewis Carroll
Dolls and dollhouses, 71, 73, 78–84, 89, 93–94, 133, 143, 154, 232, 246
  Barbie and Ken, 257 n. 13
  puppets, 76, 129, 131
  waxworks, 87–89, 232, 266 n. 2
Dollhouse. See Joss Whedon
Double-vision, 4, 130, 132, 138, 199, 227
Drabble, Margaret
  A Natural Curiosity, 228–229
  The Witch of Exmoor, 229–230

Eagleton, Terry, 54–55, 72, 255 n. 17
Ecclesiastes, 42, 65
Edison, Thomas, 266 n. 2
Electricity, 16
  and lightning, 34, 38, 247
Eliot, George, 29–30, 95, 190–191, 239. See also *Daniel Deronda*; *Middlemarch*
  Felix Holt, 29, 212
  Romola, 220
  "Silly Novels by Lady Novelists," 112
Enlightenment thought, 16, 35–36, 39
Epistolarity. See Realism
Ermarth, Elizabeth, 4, 145
Eugenides, Jeffrey, *The Marriage Plot*, 221–222, 224
Eve, 7, 9, 18, 20. See also *Paradise Lost*

Federer, Roger, 126
Fellini, Federico, *8 ½*, 246
Female suffrage, 10, 27–28, 186
Ferguson, Frances, 252 n. 20, 262 n. 6
Fielding, Henry, 112
  Shamela, 252 n. 18
Findlen, Paula, 251 n. 14
Forster, E. M., 22–23, 57, 228
Foucault, Michel, 1, 131, 142, 163, 230, 232, 246, 260 n. 11
Fowles, John, *The French Lieutenant's Woman*, 246
Frankenstein, 16, 39
Freud, Sigmund, 59
  "Beyond the Pleasure Principle," 19
  Civilization and its Discontents, 68
  "The Three Caskets," 17, 37, 40–41
  "The Uncanny," 70–71, 72, 78, 79, 93

Galatea 2.2, 232
Gallagher, Catherine, 7, 43, 100, 255 n. 14, 262 n. 7, 263 n. 18, 264 n. 10
Gardam, Jane, *Crusoe's Daughter*, 5
Gaskell, Elizabeth, 222
  Cranford, 222
  Mary Barton, 57, 150
  Ruth, 3–4
Ghosts, 186, 189, 191, 202–203, 207, 217–218
The Golden Bowl, 7, 44, 58–68, 71, 199, 247
  film version, 58
Goodlad, Lauren, 253 n. 32
Gore, Catherine, 112
Gosling, Ryan, 266 n. 2
Gothic, 8, 9, 30, 56–57, 117, 146, 193, 235
Great Expectations, 5, 79, 94, 146, 157, 161, 162
Grossman, Jonathan, 44

Hacking, Ian, 173, 183, 261 n. 5
Hadley, Elaine, 253 n. 32
Haight, Gordon, 190
The Handmaid's Tale, 10, 11, 233, 237–242, 245
Haraway, Donna, 11
  "A Cyborg Manifesto," 230, 231, 232, 245
Hard Times, 2, 7, 25, 90, 156, 161–162, 164–188, 189, 219, 244, 247

Hardy, Barbara, 265 n. 16
Hepworth, Cecil, 70
Herodotus, 72
Hill, Rowland, 153, 260 n. 12
Hoffmann, E.T.A., 80
Holmes, Sherlock, 234
House, Humphry, 261 n. 6
Hunter, J. Paul, 260 n. 10
Humphreys, Anne, 262 n. 10

Ibsen, Henrik, *A Doll's House*, 80
Ishiguro, Kazuo, *Never Let Me Go*, 162, 233, 242–247

Jaffe, Audrey, 260 n. 11
James, Henry, 57, 70, 71, 73, 225, 249 n. 9. See also *The Golden Bowl*; *The Portrait of a Lady*
  Roderick, Hudson 40
  The Princess Casamassima, 40
James, P.D., *The Children of Men*, 222
Jane Eyre, 2, 5, 8, 9, 10, 25, 33, 38, 57, 74, 99, 131, 141, 224, 234, 236
Jay, Martin, 251 n. 13
Jed, Stephanie, 54, 252 n. 16
Jordan, John, 260 n. 5
Joyce, James, 223

Kafka, Franz, "Before the Law," 69
Kaufmann, Linda, 54, 246, 255 n. 16
Kenny, Neil, 251 n. 14
Kieslowski, Krzysztof, *The Double Life of Véronique*, 233
Kincaid, James, 257 n. 4
Kipling, Rudyard, 70

The Lady Eve, 5, 7–9, 10, 246
Lady Oracle, 233–237, 239, 245, 246
Lars and the Real Girl, 266 n. 2
Leavis, F. R., 261 n. 4
Leavis, Q.D., 9
Leguin, Ursula, 227
Leibniz, G.W., 173
Lennox, Charlotte, *The Female Quixote*, 5
Lessing, Doris, *The Golden Notebook*, 23, 80, 227
Levine, Caroline, 11
Levine, George, 4
Lewes, George Henry, 190, 217, 219
Lewis, Jayne Elizabeth, 255 n. 17
Liberalism, 253 n. 32

Lindley, David, 261 n. 5
Little Dorrit, 4, 27, 166, 203
Litvak, Joseph, 258 n. 4
Livesey, Margot, *Eva Moves the Furniture*, 228
"London" (William Blake), 27
Lumière brothers, 66
Lynch, Deidre, 255 n. 15

Macpherson, Sandra, 54, 56
Magic, 102, 105–106, 205
Magic lantern, 105–108, 124–125, 132, 134, 198
Maine, Sir Henry, 27
Malthus, Thomas, 165, 169
Marcus, Sharon, 257 n. 13
Marcus, Steven, 265 n. 18
Marr, Alexander, 251 n. 14
Marx, Karl, 102–103
Maxwell, Lily, 10
Mayhew, Henry, 109–110, 114
McKeon, Michael, 260 n. 11
McMaster, Juliet, 254 n. 36, 258 n. 6
Menke, Richard, 259 n. 3
Metropolitan Museum, 220, 246
Meyers, Susan, 264 n. 10
Michaels, Walter Benn, 263 n. 4
Michie, Helena, 250 n. 13, 264 n. 15
Middlemarch, 6, 7, 10, 11, 30, 33, 35, 38, 43, 45, 60, 78, 128, 156, 178, 187, 188, 189–205, 212, 218–221, 222, 223, 225, 247
Milet, Stanton, 264 n. 11
Mill, James, 166, 169
Mill, John Stuart, 2, 7, 9, 23–24, 27–30, 80, 166, 169, 175, 180, 181, 186, 189–195, 198, 200, 206, 208, 215–218
Miller, Andrew, 259 n. 8, 264 n. 14
Miller, D.A., *Narrative and Its Discontents*, 251 n. 10, 264 n. 12
Miller, Nancy K., 249 n. 10
Milton, John, 11, 165, 196, 239. See *Paradise Lost*
  "Areopagitica," 48
  "Doctrine and Discipline of Divorce" 46, 48
Moore, Marianne, 227
Moretti, Franco, 9, 10
Mrs. Dalloway, 3, 4

Newsom, Robert, 43, 70, 100, 261 n. 4, 262 n. 4, n. 5
NFL Draft, 237
Nussbaum, Martha, 262 n. 13
Nutshell Studies of Death, 80

Oedipus, 16–17, 251 n. 9
The Old Curiosity Shop, 65, 70, 73, 81, 84–92, 100, 101, 234
Otter, Chris, 253 n. 32

Pamela (Samuel Richardson), 25
Pandora, 7, 17–18, 24, 231–232, 242
Paradise Lost, 7–8, 16, 17, 38, 41, 42, 44, 46–48, 54, 68, 79, 165, 228, 239, 247
Paris, Bernard, 265 n. 16
Park, Katharine, 20, 251 n. 14
Pascal, Blaise, 18
Persephone, 79, 233
Peters, John Durham, 133, 259 n. 1
Phillips, Adam, 44, 56
Pomian, Krzysztof, 251 n. 14
Poovey, Mary, 261 n. 5
Pornography, 20, 36, 70, 252 n. 18
Porter, Katherine Anne, 78
Porter, Roy, 16
Porter, Theodore, 165
Portrait of a Lady, 1, 5, 6, 10, 32, 33–41, 45, 59, 61, 67, 68, 74, 84, 192, 221, 222, 223–224, 247, 256 n. 30
Postal system, 152–153
Prendergast, Christopher, 44
Prometheus, 16, 17, 24
Proust, Marcel, 100, 106
Psyche, 7, 17–18

Quickening, 92–94, 136, 141, 207, 214

Rackin, Donald, 76–77
Ragussis, Michael, 264 n. 10
Realism, 1–2
  and contract, 5, 7, 43,
  and convention, 4
  and epistolarity, 140–141, 152–159, 161–162
  as optical device, 43, 66, 100, 103, 104–110, 130–132, 245–246
  and sympathy, 180
  as test, 7, 44, 45–68

Reform Bill, 2
Rhys, Jean, 227
Richardson, Samuel, 73. See *Clarissa Charles Grandison*, 57
Ritchie, Anne Thackeray, 104, 225
   "Bluebeard's Keys," 227
Rivers, Joan, 102
Rousseau, George, 49, 58
Rukeyser, Muriel, 16

Sade, Marquis de, 16, 33, 38
Said, Edward, 264 n. 10
Sayers, Dorothy, 227
The Scarlet Letter 150
Schantz, Ned, 50, 260 n. 8
Schwartz, Hillel, 136, 260 n. 6, 7,
Sensation novel, 57–58
Shakespeare, William, 1
Shattuck, Roger, 100
Shaw, George Bernard, 261 n. 4
Silver fork novels, 112, 143
Snow, John, 77
Sondheim, Stephen, *Into the Woods*, 6, 8
Soni, Vivasvan, 256 n. 20
Sphinx, 16–17, 40, 176, 251 n. 9
Statistics, 95, 156, 163, 165, 170–173, 178–179, 183, 186, 188, 262 n. 12
Steiner, George, 3
Stephen, James Fitzjames, 153, 260 n. 12
Stephen, Leslie, 220, 221, 225
Sterne, Laurence, 112
Stewart, Susan, 73, 76, 79
Stigler, Stephen, 261 n. 5
Stockard, Janice, 263 n. 1
Stone, Lawrence, 255 n. 10
Stump, Reva, 199, 265 n. 16
Sutherland, John 254 n. 36, 259 n. 15
Svankamjer, Jan, 70

The Taming of the Shrew, 223
Tatar, Maria, 254 n. 36
Taylor, Harriet, 205
The Tempest, 230, 232
Tennyson, Alfred Lord, "The Lady of Shallot", 234
Thackeray, William Makepeace, 22, 76, 95, 99, 145, 182, 198, 225, 226, 253 n. 23. See *Vanity Fair*

Notes of a Journey from Cornhill to Grand Cairo 107–111
   sketches, 104–107, 109, 124–125
Thompson, Emma, 250 n. 25
Thorne, Mrs James Ward, 69, 82–84
Thorne Rooms (Art Institute of Chicago), 81. See Mrs James Ward Thorne
Tillotson, Kathleen, 103
To the Lighthouse, 163, 220–221
Toles, George, 12
Tolstoy, Leo, 226, 227
   Anna Karenina, 220
Tradescant's Rarities, 3, 70
Trollope, Anthony, 57, 185, 226
Tudor, Tasha, 81–82
Tussaud, Madame, 87, 232, 266 n. 2

Uncanny. See Sigmund Freud

Vanity Fair, 7, 99, 100–132, 134, 136, 139, 205, 222
Varian, Hal, 263 n. 19
Victoria and Albert Museum, 234

Warner, Marina, 259 n. 8
Warner, William Beaty, 54–55, 72, 256 n. 19
Watt, Ian, 4, 24, 43, 45, 48–49, 51, 53, 54, 57, 64, 100
Waxworks. See Dolls and dollhouses
Weldon, Fay, 22
Welsh, Alexander, 44
Whedon, Joss
   Buffy the Vampire-Slayer, 233
   Dollhouse 80, 94
   Firefly, 233
   Serenity, 232
Wiggins, Marianne, *John Dollar*, 5
Wilde, Oscar, 223
Williams, Raymond, 43, 254 n. 4
Wilt, Judith, 56, 57, 250 n. 16, 263 n. 4
Woolf, Virginia, 221, 232, 236. See also *Mrs. Dalloway*; *To the Lighthouse*
   on *Jane Eyre*, 9, 224
   on *Middlemarch* 101, 193
   Night and Day 225–227, 233
   A Room of One's Own, 224–225
   The Voyage Out 227, 246
Wycherly, William, *The Country Wife*, 99

Printed in the USA/Agawam, MA
June 25, 2014

591841.033